Studies in development and planning

This series consists of studies written by staff members of the Centre for Development Planning of the Erasmus University Rotterdam, and by others specialized in the field of development and planning. This field includes, in broad terms, methods and techniques of development planning, analysis of and policies for development, economic policies towards developing countries, as well as the economics of centrally planned systems.

Most of the studies employ a quantitative approach. The common objective of all studies in this series is to contribute, directly or indirectly, to the formulation of policies which aim at furthering the fundamental goals of socio-economic development, at regional, national, multinational and global levels. The editors express the hope that this broad objective may be reflected in the diversity of contributions to this series.

Studies in development and planning
Vol. 9

Project planning and income distribution

F. L. C. H. HELMERS

Martinus Nijhoff Publishing
Boston / The Hague / London

To Loes,
Karin,
Leslie and Leo

Library of Congress Cataloging in Publication Data

Helmers, F   Leslie C   H   1929-
  Project planning and income distribution.

  (Studies in development and planning ; v. 9)
  Bibliography: p.
  Includes index.
  1. Economic development projects. 2. Underdeveloped
areas—Income distribution. I. Title. II. Series:
Studies in development and planning (Rotterdam) ; v. 9.
HD82.H434   339.2'09172'4   79-10203
ISBN 0-89838-010-3
ISBN 90 207 0873 2

Distributors outside North America:
Kluwer Academic Publishers Group
Distribution Centre
P.O. Box 322
3300 AH Dordrecht, The Netherlands

Typeset in Malta by Interprint Ltd.
Printed and bound in the United States of America

PREFACE

In the past few years several manuals dealing with project planning for the developing countries have been published. One may therefore ask why another study on this subject has been written. The answer is that the manuals, in my opinion, do not deal adequately with the income distribution aspects of projects. This study was written to demonstrate how traditional project planning criteria can be expanded to include income distribution considerations.

Part I of the study (Chapters 1 through 6) discusses conventional project planning criteria. Chapter 1 serves as an introduction by reviewing some of the broader principles of the analysis. Chapters 2 and 3 examine in detail the valuation of benefits and costs, paying particular attention to the problems that arise in making such valuations in developing countries. While Chapter 4 is concerned with the rules to be followed for maximizing the net benefits of a single project, Chapter 5 reviews the techniques for maximizing the net benefits of a series of projects. Chapter 6 deals with a number of different topics, ranging from the practical problems posed by linkages and externalities to an examination of the usefulness of international lending agencies and problems related to divergencies from situations of internal and external balance.

Part II is concerned with income distribution, and begins in Chapter 7 with a review of the concept of a social welfare function. If one accepts this concept, it is clear that traditional project planning theory assumes a special kind of welfare function, so that the social welfare function could just as well have been discussed in Part I. Because traditional project theory developed without much reference to the concept, it was thought preferable to defer the discussion of the social welfare function to Part II. Chapters 8 and 9 are devoted to the intertemporal and interpersonal aspects, respectively, of income distribution. Chapter 10 applies the methodology developed in the previous chapters to several case studies in developing countries. Part II closes with some concluding remarks and a summary.

In writing the study, I have kept in mind that the subject is relatively new and that many who are interested in project planning are not professional economists. Several topics received, therefore, a broader discussion than would have been necessary if the study were solely addressed to economists. It is assumed, however, that the reader is familiar with the basic principles of economic analysis. I hope that the study may be of some use to the practitioners of project planning – those who have the hard task of applying theoretical principles to the actual preparation, appraisal and implementation of projects.

The study was originally published in June 1977 in the Communications Series of the University of Wageningen, but is now no longer available. I am grateful to the Editorial Board of the Centre for Development Planning of the Erasmus University Rotterdam that they have made this new edition possible.

The credit for initiating the idea of writing the study is due to Dr. J. M. van Bemmelen. I am also greatly indebted to Dr. F. P. Jansen for his thoughtful and detailed review of the study, which enabled me to clarify many of my arguments. Additional valuable comments were received from Dr. L. J. Zimmerman, Dr. H. C. Bos, Dr. Ir. A. Franke, Dr. M. T. G. Meulenberg, Drs. A. J. Butler, Dr. L. B. M. Mennes and Dr. D. J. Wolfson. Ms. Veronica Hansen and Ms. Aletha Ober are to be commended for their patience in processing the manuscript and I also appreciate the efforts of Ms. Betty Griesel and Messrs. James Brown and Keith Oblitas for editorial help and of Mr. Yo Kimura for drawing the graphs.

The experience I gained as a staff member of the World Bank underlies the tenor of the study. It should be noted, however, that the study has been written as a spare-time occupation in my private capacity and that the views expressed in the study should not be taken to represent the opinion and policies of the World Bank.

Washington, D.C.
October 5, 1978

CONTENTS

PART I

THE CONVENTIONAL PROJECT PLANNING CRITERIA

1. SOME BASIC ISSUES

1.1. BACKGROUND

Since World War II, development planning has evolved tremendously. Most countries, the major exception being the USA, publish Central Plans, setting targets in terms of national income growth, sometimes also broken down in sectors, regions or income groups. Clearly, the individual projects within the Plan determine to what extent the targets will be achieved. However, even when a country has no development plan, the choice of individual projects is important. In general, given the scarce available resources, one should ensure that each project generates maximum benefits. With this is defined the subject of this study – the theory of project planning or, as it may also be called, the theory of project analysis, project evaluation, or benefit-cost analysis.

Projects are the building blocks of plans and JANSEN[1] sees, therefore, a project as the smallest unit of activity – from a technical or economical point of view – that can be undertaken. We accept this and further define such a unit of activity as the coordinated use of scarce resources for the production of goods or services that increase national welfare relative to the situation without the project. There are several aspects to this definition that need elaboration. First, the word coordinated is used to indicate that some kind of organization – a private enterprise, a government department, a state corporation, a joint venture, or some other body – is necessary to operate the project. Second, we speak of a project only if its objective is to produce goods or services that increase national welfare. For instance, building a factory does not in itself constitute a project; since the factory should eventually produce goods or services, the project, in this case, consists not only of the investment in the factory but also of the factory's operations, in the most general sense of the word, during its economic life. Third, the word investment is intentionally not used in the definition so that also such activities as research and extension can be considered projects. Finally, the definition implies that, somehow, national welfare should be maximized.

The theory of project planning provides criteria for the design and implementation of individual projects and for the selection of a series of projects to arrive at a country's development program. The theory borrows substantially from both micro- and macro-economic analysis in that the project must be considered both as an individual entity and also within the broader perspective of the national economy. An essential element of the theory is that it focuses explicitly upon the objective of increasing national welfare. What then is national welfare? Often it is considered identical to national income. There are, however, several reasons why this is not correct as illustrated in the paragraphs below.

First, there is the problem of determining at which prices national income should be measured when the market prices of the produced goods or services

3

change. Suppose, for instance, that a crop failure has increased the price of rice. Assuming that demand for rice is inelastic, expenditures on rice and national income in current terms would increase, yet welfare has decreased. If national income were measured at the old prices, it would decline but, clearly, as indicated by the higher rice prices the decline in welfare is greater than the decline in national income. Some price between the old and the new therefore seems appropriate. Traditionally, welfare changes have been determined by evaluating the changes in consumer surplus – the amount of money the consumers are willing to pay over and above what they actually pay.

A second deficiency of the national income concept is that it does not consider leisure time. Of two economies with the same national income, the one with a fourty-hour workweek should evidently be preferred to the one with a sixty-hour week. Another example is the following. If a laborer voluntarily reduces his working hours even though he thereby reduces his income, then according to the national income concept there would be a decrease in welfare. In reality, of course, the laborer's welfare has increased because otherwise he would not have made this adjustment to his working hours. The disutility of labor effort should, therefore, be taken into account in measuring welfare changes.

Third, there are many economies where the market prices which enter into the national accounts do not reflect the real values of the factors of production or of the produced goods. The most evident examples concern labor and foreign exchange. Under conditions of unemployment, the cost of hiring an unemployed laborer is obviously not measured by the wage cost. Similarly, if a system of licensing applies with respect to imports, the price of an imported good valued at the official exchange rate is an underestimate of the scarcity value of the import.

A fourth point concerns externalities. Many production increases have side effects – pollution, noise – that are never valued in the national income accounts. It is important for an investment decision to know whether such side effects exist.

As the fifth point, it may be mentioned that the national income concept does not pay attention to the distribution of income between persons or over time. A dollar[2] accruing to a rich man is generally believed to be less valuable socially than a dollar accruing to a poor man. Hence, an increase in national income going to poor income groups would increase welfare more than if the income were to accumulate in the hands of the rich. Similar considerations may apply as regards the distribution of income between generations.

Finally, it should be noted that the national income concept does not consider such things as personal freedom and the quality of life. Of two economies with the same national income, an economy with personal freedom is, in our opinion, much to be preferred over a dictatorial one. This last point will not, however, be further reviewed in this study.

From the discussion above it is clear that there is a fundamental difference between a normal profitability analysis which uses the price data entering the national income accounts and a benefit-cost analysis. For instance, while profitability analysis as undertaken by a firm uses market prices for inputs and outputs, benefit-cost analysis uses imputed values – the real values of benefits and costs – to determine whether or not an investment is worth undertaking. It is not the intention here to provide a detailed review of how benefit-cost analysis developed, but a brief presentation of some of the principal publications is in order.

The use of consumer-surplus in investment decisions has a long history and dates back to DUPUIT's famous work[3] of 1844 on the justification of public investment. Although the concept was refined by MARSHALL,[4] HOTELLING,[5] and HICKS,[6] it was not generally accepted until the middle of the 1950s when the foundation of benefit-cost analysis, including all its other elements, was laid by a group of economists associated with or interested in the Harvard Water Program[7]. In 1958, three major publications appeared, namely, by ECKSTEIN[8] – a participant of the study group – and independently of the group by McKEAN,[9] and by KRUTILLA and ECKSTEIN.[10] These were followed in 1960 by a study of HIRSHLEIFER, DE HAVEN and MILLIMAN,[11] and in 1962 by the seminal official HARVARD study.[12] Very useful survey articles were produced by PREST and TURVEY,[13] MUSGRAVE,[14] and LAYARD.[15]

During the 1960's, benefit-cost analysis became increasingly accepted as a tool for project decision making not only in the USA but also in other countries. Following a study by TINBERGEN[16] in 1958, mainly on the use of accounting prices in public investment analysis, the World Bank gradually began to apply the new methodology, and applied it in its work throughout the developing world. Manuals to deal with the problems in the developing countries were also published by the Organisation for Economic Cooperation and Development (OECD) in 1968[17], and the United Nations Industrial Development Organization (UNIDO) in 1972[18]. A sequel to the OECD manual by its authors was also published in 1974.[19]

The above list is, of course, far from complete although it presents some of the classic works upon which recent developments have been based. Many other important works dealing with benefit-cost analysis have recently been published[20] and we will refer to a number of these in the course of this study.

Despite the volume of literature that has appeared on the subject, the core principles of benefit-cost analysis are still not fully established. The analysis has become more refined but, at the same time, the positions on basic issues seem to have widened, especially regarding such fundamental matters as consumer surplus, shadow wage rates, market distortions, and the incorporation of income distribution aspects into the analysis. This study will try to reconcile the different viewpoints and, as mentioned in the preface, will develop a theory of project planning which includes income distribution considerations. Such a theory is, in principle, applicable to all types of projects. There are, however, projects whose benefits are difficult to quantify, such as those dealing with population control, health, and education. As considerable additional work would be required to deal with the special issues these projects raise, these issues will not be discussed. The project planning criteria developed in this study should, therefore, be seen as especially relevant to projects with tangible benefits, such as those concerning agriculture, industry, public utilities, urban development and transport.

It has become the custom to refer to the traditional analysis as the economic evaluation of projects and to the equity-including analysis as the social evaluation of projects. As both bodies of analysis take as their starting point the interest of society as a whole, these terms are somewhat ambiguous. However, we do not wish to confuse the issue more by introducing new terms and will, therefore, accept the usual terminology. In this study, especially in Part II, the reader will thus encounter such terms as the social evaluation of projects and the social rate of return of a project, the word social meaning that income-distribution aspects have been taken into account.

1.2. BENEFITS AND COSTS

The fundamental principle of project planning is basically very simple and can be stated as the rule that incremental units of production should have higher benefits than costs. But what are benefits and costs? In Figure 1.1 the curve DD′ is the demand curve for a certain good, the curve SS′ the marginal cost curve. The demand curve represents the price consumers are willing to pay for an additional unit of the good and may thus be defined as the marginal willingness to pay of the consumers. It is the curve which indicates what the value is of a marginal unit of the good to the consumer, and in project-evaluation theory the sum of the marginal values represents the total value of the good to consumers, i.e. the benefit of the good. In Figure 1.1, the benefit of producing the output level OQ is thus represented by the area ODTQ. The cost of producing this output level is equal to the area OSTQ. Hence, the difference between benefits and costs equals the area SDT. Since consumers pay a total of ORTQ, whereas they would have been willing to pay ODTQ, they have a gain of RDT-the so-called consumer surplus. Producers receive a revenue ORTQ but their costs are only OSTQ and thus they make a profit of SRT. Denoting benefits by B, costs by C, revenues by R, the consumer surplus by Y and profits by P, we have the following relationship:

$$B - C = (B - R) + (R - C) = Y + P$$

Since this relationship holds at any level of output, we find by differentiating this expression that the first order condition[21] for the optimum output level is that benefits and costs of the marginal unit should be equal, or, what amounts to the same, that the consumer gain on the marginal unit should equal the loss in producer's profit on the marginal unit.

This basically elementary analysis is not accepted by a number of economists on the grounds that the consumer surplus cannot be considered to represent the

Figure 1.1.

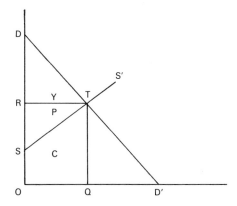

real utility gain of the consumers. When consumers do not pay what they would have been willing to pay and thus receive a gain, the effect must be that the utility levels of the consumers are larger than with payments according to willingness to pay. As the marginal utility of income of the consumers cannot be considered a constant, this means that the money gain as represented by the consumer surplus does not represent the utility gain. This criticism will be reviewed in detail in Chapter 2.

In the above discussion of the optimum output level, we lightly assumed that marginal production costs are precisely known. However, this concept is not without problems either. In a world full of distortions, costs should not be measured at market prices but at real scarcity values. This will be extensively discussed in Chapter 3. In this section we wish to review some more general problems that may arise regarding the concepts of benefits and costs.

A criticism that is often made against benefit-cost analysis is that it is a partial equilibrium analysis, which therefore cannot capture all the gains and losses that may occur in an economy due to a change in the production of a certain good. Any project will have indirect effects, in the sense that it affects others as well as the parties directly involved. Should all these indirect effects be taken into account in the evaluation of a project? The answer has been given by VINER, who in a classic article[22] has drawn the distinction between pecuniary and technological externalities. The latter do not concern us here and will be discussed in Chapter 6. The concept of pecuniary externalities, however, is of the utmost importance in the present context. An example on the demand side is the case where the tastes of a group of consumers change and their demand for, say, apples increases. The price of apples will rise and the other consumers of apples in the community will suffer a loss. The producers of apples, however, gain, and the loss of the other consumers is exactly compensated by the gain of the producers so that the pecuniary externality – the price effect on the intramarginal units – is not relevant at all in this case.

Pecuniary externalities arise also on the cost side and it was to this problem that VINER's article was in fact directed. The problem raised by PIGOU and discussed extensively in the economic literature during the first two decades of this century[23] was analogous to the demand example. Is the price increase of the intramarginal units of a certain factor of production a real production cost? Suppose that a certain enterprise needs 1,000 laborers with a certain skill. Suppose also that this type of labor can be withdrawn from other industries and that the total employed in the industry to which the enterprise belongs will increase from 50,000 to 51,000, and that the hourly wage will increase from $ 1.00 to $ 1.01. The cost of labor to the enterprise is then $ 1.01 per hour for a total of $ 1,010 per hour. However, the total marginal cost is the difference between $ 51,510 (51,000 employed at $ 1.01) and $ 50,000 (50,000 at $ 1.00). Hence, the employment of the additional 1,000 laborers in the industry has given rise to an increase in total costs per hour of $ 1,510, representing $ 1.51 per hour. Should the labor cost be calculated at $ 1.51, that is, should the price increases on the intramarginal units be taken into account, or is the real opportunity cost of labor $ 1.01 only? The answer is not difficult. The extra amount that enterprises elsewhere have to pay for a certain factor of production (in our example 50,000 hours at $ 0.01 — $ 500) is a loss to these enterprises but it represents a benefit to the suppliers of that factor. The higher price of the factor of production in question will cause all other enterprises to use less of that factor and more of other factors until a new equilibrium position is reached. There will be all kinds of price effects on factors of production and outputs. These effects are not to be taken into account because they cancel out. Similarly, a lower price for a certain factor represents a benefit to its users and a loss to its suppliers. Hence, the benefits and costs of all these indirect pecuniary spillovers compensate each other so that the true opportunity cost of labor can be set at $ 1.01 per hour in our example.

Another subject that requires a brief discussion is the distinction between short-run and long-run marginal cost, a distinction that also has given rise in the past to much controversy. In fact, the problem is straightforward. Marginal costs are the costs of additional output, which, if we consider whether an investment should be undertaken, i.e. when we consider the long run, include the costs of all additional equipment. When an investment has already been undertaken, however, its costs are sunk costs and the relevant cost concept for pricing policies is then marginal short-run costs. It would be foolish in such a case to insist on recovery of depreciation or amortization charges, since this may preclude the equipment from being utilized.

Under conditions of perfect competition, resources will have the same value in different uses. However, in the real world such conditions are often not fulfilled and resources will then have different values in their different uses. How should marginal costs then be calculated? The correct principle is to work with shadow prices which reflect the real values of the resources. If the resources are withdrawn from various uses, each with a different value, then the correct shadow price of the resources will be the weighted average of foregone values, the weights being the quantities withdrawn. This also means that when the project's inputs are imported, the relevant value is the import cost valued at the appropriate scarcity value of foreign exchange. Similarly, marginal benefit curves should be based on the values the products create, which, in case of production for the domestic market, is the gross consumer surplus – the willingness to pay – and in case of exports or import substitutes, the export earnings or savings valued at the appropriate scarcity value of foreign exchange.

Resources will be withdrawn at different periods in time and demand may change over time. To make such time dated values comparable, present values must be calculated, a procedure which may be explained as follows. Suppose the Government is willing to invest today an amount equal to K provided it obtains one year from now a return at least equal to $K(1 + q)$. Then q represents the marginal rate of return the Government expects to make. Suppose the Government expects to make the same rate of return in the second year. Then the return which should be received at the end of year two for an investment maturing in two years is $K(1 + q)^2$. Thus, in general, the terminal benefit T_n at the rate of return q of an investment maturing in n years, may be represented by $T_n = K(1 + q)^n$. It follows that the general formula for the present value of a terminal sum T_n in year n at the constant rate q is $T_n/(1 + q)^n$. Application of this formula to the various time dated costs and benefits will provide the present values of costs and benefits.

Finally, a few words about another subject that has given rise to confusion: the with and without approach. Obviously, when an investment project is considered, its costs and benefits should be determined in relation to the situation without the project. This might seem to imply that costs and benefits should be determined relative to the mutually exclusive alternative that is being considered for implementation if the project is not undertaken. Without a hydroelectric power plant, a thermal plant may be built. Should costs and benefits of the contemplated hydro investment then be calculated as incremental to the alternative investment in thermal power? Of course not. The contemplated investment and its alternative are mutually exclusive projects; each project should, therefore, be considered on its own merits compared to the without situation, and that project that has the highest value to the economy should be chosen. Calculating the cost of the investment as the incremental cost compared to the alternative could justify many unviable projects. What the with and without approach means is that costs and benefits should be determined in relation to the situation that would exist if neither the project nor its alternatives were to be implemented.

1.3. SHADOW PRICES AND OPPORTUNITY COSTS

As was briefly mentioned, in many cases market prices do not reflect the real values of goods and services because of divergences from the perfect competition situation. In such cases imputed values – also called shadow prices – should be used. Consider, for instance, Figure 1.2, which depicts the optimum situation for a monopolist. At output OB his marginal costs equal his marginal revenues, so that he will then make maximum profits. Assume now that a

FIGURE 1.2.

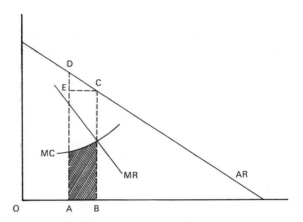

project is being undertaken which will withdraw resources from the monopolist, resulting in a curtailment of his production by AB. Then the cost of these resources should not be based on their market prices, as indicated by the shaded area in Figure 1.2. but on the value which consumers attach to the products these resources produced. which is the area ABCD. In the case of perfect competition. prices would everywhere equal marginal production costs and since there would be an infinite number of firms and consumers, the withdrawal of resources would affect these firms and consumers only infinitesimally so that then indeed the cost of the withdrawn resources would be measured by their market prices.

Considerations like those discussed above have prompted KAHN[24] to propose that the marginal costs of production of enterprises within an industry should be valued at a shadow rate exactly equal to the proportion that the value of the output in the economy is higher than its cost of production. McKENZIE[25] however. has pointed out that when an industry uses original factors of production as well as intermediate products, which is always the case, too much of the original factors will be used and too little of the intermediate products, because the first will be underpriced relative to the intermediate products. Similarly. LITTLE[26] has pointed out that difficulties will arise when goods are both final consumer goods and intermediate productive services. Also. it may be pointed out that KAHN's proposal neglects the consumer surplus; in Figure 1.2 Kahn would value the production of AB as ABCE. yet the value which consumers attach to AB is ABCD.

While this short discussion may already have shown that there are several problems regarding the determination of shadow prices when only such simple distortions as monopolies exist. it is clear that the problems are compounded when all the other possible distortions are taken into account. Monopolies. decreasing cost industries. institutional constraints. taxes and externalities are just a few of the many distortions that exist in the developed economies. In addition to these. disequilibria such as foreign exchange and capital scarcities. unemployment and underemployment may exist in the developing countries where it is, for instance, common to find government regulation of foreign exchange and capital markets and government manipulation of prices and wages.

Is it at all possible, in view of the many difficulties, to determine all the relevant shadow prices? It has been suggested[27] that they should be derived from general programming models. Such models can generate Lagrangean multipliers that represent in economic terms the shadow prices, which, given the constraints incorporated in the model, will result in an allocation of resources that will satisfy the postulated objective function. Such models should, in principle, be able to produce the real scarcity prices of the goods and services. However, although the models can provide valuable insights concerning the structural relations that exist in an economy, we seriously question on practical grounds whether all the shadow prices obtained from the models can be used for operational work. First, the models are still highly aggregated so that most of the duals they generate – the shadow prices – are extremely crude. Second, it must seriously be doubted whether the models can really depict the real world situation. It is not only that there are many distortions but also, to formulate the models, all cost and demand functions should be known. Obviously it is impossible to collect all these data. We feel, therefore, that in addition to the models approach a more practical approach must be followed.

In fact, this approach – the opportunity cost doctrine – has existed for a long time.[28] Consider an economy where only two goods – X and Y are produced. Then the calculation of the costs of an output expansion would not pose a difficult problem. For instance, if the production of X is to be increased, the cost of producing the additional quantity of X is to be found by measuring the value of the Y goods that the community will have to give up in order to increase the production of X. Analysis of the production and demand functions for goods X and Y should readily provide the required data. The situation is more complicated when a multiplicity of goods is being produced, since it will obviously be impossible to analyze the production functions and demand curves of all the different goods. The opportunity cost doctrine therefore takes as a starting point the factors of production which X uses rather than the displaced Y goods and defines the costs of these factors as the returns that the factors would earn in the next best alternative elsewhere. Or, in other words, the relevant concept for the cost measurement is that of the opportunity benefits foregone by the factors of production.

The opportunity cost approach is necessarily a detailed approach. The project analyst must investigate from where the resources for a project will be withdrawn and what their values are in those uses. As long as resources with low valued uses can be transferred to higher valued uses, the change is beneficial. This, in a nutshell, is what the theory of project planning is all about. Although the principle is simple, many problems arise in applying it to real world conditions, problems that will be discussed in detail in other parts of this study.

1.4. Optimal Policies and Actual Policies

During the last three decades, many developing countries have established elaborate systems of import controls and tariff protection, as a result of which the production of import substitution goods expanded tremendously. In an interesting study,[29] it has been contended that these policies – at least for the countries studied (Argentina, Brazil, Mexico, India, Pakistan, the Philippines and Taiwan) – have overencouraged industry in relation to agriculture. On the other hand, many developed countries have raised protective barriers around their agricultural sectors which may well have over-expanded their production of agricultural commodities. The reasons why such policies were followed may differ from country to country and may involve such considerations as the infant industry argument, notions of self-sufficiency, and employment and income distribution objectives. It is not the place here to analyze what specific reasons may have caused these in a strict economic sense perhaps non-optimal policies, or what the detrimental effects of such policies are; what we are interested in is what position the project evaluator should take vis-a-vis the created distortions. Tariffs, quotas, licenses, and such are all variables subject to Government control and can be abolished. As SEN has said, 'For a project evaluator, therefore, it is important to know which variables are within his control and to what extent...'.[30]

Let us take a specific example of a distortion in the supply of a manufactured good, say, steel. Assume that the Government has decided that the country should be self-sufficient in steel and that it has created a prohibitive import barrier through a very high duty on the import of steel, as graphically shown in Figure 1.3. The c.i.f. price of steel evaluated at the opportunity cost of foreign exchange is shown as OP_i but the tariff-inclusive market price is OP_t. As a result, domestic production of steel – the supply curve of which is SS' – has become profitable, and with a demand curve equal to DD', the price of steel has become OP_d at a production of OA. Obviously the tariff is non-optimal:

FIGURE 1.3.

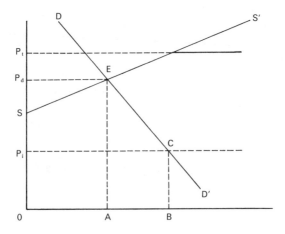

the producers of steel gain SP_dE but the users of steel lose P_iP_dEC so that the net loss to the economy is P_iSEC.

Which price should be used by the evaluator of a project which uses steel? Optimal industrial development requires that steel be imported, but the Government's policies are not optimal and steel is produced in the country. If in this situation the project evaluator were to use the real import price of steel P_i, it is clear that he would understate the cost of the resources used in the production of steel and that he could arrive at completely wrong conclusions. For instance, suppose that the project is worth undertaking if steel is imported but not when it is domestically produced. Then, if in fact only the high cost domestic steel can be used, the implementation of the project will lead to additional economic losses. Hence, to show this, the price to be used for the evaluation of the project should be the domestic price of steel. The determination of the net benefits of a project depends thus on what the costs will be in the actual situation and not on what the costs would be if optimal policies were undertaken.

This principle is not an easy one to follow. In many cases, an import duty may be the result of a haphazard historical decision and urgently in need of revision. The project evaluator should then use his influence to convince the responsible Government agencies to bring the duty in line with the overall level of tariffs. If he succeeds, he should use the real price; if he does not, the market price. Which price the project evaluator should use in the evaluation of the project under scrutiny depends thus in such cases on the outcome of his efforts. In many other cases, however, tariffs are the result of a conscientious policy, for instance, to make the country self-sufficient in a certain product. Although such policies may not be 'optimal' in a strict economic sense, they may well be 'sensible' from a national point of view, whereby what is considered sensible may be determined from the national plan or an analysis of Government actions. Clearly, if a country is determined to follow a certain policy, the price resulting from this policy is the relevant price for investment decisions rather than an imaginary optimal policy price.

1.5. NATIONAL PLANNING AND PROJECT PLANNING

In principle, the theory of project planning considers only those variables that are relevant for the project under consideration. It is possible, therefore, that one could imagine that all these variables should be determined by the project preparation agency. This would be a mistake because several project variables can be determined only at the macro level. For instance, the demand for a product depends inter alia on population and income growth; the supply situation of a project's input may depend on the growth path of the economy; the shadow price of foreign exchange and the discount rate to be used for project planning are clearly national parameters; and so on. If every project evaluator were to determine individually the national parameters, there would be quite a duplication of effort. Moreover, in all probability, one would end up with divergent estimates and misinvestments because the Government departments and public corporations that prepare the various investment projects would not have sufficient information to estimate the national parameters meaningfully. It is the task of the central authority – the Central Planning Unit or the Treasury – to review the projects prepared and proposed by the different departments and corporations and to determine after consultation with them what the final set of projects will be. But it is this final set that determines how the economy will develop, so that only the Center can really determine what the values of the national parameters are. Furthermore, it may so happen that the available investment funds will not be sufficient to undertake all the proposed projects. In such a case, it is the Center's task to set the cut-off rate of return for the individual projects at such a level that the number of acceptable projects will just exhaust the available budget.[31] This rate also can be determined only at the Center.

A national plan consists normally of sectoral plans so that the possibilities within a sector can be reviewed and misinvestments prevented. Suppose, for instance, that every region in a country plans to undertake a sugar project. Some sectoral review is then required to prevent the likely overinvestment. Also, sectoral plans will be necessary when different types of projects within a sector are interconnected. For instance, in the transport sector, a port project may necessitate improvement of road and rail connections with the hinterland, or the improvement of a certain road may necessitate a feeder road improvement program, and so on.[32] Furthermore, it is possible that a shortfall of investments in the transportation sector may hold back development elsewhere in the economy. Clearly, if the sector is so important, some long-term planning is necessary. Another example would be the following. Assume that a large power resource – hydroelectric, gas or oil – can be developed at low cost. Then it may be in the country's interest to set up a long-term plan for the promotion of energy-intensive industries. In general then, sectoral planning will be necessary where overinvestments may occur, where important inter-relations within the sector exist, or where the sector will have an important impact on the rest of the economy.

In addition to sectoral planning, plans may be required for regions or income groups. As regards regions, important interconnections may exist between agriculture, industry, transport, labor, etc., which make such plans mandatory. As regards income groups, it is now more and more accepted that for certain groups some form of planning is required. Assume, for instance, that the income level of a certain income group, say, smallholder farmers, is expected to remain depressed. Assume further that the Government has decided to remedy the situation by means of an investment program geared towards raising the income level of the group. Then also a series of projects spread out over time and interconnected, i.e., a plan, will be necessary.

Since most sectoral plans will have a substantial impact on other sectors and plans for regions or income groups will cover several sectors, the drawing up of the plans should in most cases be done jointly by the Center and the concerned

14

Government departments. The Center thus plays a crucial role. It is responsible for the macro-economic plan, it has to assure itself that the intermediate level plans relate properly to the overall plan, and it has to decide which set of individual projects will be implemented. In all of this it needs project data for the calculation of the national parameters but, at the same time, the lower levels can only provide the project data after they have received the national parameters.

Although such interactions might appear to involve an insolvable circularity, the process, if it is appropriately handled, would sharpen the understanding of the central authority as regards the desired development path of the economy. In a well run administration the interaction might take place as follows. The central authority would make, with the help of programming models, tentative projections of development objectives and national parameters, which it would submit to the various Government departments. These would use the data in the preparation of projects within their jurisdiction and submit to the Center a list of projects together with feasibility studies. The Center would review how the proposals would fit in with the initial development strategy, calculate new national parameters, including tentative cut-off rates of return in case of a shortage of available funds, and submit them to the departments, which would in turn revise their plans and submit them to the Center, and so on. As a result of these interactions, it can be expected that a well formulated national plan, including intermediate level plans, and a set of well prepared projects would emerge.

It must be remarked that the above sketch presents the target towards which the planning process should strive. In many countries we still find that the concerned Government departments have no planning unit or that the interaction between the Center and the Departments is still so rudimentary that the latter have little notion of the values of the national parameters. It is encouraging to see, however, that all this is gradually changing for the better.

In the past, many governments relied mainly on macro-economic plans for their investment strategies. Often these plans were based on estimates of simple sectoral capital-output ratios and, as a result, serious misinvestments occurred. Programming has taken great strides since then but, even so, the resource allocations emerging from the models are still so crude that the possibility of serious mistakes cannot be excluded. Project planning, on the other hand, is based on detailed investigations of the economic viabilities of individual projects, so that only projects with high priority will be selected. Also, as regards intermediate level plans, project evaluation has a fundamental task to fulfill. If a certain sector's initial set of projects includes some with low rates of return, then it would be in the national interest to transfer part of the initial budget allocation for that sector to a sector where projects have higher rates of return. Project planning thus not only increases the likelihood that the investment program will be successful, it leads also to an optimal program. Fortunately, it is becoming increasingly accepted that the basis on which macro plans as well as intermediate level plans rest are well thought out individual project proposals. Project planning theory is the tool that provides this basis.

[1] JANSEN, F. P., 'Schaarse Middelen en Structurele Samenhangen,' Thesis, Tilburg, 1969, p. 21.

[2] Reference is often made in the study to a dollar of income which should be interpreted to mean a national currency unit. Where confusion might arise, the rupee has been used as the local currency unit and the US dollar as the foreign currency unit.

[3] DUPUIT, J., 'De la Mesure de l'Utilité des Travaux Publics,' Annales des Ponts et Chaussées, 2nd series, Vol. 8, 1844. Translated by Barbach, R. H. as 'On the Measurement of the Utility of Public Works' and reprinted in 'International Economic Papers No. 2,' The MacMillan Company, New York, 1952. Also reprinted in 'Readings in Welfare Economics,' published for the American Economic Association by Richard D. Irwin, Inc., Homewood, Illinois, 1969.

[4] MARSHALL, A., 'Principles of Economics,' 8th ed., 1920; reprint ed., MacMillan and Company, London, 1962, Chapter VI and Note VI.

[5] HOTELLING, H., 'The General Welfare in Relation to Problems of Taxation and of Railway and Utility Rates,' Econometrica, 6 (1938). Reprinted in 'Readings in Welfare Economics,' published for the American Economic Association by Richard D. Irwin, Inc., Homewood, Illinois, 1969.

[6] HICKS, J. R., 'Value and Capital,' 2nd ed., Oxford University Press, London, 1946, Note to Chapter II. See also HICKS, J. R., 'A Revision of Demand Theory,' 2nd ed., Oxford University Press, London, 1959.

[7] The setting up of this study group may be seen as a successful attempt to bring uniformity to the various criteria used for evaluating water resource development projects in the USA. Under the 1936 Flood Control Act, the US Government became obliged to undertake a project only if 'the benefits to whomsoever they may accrue, are in excess of the estimated costs.' The benefit and cost valuation criteria were, however, not defined and as a result the various agencies developed a rather heterogenous mass of criteria to justify their projects.

[8] ECKSTEIN, O., 'Water Resource Development – The Economics of Project Evaluation, Harvard University Press, Cambridge, Massachusetts, 1958.

[9] McKEAN, R. N., 'Efficiency in Government through Systems Analysis, with Emphasis on Water Resources Development,' a Rand Corporation Research Study, New York, John Wiley and Sons, Inc., 1958.

[10] KRUTILLA, J. V. and ECKSTEIN, O., 'Multiple Purpose River Development,' published for Resources for the Future by The Johns Hopkins Press, Baltimore, 1958.

[11] HIRSHLEIFER, J., DE HAVEN, J. C., and MILLIMAN, J. W., 'Water Supply – Economics, Technology and Policy,' University of Chicago Press, Chicago, 1960.

[12] MAASS, A., et al., 'Design of Water Resource Systems – New Techniques for Relating Economic Objectives, Engineering Analysis and Governmental Planning,' Harvard University Press, Cambridge, Massachusetts, 1962.

[13] PREST, A. R., and TURVEY, R., 'Cost-Benefit Analysis: A Survey,' The Economic Journal, December 1965.

[14] MUSGRAVE, R. A., 'Cost-Benefit Analysis and the Theory of Public Finance,' The Journal of Economic Literature, September 1969.

[15] LAYARD, R., 'An Introduction to Cost-Benefit Analysis, Selected Readings,' ed. Layard, R., Penguin Education, reprinted with revisions, 1974.

[16] TINBERGEN, J., 'The Design of Development,' published for the International Bank for Reconstruction and Development by The Johns Hopkins Press, Baltimore, 1958.

[17] LITTLE, I. M. D. and MIRRLEES, J. A., 'Manual of Industrial Project Analysis in Developing Countries, Volume II, Social Cost Benefit Analysis,' Development Centre of the Organisation for Economic Cooperation and Development Paris, 1968.

[18] DASGUPTA, P., SEN, A., and MARGLIN, S., 'Guidelines for Project Evaluation,' United Nations Industrial Development Organisation, Vienna, Project Formulation and Evaluation Series, No. 2, United Nations, New York, 1972.

[19] LITTLE, I. M. D. and MIRRLEES, J. A., 'Project Appraisal and Planning for Developing Countries,' Basic Books Inc., New York, 1974.

[20] For instance, MILLWARD, R., 'Public Expenditure Economics – An Introductory Application of Welfare Economics,' McGraw Hill, London, 1971; DASGUPTA, A. K. and PEARCE, D. W., 'Cost-Benefit Analysis: Theory and Practice,' MacMillan Student Edition, London and Basingstoke, 1972; MISHAN, E. J. 'Cost-Benefit Analysis,' revised new edition, George Allen and Unwin, Ltd., London, 1975; and SQUIRE, L. and VAN DER TAK, H. G., 'Economic Analysis of Projects,' published for the World Bank by The Johns Hopkins University Press, Baltimore and London, 1975.

[21] Since in practice in the design of a project one knows whether one is at a maximum or minimum, second order conditions will not be discussed in this study.

[22] VINER, J., 'Cost Curves and Supply Curves,' Zeitschrift fur Nationalökonomie, Vol. III, 1931. Reprinted in 'Readings in Price Theory,' published for the American Economic Association by George Allen and Unwin, Ltd., London, 1953.

[23] For a summary of the discussion, see ELLIS, H. S. and FELLNER, W., 'External Economies and Diseconomies,' The American Economic Review, 1943, pp. 493–511. Reprinted in 'Readings in Price Theory,' published for the American Economic Association by George Allen and Unwin Ltd., London, 1953.

[24] KAHN, R. F., 'Some Notes on Ideal Output,' The Economic Journal, March 1935.

[25] MCKENZIE, L. W., 'Ideal Output and the Interdependence of Firms,' The Economic Journal, December 1951.

[26] LITTLE, I. M. D., 'A Critique of Welfare Economics,' 2nd ed., Clarendon Press, 1957; reprint ed. Oxford Paperbacks, 1963, p. 163.

[27] e.g., CHAKRAVARTY, S., 'The Use of Shadow Prices in Programme Evaluation,' in 'Capital Formation and Economic Development,' ed. Rosenstein-Rodan, P. N., George Allen and Unwin Ltd., London, 1964, pp. 48–67. See also TINBERGEN, J., 'Design of Development,' pp. 82–87.

[28] The name probably appeared for the first time in print in an article by GREEN, D. I., 'Pain Cost and Opportunity Cost,' The Quarterly Journal of Economics, Vol. VIII, 1893–1894.

[29] See LITTLE, I. M. D., SCITOVSKY, T. and SCOTT, M., 'Industry and Trade in Some Developing Countries – A Comparative Study,' published for the Development Centre of the Organization for Economic Cooperation and Development, Paris, by Oxford University Press, London, New York, Toronto, 1970.

[30] SEN, A. K., 'Control Areas and Accounting Prices: An Approach to Economic Evaluation,' The Economic Journal, Volume 82, March 1972, (Supplement), pp. 486–501. Reprinted in 'Benefit-Cost and Policy Analysis, 1972,' and Aldine manual on forecasting, decision-making and evaluation, Aldine Publishing Company, Chicago, 1973.

[31] See Section 5.5.

[32] See ADLER, H. A., 'Sector and Project Planning in Transportation,' World Bank Staff Occasional Papers, No. 4, distributed by the Johns Hopkins Press, Baltimore, 1967.

2. THE VALUATION OF BENEFITS

2.1. THE CONSUMER SURPLUS CONCEPT

The measurement of a project's benefits has been extensively discussed in the economic literature and concerns the concepts of producer surplus (profits) and consumer surplus. Should only the producer surplus be measured or the consumer surplus also? The concept of consumer surplus was discovered in 1844 by DUPUIT, who, in a path-breaking article, tried to measure the public utility of such things as roads, bridges and canals.[1] He showed that the utility which an individual obtains from the consumption of a certain quantity of a good is greater than the price he pays because the price represents only the utility of the marginal unit and not that of each intra-marginal unit. Thus, according to DUPUIT: 'To sum up, political economy has to take as the measure of utility of an object the maximum sacrifice which each consumer would be willing to make in order to acquire the object.'[2] What DUPUIT has identified is willingness to pay. What is now generally called consumer surplus is the difference between what a consumer is willing to pay and what he actually pays. To give an example: if a person would buy one pound of rice a week if the price were $ 0.20 and two pounds if the price were $ 0.15, then the individual's consumer surplus when he pays $ 0.15 is $ 0.05, since he would have been willing to pay $ 0.35 for the two pounds, whereas he pays only $ 0.30. The aggregate consumer surplus is the sum of the individual surpluses and is measured by the area under the aggregate demand curve and above the price line.

The next writer who used the concept was MARSHALL, who, in his Principles, also points out that the satisfaction a person gets from the purchase of a certain quantity of a good exceeds that which he gives up in paying away its price. MARSHALL continues: 'The excess of the price which he would be willing to pay rather than go without the thing, over that which he actually does pay, is the economic measure of this surplus satisfaction. It may be called consumer surplus.'[3] Although MARSHALL never stated explicitly how his demand curve should be drawn up, it is now generally accepted that his assumptions were that the money incomes of the consumers and the price of every commodity other than the commodity in question would be constant.[4] From this demand curve definition, it obviously follows that a consumer's real income will increase when output increases and price falls, because the lower the price, the more the consumer can buy of this or any other commodity. Thus, since a consumer's willingness to pay for commodities, including the commodity in question, will increase the lower the price of the commodity in question, it will be difficult to measure the consumer's willingness to pay on the basis of a ceteris paribus demand curve. MARSHALL was well aware of this difficulty and, therefore, makes the important qualification that the consumer's surplus can be measured only with the help of the demand curve if the marginal utility of income of the consumer is constant, i.e., if the consumer's real income does not change.[5] This will be the case when the good in question accounts for only a small part of the consumer's total expenditure. Real income changes are then negligible and the consumer's surplus can safely be measured by the difference between the area under the consumer's demand curve and the area under the price line.[6]

It appears thus that in all cases where goods have little income effect, the collective consumer surplus can be derived from the aggregate demand curve. However, in cases where the expenditure on the good accounts for a substantial part of the consumers' total expenditures. demand curve analysis is not appropriate. Because of this apparent limited application and the inherent difficulties of the concept itself, many subsequent writers – including eventually MARSHALL himself – came to believe that consumer surplus analysis was a tool of limited practical usage.

The matter had to wait until the late 1930s when HOTELLING and HICKS tried to rehabilitate the concept. HOTELLING's[7] article gives due credit to DUPUIT's work and is in fact a refinement and elaboration of the DUPUIT analysis. HICKS's analysis, on the other hand, was not so much concerned with the practical implications of the concept but with the underlying assumptions. It opens up entirely new points of view and will be discussed in the next section.

2.2. THE COMPENSATED DEMAND CURVES

The Hicksian analysis of consumer surplus advanced the understanding of the concept substantially. It appeared at first as a byproduct of the ALLEN and HICKS indifference curve analysis of consumer behavior, which was subsequently elaborated in HICKS's 1939 book, 'Value and Capital,'[8] but it was soon followed by a much more extensive series of articles in the Review of Economic Studies, which gave rise to a lengthy discussion. Most of the conclusions from this discussion are incorporated in HICKS's 1956 book on the subject.[9] Basically, what HICKS set out to prove was that the consumer surplus analysis need not be restricted to goods without income effects if a demand curve different from the Marshallian curve – a compensated curve – is introduced.

The concept of such a compensated curve may best be explained with the help of an example which refers to a demand supply situation of, say, rice in a certain country. Let us assume, as is done in Figure 2.1, that the total quantity of rice consumed in a certain year is OA at a price of BA. The curve PBC is the normal Marshallian demand curve drawn up under the assumption that money incomes remain constant and that only the price of rice and not those of other goods will change. Let us now assume that the output of rice will be increased to OD. The new price will then be CD. The consumers' willingness to pay for the additional output is ABCD but they pay only AECD and the consumer surplus on the additional output is therefore BEC. On the old output, consumers pay NKBE less than before. The total gain in consumer surplus is thus NKBC.

Thus far our example has not brought out anything that was not already

FIGURE 2.1.

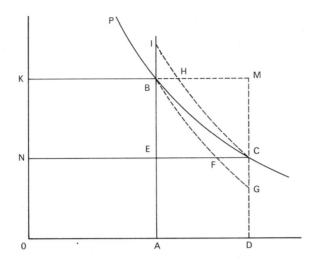

known to MARSHALL. HICKS, however, analyzed in detail how the real incomes of the consumers change when they buy the good in question. Specifically, the consumers are much better off at output point D than they were at output point A, because they would have been willing to pay a higher price than CD for each increment in output beyond A. In other words, their real income has improved. HICKS has shown that it is possible to construct a demand curve that would leave consumers' real incomes identical to what they had at point A. The easiest way to see this is to imagine that a discriminating monopolist charges the maximum price that consumers are willing to pay for every increment beyond OA. Then, because of the reduction in the consumer's income, the quantity bought at any given price will be less than that bought according to the Marshallian demand curve so that the new demand curve will be below the Marshallian curve. This new demand curve may be described as a compensated demand curve because it is the demand curve drawn up under the assumption that the person in question would have paid some maximum amount of money (a compensatory payment) to have the change undertaken. Assuming that this new – compensated – curve is BFG, then the monopolist would be able to capture an amount of money equal to the area OKBGD. Since the consumers would have been willing to pay OKBGD but pay ONCD only, the benefit of the consumers is NKBF minus FCG. In the Hicksian terminology, this is called the compensating surplus since it is the reduction in income that would be necessary to leave the consumer as well off when he buys OD units at the price CD as he was in his original position when he bought OA units at the price BA.[10]

What this analysis has shown is that one can measure, with the help of the compensated demand curve, the minimum benefit – the compensating surplus – that consumers will receive. At first sight, the consumer surplus analysis thus seemed saved. Soon, however, it became clear that the compensated demand curve discussed above could understate the benefits of a project substantially. This can be shown by constructing a demand curve under the assumption that

20

the real income of the consumer is at the level he would have had after the change had taken place (i.e. at point D in figure 2.1). Such a demand curve may be called an equilibrated demand curve because the consumer's income is equilibrated to what it would have been with the change and could be constructed as follows. Assume that the consumer has a real income as at level D and that the price is to be increased from CD to BA. Then, instead of mulcting the consumer, he should be given, if one wanted to keep the real income of the consumer unchanged from that at point D, additional amounts of money for every incremental increase in price. IHC is the demand curve under such a procedure. This demand curve can also be constructed by a reasoning analogous to the first case. One should imagine here that the consumer's demand curve is to be constructed under the assumption that the consumer's real income at level A should be the same as that which he would have if the project had already been implemented. The consumer should then be given at point A additional amounts of money equal to the difference in real income between levels D and A and the discriminating monopolist should again charge the maximum price that the consumer is willing to pay for every increment beyond OA. Also in this hypothetical case, one would end up with the equilibrated demand curve IHC. On the basis of this demand curve the gain in consumer surplus on the additional production is IEC, and on the total production NKBHC + BIH. In the Hicksian terminology, it is called the equivalent surplus[11] since it is the increase in income that would be necessary to leave the consumer as well off when he consumes OA units at the price BA as he is when he consumes OD units at the price CD.

As a result of the Hicksian analysis, it appears that there are three demand curves, each with a different consumer surplus. Consequently, it seems to have brought us back to MARSHALL's statement that the consumer surplus analysis is only valid if the good in question accounts for only a small part of each consumer's expenditure. In such a case there will be no change in the real income of the consumer and the compensated and equilibrated demand curves (BG and IC, respectively) will coincide with the Marshallian demand curve (BC). Problems arise when there are income effects, i.e., when the good in question accounts for a substantial part of consumers' expenditures because the three curves will then be far apart. The question thus arises as to which one, if any, of the three demand curves should be used for the measurement of the surplus.

It may be recalled that the compensating surplus was arrived at by measuring what consumers would have to pay in addition to the price if they were to remain as well off as they were before the project was started: in other words, what bribe the consumers can afford to offer in order to have the project undertaken. On the other hand, the equivalent surplus measures what the consumers should receive in money if the project were not undertaken so as to leave their relative well-being unchanged from the position they would have with the project: in other words, what bribe should be given to the consumers if the project were not undertaken. HICKS's two surpluses are thus compensation payments. In Chapter 7 where the compensation tests will be discussed, we will show that they cannot give the answer if we want to evaluate the distributive aspects of a project. Why is that so here? The answer is clear. The first compensated demand curve shows demand when real income is held constant at the original level A. whereas the second equilibrated demand curve shows demand when real income is held constant at the level reached after the project's implementation, the level D. But since real income at D is higher than at A, the marginal uitility of income of the consumers is lower at D than at A. In other words, while we have been trying to express the total increase in welfare in money terms, the marginal utility of income has changed. It thus appears that the consumer surplus concept involves measurement of something that is inherently impossible to measure if the values of the marginal utility of income are not known, except in the case where the goods account for only a small part of consumer expenditure.

The above short discussion cannot, of course, do full justice to the Hicksian analysis. Enough has been said, however, to show that the concept becomes less useful in the case of goods with substantial income effects. HICKS, who started to analyze the concept with enthusiasm in 1939, is hesitant about the usefulness of the concept in his 1956 book.[12]

2.3. SOCIAL WELFARE AND THE CONSUMER SURPLUS

The inherent difficulty of the consumer surplus concept is that welfare changes are being expressed in money terms. It seems to us that there is only one way out of the dilemma, namely, to express the welfare changes in utility terms. As is well-known from the theory of consumer choice, a consumer will maximize his utility by buying a quantity of a commodity such that the utility per dollar spent on the last unit will be the same as the utility per dollar spent on the unit of every other commodity: otherwise he could increase his welfare by switching expenditures from commodities where the dollar spent has a low utility to those where it has a higher utility. Denoting the utility of the last dollar spent (the marginal utility of income) by u_m, the marginal utility of commodity x by u_x, and the price of the commodity by p_x, the equilibrium position of a consumer at any price situation is $u_x/p_x = u_m$. Hence, the change in welfare due to a price change can be found by evaluating the consumer surplus change due to the price change at the appropriate marginal utilities of income. The change in the surplus can, of course, be measured only with the help of the Marshallian demand curve since the compensated demand curves by definition do not indicate what the income changes are.

An example may perhaps be useful. Assume that in figure 2.1 the demand curve BC represents the demand curve of a single consumer. Then, if the price were to be reduced from BA to CD, his additional consumer surplus would be equal to the area NKBC, which may be written as $\triangle P(Q + \frac{1}{2}\triangle Q)$. To arrive at his welfare change in utility terms this expression must be valued at the relevant marginal utilities of income (u). A good approximation will often be to value it at the average of the marginal utilities of income corresponding to the situations where the old and the new price applied, and the welfare change can then be written as $\triangle P(Q + \frac{1}{2}\triangle Q)$ $(u + \frac{1}{2}\triangle u)$. The area NKBC has thus been weighted with an income distribution weight to arrive at the welfare change.

The process is also reversible. Thus, if the welfare change in utility terms of the consumer is known, we can find the change in consumer surplus by dividing this welfare change by the factor $(u + \frac{1}{2}\triangle u)$. Hence, even when the marginal utility of income of the consumer is not constant, the consumer surplus concept, at least for the individual consumer, has relevance.

Another matter concerns whether the individual surpluses may be added. In an analysis of consumer surplus in connection with national income accounts, HARBERGER[13] arrives at the same conclusion as regards the individual surplus as above and reviews then the issue whether consumer surpluses of different beneficiaries may be added. HARBERGER believes that one might contemplate a national income measure incorporating distributional weights but that 'Two obstacles stand in the way: first, the impossibility of achieving a consensus with regard to the weights, and, second, the fact that most of the data from which the national accounts are built are aggregates in the first place and do not distinguish the individuals or groups whose dollars they represent.' Because of these difficulties, HARBERGER believes that when measuring the net benefits or costs of a given action (project, program or policy) the costs and benefits should normally be added without regard to the incomes of the individuals to whom they accrue.

We beg to differ. The last part of HARBERGER's argument is self-defeating in that if the national income accounts do not distinguish the incomes of the different income groups, then it is high time that the need for this is recognized and that changes in national accounting procedures are instigated. As regards the impossibility of achieving a consensus on weights, this concerns, of course, the issue of the construction of the social welfare function, an issue that will be extensively discussed in Part II of this study. Here, it may be mentioned that we will argue that a social marginal utility of income schedule can indeed be derived from individually held social values.

Has the HARBERGER proposal then no validity at all? In this respect, it is important to note that the traditional benefit-cost theory implicitly assumes that the marginal utilities of income of the project participants are the same, so that – as also proposed by HARBERGER – income distribution weights need not be determined. All project beneficiaries can then be treated alike and the additional dollars of benefit at different income levels will have the same value. We accept that the criteria of the traditional theory may be applied in cases where income distribution aspects are not important. In particular, we believe that the traditional approach may be followed for projects where the beneficiaries belong mainly to the middle income groups so that MARSHALL's second condition – that the different (sub)classes will be affected in about equal proportions – will be approximated. Assuming that figure 2.1 refers to such a case, the welfare change of the project beneficiaries will be NKBC, from which must be deducted the loss in income of the producers – the area NKBE – to arrive at the net welfare change of the community as a whole. The net increase in welfare

23

will then be EBC – the consumer surplus on the additional production. However, where income distribution aspects do play an overriding role such as in projects geared towards poverty eradication, we believe that project beneficiaries should be identified according to their income levels and the social value of incremental income should be estimated. To give an example: if the demand curve BC in figure 2.1 concerned a homogeneous group of low income people, then the area NKBC should be weighted with an income distribution weight to determine their welfare change. This welfare change may thus be written as $\triangle P(Q + \frac{1}{2}\triangle Q) \cdot v$ where v is the socially determined income weight. Assuming that the weight v has been determined relative to the weight of the producers, the welfare change of society as a whole is then found by deducting from the above expression the area NKBE, which may be written as $\triangle P \cdot Q$. Methods by which the income distribution weights could be determined will be extensively discussed in Part II of this study.

The relevant concept, when a project has no income distribution consequences, is thus willingness to pay as measured by the Marshallian demand curve rather than the compensated or equilibrated demand curves. A writer who also rejects the latter is WINCH.[14] Basically, what WINCH set out to prove is that the compensated and equilibrated demand curves cannot be used for the measurement of benefit increases since they do not represent the actual adjustment path. WINCH argues that the income effects and substitution effects act simultaneously and that the only way to measure them is to follow them over the range of the price change, which is what the Marshallian demand curve does. In other words, as SILBERBERG[15] phrased it: 'Winch correctly derives the "Marshallian Triangle" as the limit of a sum of compensating variations in income that a consumer would be willing to pay for the privilege of consuming at a slightly lower price, always assuming, however, that he never actually pays those amounts.' However, SILBERBERG then shows that there may be many adjustment paths so that in general one cannot accept the Marshallian area as the consumer's gain. SILBERBERG has introduced a dynamic element into the static analysis of the Marshallian triangle and there can be no doubt that within the context of a dynamic analysis the surplus may be different from the normal Marshallian surplus, Nevertheless, as noted by BURNS[16], the upper and lower limiting values of the benefit changes are the Hicksian equilibrated and compensated demand curves and the adjustment path will, in general, be very close to the Marshallian demand curve. We are therefore not concerned about what path will actually be followed. Estimates of demand curves are necessarily rough and the theoretical refinement of SILBERBERG should be treated as an application of the 'de minimus' principle.

Several writers[17] have remarked in connection with HARBERGER's analysis that the consumer surplus analysis should be rejected since it implies that the cross-elasticities of demand among products are zero. In other words, the possibility of goods being substitutes or complements is excluded. If goods X and Y are substitutes or complements, the increased production of X will not, of course, leave the price and consumer surplus of Y unchanged, but in a thorough

24

benefit-cost analysis this criticism can be discarded. One of the basic principles of benefit-cost analysis is that the system under consideration must be expanded until the major direct effects can be taken into account. Hence, if the output of a good that has a complement or substitute is changed, the analysis should take account of the effects the change will have on these goods. The basic principle to keep in mind is that the consumer surplus concept is valid provided we analyze systems that include the principal direct effects of output contraction or expansion and that can clearly be separated from the rest of the economy where the neglectable indirect effects take place.

There are, however, writers who reject the consumer surplus analysis on the grounds that the indirect effects – the effects on prices and surpluses of goods in the rest of the economy – are too important to be neglected. By reviewing this for a normal commodity, we may be able to clarify this issue. As we have discussed, the demand curve for a normal commodity is drawn up under the assumption that prices and surpluses elsewhere do not change. Is this true? Theoretically, this assumption is not correct because the increase in real income of the consumers due to a production change will cause them to change their demand for other commodities. Even if the prices of other commodities do not change measurably, theoretically the surpluses on the other commodities may change. For instance, if the price of the commodity in question falls, then its marginal utility to a consumer would be greater than its new price multiplied by the consumer's marginal utility of income. Thus, a consumer will increase his consumption of the commodity. Depending on the demand elasticity, his expenditures may increase or decrease, but this means that he should adjust his expenditures on other commodities. Hence, even if the prices of other commodities do not change, the consumer surplus on other commodities will be affected. Also, as LITTLE[18] notes, resources need to be withdrawn for the project's output. But this means that output elsewhere has to be decreased and that producer surpluses elsewhere change.

If we understand LITTLE correctly, it is because of the above arguments that he states: 'Our conclusion is that consumers' surplus is a totally useless theoretical toy.'[19] We disagree. In LITTLE's argumentation, the project evaluator measures only the financial costs of production and does not take the lost producer surplus elsewhere – which can be substantial – into account. But we will show when discussing the measurement of opportunity costs that this is automatically done. As such, the loss in producer surplus has nothing to do with the consumer surplus concept. Regarding the consumer surplus, changes will of course take place elsewhere if a project's output is expanded. However, such changes will be dispersed over many other commodities and will be negligible. LITTLE is questioning the operational significance of the partial equilibrium approach vis-a-vis general equilibrium analysis, but general equilibrium criteria are seldom operationally usable. Partial equilibrium analysis, which necessarily implies that changes of the second order of smallness cannot be taken into account, is adequate given the roughness of the estimates that are inherent in all project evaluation work and the unimportance of the second order changes relative to the direct impact.

Finally, another matter. There are writers who argue that in the measurement of benefits from public investments, consumer surpluses should not be taken into account because consumer surplus analysis is not done by the private sector. Thus WOHL and MARTIN argue in connection with highway projects: 'Because of the incomparability that would result between public and private sectors of the economy, the latter of which does not include consumer surplus in the assessment of alternative investment, and because of the indeterminate nature of consumer surplus measurement, it is our view that consumer surplus should not be included in any user trip benefit calculations to be used in assessing the economy of public projects.'[20] It is our view that the reasoning should be reversed. Consumer surplus analysis should be undertaken for private industrial projects as well as for public projects because it is only then that the social or economic priority of a project can be determined. This point is important for many developing countries because they do wish to regulate private investment. It is also ironical that WOHL and MARTIN make their suggestion in connection with road projects. As is well known, roads, bridges and the like often operate under conditions of decreasing costs, and revenues will then not be sufficient to cover investments and operating costs. As DUPUIT pointed out a long time ago, such projects would never be undertaken if the consumer surplus were not taken into account.

In concluding, we can only emphasize again what the above analysis has made clear, that there are real benefits to the consumer in all those cases where real income increases are not taken away by discriminatory charges, that is, when only one price is charged for the project's output. Hence, market prices alone cannot measure the economic or social benefits of a project.

2.4. INTERMEDIATE PRODUCTS

In the preceding discussion, consumer willingness to pay emerged as an important concept for the valuation of consumer goods. In many cases, however, the project evaluator will find himself in a position where he has to determine the value of an intermediate product which may be many production stages away from the final goods that are eventually produced. An example is steel. It may be used in the housing industry for the production of residential houses or it may be used in the tractor industry to produce tractors that will help to produce more agricultural goods, and so on.

In principle, the valuation of intermediate products is not different from that of consumer goods. Take, for instance, the case of tractors. The value of a tractor to the farmer depends on what he will obtain for his agricultural products and on what the costs of his other inputs are. Similarly, for the tractor manufacturer, the value of the steel he uses depends on what he will receive for his tractors and on what the costs of his other inputs are. Ultimately then, the value of steel used in tractor production depends on what the final consumer pays for the agricultural products which the tractor helps produce. It is thus the consumer's willingness to pay for the final product that determines the value of the intermediate product used in its production.

Often a shortcut can be used to measure the values of intermediate products. For instance, if the markets for the intermediate goods are perfectly competitive, the willingness to pay of the users of an intermediate product would represent the true value of the product and the analysis can then stop with an estimate of the demand curve for the product. Problems arise, however, where markets are not competitive, as the actual prices paid may well understate the final consumer value.

In principle, three types of distortion can be distinguished. First, the users of the intermediate product may exercise monopsony powers or, in other words, they pay less than they would be able to pay. The only way to measure the value of the intermediate product then is to determine the true capacity to pay of these users, which means that a hypothetical demand curve should be constructed, derived from the estimation of the value of the products produced by the users of the input in question, given the costs of all their other inputs. Second, it is possible that the users of the intermediate product exercise monopoly powers in their product markets. As a result of this, the final consumers would have to pay a price for the final consumer good which includes the amount of monopoly profit that is being made by the users of the intermediate product in their production process. The actual price paid for the intermediate product would then understate its value by the amount of the monopoly profit made. Finally, markets may be subject to rationing or price controls. Also, in such cases the capacity to pay will exceed the amount that is actually being paid. The task of the project analyst thus is to investigate what distortions exist and to measure in such cases by what amount true willingness to pay differs from what is actually being paid. At first sight, this may look like a formidable task. In practice, however, many inputs account for only a small portion of total costs so that rough estimates will suffice.

2.5. DOMESTIC PRICES AND BORDER PRICES

Foreign exchange can be 'produced' by a country either by expanding its exports or by reducing its imports. What are the benefit-cost evaluation rules for export-generating or import-reducing projects? Exports of a good should be expanded as long as the export earnings of the marginal unit valued at the foreign exchange shadow rate are higher than its real cost of production. Similarly, domestic production of a good should be expanded to substitute for previously imported units if the savings in foreign exchange valued at the foreign exchange opportunity rate are greater than the real domestic production cost. Note that in the latter case the consumer surplus should not be taken into account as the consumers enjoy it already on the previously imported units. Hence, in both cases, i.e., in export expansion or import substitution, the benefits are the export earnings or savings valued at the foreign exchange opportunity cost rate. In all other cases the benefits of a domestically produced good consist of the domestic willingness to pay and its costs are to be measured by the opportunity costs of the factors of production. Insofar as the project would induce additional imports, the relevant cost concept for those imports is the foreign exchange opportunity value, i.e., the c.i.f. costs in foreign currency valued at the foreign exchange opportunity cost rate.

The benefit-cost rules described in the previous paragraph are the classical rules and are also followed in the UNIDO Guidelines.[21] However, they are different from the ones LITTLE and MIRRLEES (L and M)[22] have proposed in Volume II of the OECD Manual on Industrial Project Analysis.[23] Basically, what L and M suggest is that all goods should be valued in border prices. A distinction is therefore made between tradeables – imported and exported or importable and exportable goods – for which the conversion is easy, and nontradeables – such as power, transport, construction and services. The latter are to be decomposed into their constituent inputs which, in the case of materials, are again valued in border prices and, in the case of labor, at the marginal product of labor, which is then converted into consumption so that it can also be valued at border prices. As in practice it will be difficult to decompose nontraded goods each time into their various parts, L and M suggest that conversion factors be used. Thus one may use conversion factors for construction, electricity, labor, and such, and, in cases where it is difficult to get detailed information about the methods of production, a standard conversion factor, although one should recognize that the latter is only a crude approximation. The standard conversion factor should be representative of a wide range of goods and is in practice calculated as the reciprocal of the opportunity cost of foreign exchange.

Strict adherence to L and M's methodology could lead to wrong results in all those cases where goods do not enter international trade. In a symposium on their Manual, several critics therefore took issue with L and M, and it may be useful to repeat two examples – one for tradeables, the other for nontradeables – provided by DASGUPTA, one of L and M's leading critics. The first concerns machine tools. Suppose, DASGUPTA[24] states that 1,500 units of machine tools are currently being produced annually in a country and sold at $ 20,000 each. Suppose also that the Government is considering increasing output by 300 units. If the project is accepted, the market clearing price will fall to $ 19,000. On the other hand, the import price of the 300 units is $ 15,000 each. If Government allows the units to be imported, then the normal analysis tells us that they should be produced if their production cost is lower than their import price. Suppose, however, that the Government does not allow imports of the units. Then, according to the L and M approach, the 300 units should be valued at $ 15,000, whereas, according to the UNIDO approach, they should be valued at somewhere between $ 20,000 and $ 19,000, say, $ 19,500. Which procedure is the correct one? If the Government will not allow import of the additional machine tools, then there can be no doubt that they should be valued at the domestic willingness to pay.

28

Regarding nontradeables, DASGUPTA again gave a good example, which we quote here verbatim: 'Suppose, for example, that electric power figures prominently in the operation of a project that is to produce an import substitute. If the use of electricity by the project reduces its supply in the rest of the economy by an amount that the project requires, then the UNIDO approach recommends the use of the producers' willingness to pay for electricity in order to evaluate its shadow price. The OECD approach, however, recommends the use of the marginal social cost of producing it as its appropriate shadow price. If the economy were producing efficiently, it can be shown that the two shadow prices would be equal. But, typically, the willingness to pay for a marginal amount of electricity might exceed its social cost. In such an instance it is possible for the project to be rejected by the UNIDO approach (because cost of electric power is 'high') and accepted by the OECD approach (because the cost is 'low').'

It is difficult to say whether L and M have accepted changing their appraisal methodology because they do not address themselves directly to the examples. However, the following quote seems to suggest a concession: 'Formally, we are quite prepared to settle for what Dasgupta says is the UNIDO line – that the evaluator should decide in the light of what Government policy will be, after allowing for his own influence.'[25] Also, in their sequel to the Manual, L and M appear to agree that the evaluator should evaluate what will probably happen, not what he would like to happen.[26]

If indeed L and M have accepted the above criticism, then there is not much difference any more from a theoretical point of view between the normal appraisal and L and M's methodology. Whereas normally domestic prices are used as the numéraire, L and M use foreign prices as the numéraire, but theoretically either one of the numéraires can be used with the same result. Furthermore, both methods require the same amount of information. Consider, for instance, the case where a project induces some additional production of a nontradeable input, the cost of which includes foreign exchange. Then, under the L and M method, every component of the input would be valued at border prices. Under the traditional method, all components of the input, including the foreign exchange component, would be valued at domestic prices, but to determine the foreign exchange component the same information would be required as under the L and M method.[27]

In practice there are several objections, in our opinion, to the L and M method. First, Governments in general will prefer the valuation to take place in domestic prices rather than in border prices. Second, the L and M methodology is presented in such a way that it is easy to make mistakes. As STEWART and STREETEN wrote: 'The L and M methods may themselves be stretched to cover some (possibly all) of the exceptions; in practice, as the Manual is written and applied, it is unlikely that they will be so interpreted.'[28]

Let us demonstrate a few of the difficulties of the L and M method with an example. Suppose we are to measure the values of a series of inputs to be used for constructing a dam or a factory. We can then set up the following simple table (Table 2.1) to show the difference between the normal and the L and M

TABLE 2.1.

	Normal Method		L and M Method		
	Total Cost	Foreign Exchange Component	Total Cost in Rs mil.	Conversion Factors	Total Cost in US$ mil.
	Rs mil.				
I. Equipment I (nontradeable)	30	–	30	0.80	24
II. Equipment II (imported)	30	30	30	1.00	30
III. Civil Works	40	10	40	0.85	34
Total	100	40			
Foreign Exchange Premium	10	25%			
Total	110			0.80	88

method. Since we are interested in highlighting the border price issue, we are assuming, for simplicity's sake, that there is no shadow price for labor. In this example, the official exchange rate is US $ 1 = Rs 1 and the opportunity cost of foreign exchange is US $ 1 = Rs 1.25 or, similarly, the Standard Conversion Factor (SCF), being the reciprocal of the latter, is 0.8. As should be clear after the above discussion, it does not make any difference whether the costs are expressed in rupees or in US dollars: under the normal method, the costs are valued at Rs 110 million and under the L and M method, at US $ 88 million; given the foreign exchange opportunity cost rate, both are equal.

But will this be so in practice? It seems to us that the L and M method will lead much easier to mistakes than the normal method. Let us take Category I, the nontradeables, first. In the above example, the conversion was easy: we used the SCF. But what will happen when we follow the decomposition method of the L and M manual to convert domestic values into foreign exchange? One may well arrive at very wrong values. Category II should not cause problems: imports and exports are valuated at border prices. But what about Category III and all the other categories that include a mixture of foreign exchange and local costs? L and M see the danger and recommend the use of as many conversion factors as possible. But what will happen in practice is that one will group categories together, calculate a conversion factor for them, and then always use the same conversion factor. For instance, L and M mention specifically that when information on construction is not available it will be useful to have available the construction conversion factor. It seems to us that there are dozens of techniques to construct things and that the project analyst should base his cost estimate on the construction method that actually will be followed rather than on some average technique. Finally, there are serious difficulties with the L and M

30

method if one takes into account that the opportunity cost of foreign exchange may change during the life of the project. If we follow L and M, then one must review and recalculate all the conversion factors if one expects that trade policy will change. Under the normal method we can easily adjust the foreign exchange shadow rate.

A criticism that may be made about the normal method is that many governments have objected to the use of a foreign exchange shadow rate. This is quite true, but it was caused by the way it was presented. In the past, many economists have been guilty of inferring that the foreign exchange rate under free trade – that is, the rate in the absence of exchange controls and tariffs – is the rate at which the official exchange rate should be set. This is, of course, not correct. If we make clear to governments that the opportunity cost of foreign exchange is essentially an exchange rate adjusted for the difference between domestic and international prices,[29] probably no government would object to such a rate.

Benefit-cost analysis is just taking off and it is only recently that some of its principles are becoming accepted as core principles. The normal appraisal methodology is theoretically correct; moreover, it has proven itself workable. The L and M method is complicated and easily leads to wrong results. We see no reason to change horses in mid-stream.

[1] DUPUIT, 'On the Measurement of the Utility of Public Works' in 'Readings in Welfare Economics.'

[2] Ibid., p. 262.

[3] MARSHALL, 'Principles of Economics,' p. 103.

[4] For a different interpretation, see FRIEDMAN, M., 'The Marshallian Demand Curve' in 'Essays in Positive Economics,' University of Chicago Press, Chicago, 1953, pp. 47–49.

[5] MARSHALL, 'Principles of Economics,' Mathematical Appendix, Note VI, p. 693. MARSHALL speaks of the marginal utility of money of the consumer, but it is now generally accepted that what he meant is the marginal utility of income.

[6] Before proceeding from the individual surplus to the collective consumer surplus, MARSHALL makes another qualification. He points out that 'the same sum of money represents different amounts of pleasure to different people.' However, he then adds that it is seldom necessary to consider this matter because 'by far the greater number of the events with which economics deals, affect in about equal proportions all the different classes of society.' Subsequent writers have not paid much attention to this qualification because it was not believed necessary. As will be discussed in section 2.4, we attach, however, great importance to it because we believe that the condition applies only to the middle income groups.

[7] HOTELLING, 'The General Welfare in Relation to Problems of Taxation and of Railway and Utility Rates.'

[8] HICKS, J. R., 'Value and Capital,' Note to Chapter II.

[9] HICKS, J. R., 'A Revision of Demand Theory.'

[10] It should be noted that in the Hicksian terminology, the compensating surplus is not equal to the compensating variation in income; the latter is the reduction in income that would be necessary to leave the consumer as well off when he buys as much as he likes at the price CD as when he was in his original position. The compensating variation in income is thus equal to the strip NKBF. If this were mulcted from the consumer, he would buy the quantity NF at the price CD. If, however, in addition, he is obliged to buy the additional quantity FC at the price CD, he will be worse off as measured by the triangle FCG. The compensating surplus (NKBF-FCG) is thus smaller than the compensating variation in income (NKBF).

It is the compensating variation in income which forms the basis for the Hicks equation. When the compensating variation in income is mulcted from the consumer, he will buy the additional quantity EF – the so-called substitution effect because it represents the quantity the consumer substitutes for other goods when he is constrained to remain at his initial real income level – at the price CD. When the mulcted amount is returned to the consumer, he will end up buying the additional quantity FC – the so-called income effect because it represents the quantity the consumer buys because of the increase in his real income. The total effect of the lowering of the price from BA to CD is that the consumer ends up buying the additional quantity EC and this may thus be considered to consist of the substitution effect EF and the income effect FC.

The Hicks equation is written as:

$$\frac{\delta Q}{\delta P} = \frac{\partial Q}{\partial P}\bigg|_{U=\text{const.}} + \frac{\partial Q}{\partial Y} \cdot -\frac{\partial Y}{\partial P}\bigg|_{Prices=\text{const.}}$$

The term on the left-hand side represents the total quantity effect of the price change, and the two terms on the right-hand side the substitution effect and the income effect, respectively.

Multiplying by P/Q and remembering that the compensating variation in income ∂Y is equal to $Q.\partial P$ for small price changes, we get

$$\frac{P}{Q} \cdot \frac{\delta Q}{\delta P} = \frac{P}{Q} \cdot \frac{\partial Q}{\partial P} - \frac{P}{Q} \cdot \frac{\partial Q}{\partial Y} \cdot \frac{Q\partial P}{\partial P}$$

for which we may write:

$$e_1 = e_2 - \frac{PQ}{Y} \cdot \frac{Y}{Q} \cdot \frac{\partial Q}{\partial Y} \text{ , or}$$

$$e_1 = e_2 - \frac{PQ}{Y} \cdot e_3$$

In this formula, e_1 is the elasticity of demand of the normal Marshallian demand curve, e_2 the elasticity of demand when real income is kept constant (i.e., when only the substitution effect is considered), e_3 the income elasticity of demand, and PQ/Y the fraction of income spent on the particular good.

[11] The equivalent surplus is not the same as the equivalent variation in income. The latter represents the addition to income that would be necessary to leave the consumer as well off when he is free to consume what the wants at the price BA as when he consumes OD units at the price CD. The equivalent variation in income is thus equal to the area NKHC. Since the consumer is worse off when he is constrained, the equivalent surplus is larger by the triangle BIH than the equivalent variation in income.

[12] HICKS, 'Revision of Demand Theory,' pp. 106–107.

[13] HARBERGER, A. C., 'Three Basic Postulates for Applied Welfare Economics – an Interpretive Essay,' The Journal of Economic Literature, September 1971, pp. 785–797.

[14] WINCH, D. M. 'Consumer Surplus and the Compensating Principle,' The American Economic Review, June 1965, pp. 395–423.

[15] SILBERBERG, E., 'Duality and the Many Consumer's Surpluses,' The American Economic Review, December 1972, pp. 942–952.

[16] BURNS, M. E., 'A Note on the Concept and Measure of Consumer's Surplus,' The American Economic Review, June 1973, pp. 335–344.

[17] e.g. BERGSON, A., 'On Monopoly Welfare Losses,' The American Economic Review, December 1973, pp. 853–870; and REAUME, D. M., 'Cost-Benefit Techniques and Consumer Surplus – A Clarificatory Analysis,' Public Finance No. 2, 1973, pp. 196–211.

[18] LITTLE, 'A Critique of Welfare Economics,' p. 175.

[19] Ibid., p. 180.

[20] WOHL, M. and MARTIN, B.V., 'Evaluation of Mutually Exclusive Design Projects,' Special Report 92, Highways Research Board, Washington, D.C., 1967.

[21] DASGUPTA, SEN and MARGLIN, 'Guidelines for Project Evaluation,' p. 47.

[22] LITTLE and MIRRLEES, 'Manual of Industrial Project Analysis,' Chapter XII.

[23] The OECD methodology is also followed by SQUIRE and VAN DER TAK, 'Economic Analysis of Projects.'

[24] DASGUPTA, P., 'A Comparative Analysis of the UNIDO Guidelines and the OECD Manual,' Bulletin of the Oxford University Institute of Economics and Statistics, February 1972, pp. 33–52.

[25] LITTLE, I. M. D. and MIRRLEES, J. A., 'A Reply to Some Criticisms of the OECD Manual,' Bulletin of the Oxford University Institute of Economics and Statistics, February 1972, p. 158.

[26] LITTLE and MIRRLEES, 'Project Appraisal,' Chapter VI, passim.

[27] For a detailed review of the equivalence of the two methods under various assumptions regarding the type of trade policy actually followed, see BALASSA, B., 'Estimating the Shadow Price of Foreign Exchange in Project Appraisal,' The Economic Journal, July 1974.

[28] STEWART, F. and STREETEN, D., 'Little-Mirrlees Methods and Project Appraisal,' Bulletin of the Oxford University Institute of Economics and Statistics, February 1972, p. 76.

[29] See Chapter 3, section 2.

3. THE VALUATION OF COSTS

3.1. INPUTS

The cost concept that is used in this study regarding the resources used in a project is that of the maximum benefits foregone. Suppose that a project's input of, say, steel reduces the quantity of steel available in the rest of the economy. Then the cost of this steel is to be measured by the value it had to its users. Suppose, however, that the project's demand for steel results in an increase in steel production rather than a reduction in the use of steel in the rest of the community. Then the steel producer would need to withdraw resources from the rest of the economy and the cost of the additional steel production would then be represented by the value of these resources. Or, in other words, the value of the additional steel produced would, in this case, be its opportunity cost of production.

The above analysis is especially relevant in the case of distortions which drive a wedge between prices and costs. HARBERGER[1] has done path-breaking work in this field and it will be useful to review his analysis of the opportunity cost of an input in the presence of an indirect tax. In figure 3.1 the curve DD' represents the normal market demand curve and the curve SS' the normal marginal cost (supply curve) for steel. An indirect tax on the price of steel would result in an equilibrium situation, indicated by the intersection of SS' with the net of tax curve KD', so that output would be OA, price received by the producers of steel AE, and price paid by the users of steel AJ.

Let us assume now that the project under consideration will need a quantity of steel equal to CB. This will shift the demand as well as the net of tax curve by CB to the right, so that the new production will be OB, the supply price of

FIGURE 3.1.

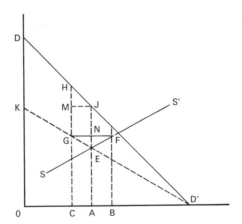

which is BF. But it is clear that this is not the opportunity cost of steel to be used in the cost calculation of the new project. The extra demand of CB has displaced demand equal to AC, the opportunity cost of which is AJHC, and has increased production by AB, the opportunity cost of which is AEFB. Hence, the true opportunity cost of the quantity CB is equal to AJHC plus AEFB.

The above can also be expressed in algebraic terms. If the additional quantity demanded is small in relation to the total market, the triangles MHJ and NFE can be neglected so that the opportunity cost consists of AJMC + ANFB. Using P_o as the general symbol for the opportunity cost of CB, we may write:

$$P_o = (AJMC + ANFB)/CB$$

$$(3.1.) = \frac{-\frac{\partial Q_d}{\partial P} \cdot P_d + \frac{\partial Q_s}{\partial P} \cdot P_s}{-\frac{\partial Q_d}{\partial P} + \frac{\partial Q_s}{\partial P}}$$

Since $-\frac{\partial Q_d}{\partial P} = e_d \cdot \frac{Q_d}{P}$ and $\frac{\partial Q_s}{\partial P} = e_s \frac{Q_s}{P}$ we may write

$$(3.2.) \quad P_o = \frac{e_d \, Q_d \, P_d + e_s \, Q_s \, P_s}{e_d \, Q_d + e_s \, Q_s}$$

Or, in words, the opportunity cost of an input is the weighted average of the demand and supply prices, the weights being the fractions of demand displaced and supply induced to additional demand.[2] This is an extremely valuable formula, which, in many cases, will give a good approximation of the cost of an input. It should be noted, however, that this result is based on two implicit assumptions. On the demand side, it was assumed that the market for steel is perfectly competitive. If, as discussed in the previous chapter, the market is distorted, it is not the actual demand price which is relevant for the analysis but the real willingness to pay of the users of steel. The second assumption was that the steel manufacturers' cost of production could be taken as the true value of the cost of producing the additional steel. Suppose, however, that the market price of the electricity the industry consumed does not reflect the real cost of electricity production or that the coal imported for the steel industry is bought by the industry at a price not reflecting its foreign exchange value. Then the true opportunity cost of the additional steel production should not be based on what is actually paid but on the real cost of the resources used. The cost of electricity should thus be calculated on the basis of its real opportunity cost of production and the cost of coal on the basis of the real opportunity cost of foreign exchange.

The principle that emerges is that one should attempt to measure the real possible willingness to pay in cases of the project displacing demand, and the real opportunity cost of production if the production of an input is increased in response to the project, and in cases where both occur, the weighted average of the two opportunity costs. This analysis may seem a hard task because, for a precise estimate, the relevant elasticities must be determined. In practice, however, the rate of return of the project may not be sensitive to the values of the input in question, so that rough estimates will suffice.

3.2. FOREIGN EXCHANGE

In many cases projects are planned because they produce products for export or for import substitution, or, in other words, for the foreign exchange earnings or savings they generate. Also, many projects – even when producing for the local market – may cause an increase in imports to be used as project inputs. Under conditions of trade equilibrium and in the absence of export duties (subsidies) and import duties (subsidies), the domestic value of the foreign exchange earnings or expenditures is found by multiplying the amount of foreign exchange by the official exchange rate. However, most countries impose import and export duties and many also have quantitative restrictions and foreign exchange controls. In such circumstances, the official exchange rate will understate the domestic value of the foreign exchange generated or used by a project.

The question thus is: Can we find criteria for measuring the domestic value of foreign exchange in cases where we suspect that the official rate does not represent the domestic value? To answer the question we should use the opportunity cost principle: for what purpose is foreign exchange used, and what is its value in such uses? A dollar of foreign exchange can either be added to a country's foreign exchange reserves or used for increasing imports or for reducing exports. Under normal circumstances a country's objective is not to earn foreign exchange for the sake of increasing its reserves so that the value of a dollar of foreign exchange is then immediately derived from the import-increasing or export-reducing objectives. But also if the reserves were to be increased, the value of a dollar of foreign exchange is determined by the opportunity-cost principle – i.e. by the alternative cost of increasing the reserves – and its value is therefore also then derived from the import-increasing or export-reducing possibilities. Hence, for the determination of the shadow price of foreign exchange it suffices to analyze what happens to the dollar when imports are increased or exports are reduced.

Suppose that a dollar of foreign exchange will be used entirely for increasing imports. Then its value is the domestic willingness to pay for such imports. To the extent that there are no quantitative restrictions, this domestic willingness to pay is the sum of the foreign price valued at the official exchange rate and the import duties. Hence, if the official exchange rate is US $ 1.00 = Rs 2.00, and the import duties are 30 percent, the domestic value of US $ 1.00 of imports is Rs 2.60.

36

Suppose that the additional dollar of foreign exchange will be used to reduce exports. Then, either more exportable goods will become available in the country or the resources otherwise used to produce export goods will be used to produce home goods. Hence, the domestic value of the additional export goods or the freed resources that become available in the home market can be found by considering the level of export duties and subsidies. In many developing countries, export duties are an important source of revenues in addition to import duties.[3] Let us assume therefore that, in our hypothetical country, export duties average 10 percent of f.o.b. value. Then the domestic value of US $ 1.00 of exports in f.o.b. prices is Rs 1.80.

We have thus found two values for the opportunity cost of foreign exchange, the first related to imports of Rs 2.60 and the second related to exports of Rs 1.80. It should be noted that we have here the same problem we discussed in Section 3.1 regarding the opportunity cost of an input, and we may therefore apply the same analysis. HARBERGER's formula (3.2) can thus be written as:[4]

$$R' = \frac{\eta . M . (1 + T)R + \varepsilon X (1 - D)R}{\eta M + \varepsilon X}$$

where R' = Shadow price of foreign exchange and R = official exchange rate, both exchange rates expressed in terms of units of local currency per unit of foreign currency

M = c.i.f. value of imports in terms of foreign currency
T = Import duties
η = Elasticity of demand for foreign exchange with respect to changes in the exchange rate
X = f.o.b. value of exports in terms of foreign currency
D = Export duties
ε = Elasticity of supply of foreign exchange with respect to changes in the exchange rate.

The foreign exchange opportunity cost is thus the weighted average of the domestic values of the country's import and export prices, the weights being the fractions in which an additional dollar of foreign exchange will be used for increasing imports and reducing exports, respectively.[5] In case of export subsidies the sign of D has, of course, to be reversed. In case of quantitative restrictions, the formula remains valid except that then T should be interpreted as representing the tariff equivalent of the restrictions. In such a case, importers may make a more than normal profit and this should be considered as if it were a tariff. Hence, the tariff equivalent is to be found by comparing the domestic prices of the restricted goods with their world prices valued at the official exchange rate. The formula thus has quite some generality. Furthermore, it may be noted that when the country in question is a price-taker, demand and supply of foreign exchange is determined by physical imports and exports, so that the demand and supply elasticities of foreign exchange can be replaced by the import demand and export supply elasticities.[6] It should also be noted that the formula is based on existing distortions and that it does not represent the shadow price of foreign exchange under free trade conditions.[7] As discussed in Chapter 1, it is therefore the correct formula to use if indeed the Government is not willing to abolish the duties, which is what one can generally expect.

A problem that remains with the HARBERGER formula is, of course, that complicated econometric studies will be necessary to find the relevant elasticities. It is therefore useful to review whether the formula can be simplified. The UNIDO Manual suggests that the opportunity cost of foreign exchange should normally be calculated as the average of the ratios of domestic clearing prices of consumption goods to c.i.f. prices calculated at the official rate of exchange. Exports would be left out of the formula as, in the opinion of the authors of the UNIDO Manual, it is unlikely that increased earnings of foreign exchange will lead to a reduction in exports. Furthermore, capital goods would not be included in the imports in the formula because the authors feel that the rate of investment is not constrained by a country's balance of payments but by political and institutional conditions. Hence, foreign exchange has a higher value than that indicated by the official exchange rate only to the extent that it increases domestic consumption.

It is difficult to reject the UNIDO proposal out of hand because it all depends on what will happen in practice when additional foreign exchange becomes available. Enhanced foreign exchange availability will often lead to increased consumption of exports when such exports are suitable for domestic consumption, such as when the exports consist of manufactured consumer goods. Where the exports consist of agricultural raw materials or minerals, the additional foreign exchange availability will not, in general, lead to home consumption of these products, but the pressure to export may well be reduced and the resources otherwise used for exports may then be used for the production of home goods. Excluding capital goods from the formula may be justified in special cases where indeed investments are constrained by political conditions. But if this is not the case, the increased availability of foreign exchange may well increase the demand for imported investment goods when such goods are not available in the country. To follow UNIDO's suggestion probably implies that the opportunity cost of foreign exchange will be overestimated. On the export side, many developing countries impose export duties, so that, in general, the exclusion of exports from the formula will tend to increase the estimate of the opportunity cost of foreign exchange. Excluding investment goods from imports will have the same effect, as import duties on capital goods are normally much lower than those on consumption goods.

Because UNIDO's suggestion is not very realistic, we may ask whether there exists another shortcut method of estimating the opportunity cost of foreign exchange. In this respect it may be noted that if the demand and supply elasticities are the same, the Harberger formula reduces to a simple ratio of the sum of domestic values of imports and exports to their world values. Thus, in our example, if exports equal imports, the opportunity cost of foreign exchange would be Rs 2.20. If it is likely that the demand elasticity for foreign exchange is higher than the supply elasiticty, a reasonable estimate will often be to take the average of the foreign exchange opportunity cost of imports (Rs 2.60) and the unweighted Harberger formula rate (Rs 2.20). Thus in our example, the base estimate of the foreign exchange opportunity cost would be Rs 2.40. On the other hand, if the supply elasticity is expected to be higher than the demand elasticity, the average of the foreign exchange opportunity cost of exports (Rs 1.80) and the unweighted Harberger formula rate (Rs 2.20) may be a good approximation. In all cases, it is recommended that sensitivity tests be undertaken. In Chapter 6 of this study, where the subject of macro-economic imbalances is discussed, more information is given on the likely values of the elasticities.

3.3. LABOR

The production factor labor has the feature, distinct from all other production factors, that the laborer's services are tied to the laborer. This feature has important implications as regards the supply price of labor and it will be useful, therefore, to review briefly how this supply price is determined.

The reader is first referred to Figure 3.2A, which presents the well-known indifference curve analysis. The horizontal axis represents the number of labor hours the worker can provide up to the physiologically maximum OA and the vertical axis represents his income. It is assumed that the laborer has a non-labor income of OR and that any addition to OR is labor income. Two of the possible indifference curves of the worker are drawn (U_1 and U_2), each presenting a line of equal utility achieved by substituting additional utility in the form of leisure for a reduction in utility in the form of income. The slope of an indifference curve at any one point is therefore $-\partial U/\partial A : \partial U/\partial M$, where $\partial U/\partial A$ is the marginal disutility of labor (or marginal utility of leisure when the sign is reversed) and $\partial U/\partial M$ the marginal utility of income. The slopes are increasing along an indifference curve from left to right, indicating that progressively increasing increments of income are needed to compensate the worker for each incremental reduction in leisure. When the worker reaches the maximum number of labor hours, the slopes become infinite. At the extreme left of the figure, the slopes are assumed to be horizontal, indicating that no disutility of labor exists when only small amounts of labor are applied.

The laborer's supply position can now be determined as follows. Suppose that the wage rate is w_1 as indicated by the slope of the line RY_1. Then the laborer's equilibrium position will be at point A, i.e., the point where the wage rate w_1 equals the marginal valuation of labor ($-\partial U/\partial A : \partial U/\partial M$), or, in perhaps more familiar terms, where the marginal disutility of labor ($-\partial U/\partial A$) equals the wage rate w multiplied by the marginal utility of income ($\partial U/\partial M$). At a wage rate of w_1 the laborer will thus work a total of OA' hours, earn AA' of income and have a welfare position equal to U_1. Increasing the wage rate to w_2 – the

FIGURE 3.2A.

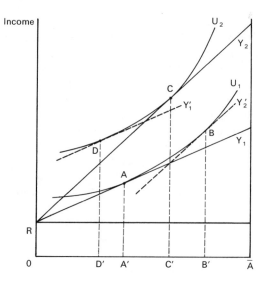

FIGURE 3.2B.

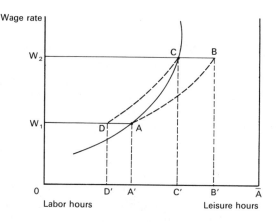

level indicated by the slope of the line RY_2 – will result in a new equilibrium position C, so that he will then work a total of OC' hours, earn CC' of income, and have a welfare position equal to U_2.

The increase in the welfare position of the worker due to a wage rate increase is often defined with the help of either the compensating variation or the equivalent variation of income. The compensating variation[8] is the amount of income that should be taken away from the worker in order to keep him when he works at the wage rate w_2 at his original welfare level U_1. This is thus equal to the difference between the Y_2 and and Y_2' lines. The equivalent variation, on the other hand, is the amount of income that should be given to the worker to bring him to the welfare level U_2 if he has to work at wage rate w_1. This amount of income is thus equal to the difference between the Y_1' and Y_1 lines.

However, neither the compensating not the equivalent variation is, in our

40

opinion, a correct measure of the increase in welfare. This may perhaps best be shown with the help of Figure 3.2B, which presents the same analysis in a slightly different form. The line AC is the laborer's supply curve and the curves AB and DC the compensated and equilibrated supply curves corresponding to the U_1 and U_2 curves of Figure 3.2A, respectively. The compensating variation in income is thus represented by the area $w_1 A B w_2$ and the equivalent variation in income by the area $w_1 D C w_2$. Neither of the two areas however, as discussed in Chapter 2 where the consumer surplus was reviewed, measures the real welfare increase of the worker. In case income distribution does not count, the exact measure is the area left of the laborer's supply curve, i.e., the area $w_1 A C w_2$. This area can also be found by considering the disutility of the extra work that the laborer undertakes when the wage rate is increased. The supply curve shows that if the wage rate increases from w_1 to w_2, the worker's income increases by a total of $0 w_2 C C'$ minus $0 w_1 A A'$. An amount equal to $A'ACC'$ is necessary to compensate the worker for his additional work and the net welfare increase is therefore $w_1 A C w_2$, or, algebraically, $\triangle w(L + 1/2 \triangle L)$. In case income distribution counts, the total increase in income as well as the leisure foregone should be evaluated at the marginal utilities of income corresponding to each of the different points on the supply curve AC, so that the welfare increase of the worker equals $\triangle w(L + 1/2 \triangle L)$ evaluated at the different marginal utilities of income.

We may now formalize the argument as follows. Suppose that we are considering the hiring of an individual worker for a new project and that

m = income of the worker in his present occupation
a = extra disutility of effort if the worker accepts the new job
w = wage the new project pays
x = product of the worker in the new project.

Then we can set up the following table to show the welfare effects of the hiring of an employed worker.

TABLE 3.1. Welfare Effects of Hiring an Employed Worker.

	Economically	Socially
Income gain of project	$x - w$	$(x - w) v_p$
Income gain of worker	$w - m$	$(w - m) v_w$
Compensation for harder work	a	$a v_w$
Net gain of worker	$w - m - a$	$(w - m - a) v_w$
Total gain of society	$x - (m + a)$	$(x - w) v_p + (w - m - a) v_w$

Economically, the benefit is simply the difference between the product of the worker in his new occupation and the worker's old income plus the value of the extra disutility of effort. For a social evaluation, however, the benefits must be valued at the relevant marginal utilities of income, and the benefit expression is then as in the right hand column of the table, whereby v_p and v_w represent the

41

income distribution weights derived from the marginal utility of income schedule applicable to the project owners and workers, respectively.

Let us consider now the case where an unemployed laborer is hired, and let us assume that the worker receives from Government unemployment benefits or from his family an income equal to y. Then the following table may be established.

TABLE 3.2. Welfare Effects of Hiring an Unemployed Laborer.

	Economically	Socially
Income gain of project	$x - w$	$(x - w) v_p$
Income gain of worker	$w - y$	$(w - y) v_w$
Compensation for harder work	a	$a v_w$
Net gain of worker	$w - y - a$	$(w - y - a) v_w$
Gain rest of society or family	y	$y v_f$
Total gain of society	$x - a$	$(x - w)v_p + (w - y - a)v_w$ $+ y v_f$

Economically, the unemployment benefits are thus not to be considered, since they are mere transfer payments. The worker loses y when he becomes employed, but the rest of society gains y, so that the net effect is nil. From a social point of view, however, when income distribution counts, the loss and the gain are to be valued at the marginal utilities of income of the different parties, so that the loss and gain do not cancel. As regards the valuation of a, it needs to elaboration that the supply price of the worker depends on his initial welfare position. For instance, it is a well known phenomenon in the developed countries that some workers prefer to remain unemployed for extended periods than to accept a job at a wage rate slightly higher than the unemployment benefits, and the value of a may then be quite high.

We attach considerable importance to the above analysis, since most of the development literature does not consider the welfare position of the worker. It is often postulated that the foregone marginal product of the worker is the opportunity cost of labor or, similarly, that when a worker is unemployed, the opportunity cost of labor is zero. This does not acknowledge that the laborer may incur an extra disutility of effort when he moves to another position or that he may have a certain reservation wage below which he is not willing to work. For the determination of the real cost of labor, the relevant concept is not that of m – the foregone marginal product, but rather of $m + a$ – the voluntary supply price of labor. Only this concept can explain, for instance, that an additional wage or salary should be offered to induce a rural laborer to move to the city or, in general, to a job where he has to work harder or where conditions are more unpleasant.

After this introduction to the subject, we can turn to the question of how in practice we should determine the real cost of labor. The number of possible cases that can be studied is almost unlimited, depending on the actual circumstances, and we will therefore restrict our analysis to three institutional frameworks which are generally believed to be relevant for the developing countries. The principles which will emerge from our analysis are, however, applicable to other situations.

The first case which we would like to review is that of the over-populated developing countries, the so-called labor-surplus countries. Lewis[9] has offered a model of such an economy which has had, and still has, substantial impact on the economic development and project evaluation literature, and it, therefore, appears well worthwhile to start our analysis with a review of his work. The Lewis model distinguishes a capitalist sector (factories, mines, plantations, and such), where labor is paid the marginal product, and a subsistence sector (of which agriculture is the most important), where labor receives the average product. The reason that the average product is paid in the agricultural subsistence sector is that the land-to-population ratio in these countries is so low that the marginal productivity of labor in agriculture is zero or even negative. Hence, labor would starve if it were paid the marginal product. However, if each member of the farm household shares equally in the total product, i.e., if each member is paid the average product, the household can continue to operate although, due to population pressures, the average product will soon equal the subsistence level. Since the marginal product of labor in the subsistence sector is zero, labor can be withdrawn from there without reducing the volume of farm output. Farm labor will be willing to move to the capitalist sector, provided the wage rate there is sufficiently above the subsistence wage of the agriculture sector to compensate the laborer for his moving. According to Lewis, this minimum wage level is reached when it is about 30 to 50 percent above the subsistence level and the labor supply curve for the capitalist sector will then be perfectly elastic. The capitalist sector has a high marginal productivity of labor due to its use of capital and can thus easily absorb some of the surplus labor of the agricultural sector at the going wage rate. Since the capitalist sector will reinvest its profits, the marginal productivity of labor curve will shift upwards, resulting in more labor employment, more profits and reinvestments, more labor employment, and so on. Industrialization is thus in the Lewis model the key to economic expansion. The process will come to an end only when the supply function of labor starts to rise. This can happen for various reasons. For instance, the number of people in the subsistence sector may be reduced so far that the average product there will rise. Alternatively, labor productivity in the subsistence sector may rise because of additional capital and new technology, or because of a rise in the relative price of agricultural products due to the additional demand of the workers in the capitalist sector. Thus, eventually, the whole process will result in an equilibrium situation, but this is so far away in time that for all practical purposes the opportunity cost of labor can be assumed to be zero.

The analysis can readily be presented graphically. In Figure 3.3A, the curve PQ represents the marginal producitivity of labor schedule in the subsistence

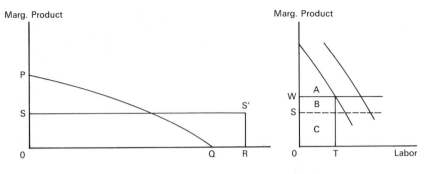

FIGURE 3.3A.   FIGURE 3.3B.

sector. Beyond the labor level OQ, it is assumed that the marginal product of labor is zero. There are, however, OR laborers who will share equally in the total product OPQ. Let OSS'R equal OPQ. Then the subsistence level is OS. Hence, out of a total of OR laborers, only OQ do productive work and QR can therefore be withdrawn from the agricultural sector without reducing the farm output: in other words, the opportunity cost of QR is zero.

Figure 3.3B presents the situation in the capitalist sector, whereby it should be noted that the labor axis is drawn on a larger scale than in Figure 3.3A. Since the supply price of labor withdrawn from the subsistence sector is OW (which is about 30 to 50 percent above the subsistence level according to Lewis), capitalists will hire laborers up to the point where the supply curve W intersects the marginal productivity of labor curve, i.e., they will hire OT Laborers. The opportunity cost of this labor is zero (OT is a fraction of QR) and the real value of the total product in the capitalist sector is therefore A + B + C, of which A accrues to the capitalists in the form of profits and B + C to the laborers in the form of wages. Whereas the wages will be consumed, the profits will be reinvested, so that the marginal productivity of labor curve will shift to the right. More laborers will then be hired, more profits will be made and reinvested, which again raises the marginal productivity of labor curve, resulting in the hiring of more laborers, and so on until the perfectly elastic labor supply curve starts to turn upward.

A problem with the model is, of course, that the capitalist sector can expand only if it has a market for its products. But in a closed economy, the markets for the capitalist sector's manufactures will be quite limited unless at the same time the productivity of the subsistence sector is raised. In an open economy, import substitution and export expansion may allow a somewhat longer expansion of the capitalist sector. However, the process may soon come to a halt if agricultural productivity is not increased since the possibility of import substitution is quite limited, and export expansion in countries at a low stage of development encounters difficulties in view of the poor quality of the manufactures produced. As a side remark, it may be noted that all this underlines once more the necessity of the interaction between national planning and project planning. The short-

44

comings of a national plan based on the model would be immediately obvious if the rates of return of the individual investment projects were calculated.

While the LEWIS model thus needs amendment, and this has been done by the so-called balanced growth theories which emphasize the necessity of raising the productivity of the agricultural sector, the question that still needs to be discussed is whether marginal labor productivity in the agricultural sector can indeed be zero. MYINT[10] has made the remark that employment in the capitalist sector of the surplus laborers will lead to extra consumption out of the expanded wage incomes (the area B in Figure 3.3B) and that this will lead to a social cost in case the projects in the capitalist sector do not yield a consumable output immediately. We believe that this argumentation is not correct. Infrastructure and heavy industry investments have indeed an element of waiting, but this should not be considered a social cost when the social rates of return of these investments exceed those of light industry investments where no waiting takes place. Furthermore, in an open economy, capital goods may be exported or used for import substitution, so that foreign exchange resources would be freed to satisfy the demand for consumption goods. Again, this would be justified as long as the social rates of return of the capital goods projects exceed those of the projects geared towards the immediate provision of consumption goods. The question which should be asked immediately in reply to this criticism is how these social rates of return should be calculated. This matter will be discussed in detail in Part II of this study. Meanwhile, it may suffice to mention that the element of waiting will indeed enter into the calculation of the social rate of return of a project, but only as long as there is a consensus in the economy that waiting is justified or, in other words, that the optimal income growth path has not yet been reached in the conomy and that investments should be stepped up. Part II will discuss the literature which proposes to deal with this matter by putting a premium on investments vis-a-vis consumption, and will show that this concept is not correct, since it does not recognize that growth in total national income is composed of the income growth of different income classes. Hence, when the distribution of income between persons and over time is not optimal, the proposal of MYINT – that it is the type of project output (heavy industry or infrastructure output vis-a-vis output of consumption goods) that counts – as well as that of others – that it is the distribution of project benefits between consumption and investment that counts – should be rejected and replaced by an analysis of the distribution of project benefits between income classes. In this part of the study, however, it is assumed that the interpersonal as well as the intertemporal distribution of income is optimal, so that the matter of waiting does not arise. Hence, if the opportunity cost of labor were zero, the benefits of a project in the capitalist sector would be A + B + C (Figure 3.3B) and there would be no need to analyze either the type of output or the distribution of the benefits.

Returning again to the matter of the zero marginal productivity of labor, MYINT has also made the remark[11] – an observation previously made by SEN[12] – that it is not the marginal product of a laborer which is relevant but the marginal product of labor time. As MYINT sees it, there is nothing wrong with applying labor time until its marginal product is zero since, according to him, it is a free good within the family. Hence, while labor time per farm household is applied until its product falls to zero, the total available labor time of all the workers exceeds what is being applied, and none of the workers will do a full day's work. As a consequence, if laborers are moved from agriculture to industry, those remaining behind will have to work harder, i.e., accept less leisure, if the total agricultural output is to remain unchanged. It is likely that this harder work will be undertaken only if economic incentives are provided, i.e., if those remaining behind receive a reward for their harder work. But if this is so, then, according to MYINT, there will be additional claims on the total resources of the country – either agricultural products or manufactures – and one cannot then speak of a zero shadow wage rate of those moving out of agriculture. Thus, even if the marginal product of labor time were zero, there would be a positive opportunity cost of labor.

MYINT's analysis is interesting but, in our opinion, not correct. First, it may be remarked that when the workers have to work harder their additional claim on the resources of the country should be considered the reward and not the cost of this harder work. The cost of the extra work is the disutility of the extra labor effort. Second, one wonders why in principle labor time should be considered a free good within the family. MYINT's assumption is certainly not correct if labor has a disutility of effort. Finally, the falling to zero of the marginal product of labor time should be seriously questioned on the basis of production principles. In a frequently quoted passage, VINER writes: 'As far as agriculture is concerned, I find it impossible to conceive of a farm of any kind on which, other factors of production being held constant in quantity and even in form as well, it would not be possible by known methods to obtain some addition to the crop by using additional labor in more careful selection and planting of the seed, more intensive weeding, cultivation, thinning and mulching, more painstaking harvesting, gleaning, and clearing of the crop.'[13] There is much to this criticism, and experience seems to bear VINER out. Even in the most overpopulated countries, one finds that positive wages are paid for rural landless workers and this phenomenon can, of course, be explained only if labor time has a positive marginal product.

Accepting then that the marginal product of labor time is in all likelihood positive, the opportunity cost of labor would be positive in the MYINT model. SEN,[14] however, has argued against such a conclusion and believes that, even if labor time has a positive marginal product, peasants will make up for the foregone output of those leaving the farm by working harder without asking for additional incentives. The assumptions SEN must make to arrive at this conclusion are that the marginal utility of income schedule of the family and its marginal disutility of labor schedule are flat in the relevant region. Similar to the analysis of the equilibrium position of a laborer at the beginning of this section, we may define the equilibrium position of the family-farm as the position where the marginal productivity of family labor ($P \cdot \partial X/\partial A$, where P is the market price, and $\partial X/\partial A$ the marginal physical product) equals the marginal valuation of family labor ($-\partial U/\partial A : \partial U/\partial M$, where $\partial U/\partial A$ is the disutility of family labor and $\partial U/\partial M$ the marginal utility of income)[15]. Under SEN's assumption, the marginal valuation of family labor curve would be horizontal so that indeed the rest of the family would work harder if a member leaves the farm. In the SEN model there is thus a positive marginal product of labor time, but there is also surplus labor because a number of workers can be withdrawn from the farm without reducing total output.

SEN regards his hypothesis as not implausible. It seems to us, however, that SEN's model is highly unrealistic. SEN's assumption that the marginal utility of income schedule is constant is rather farfetched,[16] and the assumption that the marginal disutility of labor does not increase in case of harder work is also unlikely. SEN's model leads to the conclusion that the supply function for labor would be flat. This is in contradiction with empirical observation. The facts are that during the busy seasons of planting and harvesting, even in countries such as India and Egypt – where LEWIS believes surplus labor exists – the labor supply curve turns upwards, so that in the busy season higher wages must be paid for hired labor than in the slack season. But if that is so, then there is clearly no surplus of labor. The doctrine of the zero opportunity cost of labor must thus, on this ground alone, be rejected.[17]

It remains to be analyzed how family and landless labor employment as well as the rural wage rate is determined during the various seasons. HANSEN[18] has analyzed this matter in detail. In Figure 3.4A, the supply curve of landless laborers is S_l, and of family labor S_f. It should be noted that only the short-run is considered so that the supply curve may start at a high positive level. The supply curve for family labor starts at a lower level than the one for landless labor, in line with the assumption that self-employment is considered more respectable and enjoyable than work for others. The total supply curve for labor is the horizontal summation of the two curves and is thus the curve S. Let MP_1 be the marginal productivity of labor curve (at given farm product prices) during the busy season. Then total labor input will be W_1C, of which W_1A are landless laborers hired at the wage rate OW_1 and W_1B family laborers. Similarly, if MP_2 is the marginal productivity of labor curve during one of the slack periods, the total labor input will be W_2F, of which W_2D is landless labor and W_2E is family labor, while the labor wage rate will be OW_2. The analysis is presented on a net basis in Figure 3.4B. The supply of landless laborers is S_l, while the demand curves for these laborers in the different seasons are represented by the D curves (found by deducting S_f from the MP curves). It is interesting to note that if the MP curve falls below the point G in Figure 3.4A, as it may well do during an extremely slack season, no labor can be hired. For instance, with a marginal productivity of labor curve equal to MP_3, labor input OL_3 will consist entirely of family labor. Although there exists then no market wage rate, this does not mean that labor has a zero shadow wage rate. The hiring of an unemployed worker has, as a consequence, the fact that the worker has to forego a certain amount of leisure and, as discussed, it should be recognized that this is

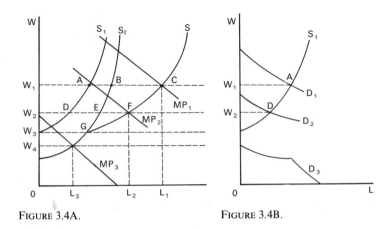

FIGURE 3.4A.   FIGURE 3.4B.

a social cost. Therefore, during the extremely slack season, the opportunity cost of landless laborers is OW_3 and of family labor OW_4.

With the above analysis we have come to an end as regards our review of how the opportunity cost of labor should be determined in the rural sector of the land-scarce developing countries. As we have seen, the problem of labor surplus is not a matter of a continuous surplus during the entire year but a matter of seasonality, with shortages during the peak periods and surpluses during the slack periods. On an aggregate basis, the overall opportunity cost of agricultural labor is simply the weighted average of the rural wage rates (OW_1 and OW_2), the reservation wage at which landless labor is not willing to work (OW_3) and the marginal product of family labor to the extent that it falls below the reservation wage (OW_4), the weights being the relevant quantities of labor. In the case of individual projects, however, a more detailed analysis will be necessary, as the withdrawing of labor will not necessarily take place in the quantities in which the different types of labor are applied on average. Although a precise analysis may be difficult, rough indications of the order of magnitude will often be sufficient to arrive at reasonably good estimates of the opportunity cost of labor. For instance, in the case of a rural works program to be undertaken mainly during the slack season, the average of the subsistence wage and the lower end of the rural wage scale will be a good indicator of the opportunity cost of the rural labor. Additional use of hired labor for irrigation projects during the entire year can be costed at the average of the rural wage rates throughout the year. The opportunity cost in the case of resettlement of non-viable farmers can often be estimated as equal to the minimum subsistence wage rate. And so on. In principle then, the opportunity cost of labor for rural projects can be reasonably well approximated and it is definitely not zero, as the LEWIS model would lead us to believe.

Although we thus reject the LEWIS doctrine, we would like to mention, however, that this does not mean that we believe that rural incomes in the developing countries are adequate. On the contrary, in many developing countries rural

48

productivity is low and many people live there at the margin of physical existence. What the development process is all about is that such poverty should be eradicated. This subject will be discussed in detail in Part II of this study.

As the second case study, we would like to analyze whether the rural opportunity cost of labor also determines the urban opportunity cost of labor. If we were to follow LEWIS, we should increase the former by about 30 to 50 percent to induce rural workers to migrate to the cities. Others believe a differential of about 100 percent would be necessary. Whatever the exact figures, the reason why this differential is necessary is obvious. A rural worker will migrate to the city only if his real income there is at least equal to his real rural earnings, and, in making the comparison, he will take into account that the cost of living in the city (food, rent, transportation) is more expensive than in the rural areas, that he may have to work harder if employed, that he may risk becoming unemployed, but that he may then have more leisure, etc.

Denoting the rural opportunity cost adjusted for the city differences and hence the worker's voluntary supply price by $\bar{m}$, the urban opportunity cost of labor would be equal to $\bar{m}$ if the wage rate in the urban sector were free to find its own market-clearing level. In most developing countries, however, the urban wage rate is institutionally determined, sometimes even at levels three to four times higher than the average rural wage rate. As a result, rural workers are willing to migrate to the urban centers, even though large pools of unemployed may exist there. If the number of unemployed in the urban sector were constant, the opportunity cost of a worker hired in the urban area would be equal to $\bar{m}$ because the hired unemployed worker would be replaced in the unemployment pool by a worker from the rural area. There is, however, as HARRIS and TODARO[19] and HARBERGER[20] (H-T-H) have shown, no reason why the number of unemployed should remain constant.

The H-T-H- model is basically very simple. Migration from the rural areas to the urban areas is a function of the expected earnings in the urban areas, while the expected earnings are a function of the urban wage rate as well as the probability of getting employed at this wage rate. In the H-T-H model, this probability is presented by $p = N/L$, where N is the number of laborers employed at the institutionally determined wage rate and L the total number of laborers in the urban area. From this follows that $dL/dN = 1/p$, or, in other words, that the creation of one urban job results in an inmigration of $1/p$ rural workers. The opportunity cost of hiring a worker in the urban area is thus $(1/p) \cdot \bar{m}$. As a rural worker will migrate to the urban areas only if the probability of obtaining the urban wage rate multiplied by this rate w equals $\bar{m}$, we may also write $\bar{m} = p_{eq}w$. Substituting this in the previous expression, it is immediately seen that in the equilibrium situation where $p = p_{eq}$, the opportunity cost of a worker hired in the urban area equals the going urban wage rate w.[21]

The rate of unemployment is in this model the mechanism that keeps the migration rate down. Suppose that the pool of unemployed in the urban area is small, so that the probability of getting a job as well as expected earnings $(N/L) \cdot w$ are high. Then there will be an inflow of migrants, which will increase the number of unemployed. As a result, the probability of obtaining a job will be reduced. This process will go on until the probability of obtaining a job N/L just equals $\bar{m}/w$. At that equilibrium level, the average unemployment rate $(L - N)/L$ is equal to $1 - p$. As the hiring of one laborer will result in an increase in the total labor force of $1/p$ persons and an increase in unemployment of $(1/p) - 1$ persons, the marginal rate of unemployment is presented by $[d(L - N)]/dL = (1/p - 1)/(1/p) = 1 - p$, and is thus the same as the average rate. Hence, in the H-T-H model the rate of unemployment in the equilibrium position is constant. The hiring of additional persons will lead to an increase in absolute numbers of the unemployed but not to an increase in the rate of unemployment.

The opportunity cost of labor must be equal to the urban wage rate in this model because the hiring of one worker whose supply price is pw will lead to an inflow of $1/p$ workers, so that the total welfare foregone equals exactly w. This can also be shown as follows. Suppose that $p = 0.5$, so that two workers will migrate to the city if one worker is hired. As a result, one worker will become unemployed and his loss in welfare is thus $\bar{m}$. This must be added to the opportunity cost of the hired worker, which is also $\bar{m}$. Hence, the total opportunity cost equals $2\bar{m}$, which, because $\bar{m} = 0.5w$, equals exactly the urban wage rate.

While the H-T-H model makes it very clear that in addition to the supply price of the individual worker, the loss in welfare of those workers who become unemployed must also be considered, the model is not very realistic in several respects. First, as STIGLITZ[22] has observed, the definition of the probability of obtaining work in the urban area, $p = N/L$, implies that 'individuals go to the hiring hall every day' or, in other words, that all the individuals – employed and unemployed – compete constantly with each other for the jobs. Since this is unrealistic, STIGLITZ replaces the one-period H-T-H model with a multi-period model where the probability of being hired depends on the length of time in the unemployment pool. STIGLITZ, however, then arrives at the same result as the H-T-H model. He recognizes as a possible objection to this result that the predicted unemployment rates are much too large. For instance, if the urban wage rate is about twice the level of $\bar{m}$ – which it often is – it follows from $\bar{m} = p_{eq}w$ that p_{eq} and hence the employment rate N/L is only about 50 percent, clearly an unacceptable prediction. The models may thus imply, in STIGLITZ's opinion, a much higher unemployment rate than is actually the case.

MAZUMDAR[23] makes the same criticisms and, following an earlier model of TODARO,[24] suggests that a more realistic probability function would be $p = (\gamma N)/(L - N)$, where as before N represents the number of urban jobs, L the number of urban job seekers, and γ the rate of growth of the urban jobs N. The probability of finding a job in the urban area is thus a function of job openings and the absolute number of unemployed. The function can also be written as $L = \{(\gamma/p) + 1\}N$ from which follows that the migration function is presented by $dL/dN = (\gamma/p) + 1$. The opportunity cost of hiring a worker is thus

50

$\{(\gamma/p) + 1\}\bar{m}$. Since a rural worker's supply price in the equilibrium situation will be $\bar{m} = p\,w$, we may write:

$$\frac{\text{opp. cost of labor}}{\text{wage rate}} = \frac{(\gamma/p + 1)\bar{m}}{(1/p)\bar{m}} = \gamma + p$$

$$= \gamma + \frac{\gamma N}{L - N} = \frac{\gamma L}{L - N} = \frac{\gamma}{(L - N)/L}.$$

Thus if the growth rate of urban jobs is 5 percent and the unemployment rate about 9 percent, the opportunity cost of labor would be about 55 percent of the urban wage rate. The average rate of unemployment is presented by

$$\frac{L - N}{L} = \frac{\gamma N/p}{\{(\gamma/p) + 1\}N} = \frac{\gamma}{\gamma + p}$$

and the marginal rate by .

$$\frac{d(L - N)}{dL} = 1 - \frac{1}{(\gamma/p) + 1} = \frac{\gamma}{\gamma + p}.$$

Since the two are equal, the rate of unemployment will not change in the MA-ZUMDAR model, just as in the H-T-H model. The MAZUMDAR model gives, however, much more reasonable predictions as regards the level of the rate of unemployment.

Rather than having large pools of unemployed in the urban areas, many developing countries appear to have an urban informal sector where the migrants can earn at least some money by working as casual laborers, street vendors, rickshaw drivers, house servants, and the like. HARBERGER has argued that in such cases the informal sector wage rate represents the supply price $\bar{m}$ of the migrants and that therefore the opportunity cost of a laborer hired by the formal sector is equal to his informal sector earnings. This argumentation, however, overlooks the point that the migrants will be willing to work for less than the going wage in the informal sector because they expect to obtain a job in the formal sector later at the higher urban wage rate. The MAZUMDAR model can easily take account of this point. In the presence of an informal sector, the equilibrium condition for a rural worker who considers migrating to the city is presented by $m = p^*_{eq}w_f + (1 - p^*_{eq})w_i$, where m is the supply price of the migrant, migrant, p^*_{eq} the probability of obtaining a job in the formal sector, w_f the wage rate in the formal sector. $(1 - p^*_{eq})$ the probability of working in the informal sector, and w_i the average earnings of the migrant in the informal sector. From this, it follows that $p^*_{eq} = (\bar{m} - w_i)/(w_f - w_i)$. Denoting the number of people in the informal sector by $L - N$, the probability function is as before $(\gamma N)/(L - N)$. Hence, rural workers will migrate to the city as long as $\gamma N/(L - N)$ is larger than p^*_{eq}. The inflow of migrants will, however, increase the number in the informal sector and also reduce the earnings w_i of the workers in the informal sector. This process will go on until the equilibrium position is reached where $\gamma N/(L - N) =$

51

p^*_{eq}. At that point the migration function is the same as in the previous model and the hiring of one person by the formal sector will thus result in an inflow of $(\gamma/p^*) + 1$ persons. It should be noted, however, that in this case p^* has a lower value than the p in the previous model, so that the opportunity cost of labor for the formal sector is higher than in the previous model. This is logical because the possibility of earning w_i will result in a larger inflow than before. The informal sector will also, therefore, account for a larger percentage of the total labor force than the unemployed in the previous model.

The last model can also be refined by means of a multi-period analysis. Furthermore, the analysis has not been entirely correct, in that the value of $\bar{m}$ will of course change during the migration process. It must, however, seriously be questioned whether sufficient empirical data will be available to determine the required migration function with any precision. Estimating the opportunity cost of labor for the formal sector in the urban area is therefore often a rather arbitrary undertaking. The upshot of the above discussion is that at least some limits can be indicated, in between which the opportunity cost will lie. It is definitely not zero, as the LEWIS model would lead us to believe, but substantially larger than the rural earnings. It is also larger than the earnings in the informal sector. On the other hand, it will be lower than the institutional wage rate. In the presence of an informal sector, a good approximation will often be to calculate the value of $\{(\gamma/p^*) + 1\}\bar{m}$. For instance, if γ equals 5 percent and the informal sector accounts for about 17 percent of the total labor force, it follows from $p^* = \gamma N/(L - N)$ that $p^* = 0.25$. Hence, the opportunity cost of labor can with reasonable accuracy be put at 1.20 times $\bar{m}$. If $w_i = 0.5\,w_f$, then $\bar{m}$ will be $0.625\,w_f$ [25] and the opportunity cost of labor will thus be 75 percent of w_f and 150 percent of w_i. Often, however, no reliable data will be available as regards p^*. The best one can do in such a case is to estimate the values of w_i and w_f and to consider these the minimum and maximum values, respectively, of labor's opportunity cost. The use of both values will show how sensitive the rate of return of the project is with respect to this variable and in cases where the value of the opportunity cost of labor appears to be important, a range of rates of return should be calculated rather than a single-valued rate of return.

The third case we would like to review is how the opportunity cost of unskilled labor should be determined in the so-called primitive affluence countries. Our attention so far has focused on the determination of labor's opportunity cost in those countries where the land-to-population ratio is low. In general, even though the subsistence sector may be quite large in such countries, the modern sector-plantations, mines and industry-does not encounter any difficulty in hiring the labor it requires. But there are quite a number of countries where the modern sector encounters substantial problems in obtaining labor. These countries also have a large subsistence sector, but the land-to-population ratio is high and the subsistence farmer does not seem to work unduly hard to obtain a reasonable living. This is all to the good, but what appears to be a perverse reaction is that even at relatively high wages, labor does not appear to be willing to work in the modern sector. Such a situation seems to have existed in countries like Malaysia, Sri Lanka, Fiji, Mauritius and some Eastern and Central African nations – to the point even that the modern sector opted to import immigrant labor from India and China. In the present time this situation exists, according to FISK[26], in the Pacific Region, including Papua New Guinea and several other Melanesian and Polynesian islands and, according to others[27], in parts of Africa. The problem of the unresponsive subsistence farmer is important because the level of participation in the monetary economy determines to a large extent the overall economic development of the country.

What then are the reasons for the unresponsive conduct of the subsistence farmer? According to FISK, the situation of many groups of peasants in the countries in the Pacific Region can be characterized as one of 'primitive affluence'. The peasants 'are able to provide, from their own resources, as much as they can consume of the normal staple foods that they are used to, together with a reasonable surplus for entertainment, display and emergency, and a standard of housing, clothing and entertainment requisites that is traditionally acceptable, with an employment of a relatively small part of the total potential resources of labor and land available to them. This means that within their self-non-monetary system the productivity of their labor is very high, and it is still quite common in these countries to find substantial groups of peasants able to sustain this level of consumption from their own resources at the cost of an average labor input of about three hours per man-day or less.'

Illustrative in this respect are the findings of MOULIK[28], who collected, inter alia, data on the daily activity patterns of sixty-seven subsistence farmers in three districts in Papua New Guinea. Out of a normal weekly activity time (including leisure) of 77 hours (11 hours per day), the productive activities – as MOULIK calls it – appeared to account for only some 19 to 25 hours. These activities included subsistence production and a very limited amount of cash cropping and paid work. Leisure accounted for about 40 to 48 hours per week, while social obligations, ceremonial activities, the meeting of Administration officials, and such, accounted for the rest of the available weekly activity time.

It is not clear from MOULIK's report where he has drawn the distinction between leisure and the social obligation type of activity. Furthermore, his definition of productive activities (subsistence production, cash cropping and paid work) is unfortunate, since many of the so-called non-productive activities definitely have an economic function. Story-telling and singing are a form of education of the young; palavers are a means of arriving at consensus and settling disputes; and the making of ceremonial masks is just as productive an action as that of a sculptor in the Western world. The way the family allocates its time between these different types of activities can still be based on marginal principles so that the utility from an hour's work in subsistence farming will be equal to the utility from an hour of leisure or any ceremonial or educational activity. What MOULIK's investigation has confirmed, however, is that the peasant farmer in Papua New Guinea appears indeed to live in a situation of primitive affluence, a situation where the agricultural work week is short and the marginal utility of additional agricultural staples is low.

The subjective equilibrium position of the peasant farm in primitive affluence has been analyzed in detail by NAKAJIMA[29] and the following analysis is based on his work. The model we will use has three special features. First, in view of the difficulty of measuring the value of ceremonial activities and the like, we define income as the value of the agricultural subsistence products, and assume that there are some outside markets for agricultural products so that the family is able to impute a price to these products. Second, as confirmed by empirical data, the equilibrium position of the farm as regards agricultural production will be reached when only a very low amount of labor is applied, say 20 to 25 hours per week. Third, the indifference curves will assume a vertical slope soon after the subsistence level of living has been reached. NAKAJIMA calls the level of income at which the curves turn upward the achievement standard of income, but this is, in our opinion, a rather unfortunate term as it does not acknowledge that the peasants may have substantial aspirations outside the subsistence farming field. NAKAJIMA's achievement standard is very similar to what FISK has called the demand-ceiling or, in a slightly different context, the full-belly situation. Whichever name is used, it is clear that in a primitive affluence type of society, the marginal utility of additional staples will become negligible at a satisfaction level close to the subsistence level.

The model is presented in Figures 3.5A and 3.5B. The horizontal axis OA represents in both figures the maximum possible labor hours of the family, while the vertical axis in Figure 3.5A represents total family income and in Figure 3.5B the marginal productivity and the marginal valuation of family labor. In Figure 3.5A the subsistence level of income is OM_0 and the full-belly level is OM_2, the latter being only slightly above the subsistence level. As mentioned above, the indifference curves (not drawn between OM_0 and OM_2) have a vertical slope above the level OM_2. Equilibrium will be reached where the family income curve OL_1 touches an indifference curve, which is assumed to be at the point Q. This equilibrium position is also shown in detail in Figure 3.5B, where the curve L_3 is the marginal productivity of labor curve and L_2 is the marginal valuation of labor. It should be noted that L_2 assumes an infinite value for work beyond M_2C. The equilibrium position is Q' and a quantity of labor equal to OA_1 will be applied, representing about 20 or 25 hours of adult male work per week.

Between the levels OM_0 and OM_2 (Figure 3.5A), the peasant farm will act as a normal economic unit. For instance, let us assume that the possibility of outside wage work has been opened. Its marginal valuation curve is then no longer determined by the production possibility curve OL_1 but by the wage income curve. In Figure 3.5B there will be a new marginal valuation curve and a new subjective equilibrium. Whether this new equilibrium will be to the left of OA_1 or to the right, depends on the slopes of the indifference curves between Q and C. Let us assume, however, that there will be a positive response towards higher wage rates and let us assume that the family will follow the curve $Q'E'$ in supplying its labor. With a wage rate equal to OW_1 the new equilibrium will

FIGURE 3.5A.

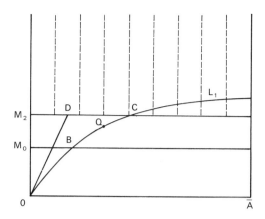

FIGURE 3.5B.

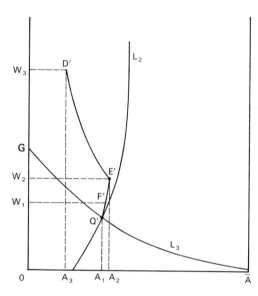

be at the point F′, so that the family works partly on the farm and partly out-side. However, the maximum the family would be willing to work would be determined by its full-belly income level, OM_2. In Figure 3.5B this occurs when the wage rate is at the level OW_2. An amount of labor equal to OA_2 will then be supplied and the family's income $OGE′A_2$ is then equal to OM_2. Above point E′ the supply curve will take the form of a hyperbole and will be back-ward sloping. This is readily seen. For instance, at the wage level OW_3 (the slope of OD in Figure 3.5A), the labor supply will be OA_3 and no more be-cause only an income of OM_2 is sought. The labor supply curve of the farm over the entire wage range is thus equal to $Q′E′D′$.

It should be noted that there is nothing unique about this backward sloping

55

labor supply curve. One will find it even in the developed countries, as the rise in income due to higher wage rates will eventually lead an individual to buy more leisure, even though the price of leisure – the hourly wage rate – has become more expensive. The income effect has then won over the substitution effect. What is unique, however, in the context of the primitive affluence society is that the backward bending takes place at, by Western standards, a minimum effort level. This has important consequences for the determination of labor's opportunity cost. Assume that at a plantation wage rate of US $ 300 per annum, the peasant farmer is willing to work only 20 hours per week rather than the 40 hours per week the plantation requires. Then the opportunity cost of labor will not be US $ 300 but US $ 600 per annum, because the plantation would need to hire two men rather than one to obtain its 40 hours of work per week.

Thus, labor in primitive affluence societies is not cheap. It is, therefore, not surprising that in the past many plantations – with the consent of the colonial governments – preferred to import cheap labor from abroad. As a result, the subsistence sectors in such countries never became developed while the immigrants, however, became used to the modern sector with its longer working hour weeks. Eventually, when the numbers of the immigrants increased, they took over many of the more lucrative jobs (trade, service, money-lending), thus exacerbating the socio-economic problems of these ethnically mixed societies. In Malaysia in the present day, for instance, the average income of the Chinese – representing 34 percent of the population – is about double that of the indigenous Malays, accounting for 55 percent of the population.

In most countries immigrant labor policies are now no longer acceptable. Another alternative to obtaining cheap labor for the modern sector – also used in the past – is to impose corvées or to use the always available casual labor, which, after a spell in the modern sector, reverts to the subsistence farm. But the former, very rightly so, is unacceptable nowadays and cheap labor policies will never lead to an increase in productivity of the subsistence sector. It should, therefore, be recognized that only a policy of relatively high wages will lead to the development of the primitive affluence societies. But such policies alone are not enough. The objective must be to shift the peasant labor supply curve $Q'E'D'$ upwards to such an extent that it will cross the line of the 40–45 hours workweek. The policy prescription for achieving this objective may be summarized as follows: (a) create work opportunities for less than 40 to 45 hours per week at relatively high wage rates; (b) increase the labor productivity curve by means of integrated rural development projects; and (c) increase farmers' demand by introducing consumer goods (kerosene lamps, tin roofs, radios, sewing machines, bicycles, and such) and by bringing the farmers into contact with the modern world (education). There is much more that can be said about the subject. We hope, however, that we have made it clear that cheap labor policies are not the answer for the development of the primitive affluence type societies and that if one really wishes to make a modern man out of the subsistence farmer, a comprehensive policy package as outlined above is necessary. Basic to the formulation of this package is the labor response of the farmer,

56

showing once more that, in the formulation of a national plan, the micro-economic data used for project evaluation purposes cannot be neglected.

3.4. CAPITAL

Capital theory is a controversial subject[30] and this applies also to the concept of the opportunity cost of capital. The determination of the opportunity cost of capital is, of course, of crucial importance for the evaluation of Government projects. If the opportunity cost of capital and therewith the cut-off rate of return for Government projects is set too high, a number of projects may need to be rejected. If the rate is set too low, inefficient projects may be accepted.

We will discuss budget constraints in Chapter 5 and assume in this section that there is no budget constraint on Government funds so that Government can obtain the funds it needs for a particular project from the private sector or, alternatively, if it has too many funds in relation to projects, that it can transfer the surplus funds to the private sector. Even under these circumstances, the economic literature in the past has taken diametrically opposite views as to how the opportunity cost of capital is to be found. On the one hand, for instance, KRUTILLA and ECKSTEIN[31] feel that the opportunity cost of capital is determined by consumers' marginal time preference rates. On the other hand, there is the view of HIRSHLEIFER, DE HAVEN and MILLIMAN[32] that it is the rate of return on private investments that counts. BAUMOL[33] takes a kind of middle position. He first argues that the relevant cut-off rate for Government projects is the marginal rate of return on investments in the private sector, but then argues that the subjective time preference rate is also relevant. The subject is thus full of controversy and it is well worth our effort to review briefly how these writers arrived at their conclusions.

KRUTILLA and ECKSTEIN argue that the true opportunity cost of capital cannot be the rate of return earned on the marginal investment of the most successful private firms since a reduction of the Government program by, say, US $ 100 million would not result in expansion of investment by such firms of an equal amount[34]. Their approach is therefore to trace how the capital for a Government project would otherwise be used and to determine its value in those uses. Two models concerning the United States are analyzed, both models assuming that the public investment forestalls cuts in taxes. Model A assumes that the tax cuts would be in sales taxes and in the personal income tax, which benefits low-income families most so that consumption would be boosted. Model B consists of a reduction of the personal income tax with emphasis on upper-income brackets and of a reduction of the corporate tax so that investments would increase. Regarding the cuts in the personal income tax and the sales taxes, the tax savings per income class are calculated and the after-income tax interest rates facing households in their saving-spending decisions estimated so that the weighted average of the after-tax interest rates can be found. Regarding the cut in the corporate income tax, it is assumed that 45 percent would be passed on immediately to consumers and wage and salary earners, and about 37.5 percent over a period of 100 years – the economic life of water resource projects – to dividend recipients. The remainder would stay with the firms in the form of retained earnings but would mainly be invested in liquid assets at low rates of return. Of the entire cut in the corporate tax, only about 3.5 percent is valued at the rates of return that firms in the private sector normally make. Since the two models calculate the cost of capital mainly on the basis of the low interest rates at which consumers undertake their savings and borrowing decisions, i.e., the consumers' marginal time preference rates, extremely low values were found for the opportunity cost of capital. Model A estimates the cost of capital at 5.29 percent, Model B at 5.44 percent.

HIRSHLEIFER, DE HAVEN and MILLIMAN point out that in a perfect competition equilibrium situation, the rate of interest measures the marginal time productivity of capital as well as the marginal rate of time preference of lenders[35]. If Government projects are not subject to risk, then the prime – riskless – rate of interest can be used for discounting the benefits of Government projects. However, in their view, Government projects have at least the same risk as private projects and perhaps even more because most Government agencies have a record of overoptimism in cost-benefit determinations[36]. On practical grounds, they feel, therefore, that the Government's discount rate for water resource projects should at least be equal to the returns that private utilities pay to their bondholders and equity owners. There is the additional complication that a corporate tax must be paid on the profits of private utilities. HIRSHLEIFER, DE HAVEN and MILLIMAN see this tax as a price which equity investors are willing to pay to avoid the risk of bearing unlimited liability[37]. Thus the marginal rate of return of private projects includes the various degrees of risk that investors face. The marginal private rate of return can be found by analyzing how private utilities are financed, which is typically with debt and equity in about equal proportions. If bonds yield 4.7 percent and equity 5.7 percent (1959 averages) and if it is assumed that no surpluses remain in the company, the marginal private rate of return will be 8.3 percent[38]. Property and other taxes raise the return to over 9 percent, and, taking into account that Government projects are riskier projects than private projects, they recommend that 10 percent should be used as the Government's discount rate.

BAUMOL starts his analysis by underlining that investment in a Government project should be undertaken only if the benefits of the project are greater than the loss sustained by removing the investment resources from the private sector. If all the goods and services in the economy other than those provided by Government are supplied by corporations, the opportunity cost of the Government funds will be equal to the return these corporations make. For instance, if the corporations must return 5 percent to their stockholders and the corporation tax is 50 percent, the opportunity cost of Government funds will be 10 percent. In the real world there may of course also be risk elements, and corporations must then make an additional rate of return sufficient to compensate the stockholders for the risks they take. For instance, suppose that the private investors need 8 percent rather than 5 percent to be induced to invest in the risky undertaking. Then the rate of return of the corporation must be 16 percent. From the point of view of society as a whole, it is this yield that will be foregone if resources are transferred to Government, and the opporutnity cost of Government funds must thus be set at 16 percent. There is no need to differentiate between the riskiness of Government projects compared to private projects since, from the point of view of society as a whole, public as well as private projects have low risks because of the law of large numbers. The opportunity cost of capital to Government consists thus of the rates of return foregone in the private sector.

BAUMOL then goes on, however, to argue that consumers' time preferences – which are, as discussed, much lower than the opportunity cost of capital because of the tax factor – also should play a role as otherwise one allocates to the future, resources much smaller than the amount consumers would be willing to allocate, as indicated by their individual subjective time preference rates. BAUMOL does not enter into the issue that the individual time preferences may not reflect adequately the social time preference rate of society as a whole. He assumes thus implicitly that the individual rates are the relevant ones for determining the optimal investment program. We will follow BAUMOL for the moment, but will criticize him later on in this section. According to BAUMOL then, there is an unavoidable indeterminancy in the choice of the discount rate to be used for Government projects. 'The figure which is optimal from the point of view of allocation of resources between the private and public sectors is necessarily higher than that which accords with the public's subjective time preference. As a result, neither the higher nor the lower figure that has been proposed can, by itself, satisfy the requirements for an optimal allocation of resources, and we find outselves forced to hunt for a solution in the dark jungles of the second best.'[39]

BAUMOL's analysis is elucidating. It makes clear that the HIRSHLEIFER, DE HAVEN and MILLIMAN construction of treating the corporate tax as a price for risk aversion is farfetched. The corporate tax is simply part of the rate of return in the private sector. That different parts of that rate of return accrue to different parties – Government, lenders, equity investors – is not important; it is the total rate of return that is foregone if funds are transferred from the private sector to the Government sector. As regards the dichotomy whether the subjective time preference rate or the private rate of return should be used as the cut-off rate for Government projects – all the time still assuming that the individual rates reflect the social time preference rate –, the matter was analyzed in detail by RAMSEY[40] and USHER[41] in their comments on BAUMOL's paper and by HARBERGER[42] in the context of his analysis of the opportunity cost of capital in an economy with a reasonably well functioning capital market.

RAMSEY uses an elegant and simple notation and it will be useful to review his analysis briefly. If resources are transferred from the production in the private sector of goods X and Y to the production in the Government sector of good Z, the value of Z production must at least be equal to the value of the foregone X and Y production. Let MC_x, MC_y and MC_z be the marginal resource cost of X, Y and Z, respectively, excluding cost of capital, and $r_x I_x$, $r_y I_y$ and $r_z I_z$ the cost of capital of X, Y and Z, respectively, then we must have (in absolute terms):

$$(MC_x + r_x I_x) \cdot \triangle X + (MC_y + r_y I_y) \cdot \triangle Y \le (MC_z + r_z I_z) \cdot \triangle Z$$

The two terms on the left-hand side represent the value of the foregone X and Y production, respectively, and the term on the right-hand side the value of the Z production. Furthermore, we may write: $MC_x \cdot \triangle X + MC_y \cdot \triangle Y = MC_z \cdot \triangle Z$ and $I_x \cdot \triangle X + I_y \cdot \triangle Y = I_z \cdot \triangle Z$, or in words, the resources other than capital and the capital, respectively, which are being transferred from the X and Y industry to the Z industry must equal the resources other than capital, and the capital, respectively, which will be used by the Z industry. Thus we get: $r_x I_x \cdot \triangle X + r_y I_y \cdot \triangle Y \le r_z I_z \cdot \triangle Z$, which when divided by $I_z \cdot \triangle Z$ gives $a_x r_x + a_y r_y \le r_z$, where $a_x = (I_x \cdot \triangle X)/(I_x \cdot \triangle X + I_y \cdot \triangle Y)$ and $a_y = (I_y \cdot \triangle Y)/(I_x \cdot \triangle X + I_y \cdot \triangle Y)$. In words this equation tells us that the opportunity cost of capital to Government is the weighted average of the rates of return foregone in the private sector, the weights being the capital which would have been necessary to produce the foregone private sector products.

Suppose that, as in our example above, the X good is produced by corporations and subject to risk so that the rate of return there is 16 percent and that the Y goods are produced in the noncorporation sector so that the rate of return there is only 5 percent. Suppose further that if the Z goods – the Government sector goods – are not produced, 80 percent of the Government funds would be used for the production of the X goods and 20 percent for the production of the Y goods. Then the opportunity cost of the Government funds would be $(0.8 \times 16\%) + (0.2 \times 5\%) = 13.8$ percent. It may be noted that, in this model, the subjective time preference rates do not enter into the picture at all. The net of risk rate of return of 5 percent which borrowers require is the before-income tax rate of return, while the subjective time preference rate is, of course, the corresponding net-of-income tax return. For instance, if the income tax rate is 30 percent, the subjective time preference rate would be 3.5 percent. In RAMSEY's model, this rate is not relevant at all since the Government funds are all obtained by displacing the investments for the production of the private goods X and Y.

In HARBERGER's capital markets model, however, additional savings will be induced and their value in terms of yield is the subjective time preference rate. HARBERGER's model is basically the same as the one he uses for analyzing the opportunity cost of an input (Section 3.1) and is as follows. Suppose that the capital market functions reasonably well and that Government borrows the funds required for a certain project in this market. Then there will be a reduction in private investment, the value of which in terms of yield is the before-tax rate of return (i.e., the amount accruing to Government in the form of taxes and to the private investors in the form of dividends and retained earnings). This is thus exactly the same as in the RAMSEY model. However, the additional borrowing of Government will increase the interest rate and this will induce private savings to come forward, the value of which in yield terms is the net of personal income tax return. The opportunity cost of the Government funds thus consists in this case of the weighted average of the private sector rate of return and the subjective time preference rate, the weights being investments displaced and savings induced.

What has become quite clear from the RAMSEY and HARBERGER analyses is that in their models the opportunity cost of Government funds is determined by the method of resource transfer which the Government uses. Public funds can be raised by taxation or by borrowing. The taxes can be designed to obtain the resources from the corporate or high-risk areas or they can be designed to obtain the resources from the unincorporated or low-risk areas, and so on. Each of the different ways in which the Government can raise its funds will have a different impact and there will thus be as many different opportunity costs as there are ways of raising money.

HARBERGER very rightly points out that we will never be able to get the information to calculate the multiplicity of possible opportunity costs and proposes therefore to use only one opportunity cost, namely, as determined by his capital market model, which he denotes by the symbol ω. He sees the capital market as a sponge which can absorb any tax revenues above anticipated levels or yield up the funds required for an increment in Government expenditures if taxes fall short. In this sense, incremental tax funds can then be said to have a yield of ω and incremental Government expenditures an opportunity cost of ω. Those who are responsible for project evaluation can thus evaluate whether a project is justified in the light of an opportunity cost of ω, so that decentralized decision making will be possible. As regards the value of ω, HARBERGER notes that savings are in general not very sensitive to interest rate changes. Hence, the weighted average of the private sector rates of return and the subjective time preference rates 'will be reasonably close, if not precisely equal, to the marginal productivity of capital in the private sector.'[43]

HARBERGER's proposal is interesting. Unfortunately, however, most developing countries do not have a well developed capital market, and the sponge concept of the capital market, therefore, breaks down. It is clear, however, that the administrative Government apparatus can only function if projects are evaluated with respect to one single opportunity cost. As the HARBERGER shadow rate cannot be used, the question arises whether there is another shadow rate that would allow such decentralized decision making.

In reviewing this matter, it is essential to recollect that all the writers so far discussed assume implicitly that the individual subjective time preference rates reflect the social time preference rate of society as a whole. However, there is, in our opinion, no reason why this should be so as it should be recognized that the consensus value of the individuals in the economy as regards the value of the social time preference rate – and, hence, as regards the optimum growth path of the economy – differs, in all probability, from the values of the time preference rates they use in making their personal investment-saving decisions. The dichotomy and the indeterminacy, to quote BAUMOL, of the choice of the discount rate to be used for evaluating projects thus does not exist. The discount rate to be used is the social time preference rate, or, as it is also called, the social discount rate.

In this part of the study, we do not consider income distribution aspects and we are analyzing, therefore, situations of optimal growth where the investment program of the economy is optimum, so that the right trade-off between current and future consumption takes place. In such cases, the social discount rate to be used for evaluating Government projects may be defined as the cut-off rate of return for Government projects that would keep the economy on the optimal growth path. Hence, if capital is to be transferred from the private sector to the Government sector, the relevant discount rate will be the weighted average of the rates of return foregone by the private sector. In this respect, it is important to note that traditional benefit-cost theory does not consider the distributive aspects of such transfers because this is considered the domain of the distribution branch of Government. The allocative branch of Government – the one that makes investment decisions – is assumed to follow economic efficiency principles only and it is assumed, therefore, that the capital foregone in the private sector is proportional to the capital employed. The opportunity cost of capital of the private sector has, therewith, become the relevant discount rate for evaluating Government projects. However, the existence of situations where the investment program of the economy cannot be considered optimal and, hence, where the traditional benefit-cost theory cannot be applied, needs no elaboration. How to evaluate projects under such circumstances will be discussed in part II of this study.

We may now turn our attention to the matter as to how, when income distribution aspects are not important, the opportunity cost of capital, which as discussed should be the same for the Government as it is for the private sector, should be estimated, and we will start our discussion by reviewing the so-called production function approach.

One of the most simple production functions is the one which is generally used in macro-planning. Output Y is seen here as a function of capital K only. and the function can thus be written as $Y = f(K)$. It is furthermore assumed that dY/dK is constant. As there is one variable only, the marginal product of capital which we write as $q = \partial Y/\partial K$ will therefore equal dY/dK. There are several objections to the use of this function. First, it is a static concept that does not take into account the time element. For instance, if $dY/dK = 1/3$, it would appear as if the rate of return were 33 percent. In reality, of course, the increment in income will not be produced immediately and the rate of return will then have a much lower value. For instance, if dY were to materialize after four years and then continued to be produced in perpetuity, the rate of return q should be calculated from $dY/[q(1 + q)^4] = dK$. If the incremental output-capital ratio is again $1/3$, the rate of return would appear to be about 19 percent[44]. However, this calculation is not correct either because (a) projects do not have infinite lives and (b) output is not only a function of capital but also of labor. The incremental output-capital formula assumes that the opportunity cost of labor is zero and, as discussed, this is a very unrealistic assumption.

A slightly more realistic approach is followed in the UNIDO Guidelines by DASGUPTA, SEN and MARGLIN. They see output determined by capital as well as labor, but do not specify the production function, so that it may be written as $Y = f(K, L)$. The function's total differential is $dY = (\partial Y/\partial K)dK + (\partial Y/\partial L)dL$, for which we may write $q = (dY/dK) - [(\partial Y/\partial L)(dL/dK)]$ where as above q is the marginal product of capital $\partial Y/\partial K$. In words, the formula suggests that the rate of return per unit of investment (i.e., the ceteris paribus rate of return $q = \partial Y/\partial K$) equals the total increase in national income per unit of investment (i.e., the mutatis mutandis rate of return dY/dK) minus labor's share of that increase. Labor's share is calculated by multiplying the opportunity cost of labor $\partial Y/\partial L$ by the number of additional laborers that are required per unit of investment dL/dK. The data regarding investments and labor can be taken from national plans. In an example in the Guidelines,[45] it is expected that at the end of a postulated country's five-year plan period, national income will be increased by £ 480 million, labor by 1.2 million workers, and that the net investment during the plan period is £ 1200 million. dY/dK is then estimated at $480/1200 = 0.40$ and dL/dK at $1.2/1200 = 0.001$. The opportunity cost of labor has to be estimated directly from micro-economic data and is assumed to be £ 100. Consequently, the opportunity cost of capital would be 30 percent $(0.40 - 100/1000)$.

Another approach commonly found in the economic literature is based on the so-called COBB-DOUGLAS production function[46]. The relationship between national income and the production factors is then presented as $Y = A K^{\alpha} L^{1-\alpha}$, where A is a constant. This is a so-called linearly homogeneous function because multiplication of each independent variable by a factor k will change the value of the dependent variable by exactly k-fold. In economic terms, this means that output is being produced under conditions of constant returns to scale. As is well-known from Euler's theorem, under such conditions, if each factor is paid its marginal product, the total product will be exactly exhausted by the distributive shares of the factors. Euler's theorem is written in its general form as $Y = (\partial Y/\partial K)K + (\partial Y/\partial L)L$. As under the Cobb-Douglas function, the marginal product of capital $\partial Y/\partial K = \alpha Y/K$ and the marginal product of labor $\partial Y/\partial L = (1 - \alpha)Y/L$, it is readily seen that Euler's theorem applies indeed to this function[47]. Assuming that the COBB-DOUGLAS function represents the actual production possibility of the economy, the marginal product of capital or of labor can easily be determined. The opportunity cost of capital is a function of its share of national income and the output-to-capital ratio, and the opportunity cost of labor is a function of its share of national income and the output-to-labor ratio. Suppose that capital's share in national income is about 30 percent and that the average output-to-capital ratio is 0.4. Then the opportunity cost of capital is 12 percent.

Finally, an example which is taken from growth theory[48]. Under conditions of balanced growth, and assuming that the average output-to-capital ratio is constant and that both profit earners and laborers save a constant proportion of their income, the following relationship holds:

$$g K = S_q \cdot q K + S_w \cdot wL$$

where g = growth rate of national income and of capital
S_q = savings coefficient of profit earners
S_w = savings coefficient of laborers
w = opportunity cost of labor, q = rate of profits
and K and L, as before, total capital and labor force, respectively.

In words, the growth of capital equals the sum of the savings of profit earners and laborers. If $(1 - D)$ represents the share of the laborers in national income we can write $S_w \cdot w L = S_w[(wL/Y)/(qK/Y)] q K = S_w[(1 - D)/D]q K$ and the formula becomes $g = [S_q + S_w \cdot (1 - D)/D]q$. Since $S_q D + S_w (1 - D)$ represents the weighted average of the two savings coefficients, which, of course, is the savings coefficient for the economy as a whole (s), the formula may be written as: $g = sq/D$ or $q = D \cdot g/s$. Thus, if capital's share of national income is 0.30, the growth rate of national income 8 percent, and the average savings rate 20 percent of national income, then the opportunity cost of capital is 12 percent.

It is interesting to note that the formulas are very similar, since the growth-theory formula is $q = D \cdot g/s$, while the UNIDO formula may be written as $q = D \cdot dY/dK$ and the COBB-DOUGLAS formula as $q = D \cdot Y/K$. Under balanced growth conditions, the formulas are equal, differing only in form, since then $dY/dK = Y/K = g/s$. How useful are the formulas? In our opinion, not very useful. The UNIDO formula has the disadvantage that a single value for the opportunity cost of labor must be estimated, which, in practice, will be purely a guess. The COBB-DOUGLAS formula uses the Y/K ratio and it needs no elaboration that it is very difficult to make an estimate of the total capital stock in a country, especially in a developing country. The formula has the further disadvantage that empirical tests have shown that increases in capital and labor lead to a greater increase in national income than the formula implies. The COBB-DOUGLAS function can, of course, be amended[49] by including in the formula a trend factor to explain that technical progress, economies of scale, improved education and the like also contribute to increases in national income, but such a trend factor would be difficult to estimate. The growth theory formula applies only under balanced growth conditions. Among other things, it assumes that capital's and labor's share of national income remain the same and that the rate of savings and investment is constant, assumptions that are clearly unrealistic. All in all, it is clear that the above discussed formulas will all arrive at different results and that they cannot lead to realistic estimates of the opportunity cost of capital.

There is further the very important point that at present it is being seriously questioned whether a production function for the economy as a whole can be constructed. It is not the intention to discuss here the recent controversies regarding capital theory, but a few words may be useful. The controversy is basically about whether there exists such a thing as the marginal product of capital, which is, at the same time, the rate of profit, or whether there is no such thing. In the first case, we have $\partial Y/\partial K = q$, where q is the rate of profit, as well as $\partial Y/\partial L = w$, where w is the wage rate, and the distribution of income between persons is thus determined by the marginal productivity relationships. If no such thing as an overall production function exists, however, we no longer have a marginal productivity theory of distribution and it must then be accepted that either the profit rate or the wage rate is determined by outside forces.

SAMUELSON[50] has shown that under certain assumptions the marginal productivity relationships do exist in an economy. First, he constructed a production function – the so-called surrogate production function – by assuming that capital and labor are malleable – like jelly – and that they produce jelly under constant returns to scale. Then he showed that the same production function can be constructed by assuming that the capital goods in the economy are entirely different from each other but that each needs labor to work with it in a fixed proportion. With such a production function the wage and profit rates are equal to the marginal product of labor and capital, respectively, and the ratio of the relative shares of profits and wages is equal to the elasticity of wages with respect to profits, i.e., $qK/wL = (-q/w)\cdot(\mathrm{d}w/\mathrm{d}q)$.

That SAMUELSON's function is rather unrealistic was shown by BHADURI[51] in probably the simplest and most direct way. The definitional relationship of national income is $Y = Kq + Lw$ where $Y =$ national income, $K =$ the value of capital, $q =$ the rate of profit or, as we called it, the rate of return, $L =$ the number of employed workers, and $w =$ the wage rate per worker. Dividing by L we get the per worker measure $y = kq + w$. Differentiating totally we obtain $\mathrm{d}y = q\,\mathrm{d}k + k\,\mathrm{d}q + \mathrm{d}w$. SAMUELSON's condition may be written as $(-q/w)\cdot(\mathrm{d}w/\mathrm{d}q) = (q/w)\,k$ because $k = K/L$. Dividing this by q/w gives $-\mathrm{d}w/\mathrm{d}q = k$. Substituting this in the expression of the total differential, we get $\mathrm{d}y/\mathrm{d}k = q = \partial y/\partial k$.

That SAMUELSON's production function is a very special one is thus clear. It implies that the marginal product of capital $\partial y/\partial k$ equals $\mathrm{d}y/\mathrm{d}k$, and as noted before, this is a very unrealistic condition. SAMUELSON had to assume that the production processes in the economy take place in rather peculiar circumstances. But in the real world, capital, labor and output do not consist of jelly, nor will all lines of production have a uniform and constant capital-to-labor ratio.

If we are then to reject the production function approach of estimating the opportunity cost of capital on practical as well as on theoretical grounds, what is left? It seems to us that there is only one way to get out of the impasse, namely, to estimate the rate of return of the private sector directly. In this respect, HARBERGER's India study[52] is an interesting attempt to measure the rate of return of the private sector from micro-economic data. The data he used were collected by the Reserve Bank of India for the period 1955–59 and covered some 1,000 companies, accounting for more than two-thirds of all gross capital formation in the corporate sector. Using different methodologies as regards the concepts of income and capital, HARBERGER arrives at rates of return varying from 10.4 to 19.3 percent. Leaving out the stock market approach, which covered only one year, and taking the most refined adjustment of capital and income, the rates of return range from 13.0 percent to 14.4 percent. Assuming that the opportunity cost of labor is 80 percent of the actual wage bill, the rates of return range from 17.2 percent to 21.3 percent.

It seems to us that HARBERGER's approach needs amendment. There is, of course, the criticism that the returns he has calculated are the profits of the joint stock companies only and that the profitability of these companies is probably greater than that of the non-incorporated companies, but this is not the point we wish to make. As HARBERGER himself points out, this upward bias is probably not sufficiently weighty to counterbalance the many downward biases he consciously introduced into his estimation procedure. What seems to us an oversight is that HARBERGER takes only the opportunity cost of labor into account when he corrects the found nominal rates of return. The objective of the whole exercise is to find the opportunity cost of capital, and this means, of course, that all the inputs as well as the output should be valued at their appropriate opportunity costs, which – especially in a country such as India – may differ from the market values.

In a world full of distortions, the only correct way to estimate the opportunity cost of capital is, in our opinion, by determining the real value of the rate of return of the private sector. The nominal rate of return of the private sector may be calculated from the formula

$$q_n = \frac{\sum_{i=1}^{n} (B_i - R_i - L_i w)}{\sum_{i=1}^{n} K_i},$$

but the real opportunity cost of capital will be presented by the formula

$$q = \frac{\sum_{i=1}^{n} (B_i^* - R_i^* - L_i w^*)}{\sum_{i=1}^{n} K_i^*}$$

where for each investment i:

B_i = benefits valued at market prices or at the official exchange rate in case of exports,

R_i = all inputs other than labor evaluated at market prices or at the official exchange rate in the case of imports,

w = market wage rate,

K_i = investment cost at market prices or at the official exchange rate,

L_i = annual quantity of labor used, and

the asterisked variables are the respective variables valued at their opportunity cost rates.

The above formula can be simplified when consolidated national income

66

accounts are available. The $\sum B$ in the above formulas represents the aggregate of the domestic and foreign willingness to pay for domestic consumption goods as well as for investment goods and intermediate products. Since the withdrawal at the margin of investment funds from all te various industries in the economy will not affect consumer surpluses, this willingness to pay may be measured by the aggregate of the production value of all the various industries. Deducting from this the aggregate value of the inputs ($\sum R$), we obtain the total value added in the economy. Hence, we may write $q_n = (Y - Lw)/K$ and $q = (Y^* - L w^*)/K^*$.

These two formulas show clearly that, if $Y = Y^*$ and $K = K^*$, then indeed HARBERGER's method of calculating the opportunity cost of capital would be correct. For instance, if q_n is 13 percent, labor's share of national income 70 percent and w^* about 80 percent of the actual wage bill, the real opportunity cost of capital q would be 19 percent[53]. In general, however, we cannot expect that $Y = Y^*$ and that $K = K^*$. Since $Y = C + I + X - M$, where C, I, X and M represent the domestic values of consumption, investments, exports and imports, respectively, and these values will differ from the nominal values if the opportunity cost of foreign exchange differs from the official exchange rate, Y will not in general be equal to Y^*. As regards capital, part of plant and equipment may have been imported and the real cost of capital may then well differ from the nominal cost. Furthermore, plant and equipment may well have been produced by means of labor-intensive techniques, so that if the shadow wage rate differs from the market wage rate, the real cost of capital goods will differ from the nominal cost of capital goods. In India, for instance, many irrigation dams are constructed with labor-intensive techniques. All in all, therefore, we must conclude that HARBERGER's method does not go far enough. It is not only the wage bill which should be corrected, but also the values of national income and capital.

Another interesting attempt to measure the opportunity cost of capital for India was made by LAL[54]. The source as regards aggregate census data for manufacturing industry in India was the same as HARBERGER had used, but the period is more recent, namely, 1958–1964. LAL's objective is to calculate the social opportunity cost of capital – a subject that will be discussed in Part II of this study and does not concern us here – but he also calculates the economic opportunity cost of capital. By comparing the nominal value of before-tax profits (i.e., value added less wages and salaries) with the nominal value of capital, LAL finds that the aggregate nominal rate of return of the manufacturing industries varies from 12 percent to 19 percent, which is well in line with HARBERGER's findings. The real opportunity cost of capital is calculated by LAL basically in accordance with the formulation we have given to it, namely $(Y^* - L w^*)/K^*$. However, rather than using domestic prices as the numéraire, LAL uses border prices and proceeds as follows. To arrive at the value of Y^*, he calculates the real value of output by dividing the nominal value by one plus the All-India average tariff, and deducts from that the real value of the inputs other than wages, found by dividing the nominal value by one plus the tariff that applies to the specific input. Similarly, to arrive at the real cost of capital goods, he divides the nominal value of capital goods by one plus the average tariff on non-agricultural machinery. As regards the value of w^*, LAL assumes that the opportunity cost of unskilled labor is 0.4 of the unskilled wage bill. After all these corrections have been made, the surprising result is that the rates of return are almost the same as the nominal before-tax rates of profits, i.e., 12 percent to 19 percent. An example of the calculation for the year 1964 is given below.

Rate of Return in Indian Manufacturing, 1964 (Rs million).

	Nominal	At Border Prices and Shadow Wage Rate
A. Gross Output	56,272	36,305
Fuel and Electricity	2,892	2,053
Materials	32,413	21,609
Other Inputs	5,933	3,490
	41,238	27,152
B. Value Added	15,035	9,153
Salaries	2,054	2,054
Wages	6,241	2,496
C. Salaries and Wages	8,295	4,550
D. Before-Tax Profits	6,740	4,603
E. Capital	52,756	35,725
Rate of Return D/E	0.128	0.128

Unfortunately, LAL's approach is also subject to criticism. LAL sets the opportunity cost of unskilled labor at 0.4 of the unskilled labor bill and justifies this by arguing that in 1964 the average agricultural wage of Rs 600 was in fact only 40 percent of the average industrial wage of Rs 1,500. As discussed in the previous section, it may be expected that the opportunity cost of labor in the urban area is a multiple of the agricultural wage rate, and HARBERGER's assumption that the opportunity cost of labor should be set at 0.8 of the wage bill appears, therefore, much more realistic to us. A second point is that LAL takes border prices as the numéraire. Although we prefer the use of domestic prices, there is no theoretical objection to the use of border prices as long as it is done consistently, since, as was discussed in Chapter 2, the two methods will theoretically lead to the same result. Unfortunately, it seems to us that LAL has not been consistent in his approach. He should have decomposed the outputs and inputs into their tradeable and non-tradeable components and should have valued each component at its border price. For instance, a large part of the output must certainly consist of non-tradeable goods, but LAL evaluates the total as if it were tradeable. Furthermore, if one evaluates outputs and inputs at border prices,

68

then one should certainly also evaluate the wage and salary bill at border prices, and this last element alone would cause the rate of return to be higher than calculated by LAL.

Neither HARBERGER nor LAL has, in our opinion, calculated the opportunity cost of capital for India correctly, but it must be said that it is difficult to obtain the data base for such a correct calculation. In practice, one has to work with rough estimates, and the HARBERGER and LAL esimates are very helpful in this respect. HARBERGER's cost of labor correction is more realistic than LAL's and this will result in an upward adjustment of the nominal rates of return. However, when the opportunity cost of foreign exchange is introduced into the calculations, it appears likely that a downward adjustment must also be made. In a country such as India, we may expect that the ratio of K^* to K will be higher than that of Y^* to Y because export trade is not that important, while capital goods account for a relatively high proportion of the import bill. This would tend to reduce the opportunity cost of capital. On the other hand, part of the plant and equipment may have been produced with labor-intensive techniques and this may tend to mitigate the downward adjustment. Taking all these considerations into account, we would expect, as a rough guesstimate, that the opportunity cost of capital in India is probably of the order of 15 percent.

With this we have come to an end of our discussion of how the opportunity cost of capital should be determined when no budget constraint operates on Government funds, and when the total investment program in a country is considered optimal. In such circumstances, the opportunity cost of capital to Government consists of the real rates of return in the private sector. The way to find these is to analyze in detail the microeconomic data as found in industrial surveys and to correct the nominal rates of return for divergences between the market wage rate and the opportunity cost of labor and for divergences between the official foreign exchange rate and the opportunity cost of foreign exchange. It must be recognized that, although theoretically the approach is clear, the lack of empirical data will often result in rather rough estimates. Sensitivity tests should therefore be applied in all project evaluation work.

[1] HARBERGER, A. C., 'Professor Arrow on the Social Discount Rate,' in 'Cost-Benefit Analysis of Manpower Policies,' eds. Somers, G. G. and Woods, W. D., Industrial Relations Centre, Queen's University, Kingston, Ontario, 1969. Excerpted in Harberger, A. C., 'Project Evaluation – Collected Papers,' Markham Publishing Company, Chicago, 1974, pp. 123–131.

[2] It may be noted that in case the additional demand is small and the distortion consists only of an indirect tax at the rate of $t \%$ on the price of the product, formula (3.1) reduces to a very simple expression. In such a case, for any given quantity, the elasticity of the net of tax curve is the same as the demand curve. Hence, by multiplying the nominator and denominator of (3.1) by P_s/Q_s and noting that $(\partial Q_d/\partial P) \cdot (P_s/Q_s) = e_d$ for marginal changes we obtain

$$P_o = \frac{e_d \, P_d + e_s \, P_s}{e_d + e_s}$$

or in words, the opportunity cost of an input is the elasticity weighted average of the demand and supply prices.

[3] As HINRICHS has investigated, import duties and taxes on exports, taxes on exporting companies or government marketing board arrangements are a chief source of revenue of more than two thirds of the less developed countries. (HINRICHS, H. H.,: 'Determinants of Permanent Revenue Shares Among Less Developed Countries,' The Economic Journal, Sept. 1965, pp. 546–556).

[4] See HARBERGER, 'Professor Arrow on the Social Discount Rate' in 'Collected Papers,' pp. 124–125. Other writers in addition to Harberger arrived at similar results, namely SCHYDLOWSKY, D. M., 'On the Choice of a Shadow Price for Foreign Exchange,' Harvard University Development Advisory Service, Economic Development Report No. 108, Cambridge, Massachusetts, 1968; and BACHA, E. and TAYLOR, L., 'Foreign Exchange Shadow Prices: A Critical Review of Current Theories,' The Quarterly Journal of Economics, No. 2, May 1971, pp. 197–224; reprinted in 'Benefit-Cost Analysis 1971,' Aldine-Atherton, Inc., Chicago, New York, 1972, pp. 29–59.

[5] The UNIDO Guidelines writes the formula as

$$R' = \frac{\partial M}{\partial B} (1 + T)R + \frac{\partial X}{\partial B} (1 - D)R,$$

where ∂B stands for the additional foreign exchange.

Since $\partial M = M \cdot \partial R \cdot \eta/R$, $\partial X = X \cdot \partial R \cdot \varepsilon/R$ and $\partial B = \partial M + \partial X$, so that

$$\frac{\partial M}{\partial B} = \frac{\eta M}{\eta M + \varepsilon X} \text{ and } \frac{\partial X}{\partial B} = \frac{\varepsilon X}{\eta M + \varepsilon X}$$

it is readily seen that the two formulas are equivalent.

[6] The relationship between the various elasticities will be further discussed in Section 6.4.

[7] For a discussion of the free trade exchange rate, see BALASSA, B. and Associates, 'The Structure of Protection in Developing Countries,' published for the International Bank for Reconstruction and Development and the Inter-American Development Bank by the Johns Hopkins University Press, Baltimore and London, 1971, pp. 326–328. The relevant formula is derived as follows. Assuming that tariffs will be abolished and that a free trade exchange rate R'' will be introduced, the change in the value of imports is:

$$-\frac{R'' - (1 + T)R}{(1 + T)R} \cdot \eta \cdot M$$

Similarly, the abolition of export duties will lead to a change in the value of exports of:

$$\frac{R'' - (1 - D)R}{(1 - D)R} \cdot \varepsilon \cdot X$$

Since balance of payments equilibrium must continue after the introduction of the free trade exchange rate, the change in the value of imports must equal the change in the value of exports. Solving for R''/R, we obtain:

$$\frac{R''}{R} = \frac{\eta M + \varepsilon X}{\dfrac{\eta M}{1 + T} + \dfrac{\varepsilon X}{1 - D}}$$

whereby it should be noted that all the elasticities are expressed as positive values. Furthermore, it may be remarked that the BALASSA free trade exchange rate will not differ significantly from the HARBERGER shadow rate as the former is a harmonic mean, while the latter is an arithmetic mean of import and export duties.

[8] It may be of interest to point out that in terms of working hours, the effect of a compensating variation in income – the so-called income effect – equals $C'B'$, while the substitution effect – the movement along the indifference curve – equals $A'B'$. Thus, in contrast to the consumer surplus diagram in Chapter 2, where in the case of normal goods the income effect is always additive to the substitution effect, the income effect in the case of labor is always the opposite of the substitution effect. The Hicks equation should thus be written as:

$$\frac{\delta L}{\delta w} = \frac{\partial L}{\partial w}\Big|_{U=\text{const.}} + \frac{\partial L}{\partial Y}\frac{\partial Y}{\partial w}\Big|_{Prices=\text{const.}}$$

Multiplying by w/L and remembering that $\partial Y = L\partial w$, we obtain

$$\frac{w}{L} \cdot \frac{\delta L}{\delta w} = \frac{w}{L} \cdot \frac{\partial L}{\partial w} + \frac{w}{L} \cdot \frac{\partial L}{\partial Y} \cdot \frac{L\partial w}{\partial w}, \text{ for which we may write:}$$

$$e_1 = e_2 + \frac{wL}{Y} \cdot \frac{Y}{L} \cdot \frac{\partial L}{\partial Y}, \text{ or}$$

$$e_1 = e_2 + \frac{wL}{Y} e_3$$

where e_1 is the elasticity of supply of labor, including the income and substitution effect; e_2 the elasticity of supply of labor including the substitution effect only; e_3 the elasticity of supply of labor, including the income effect only; and wL/Y the proportion wage income is of total income. Hence, in case a worker has only labor income, the expression is simply: $e_1 = e_2 + e_3$.

While e_2 is positive, e_3 is negative, so that e_1 will be negative (the supply of labor will be backward sloping) if the income effect is dominant.

[9] LEWIS, A. W., 'Economic Development with Unlimited Supplies of Labor,' The Manchester School of Economic and Social Studies, May 1954, and 'Unlimited Labor – Further Notes,' The Manchester School of Economic and Social Studies, January 1958.

[10] MYINT, H. 'The Economics of the Developing Countries,' 4th (revised) ed., Hutchison University Library, London, 1973, p. 71.

[11] Ibid., p. 86.

[12] SEN, A. K., 'Choice of Techniques,' 3rd ed., Basil Blackwell, Oxford, 1968, p. 3.

[13] VINER, J., 'Some Reflections on the Concept of Disguised Unemployment,' in 'Contribuicoes a Analise do Desenvolvimento Economico,' Livraria Agir Editora, Rio de Janeiro, 1957. Reprinted in 'Leading Issues in Development Economics,' ed. Meier, G. M., Oxford University Press, New York, 1964.

[14] SEN, A. K., 'Peasants and Dualism with or without Surplus Labor,' The Journal of Political Economy, October 1966.

[15] For a more detailed discussion of the farm-household, the reader is referred to 'NAKAJIMA, C., 'Subsistence and Commercial Family Farms' in 'Subsistence Agriculture and Economic Development,' ed. Wharton Jr., C. R., Aldine Publishing Company Chicago, 1969, pp. 165–185.

[16] A detailed discussion of the marginal utility of income schedule is in Chapter 9.

[17] For a refutation of empirical studies trying to prove the existence of surplus labor, see KAO, C. H., ANSCHEL, K. R., and EICHER, C. K., 'Disguised Unemployment in Agriculture: A Survey' in 'Agriculture in Economic Development,' eds. Eicher, C. K., and Witt, L. W., McGraw-Hill, New York, 1964; and JORGENSON, D. W., 'The Role of Agriculture in Economic Development: Classical versus Neoclassical Models of Growth' in 'Subsistence Ariculture and Economic Development,' ed. Wharton Jr., C. R., Aldine Publishing Company, Chicago, 1969.

[18] HANSEN, B., 'Employment and Rural Wages in Egypt: Reply,' The American Economic Review, June 1971.

[19] HARRIS, J. R. and TODARO, M. P., 'Migration, Unemployment and Development: A Two Sector Analysis,' The American Economic Review, March 1970.

[20] HARBERGER, A. C., 'On Measuring the Social Opportunity Cost of Labor,' Paper presented at a meeting of experts on Fiscal Policies for Employment Promotion, sponsored by the International Labor Office at Geneva, Switzerland, January 1971. Reprinted in 'Project Evaluation-Collected Papers,' Markham Publishing Company, Chicago, 1974, pp. 157–183.

[21] If may be noted that HARRIS and TODARO set $\bar{m}$ at the foregone marginal product of the worker. Although this is not correct, it does not affect the result that w is the opportunity cost of urban labor.

[22] STIGLITZ, J. E., 'Alternative Theories of Wage Determination and Employment in LDC's: The Labor Turnover Model,' The Quarterly Journal of Economics, May 1974.

[23] MAZUMDAR, D., 'The Rural-Urban Wage Gap, Migration and the Shadow Wage,' World Bank Staff Working Paper No. 197, Washington, D.C., February 1975.

[24] TODARO, M. P., 'A Model of Labor Migration and Urban Unemployment in Less Developed Countries,' The American Economic Review, March 1969.

[25] This follows from the formula for the equilibrium position of a rural worker.

[26] FISK, E. K., 'Response of non-Monetary Production Units to Contact with the Exchange Economy,' Paper presented at the Conference on Agriculture in Development Theory at Villa Serbilloni, Bellagio, Italy, May 23–29, 1973.

[27] HELLEINER, G. K., 'Peasant Agriculture, Government and Economic Growth in Nigeria,' Richard D. Irwin, Inc., Illinois, 1966.

[28] MOULIK, E. K., 'Money, Motivation and Cash Cropping,' New Guinea Research Unit of the Australian National University, Bulletin No. 53, Port Moresby and Canberra, 1973.

[29] NAKAJIMA, 'Subsistence and Commercial Family Farms.'

[30] For a summary of the recent controversies in Capital Theory, see HARCOURT, G. C., 'Some Cambridge Controversies in the Theory of Capital,' Cambridge University Press, London, New York, 1972.

[31] KRUTILLA and ECKSTEIN, 'Multiple Purpose River Development.'

[32] HIRSHLEIFER, DE HAVEN and MILLIMAN, 'Water Supply-Economics, Technology and Policy.'

[33] BAUMOL, W. J., 'On the Social Rate of Discount,' The American Economic Review, September 1968.

[34] KRUTILLA and ECKSTEIN, 'Multiple Purpose River Development,' p. 91.

[35] HIRSHLEIFER, DE HAVEN and MILLIMAN, 'Water Supply,' p. 116.

[36] Ibid., p. 145.

[37] Ibid., p. 147.

[38] This follows from the formula $p - (p - 0.047\,d)(t) = 0.047\,d + (1 - d)e$ where p = project yield, d = proportion financed by debt, e = after tax equity yield, and the corporation income tax t = 52 percent (Ibid., p. 142).

Hence: $p - \left(p - \dfrac{0.047}{2}\right) 0.52 = \dfrac{0.047}{2} + \dfrac{0.057}{2}$, so that $p = 8.29\%$.

[39] BAUMOL, 'On the Social Rate of Discount,' The American Economic Review, September 1968, p. 78.

[40] RAMSEY, D. D., 'On the Social Rate of Discount – Comment,' The American Economic Review, December 1969, p. 919.

[41] USHER, D., 'On the Social Rate of Discount – Comment,' The American Economic Review, December 1969, p. 925.

[42] HARBERGER, A. C., 'On Measuring the Social Opportunity Cost of Public Funds,' in 'The Discount Rate in Public Investment Evaluation,' Conference Proceedings of the Committee on the Economics of Water Resources Development, Western Agricultural Economic Research Council, Report No. 17, Denver, Colorado, 17–18 December 1969. Reprinted in Harberger, A. C., 'Project Evaluation – Collected Papers,' Markham Publishing Company, Chicago, 1974, Chapter IV.

[43] HARBERGER, 'On Measuring the Social Opportunity Costs of Public Funds,' in 'Project Evaluation – Collected Papers,' p. 108.

[44] Applying Newton's binomial formula to the above expression, we get $q + 4q^2 + 6q^3 + 4q^4 + q^5 = \frac{1}{3}$. Since we may neglect the last three terms on the left-hand side without causing a large error, we get $12q^2 + 3q - 1 = 0$ which when solved with the standard algebraic formula gives
$$q = \frac{-3 \pm \sqrt{9 + 48}}{24} = \frac{4.55}{24} \text{ and } \frac{-10.55}{24}.$$
As we cannot have a negative rate of return, we find that q is about 19 percent.

[45] DASGUPTA, SEN and MARGLIN, 'Guidelines,' pp. 234–235.

[46] The pioneers of the approach were DOUGLAS, P. H. and COBB, C. W., 'A Theory of Production,' The American Economic Review, Vol. 18, 1928, supplement. Subsequently discussed in DOUGLAS's pioneering work: 'Theory of Wages,' The MacMillan Company, New York, 1934.

[47] The relationships may be shown by differentiating the Cobb-Douglas function with respect to K and L. The first differentiation gives $\partial Y/\partial K = \alpha A K^{\alpha-1} L^{1-\alpha} = \alpha Y/K$ and capital's share of national income is thus: $[K.\alpha Y/K]/Y = \alpha$. Similarly $\partial Y/\partial L = (1-\alpha)A K^{\alpha}L^{\alpha} = (1-\alpha)Y/L$ and labor's share of national income is thus $[L(1-\alpha)Y/L]/Y = 1-\alpha$.

[48] CHAKRAVARTY, S., 'The Use of Shadow Prices in Programme Evaluation,' in 'Capital Formation and Economic Development,' ed. Rosenstein-Rodan, P. N., George Allen and Unwin, Ltd., London, 1964, p. 60.

[49] As done by SOLOW, R. M., 'Capital Theory and the Rate of Return,' Professor Dr. F. de Vries Lectures, North-Holland Publishing Company, Amsterdam, 1964. Solow found a rate of return of 23 to 25 percent in the US and about 19 percent in Germany.

[50] SAMUELSON, P. A., 'Parable and Realism in Capital Theory – The Surrogate Production Function,' The Review of Economic Studies, Vol. 39, 1962, Reprinted in 'Capital and Growth – Selected Readings,' eds. Harcourt, G. C. and Laing, N. F., Penguin Books, 1971.

[51] BHADURI, A., 'On the Significance of Recent Controversies on Capital Theory: A Marxian View,' The Economic Journal, Vol 79, 1969. Reprinted in 'Capital and Growth – Selected Readings,' eds. Harcourt, G. C. and Laing, N. F., Penguin Books, 1971.

[52] HARBERGER, A. C., 'Investment in Men versus Investment in Machinery: The Case of India,' in 'Education and Economic Development,' eds. Anderson, C. A. and Bowman, M. J., Aldine Publishing Company, Chicago, 1965. Reprinted in Harberger, A. C., 'Project Evaluation – Collected Papers,' Markham Publishing Company, Chicago, 1974, Chapter VI.

[53] In this case $q = (Y - 0.56 Y)/K$ while $K = 0.3 Y/0.13$. Hence, $q = 0.19$.

[54] LAL, D., 'Wells and Welfare – An Exploratory Cost-Benefit Study of the Economics of Small-Scale Irrigation in Maharashtra,' Series on Cost-Benefit Analysis, Case Study No. 1, Development Centre of the Organisation for Economic Cooperation and Development, Paris, 1972, pp. 154–158.

4. THE ANALYTICS OF PROJECT PLANNING

Having reviewed how the benefits and costs of a project should be valued, we are now in a position to discuss more fully than we did in Section 1.2 how the optimum production scale of a project should be determined. In Section 1.2 we showed that marginal costs should be equal to marginal benefits. Nevertheless, the project evaluation literature has often suggested that other criteria should be used and it is, therefore, well worthwhile to review in this section the various possible criteria in some detail. We will assume during the first three sections of this Chapter that Government is in a position to implement the optimum conditions and that it can ensure that they will continue to be implemented. In the fourth section, we will review how projects should be evaluated if the optimum conditions cannot be fulfilled.

The analysis of the optimal scale of a project can be done either in present value or in annual terms and is, of course, completely equivalent. For exposition purposes, however, it is easier to work with annual values. Long-run marginal cost then consists of the addition to annual capital recovery cost (depreciation plus interest)[1] and to annual short-run operating cost, which are incurred when output is increased by one unit. We will start with the assumption that the plant is perfectly divisible and that the demand curve does not shift over time. Reference is made to Figure 4.1, which shows the relevant long-run average and marginal cost curves as well as the demand curve as they would appear in a certain period. Six positions indicated by X_1 through X_6, corresponding to the various optimization criteria, will be analyzed.

The first position X_1 is based on a rule that was popular for a long time in

FIGURE 4.1.

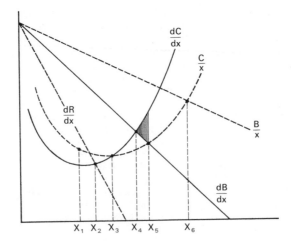

engineering circles. The rule states that the benefit-cost ratio of a project should be maximized. The first order condition for the maximization of B/C is: $[d(B/C)]/dx = 0$. Using the quotient differentiation rule, we obtain: $(C \cdot dB/dx - B \cdot dC/dx)/C^2 = 0$, which implies $(dB/dx)/(dC/dx) = B/C$. For the remainder of this study, it will often be convenient to use a shorthand notation and to write dB for dB/dx and dC for dC/dx. The above equation can thus be written as $dB/dC = B/C$, or, alternatively, $(dB/dC) \cdot C/B = 1$. In words, the criterion tells us that the elasticity of benefits with respect to costs should equal unity. Geometrically, the point X_1 can be found by extending the B/x curve to the X-axis and by drawing from that intersection the tangent line to the C/x curve.[2] As Figure 4.1 shows, it is clear that this point can never represent an optimum position if the objective is to maximize welfare since incremental production has larger benefits than costs up to the point X_4.

The second point X_2 is the so-called monopoly position. It is the optimum scale when the criterion is to maximize profits – the difference between revenues R and costs C – and the first order condition is then $dR - dC = 0$. This criterion can be expanded in the following manner. Since $R = x \cdot dB$, it follows from the product differentiation rule that

$$
\begin{aligned}
dR &= x[d \, (dB)]/dx + dB \\
&= x \, dp/dx + p \\
&= p[(x/dx) \cdot (dp/p) + 1)]
\end{aligned}
$$

The elasticity of demand with respect to price is $(-dx/x) \cdot p/dp$ and we may thus write for the above expression $dR = p \cdot (e - 1)/e$. At the optimum point $dR = dC$ and by substitution, we get $p = dC \cdot e/(e - 1)$. From this follows the well known theorem that a monopoly equilibrium position can be possible only if the elasticity of demand is greater than unity. Otherwise, i.e., if $e < 1$, p would be negative, which is evidently not possible. However, the point X_2 is not of interest to us, since it is a point of profit maximization rather than welfare maximization.

The third position X_3 is obtained when the criterion is to minimize average costs. The first order condition is: $[d \, (C/x)]/dx = (x \, dC - C)/x^2 = 0$. Hence, this condition is fulfilled when $dC = C/x$, or, in words, marginal costs should equal average costs. It is one of the perfect competition conditions.

The fourth criterion is to maximize the difference between benefits B and costs C. Hence, the criterion is $dB = dC$. Price should equal marginal costs. Since under perfect competition, marginal costs equal average costs as well as price, this condition is also fulfilled under perfect competition.

A fifth possible criterion that is sometimes defended is that the size of the project should be maximized subject to the condition that revenues should cover costs. This is the case when average costs C/x equal price dB. In Figure 4.1, this happens at scale X_5.

Finally, one may decide to push the size of the project to the point where total costs are just covered by benefits. This takes place in Figure 4.1 at the point where $C/x = B/x$.

75

FIGURE 4.2.

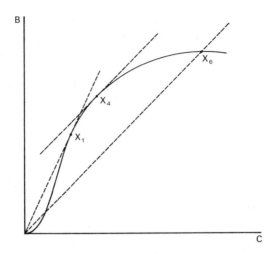

Only the point X_4 fulfills, of course, the condition of welfare maximization, given the existing income distribution. It is only at that scale that marginal costs equal marginal benefits, so that any divergence from that situation would lead to a welfare loss. For instance, at X_5 the welfare loss would equal the shaded area in Figure 4.1.

The preceding analysis can be elucidated even more succinctly if the relationship between total benefits and total costs is analyzed. This is shown by means of the benefit curve in Figure 4.2. The point X_4 – the optimal scale when the objective is to maximize the difference between benefits and costs – is now found by drawing a tangent line with a slope of 45° to the benefit curve. Clearly, X_4 is the point of welfare maximization. The vertical distance between the benefit curve and the 45° line from the origin – which represents zero net benefits – is greater at X_4 than at any other point along the curve, so that net benefits are at a maximum at X_4.

We are now in a position to review the case where the demand curve shifts over time, a phenomenon that is quite common. Suppose, for instance, that the income elasticity of demand for a certain product equals 0.5 and that per capita incomes grow at 4 percent per annum. Suppose further that population grows at the rate of 3 percent. Then the demand curve will shift over time at the rate of 5 percent per annum. In Figure 4.3, four demand curves are shown, the first one D_0 corresponding to the initial equilibrium situation. If the demand curve shifts to the position D_1, production should be increased by Q_0Q_1. The net benefit of this increase is equal to the area ABC, the difference between the willingness to pay (Q_0CBQ_1) and costs (Q_0ABQ_1). If now, during a subsequent period of the project's life, the demand curve shifts to the D_2 position, output should be increased by Q_1Q_2. The total willingness to pay during this period is Q_0EDQ_2, total costs Q_0ADQ_2, and net benefits thus AED. The net benefits of the project are thus represented by ABC in period 1, ADE in period 2, AFG in

FIGURE 4.3.

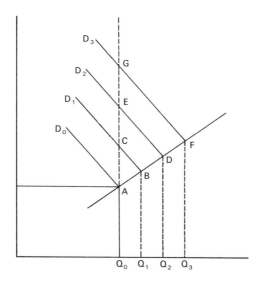

period 3, and so on. Discounting of these net benefits will present the net present value of the project. It may be noted that in case the demand curve was constant over time, the net benefit during each period would equal ABC only, so that the present value of the project would be substantially smaller. In projecting the benefits and costs of a project over time, the benefits of additional demand, and the costs which must be incurred to satisfy this additional demand, can thus not be neglected.

Finally, let us drop the assumption that the plant is perfectly divisible. The economic literature has struggled for a long time with the indivisibility problem, but the solution is fairly straightforward. A very elegant analysis regarding the case where additional electricity can be generated only in indivisible units is presented by WILLIAMSON.[3] Consider Figure 4.4. The existing capacity is $0 Q_1$, and can only be increased by the indivisible unit Q_1Q_2. Short-run marginal costs are mainly the energy costs of generation and transmission and equal b per unit. The short-run marginal cost curve is thus constant up to Q_1 and assumes at Q_1 a vertical slope because of the capacity constraint. In line with the dictum that price should equal short-run marginal cost to clear the market, the price at Q_1 is set at P_1. Long-run marginal costs are also constant and equal $b + \beta$ per unit, where β represents the capacity cost per unit. With output of $0Q_1$ at price P_1, the plant thus earns B while consumers receive a surplus equal to A. Should the capacity unit Q_1Q_2 be added to the plant? At the new position, the price will be P_2 and producers thus incur a loss of C + E + F. On the other hand, the consumer surplus is now A + B + C + D + E. Hence, the net result of the plant expansion is a benefit of D − F. The plant should thus be expanded when D exceeds F, or, in other words, when the willingness to pay for the additional output (D + E + G + H) exceeds the costs of its production (E + F + G + H).

77

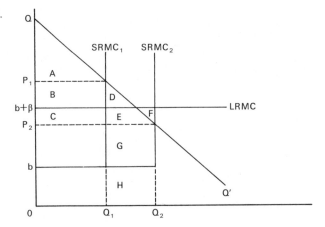

FIGURE 4.4.

Tabulation of Consumer and Producer Surpluses

	Situation at Q_1	Situation at Q_2	Gain
Consumer Surplus	A	A+B+C+D+E	B+C+D+E
Producer Surplus	B	−(C+E+F)	−B−(C+E+F)
Total Economic Surplus	A + B	(A+B) + (D−F)	D − F

The above analysis needs an explanation in that the prices in positions Q_1 and Q_2 are higher than the really incurred short-run marginal costs. Or, in other words, can one really say that the short-run marginal cost curve assumes a vertical slope at the position where the capacity constraint becomes binding? If the size of the plant is given, we should maximize benefits (*B*) minus short-run marginal costs (*b Q*), subject to the condition that *Q* will be smaller than or equal to $\bar{Q}$ – the maximum production at that plant size. The Lagrangean is thus:

$$\max L = B - bQ - \lambda (Q - \bar{Q})$$

The first order conditions are

$$dL/dQ = P - b - \lambda = 0, \text{ and } dL/d\lambda = -Q + \bar{Q} = 0$$

If $Q = \bar{Q}$, then λ has a positive value and $P = b + \lambda$. The economic interpretation of λ is straightforward: it is the scarcity premium that must be added to short-run marginal costs to clear the market. The value of $b + \lambda$ is what a single consumer is willing to pay to have a unit of electricity and it is an opportunity cost in the sense that, if he gets that unit, another consumer would be deprived of it because production cannot be expanded. In this sense, therefore, $b + \lambda$ must be seen as the real marginal cost of providing a unit of a

78

commodity when a capacity constraint exists. On the other hand, if $Q < \bar{Q}$, then there is no scarcity problem and obviously the value of λ is then zero so that $P = b$.

The question whether tolls should be levied on a bridge, which has also been a source of dispute in the economic literature for a long time, can likewise be solved readily. We assume now that the horizontal axis of Figure 4.4 is the traffic flow over the bridge. Furthermore, since a bridge has negligible short-run marginal costs, we assume that the b curve does not exist. If the demand curve is as shown in Figure 4.4 so that D is larger than F, the bridge should be constructed to capacity Q_2 and a toll equal to P_2 should be charged to the users of the bridge.[4] However, if the demand curve were to intersect the horizontal axis between Q_1 and Q_2, and the area D were still larger than F, the bridge should also be constructed to capacity constraint and, with zero short-run marginal costs, any charge would be non-optimal.

We hope to have shown in this section that the rule for determining the optimal scale of a project that still must be constructed is straightforward. Long-run marginal costs must be covered. On the other hand, once the project has been constructed, long-run marginal costs are not relevant at all since they include sunk costs, and the relevant cost concept for the pricing of the output becomes then short-run marginal costs. In case no capacity constraint exists, these are simply the really incurred costs; in case of capacity constraints, however, the short-run marginal costs are presented by the opportunity cost of not satisfying another customer.

4.2. THE OPTIMAL TIMING OF A PROJECT

This section is based upon the work of MARGLIN[5], who was the first to distinguish project time from calendar time. Suppose the demand for a project's output and the project's operating costs are constant over calendar time so that its net benefit rate depends only upon project age, i.e., in this case upon the date when the project's construction is finished and it starts to produce. Then, there would be no special problem: the project should be constructed if it has a positive present value. Neither would a special problem arise if a project has a net benefit rate that decreases as calendar time passes. If this project has a positive present value, then it should be constructed immediately because any postponement would result in a lower present value. Suppose, however, that a project's net benefit rate increases over calendar time. Then the project's net present value can perhaps be increased by postponing it. In other words, in maximizing benefits minus costs, time should also be considered an instrument variable. The optimum construction date is the date at which the present value of the derivatives with respect to time of benefits and cost are equal, i.e., when $dB/dt = dC/dt$.

A simple example may illustrate this. Suppose a project with increasing net benefits $N_1, \ldots, N_n$ can be constructed in one year at capital costs K. Postponement by one year means, on the cost side, that the project's capital costs could have been invested in alternative investment, so that there will be a saving of qK, where q is the opportunity cost of capital. The present value of this saving equals $qK/(1 + q)$. On the benefit side, postponement by one year results in the loss of the first year's benefits, the present value of which is $N_1/(1 + q)$ and the gain of the $(n + 1)$th year's benefits, the present value of which is $N_{n+1}/(1 + q)^{n+1}$. The overall net gain in present value due to a one-year postponement is thus:

$$\frac{qK}{1+q} - \frac{N_1}{1+q} + \frac{N_{n+1}}{(1+q)^{n+1}}$$

By repeating the calculation for postponements of two years, three years, and so on, the optimal construction year can be found. The optimal date is when the marginal saving in interest costs is absorbed by the marginal loss in net benefits.[6]

This is the most general formulation. Sometimes, for certain projects, it may be possible to simplify the calculation. Suppose that a project has a very long life. Then the present value of the $(n + 1)$th year's benefit will be negligible and the optimal time for project construction occurs at the date when the first year's benefit equals the rate of return q on the project's capital cost. This rule has become quite popular for road and mass transit projects in consultant engineering circles, but it should be immediately remarked that a naive application of the rule can lead to some disastrous results. If it would take, for instance, two or three years after construction before benefits would be produced, the rule would lead to the untenable result that the project in question should be postponed indefinitely since the first year's benefit would remain zero whatever the postponement period. In general, therefore, if we are to consider the optimal timing of a project, it is better for the determination of the construction period to calculate the present value of the project's net benefits directly rather than to use short-cut methods.

How important is the time phasing of projects? As mentioned, the problem arises only with projects whose benefits increase over time. It will be seldom indeed that such projects are prematurely submitted because, normally, postponement by one or two years does not affect significantly the net present value of a project. Timing is important if at a certain moment in time a sudden increase in benefits occurs. But such cases are not frequent and it is not likely that errors in timing will then be made. For instance, it is quite obvious that there is no sense in building a speedway from city A to city B when city B has not yet been constructed. In general, therefore, the optimal timing of a project is not that important. Nevertheless, the project analyst should satisfy himself that no timing errors are being made.

4.3. FURTHER EXAMPLES OF CONSUMER SURPLUS ANALYSIS

We have so far reviewed the benefits of an output expansion but there are quite a number of cases more complicated than this one, and it will be useful to review briefly how they should be treated. As a first case, we would like to review the benefits of a cost reduction due, for instance, to a technological innovation. To show the difference from the output expansion case, the cost reduction figure (Figure 4.6) has been set beside the output expansion figure (Figure 4.5). The figures speak for themselves and, rather than describing the gains and losses of the parties involved, it is believed more useful to present the analysis in tabular form immediately below the figures.

As discussed previously, in the case of a social analysis, the benefits of each of the two groups – consumers and producers – must be evaluated at the respective income distribution weights before they can be added up, whereas in the case of an economic efficiency analysis, the benefits may be added up directly. It should also be pointed out that in the case of an economic efficiency analysis it is not necessary to analyze the gain of each of the two groups as the economic benefit of the output increase can be found directly by measuring the willingness to pay for and the costs of the output. Thus in Figure 4.5, the willingness to pay increases by E + F + G, while the cost of production increases by G, resulting in a net benefit of E + F. Similarly in Figure 4.6, the willingness to pay increases by F + G + H, while the cost of production decreases by C + D and increases by H. The net benefit is thus (C + D), which is the cost saving on the old production, plus (F + G), which is the gain on the new production.

In any analysis like the above, care should be taken that the appropriate cost and demand concepts are used. In Figure 4.6, the relevant cost concept depends on what we wish to analyze. If a choice is to be made between two prospective investment opportunities, the comparison should be between the long-run marginal costs of each of the two production possibilities. On the other hand, if the choice is whether an existing production proces should be continued or replaced by a new production process, the comparison should be between the short-run marginal costs of the existing process and the long-run marginal costs of the new process. In this case, the long-run marginal costs of the existing process are clearly not relevant at all: bygones are bygones, and only short-run marginal costs for the existing plant should, therefore, be considered.

Often one finds that in analyses like the above, mistakes are made. ECKSTEIN[7] has given an interesting example as regards the procedure followed in the past by the Corps of Engineers in the USA for the estimation of the benefits of navigation. All of the benefits of such projects are of the same type – savings in transportation costs – and the procedure should be to compare the costs of river shipment with the costs of the cheapest alternative. Suppose the long-run marginal cost of shipping a commodity by water is $ 1.50 a ton, while the cheapest alternative is to ship it by railroad, for which the railroad would charge $ 3.60 a ton, although its short-run marginal cost is only $ 2.40 a ton. The Corps

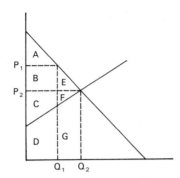
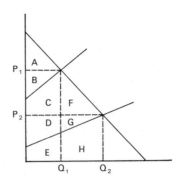

FIGURE 4.5.   FIGURE 4.6.

FIG. 4.5. Analysis of Benefits due to an Output Expansion.

	Situation at Q_1	Situation at Q_2	Gain
Consumer Surplus	A	A + B + E	B + E
Producers Surplus	B + C	C + F	F − B
Total Economic Surplus	A + B + C	A + B + C + E + F	E + F

FIG. 4.6. Analysis of Benefits due to a Lowering of Costs.

	Situation at Q_1	Situation at Q_2	Gain
Consumers Surplus	A	A + B + C + F	B + C + F
Producers Surplus	B	D + G	D + G − B
Total Economic Surplus	A + B	A + B + C + D + F + G	C + D + F + G

of Engineers calculated the benefit of the navigation project at $ 2.10 a ton –
the difference between the price charged by the railroad and the cost of water
shipment. In reality, of course, the benefit of the project is the cost difference –
$ 0.90 a ton – plus the user's benefit on the induced additional transport volume
which must also be estimated. This conclusion can be inferred from Figure 4.6
if we imagine that the two cost curves assume a horizontal slope.

The second type of complication which we would like to review is that of
production processes where joint products are produced or where peak load
demands exist. As will be shown, the analysis is quite similar in both cases.
Many production processes produce, of course, more than one type of good,
and sometimes the same equipment is used to produce good A as well as good B.
So long as the quantities of goods A and B can be varied, the calculation of the
marginal costs – either short run or long run – does not present a problem. To

FIGURE 4.7.

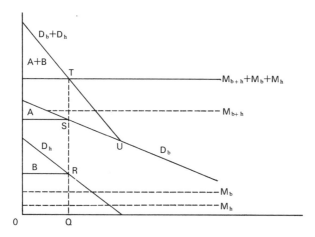

find the short-run marginal costs of product A, we should ask what the addition to the direct costs will be to increase the output of A when the output of B remains unchanged. Similarly, to determine the long-run marginal cost of A, we should ask what additions to capacity plus direct costs are necessary to increase the production of A when the capacity to produce B remains constant. The optimization rules remain as before: the intersection of the marginal cost curve of any of those goods with its demand curve represents the optimum production level of that good. A problem arises, however, when the proportions of A and B cannot be varied, i.e., when they can be produced only in fixed proportions, for then, clearly, the marginal costs can be determined only for both goods combined. The classic examples of such cases of joint production processes are beef and hides, mutton and wool, cotton fiber and cotton seeds, and wheat and straw. The technique for determining the optimal production scale for such products is as follows.

Consider Figure 4.7. The demand curves for beef and hides are D_b and D_h, respectively. For simplicity's sake, it is assumed that the marginal costs are constant. M_{b+h} represents the marginal joint cost of producing the fixed proportion of beef and hides (the cattle), M_b the marginal cost of processing beef, and M_h the marginal cost of the separate processing of hides. What is the optimum position? The solution is clear if we think of the output as a composite unit, determined by a fixed proportion such as X tons of beef plus Y hides. The price that will be paid for any quantity of such a composite unit is then found by adding vertically the demand curves for beef and hides. In Figure 4.7 this is the curve $D_b + D_h$ up to point U, and from then on, the curve D_b. Similarly, the marginal cost of producing the composite unit is found by adding vertically the three marginal cost curves. The optimum production quantity is then at the intersection of the marginal cost curve of the composite unit with the demand curve of the composite unit, and is thus equal to OQ. At this output level, the producer receives a price of QR for hides, a price of QS for beef, and a price of QT (= QR + QS) for the composite unit.

83

The principle followed in this simple example applies also to the so-called peak-load problem, which most public utility companies as well as airlines and railroads face. An airline and a railroad, for instance, face peak demands during the holiday season, an electric utility company has a slack period during the night hours, more phone calls are made during working days than during the weekends, and so on. Capacity that is necessary to satisfy demand during the peak periods is thus not necessary during the slack periods. The solution to the problem is clear if we interpret the overall demand curve as the demand for the flow of services that a capacity unit provides during an entire period, including slack and peak load periods. Take for instance an electricity undertaking. When the plant is perfectly divisible, we may define a unit of capacity as the unit which produces 1 kwh during 24 hours. Say that there is a peak period of 16 hours and a slack period of eight hours. Then we can draw up a demand curve representing the amount of money consumers are willing to pay for a marginal kwh during 16 hours, and a demand curve representing the amount of money consumers are willing to pay for a marginal kwh during eight hours. Let D_b and D_h in Figure 4.7 represent these demand curves, respectively. Then the overall demand curve $D_b + D_h$ represents the price consumers are willing to pay to use a marginal kwh during the entire period and its intersection with the long-run marginal cost curve determines what quantity should be produced. In Figure 4.7, this quantity is equal to OQ and at the point Q we may then find, for instance, that QS is equal to ¢ 160 (16 hours consumption at a price of ¢ 10 per kwh), that QR is equal to ¢ 40 (representing eight hours consumption at a price of ¢ 5 per kwh) and that QT is equal to ¢ 200. The price QT will thus be sufficient to cover all the marginal costs of production. By carefully defining the demand and cost relationships so that they refer to the relevant flow of services during the respective periods, the analysis of peak load demand becomes thus the same as the analysis of joint products. Introducing indivisibility into the analysis does not present any further problems. As discussed in Section 1, it is then a matter of whether the long-run marginal costs of the indivisible unit will be covered by the willingness of the consumer to pay for the flow of services this indivisible extra unit provides.

Decreasing average cost projects present a special problem, in that at the equilibrium situation, revenues will not be sufficient to cover costs.[8] In Figure 4.8 the demand curve intersects the long-run marginal cost curve at the point R. The consumer's willingness to pay for output level OQ is ODRQ, the long-run marginal costs are OSRQ, and the net benefit of producing OQ is thus DRS, which is clearly the maximum that can be obtained. At output level OQ, however, the price will be RQ[9] so that revenues are OTRQ whereas costs are OSRQ. The production of OQ will thus involve a financial loss of STR. The financial loss can also be found, of course, by looking at average costs. In Figure 4.8, these are OVUQ, while revenues are OTRQ and the loss can thus be defined as either STR or TVUR.

It is generally believed that several public utilities industries – especially posts, telegraphs, telephones and railroads – belong to the category of decreasing

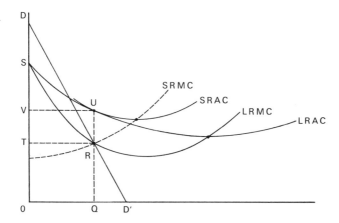

FIGURE 4.8.

average cost industries. Large economies of scale cause the average cost curve to slope downward over a substantial output range before the increased demand for additional factors of production resulting in increased factor prices overtakes this and causes the curve to slope upward. It should be noted that indivisibilities may be present, but that indivisibilities as such are not necessary to explain the phenomenon. It is rather the insufficient demand that is the cause of it.

How should the deficit be financed? It may first of all be pointed out that if one were to wait long enough, the demand curve would eventually intersect the long-run marginal cost curve at a point where average costs are increasing, so that then no problem of deficit financing would arise. This is, however, not a solution because meantime, of course, a substantial flow of services will be foregone, the value of which, as determined by the consumer's willingness to pay, is much higher than its cost of production. Should we then devise a discriminatory pricing system that will mulct from the consumer their willingness to pay? The answer depends on the distributive aspects of the project. If consumers are rich, there is no reason why we should not try to do so. If consumers are poor, however, there is no reason why we should do so. As OORT[10] has stated, if we say that the deficit of a decreasing cost industry should be charged to the consumer of its output, then logic demands that the surplus of an increasing cost industry should be refunded to its consumers.

Finally, a few words about foreign exchange earning or saving projects. There are, of course, such goods as construction, electricity, sewerage, water supply and so on that cannot be traded because the cost of transport would be exorbitantly high. Many other goods, however, such as primary products and manufactures do enter international trade. In Figure 4.9 it is assumed that the import price of such a good – the c.i.f. cost valued at the foreign exchange opportunity cost rate – equals P_m and that the export price – the f.o.b. price valued at the foreign exchange opportunity cost rate – equals P_e. Let us assume that the domestic demand curve is as indicated by the curve QQ' and that the good is entirely imported. Import substitution would then be worth-

85

FIGURE 4.9.

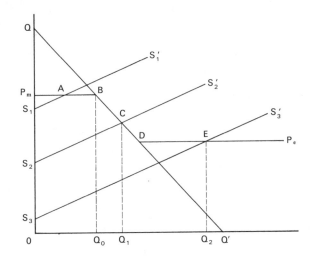

while if domestic production can substitute for imports at a cost lower than the import cost. If the good can be produced at a cost as indicated by S_1S_1', it would clearly be beneficial to produce quantity P_mA of the good, since there would be a cost saving equal to P_mAS_1. It is possible that domestic production of the good may lead eventually to a lowering of the cost curve as argued by the proponents of the infant industry argument. For instance, if the cost curve became S_2S_2', the additional net benefits would be equal to S_1ABCS_2. A further lowering of the cost curve may even lead to exports of the good. With a cost curve equal to S_3S_3', the additional net benefits would be S_2CDES_3. Any valuation of the benefits of the domestic production of a certain good should in principle take all these additional net benefits into account. However, this statement must immediately be qualified with the remark that the learning process on which the infant industry argument rests takes quite a long time, so that in practice the benefit of an import substitution project consists mainly of the immediate cost savings – the area P_mAS_1. Especially in the Latin American countries many import substituting industries were established in the 1950s which later appeared to be quite uneconomical. Extreme care should therefore be taken in projecting any additional benefits from so-called learning processes.

4.4. NON-OPTIMAL SITUATIONS

Having reviewed what the optimal production and pricing policies are for a project, the question arises as to how Government can ensure that the project will indeed be implemented in accordance with these optimal policies. The problem is that the optimum conditions are determined by the real benefits and costs of a project, while the project manager is faced all the time with benefits and costs based on market prices. As discussed in Chapters 2 and 3, there may be substantial differences between real values and market values. To repeat some examples: the benefits of a project include consumer surplus; profits do not. In the case of inputs, the real cost is the weighted average of the real supply price and willingness to pay; the cost as it appears to the project manager is, however, the market price. The real cost of an imported good is determined by the foreign exchange opportunity cost; the market price is based on the official rate and includes import duties. Similarly, the real benefit of an exported good is its shadow foreign exchange value, while the project will receive the export proceeds at the official foreign exchange rate. Differences between opportunity costs and market values may also exist as regards labor – e.g., the urban market wage rate may be higher than the real costs. Furthermore, especially as regards capital, one finds often that Governments, in order to promote investments, follow policies of providing credit at low interest rates, even though the real cost of capital may be high. We have, therefore, situations where real values and money values will not be equal so that the project manager may use the wrong values. The project manager may also see as his objective the maximization of profits rather than the maximization of welfare, and, if he is in a monopoly position and starts to act as a monopolist, the optimum may also for this reason not be reached. How should the project evaluator handle these problems?

It should first of all be noted that there are many projects that fall entirely under Government control, so that the Government can ensure that, for the design as well as the implementation of these projects, the real value of the resources will be used as a guide. Furthermore, in many cases, there may not in fact be much flexibility to change the size of a project. Roads and bridges clearly fall into this category. Also, once an irrigation dam has been constructed, it will be very costly to change the size of the dam. It must be recognized, however, that there will also be quite a number of projects, particularly commercial projects, where, indeed, plant size, as well as operations, can be set by the operators at a level different from the optimum position.

One way of letting project operations coincide with the optimum in case of divergencies is the granting of subsidies or the levying of taxes. But such incentives or disincentives, in general, cannot be applied to individual projects, except in very special circumstances that would need constant control. Suppose, for instance, that the Government were to grant a special subsidy, a wage subsidy, or an exemption from tariffs, to an undertaking that will produce a good that is in short supply. Then that particular undertaking would be able to undercut existing enterprises and eventually attain a monopoly position. Similarly, if the Government were to grant such an incentive to a particular industry, other industries would be disadvantaged. If taxes and subsidies are to be used, they should thus be applied on a factor basis. But here is a problem also, since many Governments, in view of their financial constraints, are quite willing to levy taxes but not to grant subsidies. It must therefore be accepted that in quite a number of cases it will not be possible to ensure that projects will be optimally operated.

A naive application of project evaluation rules may then lead to completely

FIGURE 4.10.

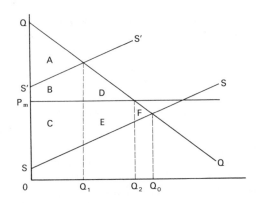

wrong conclusions[11], as was already mentioned briefly in the first chapter. Some further examples may be helpful. Let us assume that a certain good can be produced with real costs as indicated in Figure 4.10 by SS and real benefits as indicated by the demand curve QQ. Then, if there are no distortions, the project should be designed to produce an output equal to OQ_0 and the net benefit of the project would be estimated as the sum of the areas $A + B + C + D + E + F$. Suppose, however, that the project manager faces nominal costs as indicated by the curve S'S' and that the Government cannot exercise control over project implementation. The project would then be operated at an output level OQ_1 and the benefits of the project would be $A + B + C$ only. A naive benefit-cost analysis, in the sense that it does not take into account how the project will be operated, would thus lead to a substantial overestimation of the benefits.

The example can easily be extended to include the possibility of import substitution. Let us assume that the good can be imported at a real cost of OP_m. The import level would then be OQ_2 and the net benefits of importing, $A + B + D$. Should the good be locally produced or should it be imported? The answer is clear. The benefits of local production equal $A + B + C$, while the benefits of importing equal $A + B + D$. Hence, the good should be locally produced only if C is larger than D.

Divergencies between real values and nominal values may also occur on the demand side. Consider Figure 4.11, which presents the case of an exportable. SS represents the real cost of production, QQ' the domestic demand, and OP_e the real value per unit of exports. If there are no distortions, production should be OQ_0 and the net benefits will be $A + B + C + D + E + F$. Suppose, however, that exporters will receive only the price OP'_e because the official exchange rate is overvalued and the Government has no control over the project. Then output will be OQ_1 and the net benefit will be equal to $A + B + C + D + E$ only.

There are many more cases that could be studied if time and space were not a constraint. The above examples should have made it clear, however, what the

88

FIGURE 4.11.

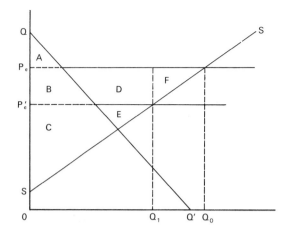

basic principles are. Furthermore, the examples have great empirical significance in that commercial enterprises are often faced with input prices which
differ significantly from the real cost of resources used and with export prices
which do not represent real export values. As Figures 4.10 and 4.11 have shown,
the evaluator must consider the actual situation within which production will
take place and can only then estimate what the real benefits and costs of this
production are. Of course, the evaluator should point out that the distortions
cause a loss to the economy. But in all cases where the Government is not
willing to eliminate the distortions, nominal prices govern the action of individuals, and the project evaluator clearly should base his analysis on the real
situation rather than on a hypothetical optimum.

[1] How the capital recovery cost should be calculated will be discussed in detail in Section 5.1.

[2] At the tangent point on the C/x curve, it holds that

$$\frac{d(B/x)}{d(C/x)} = \frac{B/x}{C/x} \text{ so that } \frac{dB}{dC} = \frac{B}{C}.$$

This can be shown as follows. For the left-hand side of the equation, we write:

$$\frac{d(B/x)}{dx} : \frac{d(C/x)}{dx} = \frac{xdB - B}{x^2} : \frac{xdC - C}{x^2} = \frac{dB - B/x}{dC - C/x}$$

This is equal to $\frac{B/x}{C/x}$. Hence, $\frac{dB}{dC} = \frac{B}{C}$.

[3] WILLIAMSON, O. E., 'Peak-Load Pricing and Optimal Capacity under Indivisibility Contraints,' The American Economic Review, September, 1966, pp. 810–827.

[4] See, however, Chapter 5, Section 2, regarding the distributive aspects of congestion.

[5] MARGLIN, S. A., 'Approaches to Dynamic Investment Planning', North Holland Publishing Company, Amsterdam, 1963.

[6] This is the optimization rule if no budget constraints exist. For a discussion of optimization rules in the presence of budget constraints see Section 5.5.

[7] ECKSTEIN, O., 'Water Resource Development,' p. 175.

[8] A monograph on the subject is provided by OORT, C. J., 'Decreasing Costs as a Problem of Welfare Economics,' Drukkerij Holland N.V., Amsterdam, 1958.

[9] It may be noted that the price R Q is equal to short-run marginal costs as well as long-run marginal costs. As a moment's reflection should make clear, when the plant is perfectly divisible, the short-run marginal costs of an additional unit of production will always equal the long-run marginal costs of the unit. This may also be shown as follows. At a point such as Q the lowest cost plant size is given by that short-run average cost curve (S R A C) that touches the envelope curve, i.e., the long-run average cost curve (L R A C). Since the slopes of S R A C and L R A C are equal, short-run marginal costs must also equal long-run marginal costs.

[10] OORT, 'Decreasing Costs as a Problem of Welfare Economics,' p. 139.

[11] A similar position is taken by JANSEN, 'Schaarse Middelen en Structurele Samenhangen,' p. 27.

5. PROJECT RANKING

5.1. COMPOUND AND DISCOUNT FORMULAS

A comprehensive discussion of the theory of project ranking requires a full understanding of the concepts of compounding and discounting. This section is, therefore, devoted to a review of these concepts and the derivation of the most frequently used formulas in this aspect of economic analysis.

As discussed in Chapter 1, the general formula for the present value of a terminal cash income T_n in year n discounted at the constant annual rate i is presented by:

$$(5.1) \quad \frac{T_n}{(1 + i)^n}$$

Where the cash income is not received as a terminal amount but in the form of a constant cash income N_A per year over n years, this cash flow can be considered as consisting of a series of n terminal sums N_A. Hence, under the assumption of a constant discount rate i, the present value of this flow is:

$$\frac{N_A}{(1 + i)} + \frac{N_A}{(1 + i)^2} + \ldots + \frac{N_A}{(1 + i)^n} = \sum_{t=1}^{n} \frac{N_A}{(1 + i)^t}$$

Using the algebraic summation rule, this expression can be reduced as follows:

$$(5.2) \quad \sum_{t=1}^{n} \frac{N_A}{(1 + i)^t} = \frac{N_A}{(1 + i)} \cdot \frac{1 - \{1/(1 + i)^n\}}{1 - \{1/(1 + i)\}} = \frac{N_A}{i} \left\{ 1 - \frac{1}{(1 + i)^n} \right\}$$

Combining (5.1) and (5.2), the present value at a discount rate i per year for n years of a terminal sum T_n and a constant flow N_A per year is thus:

$$(5.3) \quad V = \frac{T_n}{(1 + i)^n} + \frac{N_A}{i} \left\{ 1 - \frac{1}{(1 + i)^n} \right\}$$

This is an equation with five variables, which can be solved for any of the variables if the other four are known.

Table 5.1 shows the six most common compounding and discounting formulas derived from 5.3 and also their equivalent symbols. These symbols stand for the expressions between brackets in Table 5.1 and represent the discount and compound formulas when the independent variable assumes the value of 1. Table 5.1 also shows how the more complicated of these functions are derived. The values of the functions for different values of n and i can be

TABLE 5.1. A. Discount and compound functions.

Description of Formula	Given Variables in Addition to i and n		Formula	Financial Symbol for Bracketed Expression
Present value of $\$T_n$ Terminal Value	$N_A = 0$	T_n	$V = \left[\dfrac{1}{(1+i)^n}\right] T_n$	$\dfrac{1}{(1+i)^n}$
Present value of $\$N$ Cash flow per year during n years	$T_n = 0$	N_A	$V = \left[\dfrac{1 - \dfrac{1}{(1+i)^n}}{i}\right] N_A$	$a_{\overline{n}\rvert i}$
Compound Amount of $\$A$ Single Investment	$N_A = 0$	V	$T_n = [(1+i)^n] V$	$(1+i)^n$
Compound Amount of $\$N$ Invested per year during n years	$V = 0$	N_A	$T_n = \left[\dfrac{(1+i)^n - 1}{i}\right] N_A$	$s_{\overline{n}\rvert i}$
Investment required per year during n years to grow to Terminal value of $\$T_n$ (sinking fund factor)	$V = 0$	T_n	$N_A = \left[\dfrac{i}{(1+i)^n - 1}\right] T_n$	$\dfrac{1}{s_{\overline{n}\rvert i}}$
Cash flow required per year during n years to recover an Investment of $\$V$ (capital recovery factor)	$T_n = 0$	V	$N_A = \left[\dfrac{i}{1 - \dfrac{i}{(1+i)^n}}\right] V$	$\dfrac{1}{a_{\overline{n}\rvert i}}$

TABLE 5.1. B. Derivation of principal functions

If $N_A = 1$ and $T_n = 0$, then present value V is:

$$\frac{1}{(1+i)} + \frac{1}{(1+i)^2} + \ldots \frac{1}{(1+i)^n} = \sum_{t=1}^{n} \frac{1}{(1+i)^t} = \frac{1 - \frac{1}{(1+i)^n}}{i} = a_{\overline{n}|i}$$

If $N_A = 1$ and $V = 0$, then terminal value T_n is:

$$(1+i)^n + (1+i)^{n-1} + \ldots (1+i) = \sum_{t=1}^{n} (1+i)^t = \frac{(1+i)^n - 1}{i} = s_{\overline{n}|i}$$

If $T_n = 1$ and $V = 0$, then N_A is found by solving:

$$N_A(1+i)^n + N_A(1+i)^{(n-1)} + \ldots N_A(1+i) = N_A \cdot \sum_{t=1}^{n} (1+i)^t =$$

$$= N_A \cdot \frac{(1+i)^n - 1}{i} = N_A \cdot s_{\overline{n}|i} = 1$$

Hence, $N_A = 1/s_{\overline{n}|i}$

If $V = 1$ and $T_n = 0$, then N_A is found by solving:

$$1 = \frac{N_A}{(1+i)} + \frac{N_A}{(1+i)^2} + \ldots \frac{N_A}{(1+i)^n} = N_A \cdot \sum_{t=1}^{n} \frac{1}{(1+i)^t} =$$

$$= N_A \cdot \frac{1 - \frac{1}{(1+i)^n}}{i} = N_A \cdot a_{\overline{n}|i}$$

Hence, $N_A = 1/a_{\overline{n}|i}$

Furthermore, the following formulas are derived from the above:

$$\frac{1}{a_{\overline{n}|i}} = \frac{1}{s_{\overline{n}|i}} + i \text{ and } s_{\overline{n}|i} = a_{\overline{n}|i} \cdot (1+i)^n$$

found in any handbook of discount and compound tables. The reader who is not familiar with financial calculations may have some difficulty at first sight with the symbols. Once their meaning is grasped, however, it will become clear that they simplify discussions of financial matters considerably.

Some examples may be useful. Let us assume, for instance, that we wish to calculate the present value at discount rate i of a cash flow N_A per year during n years. Then by setting $T_n = 0$, and solving 5.3 (or by going back to 5.2), we

find that $V = \dfrac{N_A}{i} \left\{ 1 - \dfrac{1}{(1+i)^n} \right\}$

for which we may write $V = N_A \cdot a_{\overline{n}|i}$, where $a_{n|i}$ represents the present value at discount rate i of a \$1 cash flow per year during n years (see Table 5.1 for the direct derivation of $a_{\overline{n}|i}$).

Let us now look at the opposite case. Suppose that we wish to calculate the cash flow N_A per year that an investment should generate during n years to 'earn back' the investment in the sense that a rate of return i should be made as well as that the original sum invested should be received back. Then from the expression above, it follows immediately that $N_A = V \cdot 1/a_{\overline{n}|i}$ where the financial symbol $1/a_{\overline{n}|i}$ stands for the cash flow per year that a \$1 investment should generate during n years at rate i (Table 5.1 provides again the direct derivation of $1/a_{\overline{n}|i}$).

The other equations in Table 5.1 are derived in a similar way. The symbols used are $s_{\overline{n}|i}$, which represents the terminal value of \$1 invested per year during n years, and $1/s_{\overline{n}|i}$ which represents the investments required per year during n years to obtain a terminal value of \$1 at the end of year n.

One fundamental point needs, perhaps, further elaboration. For any investment K in a depreciating asset, net cash income (N_t) in any year consists of a return on the value of the investment in the beginning of that year (iK_t) and a depreciation part (D_t). Hence $N_t \equiv iK_t + D_t$. It should, of course, be understood that, in this identity, cash income N_t refers to gross revenues B_t minus all operating expenses O_t, to that $N_t = B_t - O_t$.

Let us review an example. Suppose an asset worth \$100,000 is expected to generate a constant cash-flow stream of \$16,274.54 per year over its useful life of 10 years. What is its rate of return? In any handbook of financial tables it may be seen that the cash flow, which is equal to $K \cdot 1/a_{\overline{n}|i}$, represents a 10 percent rate of return. Hence, the income and depreciation schedule would be as in Table 5.2.

As is readily seen, the rate of return in any one year is equal to 10 percent of the value of the asset, while the sum of the depreciation components of the cash-flow stream over the life of the project is equal to the original value of the asset.

If the same rate of return is to be earned, the factor $1/a_{\overline{n}|i}$ and the annual cash flow must be larger in the case of a short-term investment than in the case of a long-term investment. This is so, because – as the fundamental identity shows – the investment must be depreciated faster in the case of the short-term

94

TABLE 5.2. Example of Rate of Return Calculation.

	Value of Asset	Total	Cash Flow Income	Depreciation
Yrs 1	100,000.00	16,274.54	10,000.00	6,274.54
2	93,725.46	16,274.54	9,372.55	6,901.99
3	86,823.47	16,274.54	8,682.35	7,592.19
4	79,231.28	16,274.54	7,923.13	8,351.41
5	70,879.87	16,274.54	7,087.99	9,186.55
6	61,693.32	16,274.54	6,169.33	10,105.21
7	51,588.11	16,274.54	5,158.81	11,115.73
8	40,472.38	16,274.54	4,047.24	12,227.30
9	28,245.08	16,274.54	2,824.50	13,450.04
10	14,795.04	16,274.54	1,479.50	14,795.04
				100,000.00

investment. On the other hand, consideration of the formula of $1/a_{\overline{n}|i}$ in Table 5.1 shows that $1/a_{\overline{n}|i}$ will tend to i if n assumes large values. This is logical. If an investment has an infinite life, then there is no need to depreciate the investment.

Two other observations are called for. First, in accordance with the formula $1/a_{\overline{n}|i} = 1/s_{\overline{n}|i} + i$, the capital recovery factor of an investment may be considered to consist of the sinking fund factor of an equivalent loan amount and the relevant interest rate. To give an example: Suppose that we have borrowed $100,000 for 10 years at an annual interest rate of 10 percent. Then the annual amount that must be invested at an interest rate of 10 percent to be able to repay the original sum of $100,000 at the end of year 10 would be $6,274.54. As the annual interest payment is $10,000, the total annual payment is $16,274.54 which is, as shown in Table 5.2, the capital recovery factor at a rate of return of 10 percent of an investment of $100,000. It may further be noted, that if n assumes large values so that $1/a_{\overline{n}|i}$ assumes the value of i, the factor $1/s_{\overline{n}|i}$ will tend to zero. Again, this is easy to understand. If a loan has an infinite life, there is no need to establish a sinking fund.

Second, the relationship between a capital recovery factor and its terminal value is given by $1/a_{\overline{n}|i} \cdot s_{\overline{n}|i} = (1 + i)^n$. For example, if, in Table 5.2 each year's cash flow were compounded to the terminal year 10, the terminal value of the cash flow would be $259,374.25 ($16,274.54 × 15.9374), which is the same value if $100,000 were left to grow at a compound rate of return of 10 percent ($100,000 × 2.5937425). This result is, of course, not surprising because the cash flow is here assumed to be reinvested at the investment's rate of return. Problems arise, however, when this assumption cannot be made and the difference between the internal rate-of-return method and the present-value method – a subject that will be discussed in sections 5.2 and 5.4 – can basically be brought back to the assumption at which rate of return the cash flow must be valued.

In the absence of budget constraints[1] and uncertainty, two criteria[2] are generally used to evaluate whether a public investment project is justified: the internal rate of return criterion and the present value criterion.

The internal rate of return criterion consists of calculating the discount rate at which a project has a net present value of zero – the project's internal rate of return-, and accepting only those projects which have an internal rate of return larger than the pre-determined opportunity cost of capital rate q. In equation form the criterion may be presented as:

$$(5.4) \quad \text{Solve } r \text{ from } \sum_{t=1}^{n} \frac{B_t - O_t}{(1 + r)^t} - \sum_{t=1}^{n} \frac{K_t}{(1 + r)^t} = 0$$

and select only projects with $r \geqslant q$.

The net present value criterion, on the other hand, states that only those projects should be accepted for which the discounted benefits exceed discounted costs. Or, in formula form:

$$(5.5) \quad \sum_{t=1}^{n} \frac{B_t - O_t}{(1 + q)^t} - \sum_{t=1}^{n} \frac{K_t}{(1 + q)^t} \geqslant 0.$$

It may be noted that as regards formulas 5.4 and 5.5 equivalent forms of the criteria would be to add operating costs to investment costs rather than deducing it from gross benefits.

Two variants of formula 5.5 are possible. For instance, it may be written in ratio form as:

$$(5.5a) \quad \sum_{t=1}^{n} \frac{B_t - O_t}{(1 + q)^t} \bigg/ \sum_{t=1}^{n} \frac{K_t}{(1 + q)^t} \geqslant 1, \text{ or also as}$$

$$(5.5b) \quad \sum_{t=1}^{n} \frac{B_t}{(1 + q)^t} \bigg/ \sum_{t=1}^{n} \frac{K_t + O_t}{(1 + q)^t} \geqslant 1.$$

These last two formulas are not equivalent as will be discussed below.

In all these formulas, operating costs do not include financial charges and accounting items such as interest and depreciation. Financial charges and the problem of how to finance a project are not taken into account in the analysis because the analysis is concerned only with whether the project is economically justified. Since the criteria all boil down to whether the cash flow stream over the life of the project is sufficient to cover the capital investments and the opportunity cost of capital, there is no need to take account of depreciation charges separately.

At least two discount calculations are always necessary to determine the internal rate of return. The calculations are shown in the following example:

TABLE 5.3.

	Cost-Benefit Stream	Discounted at 12%	Discounted at 14%
– Year 1	– 100,000	– 89,286	– 87,719
– Year 2	– 47,000	– 37,468	– 36,165
– Year 3	– 6,000	– 4,271	– 4,050
– Year 4–32	+ 24,000	– 137,035	+113,120
Total		+ 6,010	– 14,814

Interpolation between the 12 percent discount rate (net present value +6,010) and the 14 percent discount rate (net present value – 14,814) gives a rate of approximately 12.6 percent at which the present worth of the cost-benefit stream equals zero. The internal rate of return of the project is therefore 12.6 percent.

Is the internal rate of return criterion a theoretically correct criterion? In our opinion, it is not. First, it may be pointed out that equation 5.4, from which the internal rate of return must be calculated, is a polynomial so that there may be several roots that solve the equation. Negative and imaginary numbers can be discarded and only positive roots count. However, while a normal cash-flow stream of signs –, +, has only one positive root, a cash flow stream of signs –, +, –, or +, –, + may have two positive roots and the problem then arises as to which root should be taken as the internal rate of return of that stream. We will return to this problem later on in this Chapter. Second, whereas in the absence of capital rationing, a situation which we assume throughout this section, the rate of return criterion will lead to the same projects being accepted as under the present value criterion[3], the ranking of projects will be different. Although this is not an important issue when mutually independent projects are considered because all projects satisfying the criteria can be implemented if sufficient capital is available, it may be extremely important where mutually exclusive projects are evaluated. For, in such a case, only a subset of the mutually exclusive projects can be undertaken so that then indeed only the projects with the highest values to the economy should be chosen. In this respect, it is important to be aware of the fact that ranking by rates of return may lead to wrong results.

Figure 5.1 illustrates the ranking issue. On its vertical axis are measured the present values of the cost-benefit stream of a project; on its horizontal axis the discount rates used to calculate these present values. Suppose that we are evaluating two mutually exclusive projects and that their present values at different discount rates are represented by curves A and B, respectively.[4] Then, as Figure 5.1 indicates, the net present value of Project A is zero at a discount

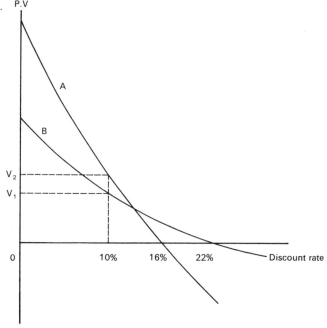

FIGURE 5.1.

rate of 16 percent, while that of Project B is zero at a discount rate of 22 percent. According to the internal rate of return criterion, Project B, whose internal rate of return is 22 percent, should thus be preferred over Project A, whose internal rate of return is only 16 percent. However, this cannot be correct. The value of a project is given by the sum of money that would be necessary to generate the project's net benefit stream at rate q, or, in other words, by the present value at rate q of the project's cost-benefit stream. In Figure 5.1, it may be seen that if the opportunity cost of capital q is, say, 10 percent, the present value of Project A equals OV_2 while that of Project B equals OV_1. Hence, Project A should be preferred over Project B, rather than Project B over Project A as the internal rate of return criterion would indicate. The internal rate of return criterion can thus lead to erroneous answers.

A variant of the rate of return method, which might be described as the alternate cost-savings method, has become quite popular in recent years for the comparison of hydro-electric and thermal power developments.[5] According to this method, the flows of investment and operating costs of the two alternative developments should be compared and the differential cost stream will then normally show that the extra investments in the hydro scheme in the earlier years will be compensated in the later years by the cost savings of the hydro alternative compared to the thermal alternative. If the internal rate of return of the extra hydro investments exceeds the opportunity cost of capital, then the extra investments are considered to be justified. Is this procedure correct? The only conclusion we can draw from the alternate cost savings analysis is that the

98

incremental investment in the hydro project results in cost savings compared to the steam program, but it does not tell us whether steam development is justified. This means that the normal present value criterion must be used to evaluate whether thermal development is justified, and there is then no reason why this procedure should not also be used to evaluate the hydro alternative.

TABLE 5.4.

	Project	
	A	B
Present Value Investments (K)	90	50
Present Value Operating Costs (O)	10	20
Present Value Benefits (B)	190	140
$(B–O)/K$ ratio (5.5a)	$180/90 = 2.0$	$120/50 = 2.4$
$B/(K+O)$ ratio (5.5b)	$190/100 = 1.9$	$140/70 = 2.0$
Present value criterion (5.5):		
$B - (K + O)$	90	70

Let us turn our attention now to the so-called benefit-cost ratios, the variants of the net present value method defined by formulas 5.5a and 5.5b. It is easy to show that ranking by ratios leads to a result different from that under the net present value method. Table 5.4 presents the ranking of two projects under the three criteria. Under the present value method, Project A should be preferred because it has the highest net present value. The ratios, however, give priority to Project B. This is clearly wrong. A's additional investment and operating costs are 30, but this gives an additional benefit of 50, resulting in an overall addition to net benefits of 20. A has thus a higher value than B.

In the absence of capital constraints, ratios are not correct ranking criteria.[6] Apart from the fact that they are wrong, it may also be pointed out that the value of 5.5a is always higher than the value of 5.5b, since transferring operating costs from the numerator to the denominator must reduce the value of the ratio. The $B/(K + O)$ ratio has found in the United States quite a range of application, especially for water resources projects. The Flood Control Act of 1936 requires that 'the benefits to whomsoever they may accrue (be) in excess of the estimated costs.' This formulation is sound in the absence of budget constraints, and means simply that projects with ratios less than 1 should be rejected. In practice, however, the ratio has also been used to rank projects and problems of consistency can then easily arise. MCKEAN[7] mentions, for example, that in the Green River Watershed project in the USA, the increased cost of cattle production was deducted from gross receipts instead of being included among the costs of the program, with the result that the ratio was higher than it should have been in that case. A further problem with the $B/(K + O)$ ratio is that it is extremely sensitive to the level of operating costs. Suppose that for a certain project B is 980, O is 800 and K is 90. Then this project, of which the relative values of the variables are well in line with those of a supermarkt or department store, would have a $B/(K + O)$ ratio of 1.1 and a net present value of 90. Project A in Table 5.4, however, has a $B/(K + O)$ ratio of 1.9 even though it is equally valuable since its present value is also 90. Thus $B/(K + O)$ ratios have a bias against projects with large operating costs.

The conclusion that, in the absence of budget constraints, only the net present value method provides the correct ranking of projects – whether mutually exclusive or not – has often encountered criticism of the sort met in the example in Table 5.5., which assumes – as we have assumed all along –

TABLE 5.5.

	Project	
	A	B
Present Value Costs: $(K + O)$	100	1,000,000
Present Value Benefits: (B)	175	1,000,100
$B/(K + O)$ ratio	1.75	1
Net Present Value: $B - (K + O)$	75	100

that costs and benefits have been determined with complete certainty. Project B has the highest net present value, but its investment costs are so large that its $B/(K + O)$ ratio is only marginally above 1. Surely, according to the criticism. Project A with its much lower investment cost and much higher $B/(K + O)$ ratio should be preferred. The apparent contradiction disappears if we focus on the fact that the discussed present value criterion applies only to situations where the Government has no budget constraint and where conditions of complete certainty exist. Project B must then have a higher ordering number than Project A because, even though its investments are larger than those of Project A, it provides a higher net present value than Project A.

The example is useful, however, because it shows that the discussed present value method, although theoretically correct, is applicable only in situations which are not realistic. Usually, we find that Governments do not have sufficient funds to undertake all projects they would like to undertake and the discussed rule then needs amendment. How this should be done in the case of a single period budget constraint as well as in the case of a multiple period budget constraint will be discussed in the next sections. The last section of this Chapter will review how uncertainties – inherent in the estimation of any project variable – should be incorporated in the analysis.

5.3. SINGLE PERIOD BUDGET CONSTRAINTS

A constraint may be said to exist with respect to a factor of production or commodity if, within a certain time period, the supply of that factor or commodity cannot be expanded to satisfy demand. In other words, part of existing demand will go unsatisfied if any additional new demand is to be served. The value of such a constrained factor or commodity is higher than its production costs by the amount of the scarcity premium it commands. Examples of how such premiums had to be calculated in the case of constraints on inputs, foreign exchange and production capacity were encountered in the previous chapters. However, many other constraints may exist; for instance, with respect to project implementation capacity, the Government budget, the number of engineers, managers or extension personnel and the like. The calculation of the relevant shadow prices is not difficult: the value of the constrained factor or commodity is the value that would be generated (or lost) if the available quantity of the factor or commodity were. increased (or reduced) by one unit. However, as regards the production factor capital some special issues arise related to the problem as to whether in cases of constraints projects should be considered discrete units or variable as regards project size, and we will, therefore, discuss these matters now in some detail.

Throughout out discussion we assume that every project variable, except capital, has been valued at its appropriate shadow price[8] and we will start our review by considering the case of the single period budget constraint. How should investments be curtailed in such a case so that their sum equals the available funds? Traditionally,[9] this is done by maximizing the Lagrangean expression of the constrained objective function. Hence, if we follow the traditional method, the present value of the net benefits of all projects should be maximized subject to the constraint that the total investment costs of all projects cannot exceed a certain given amount.

If the present value of the net benefits of the jth project is denoted by N_j and its investment costs by K_j, the problem is to maximize for a set of projects the objective function:

$$\sum_{j=1}^{n} N_j - \sum_{j=1}^{n} K_j$$

$$\text{subject to:} \sum_{j=1}^{n} K_j - \bar{K} = 0$$

where $\bar{K}$ represents the available investment funds. Hence, the Lagrangean expression that should be maximized is:

$$L = \Sigma N_j - \Sigma K_j - \lambda(\Sigma K_j - \bar{K})$$

The first order conditions are

$$\Sigma dN_j - \Sigma dK_j - \lambda \Sigma dK_j = 0 \text{ and } \bar{K} = \Sigma K_j.$$

The former may be written as $\Sigma dN_j = \Sigma dK_j (1 + \lambda)$. As we have, moreover, the normal condition that in an optimal situation dN_j/dK_j should be equal for all projects, we arrive at the rule that to maximize the net benefits of all projects, the marginal benefit of each project should be equal to that of the other projects and equal to marginal cost plus a premium λ. In other words, the marginal

FIGURE 5.2.

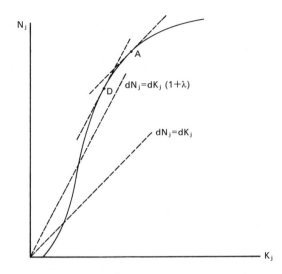

dollar invested must be valued in the case of a budget constraint at the shadow price of $1 + \lambda$. This is illustrated in Figure 5.2, where the total net benefits of a project are shown as a function of total investment costs. As discussed in Chapter 4, in the absence of budget constraints, the optimal size would be at point A where the tangent line has a slope of 1. With the budget constraint, the optimal scale would be at D, where the tangent line has the slope $1 + \lambda$.

The purpose of λ is to curtail the investment in each individual project in such a way that the sum of the investments in all projects just exhausts the available funds. Obviously, therefore, the value of λ can be found only by considering simultaneously all the investment projects. One possible way to determine λ would be by trial and error. The central planning authority could provide the different departments responsible for designing the various projects with different values of λ and then determine at what value of λ the total budget would be exhausted. Another way would consist of a bottom-up procedure. By varying, for each project, the value of λ, each department could obtain a function relating the optimal investments for the projects under its authority to various values of $1 + \lambda$. Graphically, this could be done by varying the slope of the line $dN_j = dK_j (1 + \lambda)$ of Figure 5.2. Aggregation of the investment relative to $(1 + \lambda)$ functions of the different departments would then provide the central planning authority with the function relating total optimal investments (ΣK_jopt) to $1 + \lambda$. This function is shown in Figure 5.3 as the curve ΣK_jopt.

Without budget constraints, the value of $\lambda = 0$ and the optimal total investments would be, say, K_o. With a budget constraint the total available investment funds are $\bar{K}$ and the value of $1 + \lambda$ would be read directly from the figure, where it was assumed for illustrative purposes that λ has a value of 0.3. By feeding back this value to the different departments, the Central Planning Authority would ensure that each departments project or projects would be

102

FIGURE 5.3.

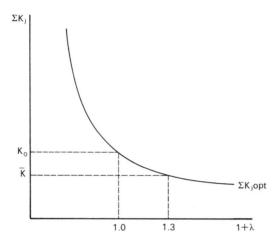

designed optimally. At the margin of each project's investment scale, each dollar invested would generate the same present value of benefits $(1 + \lambda)$. There would be no advantage in reducing any one of the projects in order to expand another project, and all available funds would be used.

The above described procedure will lead to the result that different projects will have different rates of return. This can be illustrated as follows. As discussed in Section 5.1, the present value of a constant stream of yearly net benefits N_A during n years may be represented by $N = N_A \cdot a_{\overline{n}|q}$ where N is the present value, and q the discount rate. Differentiating with respect to investment, we may write $dN = dN_A \, a_{\overline{n}|q}$. But dN_A also represents the periodic constant benefit flow of the marginal investment dK. Hence, we can also write $dN_A = dK \cdot 1/a_{\overline{n}|r}$, where r is the internal rate of return of dK. It follows that, in the case of budget constraints and constancy of benefits, $dN/dK = a_{\overline{n}|q}/a_{\overline{n}|r} = 1 + \lambda$. This expression may be written as $1/a_{\overline{n}|r} = (1 + \lambda) \cdot 1/a_{\overline{n}|q}$ or, in words, the cash flow of the marginal dollar invested $(1/a_{n|r})$ should equal the required cash flow in the absence of budget constraints $(1/a_{n|q})$ weighted with $(1 + \lambda)$.

Alternative, we may write $\{1/(1 + \lambda)\} \cdot 1/a_{\overline{n}|r} \cdot a_{\overline{n}|q} = 1$ or, in words, the cash flow stream of the marginal invested dollar should be such that its present value at discount rate q should be 1 when it is weighted with $1/(1 + \lambda)$.

If all the projects under consideration have infinite lifetimes, then $dN/dK = (1/q)/(1/r) = r/q = 1 + \lambda$, and the optimal size of each project may be determined either by using r or λ. For instance, if $\lambda = 0.3$ and $q = 10\%$, then $r = 13\%$ and the size of each project should be expanded until the rate of return on the marginal dollar invested is 13 percent. At that size level, the present value of the benefit stream of the marginal dollar invested would equal 1.3. In the case of projects with constant benefits but different lifetimes, the situation is different because the weighting with $(1 + \lambda)$ of the required cash flow for the marginal investment dollar only increases the rate of return part of the cash flow and not the depreciation part. Hence, for short life projects, the rate of

103

return would be substantially higher than the 13 percent calculated for long life projects in the example above. For instance, the rate of return on the marginal dollar invested for a project with a 10-year life would need to be about 17 percent, if the present value of the marginal benefit stream were to remain 1.3. Similar problems arise when different projects have the same lifetimes but varying benefit streams over time.

Whereas in the absence of budget constraints, the optimization rule is that a project should be expanded until the rate of return on the marginal dollar invested equals the opportunity cost of capital, this rule is apparently no longer valid in the case of budget constraints if the λ rule is followed. Although operationally difficult, the λ procedure is correct under its assumptions. But are these assumptions correct? The implicit assumption of the λ procedure is that no extra costs will be incurred if we undertake at a later date the investments eliminated at present under the λ rule. As budget constraints vary in intensity, it may well be possible that at a later date sufficient funds will be available to undertake these investments. However, as is well known, in general it will be a costly procedure to expand a project at a later date. For instance, it is very difficult to widen a bridge or a road, or to heighten an irrigation dam once construction has been completed or sometimes when construction based on a reduced design has started. As it is much more efficient to defer a marginal project than to defer last increments to projects, we would suggest for this reason that project size should be determined by the normal rule that the marginal costs of the project should equal its marginal benefits.

Once it is accepted that project size should not be tampered with, the budget constraint rule becomes a simple one. Obviously, the objective is to maximize the benefits per dollar of available investment funds. Hence, as HIRSHLEIFER, DE HAVEN and MILLIMAN[10] proposed, the procedure should be 'to compare projects on the basis of their present value as of time 1 (the value of the time stream for periods 1 through n, calculated back to time 1) per dollar of current funds.' In terms of the variables used here, the procedure is to rank projects by their N/K ratios, giving priority to the project with the highest ratio and so proceeding down the line until the budget is exhausted.

TABLE 5.6.

	Project		
	A	B	C
Present value investments (K)	90	50	140
Present value net benefits (N)	180	120	252
Present value project	90	70	112
N/K ratio	180/90 = 2.0	120/50 = 2.4	252/140 = 1.8

An example of the method is given in Table 5.6, which shows the present values and N/K ratios of projects A, B and C. Assume that there are only 140

104

units of capital available. Then according to the present value method, project C should be implemented because it has the highest present value. As Table 5.6 shows, however, it would be better to undertake projects B and A as their combined present value totals 160. Only by ranking the projects by their N/K ratio can we ensure that B and A will indeed be preferred.

Obviously, it is very important that these ratios be calculated correctly and that the K in the formula represents the real economic cost of undertaking the project during the budget constraint period. This will not be investment costs as defined by accountants or engineers, but rather will comprise all outlays that are borne by the Government budget. An example is provided in Table 5.7. The capital costs of the project during the first four years, which we assume is the budget constraint period, are 70 and the operating costs 5. However, if the Government budget has to provide only the net outlays for the project, then, as Table 5.7 shows, the investments should be taken as 68.

TABLE 5.7.

Year	0	1	2	3	4	5	6	7	8	9	10
Capital Costs	50	10	5	5							
Operating Costs	–	–	2	3	4	4	4	4	4	4	4
Benefits	–	–	3	4	34	34	34	34	34	34	34
Investment (K)	– 50	– 10	– 4	– 4							
Net Benefits (N)					30	30	30	30	30	30	30

Present Value Investments ($q = 10\%$): 65.39
Present Value Net Benefits ($q = 10\%$): 109.73
Ratio N/K: 109.73/65.39 $= 1.68$

If the ratio is calculated as shown in Table 5.7, the value of K will represent the amount of scarce capital needed for the project and the value of N the amount that will be generated. This ratio is thus a measure of the importance of the project to the national economy. The disadvantage of this formula is that it is a ratio while normal practice is to express the profitability of an investment in terms of a rate of return. We will, therefore, discuss in the next section whether it is possible to express the N/K ratio as a rate of return.

5.4. THE MODIFIED INTERNAL RATE OF RETURN

The relationship between the N/K ratio and the internal rate of return can best be shown if we assume that the benefit and operating cost streams are constant. In such a case $N = N_A \cdot a_{\overline{n}|q}$. Since $K = N_A \cdot a_{\overline{n}|r}$, it follows that $N/K = (1/a_{\overline{n}|r})/(1/a_{\overline{n}|q})$. Thus, in cases of constancy of net benefit streams, projects with the same lifetimes may be ranked either by their N/K ratios or by their internal rates of return. If, however, projects with different lifetimes are compared,

TABLE 5.8. Formula: $N/K = (1/a_{\overline{n}|r})/(1/a_{\overline{n}|q})$, where $q = 10$ percent.

Project	Lifetime	Internal Rate of Return	Corresponding N/K Ratio
A	10 yrs.	15%	1.22
B	25 yrs.	15%	1.40
C	50 yrs.	15%	1.50
D	∞ yrs.	15%	1.50

rankings under the two methods will differ from each other. An example is presented in Table 5.8 which shows the N/K ratios of four projects, each with a different lifetime, under the assumption that their internal rates of return are all 15 percent. While the N/K method would give preference to the projects with the longest lives, the internal rate of return method would consider all projects to be of equal priority.[11] Furthermore, it needs no elaboration that the ranking of projects under the two criteria may also differ in cases where the net benefits vary over time, even though all projects may have the same lifetime.

The example in Table 5.8 demonstrates that the internal rate of return criterion will lead to a different ranking from that obtained when the N/K approach is used, while the latter, as discussed in the previous section, provides the theoretically correct criterion. Nevertheless, it is possible to arrive at a correct ranking if a modified internal rate of return criterion is adopted. According to Solomon,[12] the internal rate of return criterion can be reconciled with the N/K criterion if the reinvestment of the cash flow is taken into account. He maintains that the present value criterion assumes benefits to be reinvested at the opportunity cost of capital rate, while the internal rate of return criterion assumes that reinvestment of the returns will take place at the internal rate of return. We believe this explanation to be incorrect. The internal rate of return criterion makes no assumption as regards what happens to benefits; they can be consumed or they can be reinvested. The decision between consumption and reinvestment is, of course, based on the same rate of return and in the absence of multiple period budget constraints, this rate is the opportunity cost of capital, q. Solomon is, however, on the right track and the internal rate of return criterion can indeed be reconciled with the N/K criterion if we value the cash flow at its appropriate rate. If we assume that the appropriate rate is the opportunity cost of capital, q, then the modified internal rate of return is found with the help of the formula $N(1 + q)^n = K(1 + r^*)^n$, where r^* represents the modified internal rate of return. Hence, $N/K = (1 + r^*)^n/(1 + q)^n$, so that ranking by modified internal rates of return leads to the same result as ranking by N/K ratios.

The principle is illustrated with an example in Table 5.9, which shows the investments and benefit streams of projects A and B. According to the present value criterion, project B should be chosen because its present value (13.13) is higher than that of A (9.89), whereas according to the internal rate of return

TABLE 5.9.

	Project A	Project B
Opportunity cost of capital	10%	
Investments	− 100	− 100
Net Benefits yr. 1	+ 80	−
Net Benefits yr. 2	+ 45	+136.89
Present Value Net Benefits at 10%	+109.89	+113.13
Internal Rate of Return	18%	17%
Terminal Value of Net Benefits when compounded at 10%	132.97	136.89
Modified Rate of Return	15.3%	17%
N/K Ratio	1.10	1.37

criterion A (IRR = 18%) should be chosen rather than B (IRR = 17%). If the present values of the net benefits are compounded at the opportunity cost of capital rate of 10 percent, then the terminal value of the benefits of project A will be $132.97 and of project B, $136.89. With investments of $100 this corresponds to a modified rate of return of 15.3 percent and 17 percent, respectively, which gives the same ranking as under the N/K ratios. The two approaches are therefore consistent if a common assumption is adopted with respect to the rate of return at which the benefits should be valued and both criteria – N/K ratio and modified rate of return – will then rank the projects identically.

The problem of multiple solutions to an internal rate of return function can now be addressed. This situation arises when the net cash flow changes its direction several times, as shown, for instance, in Table 5.10, which reproduces an example from GRANT and IRESON.[13] The internal rates of return in this case are approximately 25 percent and 40 percent. To solve this ambiguity the opportunity cost of capital should be used to value the cash flow. In the example, if the opportunity cost of capital is 8 percent. the modified rate of return is about 10 percent, [14] which was found by solving the equation $544.5 (1 + r^*)^{20} = 782.1 \times 1.08^{20}$. Such cases are, however, rare outside of the mineral and petroleum industries, and GRANT and IRESON[15] emphasize that even then 'cases of this type arise only in quite specialized circumstances.'

TABLE 5.10.

Year	Net Cash Flow ($'000)	Present Worth				
		at 8%	at 20%	at 25%	at 30%	at 40%
1–5	+ 50 per year	+199.6	+149.6	+134.4	+121.8	+101.8
5	− 800	− 544.5	− 321.5	− 262.5	− 215.4	− 148.7
6–20	+100 per year	+582.5	+187.9	+126.5	+ 88.0	+ 46.2
		+237.6	+ 16.0	− 1.3	− 5.6	− 0.7

The standard internal rate of return criterion, which was rejected earlier in Section 5.2 in the case of an absence of capital rationing, must also, as we have seen in Section 5.3 and this section, be rejected if budget constraints exist. Therefore, one may ask 'Under what conditions can the standard internal rate of return criterion be applied?' As LORIE and SAVAGE[16] have pointed out, there are four such situations: (a) when only one project should be compared with the opportunity cost of capital; (b) in the case of several projects when the opportunity cost of capital is zero; (c) when the opportunity cost of capital is not zero and several projects are to be compared but the time paths of the projects do not cross; and (d) when the opportunity cost of capital is not zero, several projects are being ranked and the net benefits from each of the projects can be valued at their internal rates of return.

Matters relating to case (a) will be discussed below. Case (b) is of no practical relevance since the opportunity cost of capital is always positive. Cases (c) and (d) are theoretically identical since the condition of (d) makes the time paths of the net benefits of the projects equal except for a proportionality factor. Case (d), however, is of less practical value than case (c) because, in general, benefits cannot be valued at the internal rate of return.

What about case (a)? We have discussed in Section 5.1 that in the absence of budget constraints a project should be accepted if it has either a present value at least equal to zero ($B - C \geqslant 0$) or an internal rate of return higher than the opportunity cost of capital. As in practical work we often find that the estimate of the opportunity cost of capital and, hence of $B - C$ is a rather arbitrary undertaking, we feel that the internal rate of return has great operational value in the absence of budgetary constraints. However, we have also stated that in general we would expect that the usual situation is one of capital rationing. Has the internal rate of return criterion any validity in such a case? Theoretically not. As we have discussed, the N/K approach or the modified internal rate of return approach should be followed. However, the problem is again that the opportunity cost of capital is difficult to estimate. One may attempt to calculate for each project a minimum and maximum value of the N/K ratio or of the modified rate of return by using a minimum and maximum value of the opportunity cost of capital, but where one can only estimate that the opportunity cost of capital lies between some very extreme values, this procedure is not very meaningful. In such a case the internal rate of return method may be used to establish a tentative ranking order of projects. As projects with high internal rates of return will be accepted in any case, one can then spend extra time on projects with low rates of return – those at the margin of acceptability – in order to sharpen the accept-reject decision. This may be done, for instance, by calculating probability distributions of the N/K ratios. We feel, therefore, that the internal rate of return is an important tool in practical work despite its theoretical limitations.

5.5. Multiple Period Budget Constraints

It may be recalled that the optimization rule in the case of the single period budget constraint requires that the cash flow of the marginal dollar invested must be weighted with $1/(1 + \lambda)$ before discounting, where λ is the Lagrangean shadow premium on investment undertaken during the constraint period. As the discount factor at the margin is also relevant for intra-marginal units, the result of the budget constraint is that not only the cash flow of the marginal investment dollar but any cash flow starting in the period of constraint should be weighted with $1/(1 + \lambda)$. To distinguish the constraint in period 1 from constraints in other periods, we denote this weighting factor by $1/(1 + \lambda_1)$.

Suppose now that there is a two-period budget constraint. Then any cash flow starting in period two should be weighted with $1/(1 + \lambda_2)$. It follows that, of a cash flow resulting from a marginal dollar invested in the first period, the elements that become available in years 2 through n should be valued at $1/(1 + \lambda_2)$. Let us assume that the periods of the constraints are years. Then the following tabulation (Table 5.11) may be made of how the present value of a two-year cash flow from a dollar invested in period 1 should be calculated if there were one or two period budget constraints.

TABLE 5.11.

Budget Constraint	Present Value Benefits	
	Yr. 1	Yr. 2
None	$\dfrac{N_1}{(1 + q)}$	$\dfrac{N_2}{(1 + q)^2}$
Single Period	$\dfrac{N_1}{(1 + \lambda_1)(1 + q)}$	$\dfrac{N_2}{(1 + \lambda_1)(1 + q)^2}$
Two Period	$\dfrac{N_1}{(1 + \lambda_1)(1 + q)}$	$\dfrac{N_2}{(1 + \lambda_1)(1 + \lambda_2)(1 + q)^2}$

From Table 5.11 it is clear that if the impact of the budget constraints is about equal in the different periods, i.e., $\lambda_1 = \lambda_2 = \ldots = \lambda_n$, the present value of a benefit in any year t, if there were a multiple period constraint, would be-

$$N_t / [(1 + \lambda)^t (1 + q)^t]$$

which can be replaced by

$$N_t / [(1 + b)^t]$$

where $b = (1 + \lambda)(1 + q)$. In case of continuous compounding, of course, $b = \lambda + q$.

The result derived here is intuitively simple: the discount rate to be used for

109

discounting a project's benefit and cost stream in the case of a multiple period budget constraint should be the budget constraint discount rate. This rate is higher than the opportunity cost of capital and acts as a clearing mechanism equilibrating total investments with available funds.

The optimal size of a project can now easily be determined. The project should be expanded until the rate of return on the marginal dollar invested equals b. Ranking of projects also presents no problem. If, for one reason or another, notwithstanding the use of b as a clearing rate, there would be a need to defer some projects – e.g., when there would be a temporary shortage of capital – projects should be ranked by their N/K ratios, found by discounting at rate b. and those with the lowest ratios should be the first to be deferred. Alternatively, the ranking could take place by calculating the projects' modified rates of return, whereby the rate b should be used for the evaluation of the cash flow streams. Projects that have the lowest modified rate of return should then be deferred.

MARGLIN has criticized the use of the N/K criterion because, 'It concentrates on the absolute advantage among projects within each period instead of looking at the comparative advantage among projects between periods.'[17] Suppose that in each of two budget periods only one project can be implemented out of a group of two, each project having the same investment costs. Suppose, MARGLIN continues, that construction timing is optimal for the present period, and that if the projects were undertaken in the second period, net present values will decrease, as illustrated in Table 5.12. Application of the N/K criterion would then lead us to undertake project A first. However, a glance at the table shows that the construction sequence B, A has a higher net present value than the sequence A, B so that the N/K criterion would apparently lead to the wrong result. While project A has the absolute advantage (highest present value) for 1975 construction, it has the comparative advantage (it loses the least due to postponement) for 1980 construction and should therefore be undertaken in 1980 if we are to maximize net present values simultaneously rather than serially. The problem of investment planning in a dynamic context becomes rather complicated if more than two projects are involved. However, MARGLIN has shown that it can be solved with the help of planning algorithms, following the solution method of the linear programming problem known as the Assignment Problem. The assignment of projects to the different budget periods is then essentially the same as the assignment of factories to locations or personnel to jobs.

TABLE 5.12.

	Net Present Value Today as a Function of the Construction Date	
	1975	1980
Project A	150	140
Project B	135	115

Should we follow MARGLIN's approach? The comparative advantage criterion would be entirely correct if indeed we could know which projects would come up for evaluation in the next plan period. There may indeed be such cases, for instance, when large river basins are being studied. Often, however, we find that Central Planning Authorities do not possess this knowledge. It is easy to see that, under such circumstances, the comparative advantage criterion may lead to worse results than the N/K criterion. For instance, postponement of a project from the present plan period to the next plan period could lead to its replacement in the present period by a lower ranking project, while in the next plan period it would compete with projects not yet identified so that perhaps it might not be accepted then at all. As a result, total net present value could be lower under the comparative advantage rule than under the N/K criterion. It is often not possible to consider projects of different plan periods simultaneously, and MARGLIN's approach is then not feasible. It seems to us that the best one can do in such cases is to concentrate on the projects that are known. If there is a need to postpone a project because of budget constraints, then ranking by N/K ratios would ensure the maximization of the net present values of the projects under scrutiny.

5.6. UNCERTAINTY

So far it has been implicitly assumed that inputs, outputs, costs and prices of the projects under scrutiny are precisely known. In many cases, however, these variables can only be estimated within a wide range of values. For instance, investment costs are notoriously difficult to estimate; projections of quantities produced are often subject to a wide margin of error, and prices also, in most cases, can only be forecast in the form of a range of prices.

In such circumstances, consultants and engineers often use the most likely values of the variables to calculate whether a project is acceptable. This procedure is not correct, as a simple example will show. Suppose that an agricultural engineer has estimated the probability of a project producing 10,000 tons and 15,000 tons of padi per year at 60 percent and 40 percent, respectively. Suppose, further, that the rice marketing expert has estimated the price of padi at $100, with a probability of 60 percent, and at $150, with a probability of 40 percent, the price not being affected by the project. Then the value of the gross benefits would be $1,000,000 if the calculation were based on the most likely values of quantity and price. In fact, as the table below shows, this estimate would be too conservative. The probability of the project producing a gross benefit of $1,000,000 is only 36 percent, while the probability of a gross benefit of $1,500,000 or higher is 64 percent.

In the above example, the analysis was kept simple. Only two variables and only two values for each variable were considered. In reality there will be many more variables that affect a project's rate of return and several values which each of these variables could assume. Clearly, therefore, the acceptance

TABLE 5.13.

Quantity		Price		Gross Benefits	
Tons	Prob.	$	Prob.	$	Prob.
10,000	0.6	100	0.6	1,000,000	0.36
10,000	0.6	150	0.4	1,500,000	0.24
15,000	0.4	100	0.6	1,500,000	0.24
15,000	0.4	150	0.4	2,250,000	0.16

decision of a project should include probability analysis.[18]

How should we determine which variables and values should be considered? To begin, a sensitivity analysis should be undertaken. Start the rate of return or net present value calculation on the basis of the most likely values of the variables, and then change the value of each variable one at a time by, say, 20 percent to determine whether the project's rate of return or net present value is sensitive to such variations. The next step is to choose the probability distribution of the values of each of the significant variables. In most cases these probabilities will be subjective estimates based on the consulted expert's experience and expertise. The simplest way to proceed is to have the expert indicate the probability of different interval-values of the variable rather than the probability of each single point estimate of the variable, or, in other words, to have him draw up a step rectangular distribution rather than the much more difficult smooth curve distribution of probabilities.[19] The final step then is to calculate the probability distribution of the rate of return or net present value of the project. This seems at first sight a formidable task. For instance, assuming that there are seven significant variables and that each of these has been assigned four values, the number of computations would be $4^7 = 16,384$. The procedure can, however, be simplified by using a simulation technique, known as the Monte-Carlo Method. The computer is instructed to assign random values to each of the variables which should be varied and to repeat the computations until the probability distribution of the rate of return or net present value emerges. The number of computations is a simple problem of statistics, known as the Sample Problem, and in most cases a few fundred calculations suffice to arrive at an accurate description of the probability distribution.

In the absence of a computer the calculations can be done by hand, using, for example, a table of random numbers to assign random values to the variables. Rather than a few computer minutes, the calculations may then take a few man-weeks. For many projects this is well justified, especially when the projects appear at first sight marginal, or when unusual uncertainties are present. A probability analysis may also be extremely important for optimizing the project's design. POULIQUEN,[20] for instance, mentions that a probability analysis showed that the productivity of the cargo gangs at the Port of Mogadiscio was a key factor affecting the rate of return of the planned expansion of port facilities. If the productivity could be raised to 9 or 10 tons per gang-hour, the major risk in the project would be eliminated. It was therefore recommended that a consultant be engaged to help organize cargo handling operations.

A problem for which one has to watch carefully in any probability analysis is that of correlation between the variables which are varied. For instance, in our example above, it may well be that the uncertainty in the quantity of padi production is not independent of the uncertainty in the price of padi because the price may depend on the quantity produced. The way to proceed then is to estimate the probability of the price being $150 when production is 10,000 tons, the probability of the price being $100 when production is 15,000 tons, and so on. Or, in other words, the estimates of the price probabilities should then be contingent upon the estimated quantities. In our example, the correlation between the two variables is negative, i.e., an increase in quantity leads to a lower price. Often, however, the correlation is positive. For instance, a smoother road surface (increase in costs) may lead to reduced vehicle operating costs (increase in benefits), or an increase in the productivity of the cargo gang would increase the capacity of the port. The correlation may also be caused by a third variable such as the state of the economy. In the case of a combined hydroelectric-irrigation project, an increase in the level of economic activity may well raise the demand for electricity as well as for agricultural products. In all such cases of correlation, benefits could be substantially over- or under-estimated if the correlations between the variables were neglected.

Suppose now that probability analysis has been applied to all the projects under scrutiny. How should we determine their priority? Figure 5.4 presents the cumulative probability distributions of two projects. The probability that project A will have a rate of return of 10 percent is 90 percent, whereas project B's probability of a rate of return of 10 percent is only 60 percent. On the other hand, B's chance of achieving a rate of return higher than 10 percent is much greater than A's chance, but, at the same time, B has a much greater chance

FIGURE 5.4.

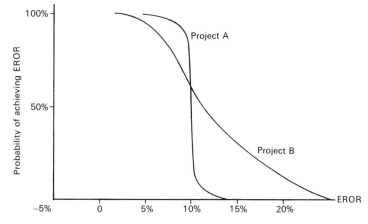

than A to end up with rates of return lower than 10 percent. In other words, the variance of the rate of return is much larger in the case of B than of A.

Preference among these projects should be determined in the following manner. Denote the probability that the utility of a project will be u_1, u_2, etc., by p_1, p_2, etc., then the expected utility value of the project will be $\Sigma p_k u_k$ where k is the kth possible outcome. This raises immediately the question of which utility should be attached to the various possible returns. In our discussion in Chapter 9 we will show that this utility depends on the project beneficiaries – whether they are the poor, the middle income group, or the rich. A dollar accruing to a poor man is generally considered to have a higher marginal utility than a dollar accruing to an average income earner or a rich man. Consequently, a project of which the beneficiaries are the poor will have a higher social rate of return than one generating benefits for the middle or high income population groups.

Let us assume for the present, however, as has been done so far, that income distribution considerations are not important, as is true for a wide range of projects. Then the marginal utility of a dollar will be the same irrespective of the individual to whom it accrues and the expected utility value of a project will be its expected economic value, i.e., the difference between the present values of the expected economic benefits and the expected economic costs. The expected (modified) economic rate of return of a project is found similarly by weighting each possible economic rate of return by its probability. Following this procedure, project A would have an expected economic rate of return of 10 percent, project B of 12 percent, and project B would thus be assigned a higher priority than project A.

An objection may be raised to this procedure on the grounds that it does not take into account the fact that project B is much 'riskier' than project A. Two approaches are commonly used to deal with risk. The first – often applied in private business – is to adjust conservatively the estimates of such variables as the discount rate, costs, benefits and project life. Theoretically, this approach leaves much to be desired. In general, risks do not increase with time, as the use of a higher than normal discount rate would imply, because steps can be taken to remedy the situation. Furthermore, over-estimation of costs or under-estimation of benefits and project life is a rather arbitrary method which can only negate the systematic evaluation of the project's net present value or rate of return. The second approach would be to use the decision maker's subjective probabilities which express his attitude toward risk rather than the subjective probabilities estimated by the project experts which do not take account of risk. A decision-maker not willing to accept risk might then well prefer project A to project B. In general, we believe that it is not necessary to follow this approach, because normally it may be assumed that there will be a large number of independent Government projects so that their risks will be pooled in accordance with the law of large numbers. There are, however, cases where the risk element should definitely be taken into account, for instance, where the variation in the net benefits of a project amounts to a substantial percentage of

TABLE 5.14.

	Flood	No Flood
Project A	200	70
Project B	140	80

a country's national income, or where the risk of a project will be borne mainly by certain income groups (e.g. the poor), or where detrimental effects may be imposed on the rest of the economy (e.g. in cases of underestimation of power needs). It would be folly then not to take account of the risk element. However, such cases do not occur often and it is then no longer a problem for the project appraiser but for the highest decision-making authority of government.

Finally, we may mention briefly that there is a substantial volume of theoretical literature about the decision rules to be followed in the case of complete uncertainty.[21] One of the more well-known of these rules is the so-called Maximin Return principle under which that alternative should be chosen which guarantees the highest minimum return. For instance, suppose that there are two states of nature about which we are completely uncertain – flood and no flood – and that two types of flood control projects are possible with net present values as presented in Table 5.14. Then the Maximin Return principle would recommend project B because the highest minimum return would be 80. The extremely conservative nature of this rule needs no elaboration. To obtain an additional minimum return of 10 in the case of no-flood, we are willing to forego a possible additional return of 60 in the case of flood. Objections of this nature can be raised to any of the various decision rules. In fact, a logically consistent system of decision rules can only be based upon judgments of the various possible states of nature, i.e., the subjective probability approach.

KNIGHT's distinction between risk and uncertainty is famous.[22] In KNIGHT's view, risk is an uncertainty which can by any method be reduced to an objective, quantitatively determinate probability. Risk is, therefore, not an uncertainty but a complete certainty. True uncertainty, on the other hand, is, in his opinion, not susceptible to any measurement at all. If we follow his approach, then it is logical that we should arrive at a theory of objective probabilities under conditions of risk and a theory of decision rules under conditions of uncertainty. But it is difficult to imagine, as KNIGHT and the decision theory do, that no opinion can be formed about the possibility of a certain state of nature. If we accept that there are no sharp boundaries between risk and uncertainty, and that decisions in real life must be based on judgments, then we must settle on a theory of subjective probability as followed here.

[1] It should be noted that we assume that the values of the project variables reflect other possible constraints. More about this will be said in Section 5.3.

[2] There are, of course, many other criteria, but they are all without theoretical foundation. An interesting rule of thumb is the so-called payback criterion, which states that a firm should recover its capital normally within a fiveyear period. If benefits are constant, the criterion is $5.1/a_{n/r} = 1$. Hence, as can be found in the compound and discount tables, if the lifetime of the investment is about 25 to 30 years, the firm's target rate of return is about 20 percent.

[3] If for a certain project $r > q$, then its net present value at discount rate q will be positive. Hence, the criteria will accept the same projects.

[4] A few words may be in order as regards the treatment of the lifetimes of projects in project evaluation. For mutually independent projects this presents no special problem, because we may assume that the cashflows of the projects under consideration may be valued at the opportunity cost of capital rate q, i.e. the cash flows may be valued at face value, and the differences in the lifetimes of the projects are then fully taken into account in the calculation of the net present values of the projects. For mutually exclusive projects, where the cash-flow streams may need to be reinvested for a specific purpose the situation is different. For instance, suppose that Project A has a life of 10 years, and Project B of 30 years. Then, to make a choice between A and B, GRANT and IRESON (GRANT, E. L. and IRESON, W. G. Principles of Engineering Economy, 4th ed., The Ronald Press Company, New York, 1960, p. 87) have suggested that we should consider what renewal investments will be necessary for Project A during the life of Project B. In case the life of Project B is not a multiple of the life of Project A, they believe that the most appropriate time period would be the least common multiple of the lives of the projects being analyzed. Thus, for instance, if two mutually exclusive projects are to be compared with lives of three and 31 years, respectively, investment costs, benefits and operating costs of each of the projects should be worked out as they appear in a 93-year period. However, as GRANT and IRESON point out, the arithmetic of discount calculations makes it possible to consider a much shorter period. For instance, at a discount rate of 10 percent, one dollar 25 years hence is worth only about $ 0.10; the same present value is found at a discount rate of 5 percent for one dollar 50 years hence.

The GRANT and IRESON procedure is complicated and we prefer, therefore, a more direct method of taking account of the differences in lifetimes, namely to attach a terminal benefit to the last year of each project's life. This terminal benefit should be found by deducting from the present value in the last year of all subsequent net benefits the present value in the same year of all subsequent reinvestments. For each project sensitivity tests should be applied with respect to lifetime and terminal benefit and we may consider the calculation to be correct if changes in lifetime and terminal benefit do not affect the present value of the project under scrutiny.

[5] See ECKSTEIN, 'Water Resource Development,' p. 239, and for a monograph on the subject. VAN DER TAK, H. G., 'The Economic Choice Between Hydroelectric and Thermal Power Developments,' World Bank Staff Occasional Papers, No. 1, distributed by the Johns Hopkins Press, Baltimore and London, 1966.

[6] See, however, Section 5.3 for a discussion of ratios in the case of budget constraints.

[7] McKEAN, 'Efficiency in Government through Systems Analysis,' p. 197.

[8] For a more detailed discussion about shadow prices in cases of constraints than in the paragraph above, the reader is referred to Jansen, 'Schaarse Middelen en Structurele Samenhangen.'

[9] See, for instance, MARGLIN, S. A., 'Objectives of Water Resource Development: A General Statement,' in Maass et al., 'Design of Water Resource Systems,' p. 34; and DASGUPTA, A. K. and PEARCE, D. W., 'Cost-Benefit Analysis: Theory and Practice, MacMillan Student Editions, London and Basingstoke, 1972.

[10] HIRSHLEIFER, DE HAVEN and MILLIMAN, 'Water Supply,' p. 161.

[11] This result may be explained as follows. Long-life projects have smaller depreciation elements in their cash flows than short-life projects. Hence, if both types of projects are to have the same internal rate of return, long-life projects will have relatively larger income elements and higher N/K ratios than short-life projects.

[12] SOLOMON, E., 'The Arithmetic of Capital Budgeting Decisions,' the Journal of Business, University of Chicago, April 1956, p. 124.

[13] GRANT and IRESON, 'Principles of Engineering Economy,' 4th ed., p. 509.

[14] It should be noted that GRANT and IRESON arrive at a different conclusion. They use 8 percent as the auxiliary interest rate to convert the positive cash flow of years 1–5 (+50 per year) to compound amount at date 5, which is 293.4. The series becomes then yr 5: −506.6 (= +293.4–800.0) yrs 6–20: +100 a year. At 18 percent the present worth of this series is zero and GRANT and IRESON conclude that the prospective rate of return is 18 percent. We believe that, to be consistent, the auxiliary interest rate should also be used to valuate the cash flow streams during yrs. 6–20, in which case the result would be a prospective rate of return of 10 percent.

[15] GRANT and IRESON, 'Principles of Engineering Economics,' 4th ed., p. 513.

[16] LORIE, J. H. and SAVAGE, L. J., 'Three Problems in Capital Rationing,' The Journal of Business, University of Chicago, October 1955.

[17] MARGLIN, 'Approaches to Dynamic Investment Planning,' p. 38.

[18] A more detailed discussion of the reasons why will be found in REUTLINGER, S., 'Techniques for Project Appraisal under Uncertainty,' World Bank Staff Occasional Papers, No. 10, distributed by the Johns Hopkins Press, Baltimore and London, 1970.

[19] See POULIQUEN, L.,'Risk Analysis in Project Appraisal.' World Bank Staff Occasional Papers, No. 11, distributed by The Johns Hopkins Press, Baltimore and London, 1970.

[20] Ibid., p. 20.

[21] A discussion of some of these decision rules is in DORFMAN, R., 'Basic Economic and Technologic Concepts – A General Statement,' in Maass et al., 'Design of Water Resource Systems,' pp. 129–158.

[22] KNIGHT, F. H., 'Risk, Uncertainty and Profit,' Sixth Impression, Houghton Mifflin Company, Boston and New York, 1946, pp. 231–232.

6. MISCELLANEOUS PROBLEMS

6.1. LINKAGE EFFECTS

Much has been written about the contribution that the so-called forward and backward linkages can make to the industrialization of developing countries. It is not our intention to review this literature; rather, we would like to review how the linkages are to be analyzed in the context of benefit-cost analysis

Backward linkages may be said to exist where the production of an industry (or a project) stimulates the activity of another industry that produces inputs for the first industry. Forward linkages may be said to exist where the production of an industry stimulates the activity of another industry that uses the outputs of the first industry. Often the two go together, and the classic examples are the cement plant, where bags for packing purposes represent backward linkage and cement block manufacturing forward linkage, and the steel plant, where coal production represents backward linkage and metal fabrication forward linkage.

The development literature has devoted its attention mainly to these backward and forward linkages, but there may, of course, be other types of connection between two industries. The classical price theory types are the cases where two industries produce goods that are substitutes or complements. Examples of substitutes are gas and electricity, rice and wheat, beef and lamb, butter and margarine. Examples of complements are housing and furniture, automobile plants and repair shops, hybrids and fertilizer. Also, it may be possible theoretically – although examples of such cases are hard to find – that the incomes that are raised by the expansion of a certain industry will be spent mainly on the products of another industry.

SCITOVSKY[1] considers all these cases of interconnection examples of pecuniary externalities and has challenged the concept that these are not to be taken into account in the evaluation of projects as the traditional benefit-cost evaluation rules tell us. SCITOVSKY draws his conclusion from the analysis of a forward linkage between industries A and B, and reasons as follows. Assume that it is advantageous for industry A to invest in a technological innovation which will lower its supply curve. A's product has then become cheaper in price and B's profits will thus rise. The increase in B's profits calls for investment and expansion in B, as a result of which B's demand for A's products increases. Hence, there will be a further increase in A's profits, leading to further expansion of A, as a result of which B's profits may increase further, and so on. Equilibrium will be reached when additional investments in each of the industries do not lead to increases in profits. The point of all this, according to SCITOVSKY, is that the amount of investment in industry A at the first stage is clearly smaller than what it will be after B has made adjustment. He concludes, therefore, that when an investment gives rise to a pecuniary external economy,

FIGURE 6.1.

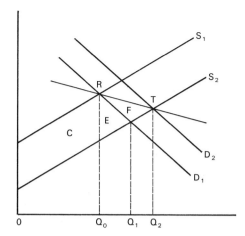

that its first stage profitability understates the real profitability of the investment.

Clearly, however, this has nothing to do with the concept of pecuniary externalities. At the first stage, the lower price of A's products leads to higher profits for B, but this is exactly compensated by the loss in income on these units of A. It is therefore not the pecuniary externality that is relevant, but the linkage. What SCITOVSKY has done is to describe how the adjustment process takes place. This is important because, for a correct investment decision, the project analyst should, of course, estimate what the cost and demand curves for the projects under scrutiny will be after the adjustment has taken place. What SCITOVSKY's argumentation boils down to is that an error will be made in estimating the benefit of a project if the analyst makes an error. Pecuniary externalities as traditionally defined are, however, not to be counted as benefits. This may also be shown with the help of a graphical presentation of his example.

In Figure 6.1 the demand curve for A's product is presented by D_1, and the cost curve of A's product by S_1. Suppose, as SCITOVSKY does, that A's cost curve is lowered to S_2. Then, if there were no linkage effects, the new production would be $0\,Q_1$ and the benefit of the cost reduction – the savings in resources – would be equal to the area C + E. A pecuniary externality arises in this case because the amount A loses on the intra-marginal units represents a gain to the users of A's product. However, the two compensate each other; the pecuniary externality is not to be taken into account, and the area C + E thus represents the exact measure of the benefits. An underestimation of the benefits will occur when B increases its production to profit from the lower costs of the A product which it uses in its production process. However, this additional benefit is due to the interlinking of the two industries rather than the pecuniary externality, and it is therefore preferable to reserve the term linkage for such effects than to see it as a new type of externality as SCITOVSKY does.

The additional benefit which is realized because B expands its production can also be measured by considering the shift in the demand curve that A faces. Let D_2 represent the demand curve in the final equilibrium situation. Then the total benefit after the adjustment has taken place will equal $C + E + F$. The area F is traced out by imagining that the cost and demand curves shift simultaneously. At any one moment the value of any of the successive units produced by A is indicated by the RT line – the quantity price locus – so that the value of the additional units is equal to the area $Q_0 R T Q_2$. With costs of this additional production equal to the area traced out by the S_2 curve, the net benefit of the additional production is $E + F$. While in the absence of linkages the benefits are represented by $C + E$, in case of linkages the benefits are larger and equal to $C + E + F$, where F represents the benefit due to B's output expansion.[2]

All the other cases of linkages discussed above can be analyzed in the same way. The approach is clear. The benefits can be found either by analyzing each of the interconnected industries separately, or by analyzing the quantity price locus which the principal industry faces because of the linkages. Which linkages should be and which should not be considered is, of course, a matter of judgment. In principle, the system under analysis should be expanded until all the principal linkage effects are captured. There is, however, no universal rule to be given and it is the task of the project analyst to ensure that significant linkage benefits are included in the estimates of the benefit of a project.

Can we normally expect that linkage effects will be substantial? In our opinion many linkage effects are so small that the estimation errors of the normal unadjusted cost and demand values may be larger than the value of the linkage benefits. Furthermore, it may be pointed out that in many cases the adjustment process will take a long time, especially in cases of forward or backward linkages so that the present value of the linkage benefits may be negligible. Also, it may be possible that the linkage benefits will materialize in any case, due to the general development of the economy, and it would then be wrong to attribute all of these benefits to the specific project being considered.

In concluding this section it may be useful to discuss briefly a slightly changed example from the OECD Manual which underlines this note of caution. Suppose that a project's investment cost in a certain year is Rs 50 million, and that its sales and current costs every year thereafter are Rs 15 million and Rs 10 million, respectively, so that its rate of return is 10 percent. Suppose, further, that a certain input accounts for 10 percent of total operating costs and that because of the increased demand of the project its cost will fall – and let us be optimistic – by some 20 percent. Then there will be a saving of Rs 200,000. But this clearly cannot be attributed to the project because in any case the general development of the economy would have caused the realization of these savings. The project has only advanced the realization of the savings and a generous estimate would therefore be that the savings attributable to the project amount to the equivalent of some Rs 100,000 per annum over the life of the project. This makes a total benefit of Rs 5.1 million per annum and the rate of return of the project becomes 10.1 percent. Hence, the OECD Manual states: 'Thus even with such a crude hypothetical example as this does one wonder whether it is worth spending a lot of time on trying to estimate external economies. It may be far more important to spend the time improving the ordinary estimates of sales and costs.'[3] Although we do not agree entirely with this and feel that the project analyst should try to estimate the linkage benefits to the fullest extent possible, the example may have made it clear that many linkage benefits will be extremely small. Because, moreover, assumed linkage benefits do not always exist in reality, we believe that one should be extremely skeptical if the justification of a project depends on the inclusion of linkage benefits.

6.2. EXTERNALITES

Any project will have indirect effects in the sense that parties other than those directly involved are affected. Examples of linkage effects were discussed in the previous section and they presented no special problems because the same analysis appeared to apply that applied in the case of a single integrated production process. Examples of pecuniary externalities were also discussed in several places in this study and they appeared not to be real externalities in the sense that they lead to an additional or a reduced use of resources. The situation is entirely different, however, with regard to technological externalities. Suppose that a new factory emits so much soot that the vegetable crops of a neighboring farmer need to be rinsed before they can be marketed. Then we would have a situation where a real cost in the sense of additional resources is incurred by the farmer as a result of the soot emission. While in the case of pecuniary externalities no shifting of production functions takes place, the externality in this example shifts the production function of the farmer. Technological externalities may also arise in the case of consumers. For instance, a new airport may produce so much noise that the utility level of neighboring households is reduced. Technological externalities may thus arise whenever a certain action affects the production or utility functions of other parties.

Technological externalities are almost unlimited. In the case of producers, we see that factories pollute the atmosphere and the waters with consequent detrimental effects on health, that farmers use chemicals and insecticides which may have the same detrimental effect, that highways cause congestion, that airports produce noise, and so on. With respect to consumers, we find that cigarette smoking irritates non-smokers, that garbage dumped on the street irritates other households, that the noise produced by mowing a lawn or turning on a radio may upset neighbors, and so on. Many of these externalities are negligible; some, however, may be substantial.

How should the technological externalities that a project generates be taken into account when evaluating the project? In many cases it may be possible that the project itself will pay its victims. For instance, in the case of the soot example

FIGURE 6.2.

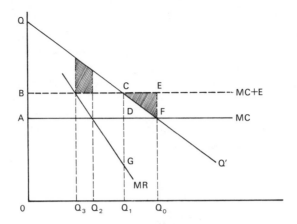

the farmer will, without doubt, ask the factory for reimbursement of his expenses. Such payments are to be considered costs of the project and the optimal scale of the project will then be reduced, so that the externality is fully taken into account. In many other cases, however, compensation payments may not be feasible, either because individuals of a large group of people are affected to a relatively small extent, or because the externality may have, as will be discussed further below, the character of a public good.

Since PIGOU's magistral work appeared,[4] it has been generally accepted that a tax on the generator of the externality equal to the damage he imposes at the margin on others will ensure an optimal allocation of resources. This is depicted graphically in Figure 6.2. The curve QQ' is the demand curve for the project's output, and the curve M C is the marginal cost curve (drawn horizontally for simplicity's sake). If the project produces in addition an externality, say, smoke, which will impose a cost on others equal to E per unit, a tax of E should be levied on the project so that the new equilibrium output will be O Q_1. The loss in consumer surplus is equal to the area A B C F, but A B C D becomes available in the form of tax revenue and the net loss is thus C D F. On the other hand, there will be a savings equal to C E F D, since this externality cost is no longer incurred. The gain of imposing the tax is thus equal to C E F.

As BUCHANAN has shown,[5] however, a conditio sine qua non for obtaining, in the case of a technological externality, an optimal resource allocation by means of a tax, is that production is organized in accordance with the optimality condition of welfare maximization. In all other cases, a single tax may lead to a loss in welfare. Suppose, for instance, that the project manager were to maximize profits rather than welfare or, in other words, that he acted as a monopolist. Then the monopoly output would be O Q_2, i.e., the output level where marginal costs equal marginal revenues. Imposition of the tax E would reduce output by Q_3 Q_2. Instead of a welfare gain, there would now be a welfare loss equal to the shaded area because consumer's value of the eliminated quantity is higher than the value of the freed resources plus the cost of the eliminated externality.

122

One should thus be extremely cautious in recommending a tax for the elimination of a technological externality. Nevertheless, the principle is correct. The reason that, in the case of the monopolist, the tax will lead to a loss in welfare is because the normal optimality condition is not fulfilled. For the elimination of such an additional distortion, an additional instrument will be needed, and, in the case of the monopolist, this will be a subsidy. By granting to the monopolist a subsidy equal to C G per unit, one would ensure again production taking place at the optimal level $0 Q_1$. The tax is thus necessary to eliminate the externality distortion, and the subsidy to eliminate the monopoly distortion. Although it is true that the simultaneous levying of a tax (CD per unit in our example) and granting of a subsidy (CG per unit) can be replaced by the granting of a smaller subsidy (DG per unit), it is clear that the latter can be found only after the externality and the monopoly distortion have been determined. Pigou's principle is thus valid even when other distortions exist, but it should be borne in mind that additional instruments will be required to eliminate additional distortions.

What should Government do with the taxes it has collected from the generator of the technological externality? It is here that the distinction made for the first time by Bator[6] between public and private good externalities becomes important in that the way the victim should be treated depends on the type of externality. First, let us consider the public good type of externality. A public good has the peculiar feature that consumption by one person does not reduce other persons' consumption (for example, TV programs, police protection, and such) and the demand curve is therefore constructed by adding vertically the individual demand curves. In principle, therefore, a series of prices rather than one single price should be charged, each one determined by each consumer's marginal willingness to pay. In practice, however, it will not be possible to determine these prices, because each consumer when interviewed may well understate his willingness to pay in the hope that then the burden will be borne by the other consumers. Since efficiency prices cannot be determined, the financing of a public good is therefore a matter of spreading the burden over consumers and then, of course, equity considerations play a primary role.

Many technological externalities may have the character of a public good in the sense that the consumption of one person does not reduce the quantity available for consumption by others. Examples of such externalities which present negative effects are smoke or water pollution generated by a factory, or the noise and fumes generated by a new highway. An example of a positive externality would be an irrigation dam or hydroelectric development which would open the possibility of gratis recreation on the created water basin. Suppose that the externality is smoke. Government should then impose on the factory a tax equal to the marginal harm done by the smoke. Should the tax revenues be used to compensate the victims? This may well lead to further harmful effects because an incentive is then offered to people to seek the externality. Coase[7] has therefore suggested that the victims should be taxed so that they will try to escape the externality. However, in general, this is not correct either, as BAUMOL and OATES[8] have shown. Since the externality has the character of a public good, the person who inhales the smoke affects only himself, and he will thus absorb the full consequences of his decision to escape or not to escape the externality. Therefore, according to BAUMOL and OATES, in cases of public good type externalities, the tax revenues collected from the generator of the externality should not be used by the Government to compensate the victims; any other use of the revenues is allowed.[9] Similarly, neither is it necessary to charge a price to the beneficiaries of a public good type externality.

In our example, we have lightly passed over the problem of how the marginal damage of the smoke can be measured. This is an extremely complicated problem because, just as with public goods, no price mechanism exists to measure the marginal valuation of the consumers, and it must therefore be accepted that the level of the taxes will be, to a large extent, determined arbitrarily. The problem is further complicated because in many cases – our smoke example is a case in point – the externality will have harmful effects on health or will even reduce life expectancy. How these matters should conceptually be dealt with will be discussed briefly at the end of this section. A further problem is that the distributive aspects of an externality may play a role. For instance, a new road may generate noise and fumes which may play a preponderant role in planning a road layout. However, it would be ridiculous to plan the road through a poor income area of a city on the grounds that the willingess to pay of the citizens in that area to escape the externality is lower than anywhere else. After our discussion in Chapter 2, it should be clear that willingness to pay should be weighted with the relevant income distribution weights, a matter which will be more fully discussed in Part II of this study.

Let us turn now to the private type of externality. In our soot example, we saw already that the factory may enter into negotiation with the farmer with regard to the compensation payment the latter should receive, and these payments will then enter into the cost function of the factory. In the case of a large number of victims, this obviously would not be possible and the Government should then impose a tax on the factory. As we have here a private good type of externality, the tax revenues should be used to compensate the victims. The principle is clear: a private externality can be regarded as a private good and, to achieve an optimal allocation of resources, the same pricing rules that apply for a private good should apply to the externality. In the case of our soot example, this means because the externality carries a disbenefit, that a negative price (the tax) should be imposed on the producers, while the victims should receive this fine. In the case of a private externality that presents a benefit, the producer should receive a positive price (a subsidy) while the beneficiary should pay this price.

A very interesting example of a private externality is the hides-meat case mentioned by MISHAN[10]. In Argentina at the end of the last century, cattle were slaughtered on the ranches for their hides, and the meat was left for whomever wanted it. Clearly, this was a beneficial externality and a private one since an individual's consumption of meat would leave less behind for others. In principle, to achieve an optimal level of cattle production a price should have been charged for this meat. This was not done because it was too costly for the ranchers either to collect the price or to transport the meat to a central marketing point. It should be noted that it would also be too costly for the Government to impose and collect these prices. When demand increased, however, the industry found it worthwhile to sell the meat and the externality therewith became captured. This example is interesting because, when demand was insufficient, neither private industry nor the Government found it worthwhile to price the meat. Thus if a dollar is counted for a dollar, there did not exist any externality at all. However, if we accept that the persons who gathered the meat had a much higher marginal utility of income than the ranchers, it becomes clear that the willingness to pay of these persons, weighted with the appropriate marginal utilities of income, represents the real value of their increase in meat consumption. Thus, when the distributive aspects count, the meat is clearly an important beneficial externality.

In all the cases so far discussed, the pricing principles when income distribution does not count are exactly the same as those that apply to the pricing of public and private goods. We will now, however, turn our attention to a group of technological externalities where these principles break down. These include the cases where the generators of the externality are at the same time the victims. Although theoretically the group should include generators that are at the same time beneficiaries, it is hard to find a concrete example. Therefore, we will limit our discussion to the frequent cases where the generators are also the victims, a phenomenon that is known as the congestion externality. Since it is such an important type of externality, we will discuss in detail the case of road congestion.

Reference is made to Figure 6.3. The Q Q' curve is the demand for trips on a highway and thus represents the marginal willingness to pay of the motorists for the privilege of making a trip. What are the costs? There are the capacity costs of the highway, the operating and maintenance costs of the highway, the operating costs of the motorists and the time costs of the motorists. To simplify the analysis, we assume that all these costs are equal to OA per trip when no congestion occurs on the highway. When congestion occurs, however, fuel and time costs of the motorists will increase and the cost of a trip will increase, as indicated by the curve A B C D. Thus, for instance, when the number of trips equals OT_2, the cost of each trip will be CT_2. It may be noted that the curve bends backward at point D since congestion has then become so severe that any additional vehicle reduces the number of trips that can be undertaken within a certain time period. The curve marginal to the average cost curve – the curve A F E – indicates what the true cost of an additional trip will be in the sense that it includes the extra cost of congestion imposed on others. For instance, if the cost of a trip is $1.00 when the number of trips is 50,000 per annum and $1.01 when the number of trips is 51,000, the marginal cost of the extra 1,000 trips is $1.51 per trip. To the motorists making the additional 1,000 trips,

125

FIGURE 6.3.

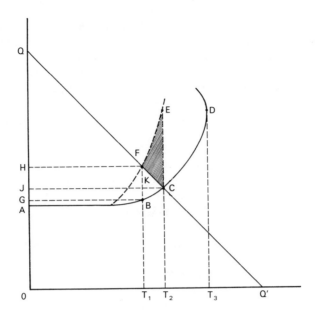

Tabulation of Benefits

	at OT_1	at OT_2	Difference
Willingness to Pay	$OQFT_1 (= OQFT_1)$	$OQCT_2 (= OQCT_2)$	$+T_1FCT_2 (= T_1FCT_2)$
Cost of Trips	$OAFT_1 (= OGBT_1)$	$OAFET_2 (= OJCT_2)$	$+T_1FET_2 (= GJKB + + T_1KCT_2)$
Net Benefit	$AQF (= GQFB)$	$AQF - FEC (= JQC)$	$-FEC (= -GJKB+KFC)$
Net Benefit Government	GHFB	–	$-GHFB$
Net Benefit Motorists	$\dfrac{HQF}{GQFB}$	$\dfrac{JQC}{JQC}$	$\dfrac{+JHFC}{-GJKB + KFC}$

however, the cost of $1.01 per trip will appear as their marginal cost. The curve A B C D is thus a marginal cost curve to the individual motorist and an average cost curve for the motorists as a whole. The curve A F E, on the other hand, includes the increase in cost of every motorist and is thus the real marginal cost curve. It shows that the real cost of the additional 1,000 trips is $1.51 per trip.

It is easy to see that the trip number corresponding to the intersection of the marginal cost curve with the demand curve represents the optimum volume of traffic. When volume of traffic is OT_1 the total cost of the trips will be O G B T_1 (which is equal to O A F T_1) while the willingness to pay is O Q F T_1. Hence, the net benefit equals G Q F B which is equivalent to A Q F. Any other position

126

will lead to a lower net benefit. For instance, at trip level OT_2, costs exceed willingness to pay by the area F E C.

How can the Government ensure that the volume of traffic will stabilize at the optimum level OT_1? Following the above discussed rules, the Government should levy a tax equal to the marginal cost which the externality imposes on others, and make a payment to the victims equal to the tax collected. Hence, the first step to be taken is to collect a toll equal to BF per trip. Motorists then pay a total of G H F B in the form of tolls, and, according to the second part of the policy prescription, the Government should use this amount to compensate the victims of the externality. But in this case the victims are the ones that produce the externality, and if the Government were to pay them back the toll, the net result would be as if no toll were levied, so that immediately the traffic volume would return to the level OT_2. Let us assume that the Government will keep the toll; then motorists would be worse off by the area J H F C (the difference between the consumer surplus at level OT_2 which equals J Q C and the consumer surplus at level OT_1 which equals H Q F). Rather than benefiting the road users, the toll thus results in a harmful effect.[11]

It remains true that society as a whole is still better off when the toll is levied than when it is not levied. Although the road users lose J H F C, the Government gains the toll amount G H F B, and the net result is thus a gain of G H F B – J H F C, which, as the tabulation under Figure 6.3 shows, is equal to F E C. It is, however, clear that the distributive aspects of the toll financing will now play an important role. For instance, a Government might want to levy a toll on a road going to an expensive holiday resort. On the other hand, when the users of a road do not belong to the higher income groups, the effects of a toll may result in a socially unacceptable loss of welfare.

Because many roads where congestion occurs are often used by average and poor income classes, it is not surprising that many Governments have not been willing to impose tolls but have preferred to let the road become congested. As we discussed in the previous Chapter, benefits and costs must then be determined with respect to the non-optimal situation rather than with respect to the optimal level.

Congestion externalities are an extremely important type of externality. In general, they occur wherever common property is being exploited. Our road is an example. Other examples would be the exploitation of fish or oil resources. In all these cases the analysis should follow the same principle as that of the road analysis. This may be shown briefly for the fisheries case. Suppose that the demand curve in Figure 6.3 represents the demand for fish and the curve A B C D the marginal cost curve of the fishermen. Assuming that there is perfect competition, the equilibrium catch rate would be at level $O\ T_2$. The correct optimal catch volume would, however, be at $O\ T_1$, the level comparable to the point where the A F E curve – the curve that includes the cost which an individual fisherman inposes on the other fishermen – intersects the demand curve. A tax equal to B F would ensure this volume but, again, fishermen would be worse off by the area J H F C and, the Government may therefore decide to leave well enough alone and to let the fishermen continue to fish at the non-optimal activity level.

A similar analysis applies to the congestion which occurs in the cities. As we discussed in Chapter 3, the distorted high wage rates in the cities cause an immigration of rural workers, many of whom will become jobless. To the extent that this immigration leads to congested living conditions and a deterioration of the city environment, the opportunity cost of labor must be increased by the cost that immigration imposes on others. The same should be done where an influx of industries would lead to such congestion or deterioration. Many cities seem to have reached a stage where any further growth will have significant harmful effects on their residents. In principle, benefit-cost analysis should try to capture these technological externalities, but, as we have seen, this is extremely difficult. That such externalities exist, however, cannot be doubted since in many cases Governments are diverting industries away from cities solely because of them.

Finally, we would like to say a few words about the evaluation of human health and lives, a subject that is important because humans may be substantially affected by environmental externalities. Although we do not wish to discuss these extremely important problems in any detail in this study, it is appropriate as the last subject of this section to comment briefly on some evaluation rules that have recently been proposed. WEISBROD[12] has suggested that the value of a human life can be measured by calculating the present value of either a person's future lifetime earnings or of a person's excess of earnings over consumption. Both methods are, however, not correct. Both methods have all the deficiencies of the national income concept. Moreover, a logical extension of the first concept would be that all those who are not able to earn a salary should be killed. Similarly, under the second method all those who consume more than they earn, for instance, retired persons, should be killed.

There is also the method proposed by some to measure the value of a person's life on the basis of what he has insured himself for. But, clearly, this is of more concern to those who survive him than to himself. MISHAN[13], therefore, has rightly pointed out that the value of a human life is the value that the person whose life is at stake attaches to it. MISHAN argues that conceptually this value is determined by the compensating variation measure, i.e., the minimum sum a person is prepared to accept in exchange for the surrender of his life, but points out that in ordinary circumstances no sum of money will be large enough to compensate a man for the loss of his life. It is never the case, however, that a specific person can be designated in advance as one who will be killed if a particular project is undertaken. According to MISHAN, this fact of complete ignorance, therefore, transfers the calculation from one of calculating the compensating variation of surrending one's life to one of calculating the compensating variation for accepting additional risk.

MISHAN is on the right track. Nevertheless, there are, in our opinion, two objections to his proposal. First, as was discussed in Chapter 2, the compensating variations are irrelevant for the valuation of a good. It is the normal demand curve for a good that indicates how a person valuates that good and also, as regards health and life, the relevant concept should be the willingness to pay of a person for a reduction in the probability of incurring a disease or losing his life. Second, just as with a normal good, it is not the money costs, but the utility value that counts, especially when such important things as health and life are at stake. For instance, the probability calculations may show that a poor man's life is worth $5,000 and a rich man's life $500,000, but, clearly, none of these figures is an appropriate measure of the utility loss. The correct calculation should be to weight both sums with the respective marginal utilities of income so that the poor man's life as well as the rich man's life will be expressed in the denominator of an 'average' man's life.

This short discussion on the value of health and life cannot do justice to the extremely difficult and intricate problems that are inherent in any attempt to measure these values. Further discussion would fall outside the scope of this study but it should be clear that any estimate will be rough. We, therefore, agree wholeheartedly with MISHAN who, at the end of his extremely useful survey, writes: 'In view of the existing quantomania, one may be forgiven for asserting that there is more to be said for rough estimates of the precise concept than for precise estimates of economically irrelevant concepts.'

As a last remark, it may be mentioned that there is, of course, always the possibility to apply a cost-effectiveness analysis. In such a case one would stipulate targets in terms of savings of lives or improvement of health and then weigh the costs of the alternative ways of achieving the objective in order to determine the least-cost solution. As this technique presents no special problems, it need not be further discussed. The difficulty of this technique is, of course, that some body politic needs to set the objective – truly, not a desirable task.

6.3. FOREIGN LABOR AND CAPITAL

In many cases, foreigners provide part of the labor and capital inputs of a project. The question which may be asked is whether the costs of the inputs provided by foreigners and the benefits accruing to foreigners should be treated in the same way as domestic costs and benefits. Or, in other words, should the nationality of the participants in a project be ignored?

In answering the question, we will not consider international aspects but analyze the issue from a purely national point of view. Moreover, we will not deal with the special problems that are created by huge influxes of foreign labor or capital,[14] but limit our analysis to marginal changes.

Let us start with the production factor labor. Two cases will be reviewed. The first is that the project authority will hire a foreigner specifically for the project. Employing the foreigner then does not have an opportunity cost in the sense that domestic output will be foregone in the host country. On the other hand, the salary received by the foreigner represents a transfer of resources from the host country to the foreigner. We may conclude, therefore, that the

TABLE 6.1. Example of the benefit of hiring a foreigner.

	Foreigner Hired From Abroad	Foreigner Withdrawn From Alternative Employment In Host Country
x = value of foreigner's product in project	5,000	5,000
w = foreigner's net-of-tax salary in project	4,000	3,000
m = foreigner's product in next best alternative	–	4,000
y = foreigner's earnings in next best alternative	–	2,500
Total cost of hiring foreigner ($w+m-y$)	4,000	4,500
Net benefit of employing foreigner in project	1,000	500

salary of the foreigner represents the costs to the host country. This salary is, of course, net of tax since the taxes the foreigner pays on his salary represent benefits to the host country.

Now consider the case where the foreigner will be withdrawn from alternative employment in the host country. It then remains valid that the net-of-tax salary the foreigner will receive from the project is a cost to the host country. On the other hand, there is now an opportunity cost in the sense that the product which he would have produced in the next best alternative employment is foregone. At the same time, however, the salary the foreigner would have earned in that alternative employment is saved. Denoting the net-of-tax salary of the foreigner in his new employment by w, the foregone product by m and the foreigner's net-of-tax salary in the next best alternative by y, the cost of the foreigner to the host country is $w + m - y$. If the product of the foreigner in his new occupation with the project is x, the net benefit to the host country of employing the foreigner is thus equal to $x - (w + m - y)$. It may be noted that if m and y are equal, the net benefit will be $x - w$, as in the first case. A simple example in tabular form is presented above to elucidate the analysis.

Let us turn now to the production factor capital. The analysis is then similar to the labor case but slightly more complicated because we need to work with present values. Let us assume that we are contemplating a project with investment costs of $300 and net benefits of $360 after one year, so that the rate of return on investment equals 20 percent. Assume further that foreign capital participation will be $200 and that a total of $224 must be repaid after one year, so that interest amounts to 12 percent. What are the benefits and costs of the project to the country?

Let us assume first that additional foreign funds are available for the project. Just as in the labor case, the benefit to the country is then equal to $x - w$, whereby x now stands for the present value of the net benefits attributable to the foreign capital and w for the present value of the foreign earnings. The calculations are presented in tabular form in Table 6.2, but a brief explanation

130

TABLE 6.2. Example of the benefit of employing foreign capital.

	Additional Foreign Capital Available	Foreign Capital Withdrawn from Alternative Employment in Host Country
Benefit Attributable to Foreign Capital		
x = present value of net benefits attributable to foreign capital	$-200 + \dfrac{240}{1.15}$	$-200 + \dfrac{240}{1.15}$
w = present value of foreigner's net earnings (12%)	$-200 + \dfrac{224}{1.15}$	$-200 + \dfrac{224}{1.15}$
m = present value of net benefits attributable to foreign capital in next best alternative (18%)		$-200 + \dfrac{236}{1.15}$
y = present value of foreigner's earnings (14%) in next best alternative		$-200 + \dfrac{228}{1.15}$
Total cost to country of employing foreign capital ($w+m-y$)	$-200 + \dfrac{224}{1.15}$	$-200 + \dfrac{232}{1.15}$
Present value of the net benefits of employing foreign capital in the project	$\dfrac{16}{1.15}$	$\dfrac{8}{1.15}$
Present value of net benefits attributable to domestic capital	$-100 + \dfrac{120}{1.15}$	$-100 + \dfrac{120}{1.15}$
Benefit of Project	$-100 + \dfrac{136}{1.15}$	$-100 + \dfrac{128}{1.15}$

is perhaps helpful. It is assumed that the opportunity cost of capital in the country is 15 percent. The x of the formula is then equal to $-200 + 240/1.15$ because the rate of return of the project is 20 percent, while the discount factor is 15 percent. The w in the formula is equal to $-200 + 224/1.15$ because the foreigner requires a return of 12 percent. Hence, the benefit to the country of the foreign participation is equal to $16/1.15$. Since we know in this case that the benefit attributable to domestic capital is $-100 + 120/1.15$, the total benefit to the country, including the benefit made on the foreign capital, is $-100 + 136/1.15$.

The case where foreign capital is withdrawn from alternative employment in the host country is also presented in Table 6.2. The total cost to the country of employing foreign capital is again, as in the case of labor, presented by $w + m-y$, whereby w is defined as in the previous paragraph, m as the present value of the foregone contribution of foreign capital in the next best alternative, and y as the present value of the earnings of foreign capital in the next best alternative.

An additional point should be noted, namely, that the total benefit to the country of a project where foreign capital is used can also be found by deducting directly from the present value of the total benefit of the project (z) – calculated under the assumption that all capital is domestic capital – the foreign costs and benefits. This way of looking at the use of foreign capital is presented

TABLE 6.3. Alternative method of calculating the benefit of employing foreign capital.

	Additional Foreign Capital Available	Foreign Capital Withdrawn from Alternative Employment in Host Country
z – present value of project if all capital domestic	$-300 + \dfrac{360}{1.15} = 13$	$-300 + \dfrac{360}{1.15} = 13$
w – present value of foreign capital in and outflow	$+200 - \dfrac{224}{1.15} = 5$	$+200 - \dfrac{224}{1.15} = 5$
$(m-y)$ adjustment for difference between earnings and opportunity cost in next best alternative		$-\dfrac{8}{1.15} = -7$
Benefit of Project	$-100 + \dfrac{136}{1.15} = 18$	$-100 + \dfrac{128}{1.15} = 11$

in Table 6.3 and leads, of course, to the same result as the previous calculation, as it is a mere rearrangement of the variables. The principle in both calculations is that foreign capital can be considered a capital inflow, which reduces the need for domestic capital, while debt service payments on foreign capital can be considered an outflow, which reduces the benefits of the project.

Table 6.3 also shows the actual present values. As may be seen, in the case where additional foreign capital becomes available, the benefit of the project is calculated as 18, whereas in the case where foreign capital is withdrawn from alternative employment, the benefit is only 11. This may at first seem surprising because in both cases foreign capital is made available on the same terms. The contradiction disappears, however, if we remember that, in the second case, a constraint exists on the availability of foreign capital. We encountered several instances of constraints earlier and saw that they increased the opportunity costs of the factor subject to the constraint. The same happens here. By withdrawing the foreign capital from its alternative employment, we lose a present value of 7 which the foreign capital would have produced. Hence, the benefit of the project is $18-7 = 11$.

Macro-economically, it will be advantageous for a country to borrow foreign capital as long as the cost of borrowing is lower than the cost of using domestic capital. In other words, the cost of borrowing should be lower than the opportunity cost of capital. Micro-economically, we can show this by considering a marginal investment project. In case such a project is domestically financed, the present value of the benefits will be equal to the present value of the investments, both values found by discounting at the opportunity cost of capital q. In symbols we may write $N_A a_{\overline{n}|q} = K$, where N_A is annual net benefits, $a_{\overline{n}|q}$ the discount factor and K the value of the investments which we assume take place in year 1. Suppose that additional foreign funds in the amount of αK can be borrowed at rate i. The debt service payments (amortization + interest) are then $\alpha K/a_{\overline{n}|i}$ and the present value of these payments $(\alpha K/a_{\overline{n}|i}) a_{\overline{n}|q}$. The present value of the benefit of the project is presented by:

$$[N_A a_{\overline{n}|q} - (\alpha K/a_{\overline{n}|i}) a_{\overline{n}|q}] - (K - \alpha K).$$

As $N_A a_{\overline{n}|q} = K$ for the marginal project, this may be written as $\alpha K - (\alpha K \cdot a_{\overline{n}|q}/a_{\overline{n}|i})$. and it can be seen immediately that this expression is positive only if $a_{\overline{n}|q} < a_{\overline{n}|i}$. This will be the case if the borrowing rate i is lower than the opportunity cost of capital q. We can illustrate the above even more clearly if we assume that the capital borrowed abroad will be repaid with interest at the end of the project's life. In order to have a positive project benefit, we should have

$$\alpha K - \alpha K \frac{(1 + i)^n}{(1 + q)^n} > 0$$

Again, this will be the case only if i is smaller than q.

The main benefit of foreign aid is that funds are made available to the recipient country at a cost lower than the country's opportunity cost of capital. As a measure of such aid, the so-called grant element of the aid[15] is often calculated. It expresses the softness of the loan as a percentage of the face value of the loan and in our example it would be equal to:

$$\frac{\alpha K - \alpha K \dfrac{(1 + i)^n}{(1 + q)^n}}{\alpha K} = 1 - \frac{(1 + i)^n}{(1 + q)^n}$$

In many cases, a grace period is given to the recipient country before payments of principal begin, something that we did not assume in our example. The principle of calculating the grant element remains, however, the same. One expresses the difference between the face value of the loan and the present value of the debt service payments as a percentage of the face value.

Unfortunately, the grant element as traditionally defined represents only a partial picture of the benefit of aid. It does not, for instance, take into account that bilateral aid is often conditional on ordering the required machinery and equipment from the donor country. Several studies have shown that in such cases the cost of the equipment may be as much as 25 percent higher than if it were procured on the basis of international competitive bidding. How should one account for the excess costs in the case of such tied loans? Let us assume that there will be an excess cost equal to βK, and that $K(1 + \beta)$ will be borrowed at rate i. with repayment at the end of the project's life. The recipient country should then accept the aid if: $K - [K (1 + \beta) (1 + i)^n/(1 + q)^n] \geq 0$. Or, in words, the borrowing rate i should be lower than q by an amount sufficient to offset the excess investment cost.

Foreign capital and foreign labor should, of course, be valued at the appropriate foreign exchange rate in the same way as the foreign exchange components of the total benefit-cost stream are valued. For instance, as regards foreign labor, the value of the foreigner's product in the project may consist of foreign exchange or the foreigner may remit his income abroad. To the extent that foreign exchange incurs a premium, the foreign exchange shadow rate rather than the official rate should be used to value these items. A similar valuation should be applied to foreign capital and debt service payments. Problems arise when the shadow rate of foreign exchange varies over time. Suppose, for instance, that foreign financing can be obtained for a marginal project, of which all costs and benefits are domestic. Should the foreign finance be accepted? Denoting by R_1 the foreign exchange shadow rate at the moment the foreign capital is received and by R_2 the shadow rate at the time principal plus interest should be repaid, we find that the recipient country should accept the foreign finance if $KR_1 - [KR_2 (1 + i)^n/(1 + q)^n] \geqslant 0$. To the extent that R_2 is higher than R_1, the borrowing rate should thus be lower to make it advantageous for the recipient country to accept the loan.

Finally, as the last subject of this section, we would like to review the practice of international aid agencies and whether their aid can indeed be expected to help the developing countries. This subject appears to be controversial and it is therefore well worthwhile to examine the matter in some detail. In an interesting study ZEYLSTRA[16] argues that development aid has been very ineffective and that its main purpose has been to preserve the existing political world order. Furthermore, he criticizes severely the policies of the international agencies. In his words: 'Since even the World Bank has been satisfied with the interpretation of repayment capacity following from the role assigned to capital imports in conventional theory, it appears fair to include creditor countries and international agencies such as the World Bank among those responsible for the alarming situation in which numerous developing countries have now found themselves for years, that they have had to borrow in order to be able to pay service costs on previous loans.' We will not comment on ZEYLSTRA's general contention that self-interest has been the main motive for providing aid, except to state that a reasonable level of aid has been far from reached. As regards ZEYLSTRA's criticism that lending by creditor countries and international agencies has exacerbated the situation of the developing countries, it seems to us that he is wrong. ZEYLSTRA is not alone in his criticism; in fact, it is inspired by LINDER's theory which he quotes wholeheartedly. As this theory has led to much confusion, we will criticize it in some detail.

Conventional theory tells us that a country can always overcome foreign exchange problems by appropriate expenditure and exchange rate policies. According to LINDER,[17] however, this theory does not apply to most developing countries because they will be faced with an import minimum as well as an export maximum which does not cover the former. Chronic foreign exchange gaps are, therefore, in LINDER's opinion quite common for the developing countries. To explain the export maximum, LINDER makes a distinction between manufactures and raw materials. As regards manufactures, he introduces the theory of representative demand, according to which a country is most efficient in the manufacture of goods that fit into the economic structure of the domestic market. Because the domestic demand structure differs greatly between advanced and developing countries, the goods that advanced countries demand are not typical of the demand structure of the developing countries so that the manufactures that developing countries are particularly adept at producing lack foreign demand. As regards the manufactures for which a foreign demand does exist the production function will be at a disadvantage and productivity will be so low that these products will not be competitive. This disadvantage does not exist, of course, with regard to primary products, but most of the primary products are faced with inelastic world demand. Therefore, LINDER concludes that developing countries have an export maximum.

On the import side, the developing countries need input imports (investment and operation imports) to avoid underutilization of existing resources. Investment imports (such as machinery and equipment), would not be necessary if simple techniques of production could be used, but such techniques do not exist. Because a substantial amount of inventive engineering work is required to develop the simpler production techniques and because this is too time consuming, it is more efficient to import modern machinery. If capital goods must then be imported for investment purposes, there must also be imports for operational purposes. There is thus a minimum amount of imports that is absolutely necessary to utilize domestic savings.

The essential point now, according to LINDER, is that the export maximum may be too low to cover the import minimum, so that a typical developing country faces a continuous foreign exchange gap. While in conventional theory, capital imports serve the function of supplementing domestic savings in order to make possible a higher rate of investment than could be realized without reducing domestic consumption, in LINDER's framework capital imports supplement not insufficient domestic savings but insufficient foreign exchange resources, which must be augmented in order to avoid making domestic savings superfluous. This analysis, according to LINDER, has important implications in all cases where service charges arise on borrowed capital. 'Capital imports made now might be impossible to service later without cutting back imports and widening a still-prevailing foreign exchange gap.'[18] LINDER, therefore, believes that it is not enough that the projects financed by a loan yield profits or add to GNP. In his opinion, every project must not only be efficient in this sense, but also when charged with the service costs of the loan. LINDER states that the World Bank has gradually increased its project lending to a much higher percentage than the foreign exchange content of a project, and he believes that this is wrong. According to him, it would be sufficient to lend only the foreign exchange content of a project.

In our opinion, LINDER's theory is extreme. Although we are willing to accept that the elasticity of demand for imports may be low, it is unrealistic to assume that a devaluation and hence an increase in the domestic value of imports will not lead to a reduction in the home demand for imports. As regards exports, LINDER assumes that the outside world will always buy the same quantity of exported goods and that the increase in domestic production of export goods brought forth by the increase in the domestic price due to the devaluation can under no circumstances be sold abroad. Again, this assumption is unrealistic. Accepting that the elasticity of export supply is positive, a devaluation will increase the amount of foreign exchange supplied in terms of foreign currency if the elasticity of foreign demand for the country's exports is greater than unity. As will be discussed in more detail in the next section, there are sound theoretical reasons to expect that the export demand elasticity is greater than unity, even for primary products. Empirical studies also confirm this. For instance, HARBERGER,[19] having reviewed a number of econometric studies, concludes that even for a country such as Brazil, which produced about half the world's coffee during the last decade, the elasticity of demand for its coffee exports can be assumed to be higher than 2. LINDER's theory of the export maximum and import minimum must, therefore, be rejected.

LINDER's ideas are, in our opinion, dangerous. As an export maximum exists, it makes no sense under his theory for the developing countries to invest in export-generating projects, and the only possible way of improving their balance of payments is to substitute domestic production for imports to the largest extent possible. The fallacy of such a strategy has been well demonstrated in the last decade: policies of export promotion have paid off handsomely vide the phenomenal growth in industrial exports of many developing countries, whereas policies of import substitution, as followed in several Latin American countries, have resulted in uneconomic industries. There is no doubt that production for export markets involves an extra effort, but the cost of this effort is often much less than the extra resources needed to produce import goods domestically. LINDER's theory underlines once again the danger of a macro-economic approach to development planning. In our opinion, it is not the conventional theory which should be held responsible for the sorry state of affairs in some of the developing countries, but the sort of policy prescriptions as advocated by LINDER.

Having rejected the theoretical basis of the LINDER theory, it may still be asked whether it makes any sense to limit project lending to those projects that earn the foreign exchange to service and repay the loan. The answer is no. As WOLFSON[20] has put it, 'It makes no more sense to link individual items in the overall assets and liabilities of a country as a whole, as reflected in its balance of payments, than it does to impute individual assets to individual liabilities in the balance sheet of a bank.' We have shown above the correct method of calculating whether a loan should be accepted. When foreign exchange is becoming more scarce, the borrowing rate should be lower to offset the increase in the scarcity premium. A loan should be accepted only if the additional resources that become available because of the loan are larger than the resources that must be used to service the loan. The shadow foreign exchange rate has the role of making foreign exchange resources comparable to domestic resources. This means that when the shadow foreign exchange rate is, say, Rs 5 per US dollar, that a project whose annual domestic benefits are equal to Rs 5 has exactly the same priority as a project with the same investments and the same lifetime, but which annual benefits of US$1. Whether a project earns foreign exchange or whether its investments absorb foreign exchange is thus completely irrelevant to the question of whether a loan should be accepted.

Finally, we can address ourselves to the matter of whether international agencies follow the right procedures. In general, institutions such as the World Bank and the Asian Development Bank use shadow prices for labor and foreign exchange in calculating the rate of return of a project. This is as it should be. However, they do not take specific account of the foreign capital in and out flows and their main economic criterion for granting a loan is that the project should earn at least the opportunity cost of domestic capital. In other words, these institutions do not pay any attention to the benefit the country will have from their soft-term loans but determine the benefit of a project to the country on the basis of the total benefit-cost stream. As their loans are indeed on soft terms compared to the terms the developing countries have to pay for normal market borrowings, this procedure may at first seem rather surprising. In reality, however, it is entirely correct. The international agencies normally allocate their limited funds on a country basis, so that for a certain country the foreign exchange that can be borrowed for a project will not be available for another project. The country then finds itself in the situation discussed above of having a constraint on the availability of foreign exchange and the benefit of a loan should then be analyzed in accordance with the formula developed for this case. Suppose that the opportunity cost of capital in the country is 15 percent, and that the lending rate of the institutions is $8^1/_2$ percent. We may then set w at $8^1/_2$ percent, m at 15 percent and y at $8^1/_2$ percent, so that the cost of the foreign assistance for the project under scrutiny $w + m - y$ equals 15 percent. To continue the example, suppose that the present value of the total cost-benefit stream of a project is $-300 +360/1.15$ so that the present value of the project is 13. Assume further that the foreign assistance is 200. Then it makes no difference whether the net present value of the project is calculated on the basis of the total cost-benefit stream or on the basis of the cost-benefit stream reduced by the foreign capital in and outflow. In the former case, the present value is $-300 + 360/1.15$, which equals 13. In the latter case, the present value of the foreign assistance equals $+200 - 230/1.15 = 0$, and the benefit of that specific project is thus presented by $-100 + 130/1.15$, which again equals 13. The appraisal procedures and the lending policies of the international agencies are thus entirely correct.

The international agencies ensure that the projects for which they lend have yields at least equal to the opportunity cost of capital in the country concerned so that their funds cannot be squandered on uneconomic projects. As the normal lending rates of these institutions are substantially below the opportunity cost of capital of the developing countries, the latter reap substantial benefits. In this respect, it should also be noted that if it is expected that a country will have repayment difficulties, loans at softer than normal terms are granted. For instance, at present the International Development Association, an affiliate of the World Bank, provides credits for 50 years with a grace period for repayment of 10 years, at a commitment charge of only 3/4 of 1 percent. This compares very favorably with the loans of the World Bank itself, which are at the time of writing this study for 20 to 25 years including grace periods of about 5 years at an interest rate of about $8^1/_2$ percent. In conclusion, it seems to us that if a developing country encounters balance of payments difficulties, this certainly cannot be attributed to the policies of the international lending institutions. On the contrary, without their assistance the developing countries would be in a much worse situation than they are at present.

6.4. MACRO-ECONOMIC IMBALANCES

We have so far assumed that neither cyclical unemployment nor balance of payments problems exist; but in the real world these conditions will not always be fulfilled. The issue which we will discuss briefly in this section is the type of stabilization policies Governments should follow to counteract such disturbances and, as a corollary, whether the project evaluation criteria so far discussed should be amended to take account of macro-economic imbalances and movements towards balance resulting from Government stabilization policies.

Since Keynes's General Theory, it is widely accepted that in order to move towards a situation of full employment without inflation or, as it is normally termed a situation of internal balance, appropriate expenditure policies may be used to correct, through the income multiplier mechanism, situations of underemployment or overemployment. More controversial still is the question of the appropriate instruments for attaining a situation of external balance, i.e., a situation where the gap between the autonomous demand and supply of foreign exchange on account of imports and exports of goods and services can be counted on to be covered by autonomous capital inflows. The literature distinguishes two approaches to balance of payments problems – elasticities and expenditure – and we will review these briefly.

The elasticities approach has been described in a seminal paper by JOAN ROBINSON.[21] She showed that the effect of a devaluation (or revaluation) on the balance of payments depends on the domestic and foreign elasticities of demand and supply for import and export goods and services. While JOAN ROBINSON presented her analysis in terms of domestic currency, it is more in line with our discussion of the opportunity cost of foreign exchange in Chapter 3 to present the analysis in terms of foreign currency, and we will therefore express the exchange rate in terms of units of local currency per unit of foreign exchange (say, Rupees per US dollar). We can then derive the relevant elasticity relationships as follows As demonstrated in Figure 6.4, a devaluation will improve the balance of payments if the slope of the supply curve of foreign exchange has a higher absolute value than the slope of the demand curve of foreign exchange. In Figure 6.4, the supply curve is negatively inclined but its slope is steeper than the slope of the demand curve, and a devaluation from R_1 to R_2 thus reduces the balance of payments gap by AB minus CE.

The stability condition can be expressed algebraically. Denoting the amount of foreign exchange supplied by X_f, the amount of foreign exchange demanded by M_f, and the exchange rate by R, a devaluation will improve the balance of

FIGURE 6.4.

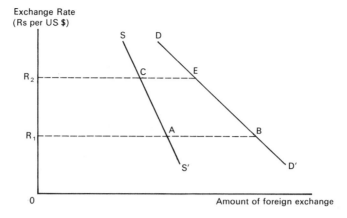

payments if:

$$\frac{dB}{dR} = \frac{-dX_f}{dR} - \frac{-dM_f}{dR}$$

is positive. This expression may be expanded as follows:

$$\frac{dB}{dR} = \frac{-dX_f}{dR} \cdot \frac{R}{X_f} \cdot \frac{X_f}{R} - \frac{-dM_f}{dR} \cdot \frac{R}{M_f} \cdot \frac{M_f}{R}$$

and may thus be written as:

$$dB = (X_f \, \varepsilon_f + M_f \, \eta_f) \, \frac{dR}{R}$$

where ε_f is the elasticity of supply of foreign exchange with respect to the exchange rate, and η_f the elasticity of demand for foreign exchange with respect to the exchange rate.[22]

Using the following elasticity definitions on the export side:

η_x = elasticity of foreign demand for export goods with respect to price in terms of foreign currency (P_x)

ε_x = elasticity of domestic supply of export goods with respect to price in terms of domestic currency $(P_x \cdot R)$,

and the following on the import side:

ε_m = elasticity of foreign supply of import goods with respect to price in terms of foreign currency (P_m)

η_m = elasticity of home demand for import goods with respect to price in terms of domestic currency $(P_m \cdot R)$

we may write the above expression as:[23]

139

$$(6.1) \quad dB = \left\{ X_f \frac{\varepsilon_x (\eta_x - 1)}{\varepsilon_x + \eta_x} + M_f \cdot \frac{\eta_m (\varepsilon_m + 1)}{\eta_m + \varepsilon_m} \right\} \frac{dR}{R}$$

Equation 6.1 is extremely valuable. As regards imports, it shows that a devaluation will always reduce the amount of foreign exchange demanded, except where the elasticity of home demand for imports (η_m) is zero, which is not to be expected. With respect to exports, a devaluation will not increase the amount of foreign exchange supplied if the elasticity of the domestic supply of export goods (ε_x) is zero but, again, this is not a realistic assumption. Accepting that the elasticity of export supply is positive, Equation 6.1 shows that a devaluation will increase, leave unchanged, or decrease the amount of foreign exchange supplied, depending on whether the elasticity of foreign demand (η_x) is greater than unity, unity, or smaller than unity, respectively. This is interesting to know but not very helpful for operational decision-making and the question thus arises of what will normally be the case. It is easy to show that the elasticity of foreign demand for a country's exports of a certain commodity is a function of the elasticities of world demand and supply[24]. For manufactures, both elasticities may be taken as substantially greater than unity, and a devaluation will thus certainly increase foreign demand. As regards primary products, world demand is generally relatively inelastic. However, provided that the country in question is not the sole producer of the commodity, the foreign demand the country faces will always be more elastic than world demand. This is logical because if only the country in question devalues while other countries do not, the country's export demand will increase by the increase in world demand as well as by the decrease in production of competing suppliers. It is generally accepted that even for primary products, export demand is greater than unity, and it may thus be concluded that according to the elasticities analysis, a devaluation will always improve the balance of payments, the degree of inprovement being determined by the values of the elasticities in formula 6.1.

It remains to be discussed what order of magnitude the elasticities normally assume. In this respect, we define normal as a situation of full employment where the Government follows appropriate policies to prevent inflation, i.e., a situation of internal balance. Furthermore, we will assume, as for instance is assumed in the BALASSA et al. study[25], that there are no quantitative trade restrictions. Otherwise, because the elasticities depend on the degree of trade restriction, a meaningful discussion of the normal values of the elasticities would not be possible.

Most developing countries are price takers on the import side, so that the elasticity of the foreign supply of import goods (ε_m) may then be set at infinity. As formula 6.1 shows, the elasticity of demand for foreign exchange (η_f) is then equal to the elasticity of import demand (η_m). The elasticity of import demand is determined by the elasticity of domestic demand and supply[26] and will be larger the more import-competing products the country produces, and smaller the smaller the share of the import goods in relation to total domestic

TABLE 6.4. Import and export elasticities according to Balassa et al.

	Elasticity of Demand for Foreign Exchange (= Elasticity of Demand for Imports)	Elasticity of Supply of Exports	Elasticity of Foreign Demand for Exports	Elasticity of Supply of Foreign Exchange
	$\eta_f = \eta_m$	ε_x	η_x	ε_f
Brazil (Appendix C)	1.5	5	7–13	2.5–3.3
Chile (pp. 164–165)	3	3	5	1.5
Mexico (pp. 197–198)	3	3	10	2.08
Malaysia (p. 218)	3–5	1–4	5–10	0.67–2.57
Pakistan (p. 253)	1–3	2–4	5	1.14–1.78
Philippines (p. 281)	4	3–5	16–20	2.37–3.8
Norway (pp. 309–310)	1.6	6	8	3

supply and demand. In the study of BALASSA et al., which analyzed inter alia the rates of protection in seven countries, η_m varied from 1 to 5, the lowest values being assumed to apply to countries that have difficulty in producing import-competing products. A summary of the assumed values of η_m is presented in Table 6.4.

Regarding exports, it may be assumed as regards the smaller developing countries that the elasticity of foreign demand for their exports (η_x) is infinite, so that the elasticity of supply of foreign exchange (ε_f) is equal to the elasticity of supply of exports (ε_x). The export supply elasticity (ε_x) depends on the elasticities of domestic supply and demand[27] and will be larger the smaller the export share is in relation to domestic supply and demand. In general, we may therefore expect that the export supply elasticity will be larger for manufactures than for primary products, the more so because a shift of resources to the production of manufactures will usually lead more easily and faster to an increase in production than if the resources were directed to the production of primary products. Nevertheless, the long-run supply elasticity of primary products will probably be well above unity. In general, the overall export supply elasticity in the case of a mixture of manufactures and primary product exports may be assumed to be at least 2.

As regards the larger developing countries or those that account for a substantial part of the world production of a certain commodity, increased exports may tend to lower the export price. It is then necessary to estimate the elasticity of foreign demand (η_x) in addition to the elasticity of export supply (ε_x) in order to calculate the elasticity of supply of foreign exchange (ε_f). The more a country's exports are concentrated in a few commodities, the lower will be the elasticity of export demand. In the BALASSA et al. study, for instance, the export demand elasticity is estimated at 5 for Pakistan, the bulk of whose exports consisted of jute and raw cotton, and at 20 for the Philippines, whose exports were quite diversified. Combining export supply elasticities of 2 to 5 with export

141

demand elasticities of 5 to 20, the elasticities of supply of foreign exchange will vary from 1.14 to 3.8.

Table 6.4 recapitulates the estimates of BALASSA et al. regarding the demand and supply elasticities in the seven countries they studied. Taking the midpoint of the elasticities where a range was estimated, it may be seen that for five countries the elasticity of demand for foreign exchange was higher than the elasticity of supply of foreign exchange, while for two countries the reverse was true. In all cases, however, the sum of the demand and supply elasticities is significantly greater than 1, so that a devaluation would substantially improve the balance of payments.

The elasticities analysis has important operational value. As discussed in Chapter 3, it enables us to calculate the opportunity cost of foreign exchange; as discussed in this section, it enables us to calculate the effect of a devaluation on the balance of payments. The following simplified example illustrates the case for a price taker. If M_f = US\$600 million per annum, X_f = US\$400 million per annum, η_m = 2, ε_x = 4 and internal balance is maintained, the effect of a 5 percent devaluation will be to reduce import payments by US\$60 million and to increase export earnings by US\$80 million, so that the gap between export and import values will be closed by US\$140 million. It should be noted, however, that the values of the elasticities are not invariant with respect to economic conditions. For instance, during periods of depression, the export supply elasticity will be higher and the import demand elasticity lower than during periods of full employment. In an already classic article,[28] ALEXANDER has argued that because the values of the elasticities depend on the behaviour of the whole economic system, it would be more fruitful to analyze the system directly by concentrating on the relationship of real expenditures to real incomes and on the relationship of both of these to price levels. It is to this subject that we will now address ourselves.

The starting point of ALEXANDER's analysis is that the national product equation may be written as $(X - M) = Y - (C + I)$, where all variables are expressed in domestic currency and X is value of exports, M value of imports, Y national product, C consumption and I investment.[29] Denoting the external balance $(X - M)$ by B and the domestic expenditure[30] on consumption and investment goods $(C + I)$, which includes imported goods, by E, the equation may be written as $B = Y - E$. Differentiating, we obtain $dB = dY - dE$ or, in words, the change in the external balance equals the difference between the change in national product and the change in domestic expenditures. As part of domestic expenditures depends on real income (= national product) while the remainder depends on other factors, we may write $E = c \cdot Y + E_o$, where c is the marginal propensity to spend on consumption and investment goods and E_o the non-income related part of expenditures. Differentiating, we obtain $dE = c\,dY + dE_o$. Combining this with the identity function, we may write: $dB = (dY - c\,dY) - dE_o$.

When resources are idle, a devaluation will lead through the foreign trade multiplier to a substantial increase in national production. This will improve

142

the external balance, provided that the marginal propensity to spend c is less than unity – i.e., saving takes place – and provided that the direct effects of the devaluation on expenditures (E_o) are not of opposite sign. As regards the marginal propensity to spend, ALEXANDER seemed initially to believe that it could be greater than unity, but this assumption has not been substantiated empirically. As regards the direct effects (cash balance, redistribution of incomes, money illusion effects, and the like), these are mainly transitory and not very large and it can thus be expected that in situations of underemployment, a devaluation will increase national income as well as the external balance. However, under conditions of full employment, a devaluation cannot, according to ALEXANDER, lead to an increase in production, as all resources are fully employed. Because the effects of the devaluation on E are negligible, a devaluation will not improve the balance of payments unless expenditures are reduced. In ALEXANDER's view under conditions of full employment the only way to improve the balance of payments is to reduce domestic expenditures.

The conclusion of ALEXANDER's expenditure analysis as regards the effect of a devaluation on the balance of payments in situations of full employment is thus completely contrary to the conclusion of the elasticities analysis. The contradiction is, however, not a real one. It is entirely correct that a deficit in the balance of payments is caused by the excess of real expenditures over real production and, at first sight, it may indeed appear that the only way to improve the balance of payments in situations of full employment is to reduce real expenditures. However this argumentation does not acknowledge that devaluations have substantial resource reallocation effects.

In the elasticities approach, it is assumed that internal balance is maintained, or, in other words, that no inflation and no reductions in real income should be allowed to occur. Thus, in situations of full employment, the increase in money incomes resulting from the improvement in the balance of payments due to the devaluation should be negated by a reduction in the money supply, so that money expenditures remain constant. In these circumstances, real expenditures will decrease because the devaluation increases the prices, in terms of domestic currency, of the internationally tradeable goods (i.e., imports and exports) relative to those of home goods and therewith the overall price level. At the same time, on the production side resources will be diverted from the production of home goods to tradeables as the latter have become more profitable. The end result of the process is therefore that, while real expenditures are brought into line with real production, the balance of payments will improve.

ALEXANDER's expenditure analysis overlooks the fact that an external deficit is caused not only by an excess of expenditure over income but also by an excess in production of home goods. The elasticities theory as well as the expenditure theory are necessary to explain why in actual fact devaluations will indeed improve the balance of payments in situations of full employment. The task at hand now is to synthesize the two approaches. ALEXANDER himself suggested at a later date such a synthesis, but his approach is rather formal and incorporates foreign repercussions.[31] For our purposes, a model without foreign repercussions suffices. We may draw up a simple model by assuming that parts of imports and consumption are functions of real income, and that the remaining parts as well as exports and investments are autonomously determined. We then have the following relationships, whereby it should be noted that all variables are expressed in real terms:

$$dM = m \cdot dY + dM_o$$
$$dC = c \cdot dY + dC_0 \text{ and}$$
$$dB = dX_o - dM = dY - d(C + I_o)$$

where m and c are the marginal propensities to import and to consume, respectively, and the subscript o indicates that the variables are autonomously determined. It follows that

$$dX_o - dM_o - m \cdot dY = dY - c \cdot dY - dC_o - dI_o$$

so that

$$dY = [1/(s + m)](dX_o - dM_o + dC_o + dI_o)$$

where the marginal savings propensity $s = 1 - c$. This expression is, of course, the well known trade multiplier. Since $dB = dX_o - dM_o - m\,dY$, we obtain

$$dB = dX_o - dM_o - [m/(s + m)](dX_o - dM_o + dC_o + dI_o)$$

which may be written as:

$$dB = [s/(s + m)](dX_o - dM_o) - [m/(s + m)](dC_o + dI_o)$$

In this formula, $dX_o - dM_o$ can be considered to represent the effect of a devaluation on the balance of payments when real incomes are being held constant. The value of $dX_o - dM_o$ can thus be found from formula 6.1 where the elasticities are assumed to be calculated under this assumption. As formula 6.1 gives the change in the balance of payments in terms of foreign currency, it will be necessary to convert the change into domestic currency by multiplying it with the new exchange rate. Denoting this change by dB_h, the change in the autonomous expenditures by dE_o and the total change in the balance of payments, including the reversal effects due to changes in income, by dB_t, we may write:

$$(6.2) \quad dB_t = \frac{s}{s + m} \cdot dB_h - \frac{m}{s + m} \cdot dE_o$$

This formula includes the effects of a devaluation as well as a change in expenditures. As an illustration, we will use it to analyze for two cases of imbalance how overall balance can be obtained. For the first case, let us assume that there is full employment but, at the same time, a deficit in the external account. If the Government devalues without a compensating expenditure reduction, the increase in money incomes of dB_h does not increase real income

144

but increases prices of home goods or imports. Thus no extra savings will be generated and s will be zero. As formula 6.2 shows, there will then be no change at all in B_t, i.e., the balance of payments does not improve. However, if autonomous expenditures are reduced by dB_h, or in, other words, if the increase in money incomes due to the devaluation of dB_h is mopped up, the balance of payments improves by $dB_h \cdot s/(s + m) + dB_h \cdot m/(s + m) = dB_h$ and the change in the balance of payments is then determined by the elasticity formula. It is the resource reallocation effect of the devaluation which ensures that the balance of payments improves.

For the second case, we assume a situation of underemployment and external deficit. In such a situation, the initial effect of a devaluation is that a surplus of dB_h arises in the balance of payments. If the Government follows appropriate policies, it will ensure that money supply is elastic so that real income ($=$ real production) increases by $dB_h/(s + m)$ and the balance of payments by $dB_h \cdot s/(s + m)$. Our function assumes that there are no other effects on the balance of payments. Very probably, however, the elasticities of supply and demand of home goods, exports and imports will be affected because the increase in real income may, for instance, increase the price of home goods further and therewith further curtail imports. As it is extremely difficult to take account of these secondary effects, we will assume that they can be neglected. In practice this means that formula 6.2 provides us with an underestimate of the effects of a devaluation on the balance of payments in a situation of underemployment, which is perhaps just as well. Assuming then that the rise in real incomes is $dB_h/(s + m)$, imports wil increase by $m \cdot dB_h/(s + m)$. The total effect on the balance of payments is therefore $dB_h - m \cdot dB_h/(s + m) = dB_h \cdot s/(s + m)$. The devaluation thus increases real incomes as well as the balance of payments but, in general, it cannot be expected that it would result in the simultaneous attainment of external and internal balance. Suppose that external balance has been attained but that there is still underemployment. Increasing autonomous domestic expenditure by dE_o will then increase real income but at the same time lead to a deterioration in the balance of payments of $m \cdot dE_o/(s + m)$. A further devaluation will be necessary to obtain external balance again plus further increases in expenditures to obtain internal balance if resources are still underemployed, and so on. Both instruments should be used to obtain overall balance, and one should try to achieve it at once without resort to miniadjustments.

A devaluation affects the balance of payments as well as national income; expenditure-changing policies have similar effects. In a pathbreaking article, SWAN[32] has shown how the attainment of external and internal balance necessitates in general the use of both policy instruments. SWAN uses a diagram in which he shows on the vertical axis a cost ratio indicating the competitiveness of Australian industries versus imports and exports, and on the horizontal axis real expenditures. Without changing the substance of SWAN's analysis, we will show in Figure 6.5, in line with our formula 6.2, the exchange rate expressed in terms of local currency units per unit of foreign exchange

145

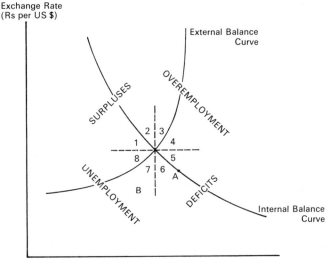

FIGURE 6.5.

Exchange Rate
(Rs per US $)

Autonomous Real Expenditures

(Rupees per US dollar) on the vertical axis and autonomous real expenditures on the horizontal axis. A devaluation is represented by an upward movement along the vertical axis and an increase in autonomous expenditures by a movement to the right along the horizontal axis. The essence of SWAN's analysis is presented by the curves of internal and external balance. Both curves show that various combinations of exchange rates and autonomous expenditures are possible to keep the economy in internal or external balance. The internal balance curve is downward sloping because the lower the exchange rate (Rs per US$) which limits exports, the higher autonomous expenditures must be to stimulate the economy to a position of full employment. The external balance curve, however, is upward sloping because if the exchange rate is increased, autonomous expenditures should be increased in order to prevent the appearance of surpluses. Noteworthy is the fact that the external balance curve turns steeply upwards as soon as full employment is reached, because infinite devaluations would at this stage be necessary to offset the adverse effects on the balance of payments of autonomous expenditure increases.

As seen in Figure 6.5, the economy may be in any of the several sectors of the diagram at any moment in time, but there is only one situation where internal as well as external balance exists. To the left of the external balance curve (Sectors 8, 1, 2 and 3), the economy has balance of payments surpluses and to the right (Sectors 7, 6, 5 and 4), deficits. On the other hand, to the left of the internal balance curve (Sectors 1, 8, 7 and 6), there is unemployment and to the right (Sectors 2, 3, 4 and 5), over-employment. The internal and external balance curves divide the diagram up into 4 zones. On the other hand, the policy instruments to be used are determined by the quadrant in which the economy finds itself. In the two western quadrants (Sectors 2, 1, 8 and 7) autonomous

146

expenditures should be increased and in the two eastern quadrants (Sectors 3, 4, 5 and 6) decreased. The production of home goods relative to that of trade-ables is too low in the northern quadrants (Sectors 1, 2, 3 and 4) and a revaluation is indicated; in the southern quadrants (Sectors 8, 7, 6 and 5) the opposite is true and a devaluation should take place. All in all, there are a total of eight sectors, each sector being described by its balance of payments (surpluses or deficits) and employment situation (under- or over-employment) and the two policy instruments to be used (devaluation or revaluation and autonomous expenditure increase or decrease). We have already discussed in detail how internal and external balance can be obtained starting from a full employment-deficit situation (Point A in Figure 6.5), and from an unemployment-deficit situation (Point B) so we will not go into any of the other possible situations. A summary describing each sector is presented in Table 6.5.

We are now finally in a position to show that the project evaluation criteria developed in this study are consistent with the macro-economic framework just described. If this is so, we should find that in each of the possible economic situations, the micro-economic values to be used for project evaluation pur-poses reflect the actual economic situation. In other words, the opportunity costs of foreign exchange, labor and capital and the price of home products versus tradeables should be such that they do not detract from the Government objective of achieving a situation of overall balance. The task at hand is there-fore to review the values of the micro-economic variables in each of the eight sectors of economic imbalance relative to the situation of overall balance.

Following the order of Table 6.5, we may start with the opportunity cost of foreign exchange. As discussed in Chapter 3, this variable is the weighted average of the domestic values of the country's import and export prices, the weights being the fractions in which an additional dollar of foreign exchange will be used for increasing imports and reducing exports. As in Sectors 7, 6, 5 and 4 the economy incurs balance of payments deficits or, in other words, as in these sectors the propensity to import is high, the opportunity cost of foreign exchange will also be high relative to a situation where the balance of payments is in equilibrium. Conversely, the opportunity cost of foreign exchange will be low in situations of surplus as exist in Sectors 8, 1, 2 and 3.

As regards labor, the opportunity cost of labor will be high relative to a situation of full employment in Sectors 2, 3, 4 and 5. The resources in the economy are over-employed; employers are competing for the available man-power and the supply price of labor will be high. In Sectors 1, 8, 7 and 6, how-ever, a downward adjustment relative to a situation of full employment must be made to the opportunity cost of labor because laborers are unemployed. Furthermore, the hiring of unemployed laborers will result in multiplier effects as the increase in their expenditures will lead to the hiring of still more unem-ployed. This external effect can be counted on the benefit side of the project under scrutiny; alternatively, the opportunity cost of labor can be adjusted further downward. However the effect is accounted for, it is clear that the hiring of unemployed laborers has substantial economic benefits.

TABLE 6.5. Values of variables in the different policy sectors.

Policy Sector	1	2	3	4	5	6	7	8
A. *Description of Actual Economic Situation*								
Balance of Payments	Surplus	Surplus	Surplus	Deficit	Deficit	Deficit	Deficit	Surplus
Employment	Under	Over	Over	Over	Over	Under	Under	Under
Expenditure	Insuff.	Insuff.	Excess	Excess	Excess	Excess	Insuff.	Insuff.
Production of Home Goods vs. Production of Tradeables	Too low	Too low	Too low	Too low	Too much	Too much	Too much	Too much
B. *Value of Variables in Project Evaluation*								
Opp. Cost of F.E.	Low	Low	Low	High	High	High	High	Low
Opp. Cost of Labor	Low	High	High	High	High	Low	Low	Low
Opp. Cost of Capital	Low	Low	High	High	High	High	Low	Low
Price of Home Goods vs. Price of Tradeables	Low	Low	Low	Low	High	High	High	High
C. *Expected Government Policies*								
Exchange Rate	–	–	–	–	+	+	+	+
Expenditures	+	+	–	–	–	–	+	+

We come now to the policy measures the Government should use to obtain a situation of overall balance. In Sectors 3, 4, 5 and 6, investments are at too high a level relative to the situation of overall balance. Expenditures will exceed the funds normally available and the Government should then use a budget constraint interest rate or a ratio of present value per dollar of investment to defer projects with low priority. In Sectors 2, 1, 8 and 7, on the other hand, the Government may wish to use a cut-off rate somewhat lower than the normal opportunity cost of capital rate to promote investments.

As regards the exchange rate, the Government should revalue in Sectors 1, 2, 3 and 4. In terms of benefit-cost analysis, this means that the price of home goods versus the price of tradeables is too low, and that it should be increased by a revaluation. The opposite holds true in Sectors 8, 7, 6 and 5; the price of home goods versus the price of tradeables is too high, and a devaluation should take place to reduce this price ratio.

Having determined the values of the various variables to be used in benefit-cost analysis, it is not difficult to see how they will promote or deter investments. For instance, let us assume that we are at position B in Sector 7 in Figure 6.5. As tabulated in Table 6.5, there are then balance of payments deficits and unemployment while, at the same time, expenditures are insufficient and too many home goods are being produced. As the actual price of home goods is too high, a devaluation should take place and it can thus be expected that the relative price of home goods will decline, making projects producing home goods unattractive and projects producing tradeables attractive. On the other hand, as the opportunity costs of capital and labor are low compared with those in subsequent periods and the opportunity cost of foreign exchange high compared with those in subsequent periods, there will be every incentive to promote investments and to choose labor-intensive projects which will produce tradeables. The projects that will be accepted under our benefit-cost evaluation criteria are thus in line with the Government's overall objective. This will, of course, hold true in each of the eight sectors. In general, we may express it in this way: that the shadow prices of capital, labor and foreign exchange are such that each time, not only will the right amount of investment be promoted, but also the right type of investment in terms of type of resources used and type of benefits produced.

We have so far assumed that the Government obtains overall balance through exchange rate and expenditure changing measures. It is also possible, of course, that quantitative trade restrictions will be used in conjunction with expenditure changes. Suppose, for instance, that in the previous example, the Government were to restrict the imports of certain goods in order to improve its balance of payments. Then the domestic prices of these goods would rise and hence also the opportunity cost of foreign exchange. As was briefly mentioned in Chapter 3, the value of the imports in the opportunity cost of foreign exchange formula is found in such cases by comparing the domestic prices of the restricted goods with their world prices valued at the official exchange rate. Thus, in principle, quantitative trade restrictions should not create any undue difficulty in the benefit-cost analysis.

Divergences from the overall balance situation are quite common. However, as these divergences are usually short-term fluctuations of one or two years around the normal situation and, moreover, as it is difficult to estimate the required adjustments, one may question whether it is worth the trouble to revise the normal values of the project variables. On the other hand, it is only by taking account of the changed circumstances that one can ensure that the right type of investment will be undertaken. It seems to us that a practical approach is necessary. In this respect it is important to remember that the initial few years of a project are the ones during which construction takes place, while the later years, representing the longest part of a project's life, are the ones during which most of the benefits are produced. As the divergences from the optimum situation are usually short-term in nature, it is mainly the investment value of a project that will be affected by the adjustments and not the benefit value. Furthermore, because it will be difficult to change the construction method from one year to another or to stop an ongoing project, it will be mainly the projects with short construction periods that will be affected by the changed circumstances. We would suggest, therefore, that, in general, project evaluation should take place on the basis of the normal values, but that in periods of divergence from the norm special attention should be paid to projects with short construction periods. The investment values of such projects should be revised to take account of the changed values of the shadow prices of labor and foreign exchange, and comparison of the revised rates of return with the adjusted cut-off rate will then ensure that the right type of investment is promoted or deterred. Following this procedure, labor-intensive public works projects will be important instruments with which to combat unemployment in periods of depression.

Finally, we would like to turn to another type of imbalance, one, which in present day circumstances especially, seems to be all-pervasive, but which we have ignored in our discussions so far by expressing all variables in real terms. The imbalance is, of course, inflation and we will now discuss how one should take account of this factor. The effects of inflation on benefits and costs can be complicated, since prices do not normally increase at the same rate. Relative prices may change substantially, and the benefits and costs of a project may differ substantially from what they would be if there were no inflation. The task of the project evaluator is, therefore, to not only estimate the general rate of inflation but also the specific rates of inflation of the project's various inputs and outputs. Suppose that he has done so; how should he then proceed?

There are, theoretically, two methods possible for taking the various inflation rates into account. The first is to calculate the values of benefits and costs in current terms, i.e., in prices of each period, and to discount at the inflation adjusted discount rate. The second is to evaluate all benefits and costs in real terms and to discount at the unadjusted discount rate.

The two methods are identical, as may be seen from the following. Suppose that all prices increase at the same rate f. Then the benefit-cost criterion will be

$$\sum \frac{B_t\,(1+f)^t}{(1+d)^t\,(1+f)^t} - \sum \frac{C_t\,(1+f)^t}{(1+d)^t\,(1+f)^t} \geq 0$$

where d is the cutoff discount rate. Since the factor $(1+f)$ drops out of the formula, it can be seen immediately that we have here the normal benefit cost formula. Suppose now that while the general inflation rate is f, the prices of B increase at the rate f_1 and the prices of C at the rate f_2. Then our formula becomes:

$$\sum \frac{B_t\,(1+f_1)^t}{(1+d)^t\,(1+f)^t} - \sum \frac{C_t\,(1+f_2)^t}{(1+d)^t\,(1+f)^t} \geq 0$$

which corresponds to the first method. Alternatively, the formula may be written as:

$$\sum \frac{B_t\dfrac{(1+f_1)^t}{(1+f)^t}}{(1+d)^t} - \sum \frac{C_t\dfrac{(1+f_2)^t}{(1+f)^t}}{(1+d)^t} \geq 0$$

which is the second method. Under both methods then, the underlying principle is to deflate the prices in each successive period by the general inflation rate. Or, in other words, the prices must be expressed in real terms, i.e., in terms of the purchasing power of the national currency unit, say, the Rupee, as it is in the base year. Thus, for instance, if the price of a certain project input or output is expected to increase at the rate of 9 percent per annum while the domestic inflation rate is only 5 percent per annun, then the real price of this item increases by 4 percent per annum.

An additional complication might seem to arise when project inputs or outputs are imported or exported and the domestic inflation rate differs from the rate of inflation of the country's trading partners. To the extent that such a differential is continuously offset by exchange rate adjustments, the ratio between domestic prices and foreign prices will not change and the project evaluator does not need to make any adjustment to the base prices. For instance, suppose that the domestic inflation rate is 5 percent per annum. Then, when the prices in foreign currency of the inputs procured from abroad or of the outputs exported increase at the rate of 2 percent per annum, the real prices of these foreign items will remain constant if the domestic currency depreciates at the rate of 3 percent per annum. Suppose, however, that it is expected that the country will not devalue its currency. We may assume then that the opportunity cost of foreign exchange will increase at the rate of 3 percent per annum, so that here also no adjustments need to be made to the base prices.

As a practical rule, we would suggest that it may be assumed that grosso modo the exchange rate or the opportunity cost of foreign exchange will tend to equalize the differential between the domestic and foreign inflation. Furthermore, as regards the specific rate of inflation of a particular input or output-only significant variances from the general rate of inflation should be considered. Where the project evaluator is at a loss as to the likely change in real prices, sensitivity tests should be applied to provide a likely range of the rates of return.

We have now come to the end of this part of the study. We have reviewed the project planning rules when income distribution does not count. However, it often does count and it is time to consider how the normal benefit-cost criteria should be amended. It is to this task that Part II of the study is devoted.

[1] SCITOVSKY, T., 'Two Concepts of External Economies,' Journal of Political Economy 17 (1954) pp. 143–51. Reprinted in 'Readings in Welfare Economics,' published for the American Economic Association by Richard D. Irwin, Inc., Homewood, Illinois, 1969.

[2] It may be noted that the total benefit is again presented in algebraic form by the familiar formula $\triangle C$ $(Q + {}^1\!/_2 \triangle Q)$, where $\triangle C$ is the unit cost reduction.

[3] LITTLE and MIRRLEES, 'Manual,' p. 218.

[4] PIGOU, A. C., 'The Economics of Welfare,' 4th ed., Macmillan and Co., Ltd., London, 1952.

[5] BUCHANAN, J. H., 'External Diseconomies, Corrective Taxes, and Market Structure,' The American Economic Review, March 1969.

[6] BATOR, F. M., 'The Anatomy of Market Failure,' The Quarterly Journal of Economics, August 1958.

[7] COASE, R. H., 'The Problem of Social Cost,' Journal of Law and Economics, October 1960.

[8] BAUMOL, W. J. and OATES, W. E., 'The Theory of Environmental Policy,' Prentice-Hall, Inc., Englewood Cliffs, New Jersey, 1975.

[9] It may be mentioned that, in our opinion, the argument of BAUMOL and OATES rests upon the assumption that the person who tries to escape the externality does not incur any costs. If there are such costs, then it seems to us that a compensatory payment would be quite justified. This remark does not detract, however, from the main line of the argument.

[10] MISHAN, E. J., 'Cost-Benefit Analysis,' 2nd ed., George Allen & Unwin Ltd., London, 1975, p. 117.

[11] According to BAUMOL and OATES, this paradoxical result was discovered independently of each other by WEITZMAN, M. ('Free Access vs. Private Ownership as Alternative Systems for Managing Common Property' – Working Draft, April 12, 1972) and REINHARDT, U. ('Efficiency Tolls and the Problem of Equity' – Working Draft, 1973).

[12] WEISBROD, B. A., 'The Valuation of Human Capital,' Journal of Political Economy, Vol. 69, 1961, pp. 425–36.

[13] MISHAN, 'Cost-Benefit Analysis,' 2nd revised new ed., pp. 290–320.

[14] For instance, some economists in the Netherlands believe that if the huge influx of low-wage migrant workers of the last decade or so had not taken place more in-depth investment would have occurred and, consequently, the country would have been in a better economic position than it is in now.

[15] For a detailed discussion, see HAWKINS, E. K., 'The Principles of Development Aid,' Penguin Books, 1970, Chapter 2.

[16] ZEYLSTRA, W. G., 'Aid or Development: The Relevance of Development Aid to the Problems of Developing Countries,' A. W. Sijthoff, Leyden, 1975, p. 161.

[17] LINDER, S. B., 'Trade and Trade Policy for Development,' Frederick A. Praeger Publishers, New York, Washington, London, 1967.

[18] LINDER, 'Trade and Trade Policy for Development,' p. 115.

[19] HARBERGER, A. C., 'Some Evidence on the International Price Mechanism,' Journal of Political Economy, Vol. 56, 1957. Reprinted in 'International Finance – Selected Readings,' ed. Cooper, R. N., Penguin Books, 1969.

[20] WOLFSON, D. G., 'Fiscal Policy and Development Strategy,' Thesis, University of Amsterdam, 1974.

[21] ROBINSON, J., 'The Foreign Exchanges' in 'Essays in the Theory of Employment,' 2nd ed., Basil Blackwell, Oxford, 1947, Part III, Chapter 1. Reprinted in 'Readings in the Theory of International Trade,' published for the American Economic Association by George Allen and Unwin Ltd. London, 1950.

[22] It should be noted that, as is the custom in balance of payments theory, the elasticities are expressed as positive numbers.

[23] The easiest way to show this is by expressing all elasticities in logarithmic form. Denoting physical exports by X_x, we have on the export side:

a) $$\eta_x = -\frac{dX_x}{dP_x} \cdot \frac{P_x}{X_x} = -\frac{d \log X_x}{d \log P_x}$$

b) $$\varepsilon_x = \frac{dX_x}{d(P_x \cdot R)} \cdot \frac{P_x R}{X_x} = \frac{d \log X_x}{d \log P_x + d \log R}$$

c) $$\varepsilon_f = \frac{d(X_x P_x)}{dR} \cdot \frac{R}{X_x P_x} = \frac{d \log X_x + d \log P_x}{d \log R}$$

Multiplying (c) by X_f and substituting into (c) the value of d log R from (b) and the value of d log X_x from (a), we obtain the first term of 6.1. Denoting physical imports by M_m, we have on the import side:

d) $$\varepsilon_m = \frac{dM_m}{dP_m} \cdot \frac{P_m}{M_m} = \frac{d \log M_m}{d \log P_m}$$

e) $$\eta_m = -\frac{dM_m}{d(P_m \cdot R)} \cdot \frac{P_m R}{M} = -\frac{d \log M_m}{d \log P_m + d \log R}$$

f) $$\eta_f = -\frac{d(M_m \cdot P_m)}{dR} \cdot \frac{R}{M_m P_m} = -\frac{d \log M_m + d \log P_m}{d \log R}$$

Multiplying (f) by M_f and substituting into (f) the value of d log R from (e) and the value of d log M_m from (d), we obtain the second term of 6.1.

[24] Denoting world demand for the export commodity by W, supply of the rest of the world by S, the price of the commodity by P_x, the exports of our country by X_x, and remembering that $W - S = X_x$, we may write:

$$\eta_x = -\frac{dX_x}{dP_x} \cdot \frac{P_x}{X_x} = -\frac{d(W - S)}{dP_x} \cdot \frac{P_x}{X_x}$$

$$= -\frac{dW}{dP_x} \cdot \frac{P_x}{\frac{X_x}{W} \cdot W} + \frac{dS}{dP_x} \cdot \frac{P_x}{\frac{X_x}{S} \cdot S}$$

$$= \frac{W}{X_x} \cdot \eta_{xw} + \frac{W - X_x}{X_x} \cdot \varepsilon_{xw}$$

where η_{xw} is the elasticity of world demand, and ε_{xw} the elasticity of supply of the rest of the world.

[25] BALASSA, B. and Associates, 'The Structure of Protection in Developing Countries.

[26] Denoting total domestic demand for the commodity by D, domestic supply by S, the price of the commodity by $P_m R$, imports by M_m, and remembering that $D - S = M_m$, we may write:

$$\eta_m = -\frac{\mathrm{d}M_m}{\mathrm{d}(P_mR)}\cdot\frac{(P_mR)}{M_m} = -\frac{\mathrm{d}(D-S)}{\mathrm{d}(P_mR)}\cdot\frac{(P_mR)}{M_m}$$

$$= -\frac{\mathrm{d}D}{\mathrm{d}(P_mR)}\cdot\frac{(P_mR)}{\dfrac{M_m}{D}\cdot D} + \frac{\mathrm{d}S}{\mathrm{d}(P_mR)}\cdot\frac{(P_mR)}{\dfrac{M_m}{S}\cdot S}$$

$$= \frac{D}{M_m}\cdot\eta_d + \frac{S}{M_m}\cdot\varepsilon_s$$

where η_d is the elasticity of domestic demand and ε_s the elasticity of domestic supply.

[27] Denoting domestic demand for the export commodity by D_x, domestic supply by S_x, the price of the commodity by P_xR, the exports by X_x, and remembering that $S_x - D_x = X_x$, we may write:

$$\varepsilon_x = \frac{\mathrm{d}X_x}{\mathrm{d}(P_xR)}\cdot\frac{(P_xR)}{X_x} = \frac{\mathrm{d}(S_x-D_x)}{\mathrm{d}(P_xR)}\cdot\frac{(P_xR)}{X_x}$$

$$= \frac{\mathrm{d}S_x}{\mathrm{d}(P_xR)}\cdot\frac{(P_xR)}{\dfrac{X_x}{S_x}\cdot S_x} - \frac{\mathrm{d}D_x}{\mathrm{d}P_x}\cdot\frac{(P_xR)}{\dfrac{X_x}{D_x}\cdot D_x}$$

$$= \frac{S_x}{X_x}\cdot\varepsilon_{xd} + \frac{D_x}{X_x}\cdot\eta_{xd}$$

where ε_{xd} is the elasticity of domestic supply and η_{xd} the elasticity of domestic demand.

[28] ALEXANDER, S. S., 'Effects of a Devaluation on a Trade Balance,' IMF Staff Papers, April 1952; reprinted in 'Readings in International Economics,' published for the American Economic Association by Richard D. Irwin, Inc., Homewood, Illinois, 1968.

[29] Following ALEXANDER, we ignore any factors affecting the foreign balance of a country other than those connected with trade in goods and services.

[30] ALEXANDER speaks of domestic absorption, i.e., the taking of goods and services off the domestic markets, but the term domestic expenditure has since then become more popular.

[31] ALEXANDER, S. S., 'Effects of a Devaluation – A Simplified Synthesis of Elasticities and Absorption Approaches,' The American Economic Review, March 1959.

[32] SWAN, T. W., 'Longer-Run Problems of the Balance of Payments.' Paper presented to Section G of the Congress of the Australian and New Zealand Association for the Advancement of Science, Melbourne, 1955. Published in 'The Australian Economy – A Volume of Readings,' eds. Arndt, H. W. and Corder, M. W., Cheshire Press, Melbourne 1963. Reprinted in 'Readings in International Economics,' published for the American Economic Association by Richard D. Irwin Inc., Homewood, Illinois, 1968.

PART II

INCOME DISTRIBUTION ASPECTS

7. SOCIAL WELFARE AND BENEFIT-COST ANALYSIS

7.1. COMPENSATION TESTS

In the first part of this study we assumed that the distribution of income in a country was optimal. In many countries, however, the distribution of income is not optimal and projects could then be used towards redressing any such imbalances. In addition, it is also possible that, when the existing income distribution in a country is optimal, projects may cause divergences from the optimum. In our opinion, therefore, if a project has distributive consequences, benefit-cost analysis should take these into account along with economic considerations in determining the priority of projects. To measure distributional effects some weighing of the gains and losses of the different income groups is required and the task at hand, therefore, is to estimate the social value of additions to income at different levels of income, i.e., to determine the social welfare function that expresses such weights.

There is a considerable body of literature that does not accept this premise. Most recently, MISHAN[1] has defended the traditional analysis by linking it to the so-called compensation criterion. Suppose, as the result of a project, the rich become better off by $ 250,000, while the poor will be worse off by $ 150,000. Then, according to the compensation criterion, there would still be a gain of $ 100,000 because the poor can be compensated for their loss. The compensation need not actually take place; the criterion states only that it should be possible. MISHAN agrees that the criterion would be much more appealing if indeed the poor were compensated for their loss, so that one can speak of a true PARETO improvement – i.e., some are made better off, no one is made worse off. In MISHAN's view benefit-cost analysis may, therefore, be accompanied by observations on the resulting income distribution, and even by recommendations, but the analysis itself should not attach different weights to the dollars lost or gained by the different income groups. These weights are, according to MISHAN, too arbitrary. Benefit-cost analysis itself can only show that the gains exceed the losses, no more.

It seems to us that MISHAN fails to address the problem. Merely noting the income effects of a project is not very meaningful. Moreover, often it will not be possible to actually compensate the losers and it may well be that a project should then not be undertaken. In our example, for instance, the social value of the $ 150,000 loss of the poor might be much greater than the social value of the $ 250,000 gain of the rich. Clearly, therefore, if income distribution is important, and he agrees that it is, one should try to measure it. In fact, the long discussion in the economic literature on the so-called compensation tests concluded that statements about income distribution are necessary and that they should be made by referring to a country's social welfare function. Since this point is crucial, it will be useful to review the discussion briefly.

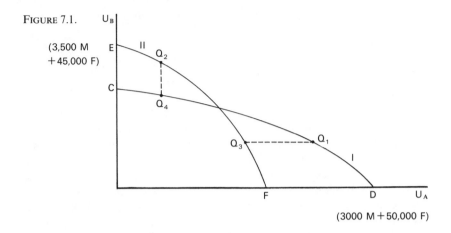

FIGURE 7.1.

(3,500 M + 45,000 F)

(3000 M + 50,000 F)

The debate on the compensation tests was essentially a debate between two schools of thought. One, influenced by ROBBINS's well-known essay[2] on the underlying philosophy of economic science, held that economic analysis should not be based on value judgments, and it was, therefore, logical that this group, including KALDOR,[3] HICKS,[4] and SCITOVSKY,[5] resorted to compensation tests. The other, including perhaps LITTLE,[6] but especially SAMUELSON,[7] felt that judgments about income distribution could and should be made.

Instead of representing all the arguments in their original form, it will be useful to summarize the discussions with the help of a device introduced by SAMUELSON: the utility-possibility curve. Analogous to the production transformation curve between two goods, it is possible to construct utility-possibility curves for two consumers. In Figure 7.1, the axes U_A and U_B represent the ordinal utilities of two consumers A and B on any arbitrary scale. Curves I and II are two utility-possibility curves, each curve representing a point on the production transformation curve, i.e., a possible production combination of two goods. Each point on a utility possibility curve represents a point of highest utility for each of the consumers, given the division of the available commodity package over the two consumers. A's utility can only increase if B's utility decreases. The curves are therefore downward sloping from left to right.

It may be useful to clarify the concept with an example. Suppose that a community consists of two homogeneous groups, A and B, each having its own preference between manufactured products and food. Assume that the community produces annually 3,000 units of manufactures plus 50,000 units of food. Then curve I may represent all the possible ordinal welfare combinations of groups A and B, depending on each one's share in the combination of manufactures and food. Thus, point C is best for Group B since it gets the entire combination, while it is worst for Group A which receives nothing. On the other hand, at point D, the reverse would apply. Along Curve I from C to D, group A receives more manufactures and food and its welfare thus increases, while Group B becomes worse off. Depending on the income of each group, a

160

position may be reached anywhere along Curve I, say, at point Q_1.

Suppose now that the Government feels that the country should strengthen its industrial sector and it, therefore, subsidizes industry and taxes agriculture. This policy would have several consequences. First, more manufactures and less food will be produced; say that the new equilibrium is 3,500 units of manufactures and 45,000 units of food. Second, the change in relative prices of manufactures and food will alter the welfare position of each of the two groups; say that Group B is now better off and Group A worse off than before the change and that the new position is Q_2. Since there is a new production combination, Q_2 must lie on a new utility-possibility curve, which is depicted as II in Figure 7.1. Curve II shows that point E is best for Group B, since it would get all of the 3,500 units of manufactures and 45,000 units of food, while point F, for the same reason, is best for Group A. Since Group B prefers E over C, while Group A prefers D over F, the two curves intersect. Is it now possible to say that Q_2 is better than Q_1 from a welfare point of view? Several criteria have been suggested.

I. PARETO's *Criterion*: An economic change is desirable if at least one person is better off while all the others are no worse off. It is clear that this criterion is very limited; it can tell us only that a new position is better than Q_1, if it is situated in the northeast quadrant with origin at Q_1.

II. KALDOR-HICKS *Criterion*: The change is an improvement if the gainers from the change could compensate the losers for their losses. It is not necessary, according to this criterion, that the compensation actually takes place because it is only the potential gain that is relevant. It will be clear from Figure 7.1 that, after the change from Q_1 to Q_2, the gainer B can only travel from Q_2 to Q_3 if he is not to give up more than he has gained. But at Q_3, loser A is worse off than he was in the initial situation. The Kaldor-Hicks criterion is thus not satisfied and it cannot be said that the new situation is better than the old one. Suppose, however, that the change involved a movement from Q_4 to Q_3. The gainer is now A, who could move to Q_2 to compensate B, so that, clearly, B would be better off while A stayed the same. The criterion would then be satisfied. However, SCITOVSKY has pointed out that this situation is reversible. Suppose Q_3 was the initial situation and Q_4 the final one. Then gainer B could move to Q_1 to compensate loser A, and A would be better off. Hence, Q_4 is better than Q_3, but at the same time Q_3 is better than Q_4. For this reason SCITOVSKY has suggested a different criterion.

III. SCITOVSKY's *Criterion*: The gainer should be able to compensate the loser but, at the same time, the loser should not be able to bribe the gainer to oppose the change. The result of this criterion is that we can only say that a change is good if (a) utility-possibility curve II cuts curve I to the right of Q_1, or (b) curve II lies outside curve I, or (c) Q_2 lies in the quadrant northeast of Q_1. The last possibility is PARETO's criterion and has thus very limited application. What about possibilities a and b? Suppose that the curves cross as depicted in Figure 7.2. Then the gainer after a change from Q_1 to Q_2 is B, who can travel to Q_3 to compensate A (Criterion II satisfied). Before the change takes place,

161

FIGURE 7.2.

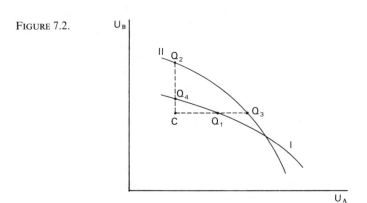

FIGURE 7.3.

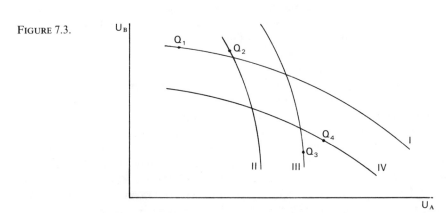

loser A can travel from Q_1 to Q_4 – he is then in the same position as if he were at point Q_2 after the change – and give a bribe $Q_1 C$ to B. But $Q_1 C$ is only worth $Q_4 C$ to B, while the change gives him $Q_2 C$ so that B will not accept the bribe. Criterion III is thus satisfied, and according to SCITOVSKY the change from Q_1 to Q_2 should be accepted. The same analysis applies if curve II lies outside curve I.

However, as GORMAN[8] has pointed out, criterion III may give rise to conflicts. This is shown in Figure 7.3, where four utility-possibility curves representing four bundles of goods and four welfare distribution situations are shown.

Suppose that the changes involve a movement from Q_1 to Q_2 to Q_3 to Q_4. Now Q_2 is better than Q_1 (II cuts I to the right of Q_1) and Q_3 is better than Q_2 (III outside II), and Q_4 better than Q_3 (Q_4 in northeast quadrant of Q_3). Thus one would have thought that Q_4 was better than Q_1, but it is clear from Figure 7.3 that Q_1 is better than Q_4 (I outside IV). Thus the SCITOVSKY criterion is not transitive and cannot be used for decision-making. The objection may be raised that the non-transitivity appears only after several changes and that for a simple decision such as whether to undertake a project, this criterion could still be used. This is, however, not valid, because there is always a whole range of projects about which decisions have to be made.

162

FIGURE 7.4.

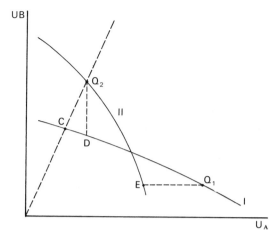

IV. LITTLE's *Criterion.* LITTLE has seen that the difficulty with criteria II and III lies in the comparison which must be made between the distributive aspects of the old and new bundles of goods. Since the first edition of his book, LITTLE has substantially changed his argument due to several criticisms, but it is not worthwhile here to repeat the whole polemic.[9] One of the initial positions which LITTLE took was that even if only the second part of the SCITOVSKY criterion (loser not able to bribe gainer) was taken into account, the change would be an improvement if it also resulted in a better welfare distribution. In Figure 7.4 the change is from Q_1 to Q_2. The broken line from the origin indicates points of equal welfare distribution, so that point C has the same distribution of welfare as point Q_2. Is it possible to arrive at point C by means of a compensation? Obviously not. The SCITOVSKY condition is satisfied: to oppose the change from Q_1 to Q_2, loser A can only move to D. LITTLE, therefore, considers Q_2 better than Q_1.

As KENNEDY[10] has pointed out, one wonders, however, why the SCITOVSKY reverse criterion is necessary. Under the SCITOVSKY criterion, to oppose the change, A can move to point D; LITTLE, however, moves directly to point C. If C is considered better than Q_1, it is evident that Q_2 is better than C on the basis of PARETO's criterion. What LITTLE has done implicitly is to introduce a social welfare function, whereby C represents a point on a higher welfare function than Q_1, and Q_2 a point on a higher welfare function than C.

The inherent difficulty of the compensation tests is that they measure only one thing, whereas there are two things which must be measured. In Figure 7.2, for instance, after the change from Q_1 to Q_2 gainer B can travel to Q_3 and give Q_2C to A. When measured by curve II, this is worth Q_3C to A but when measured by curve I it is worth a different amount. This means that we must give an opinion as to whether the new welfare distribution is better or worse than the old one.

The entire discussion so far has been quite formalistic, and it is now time to rephrase the argumentation. What it all boils down to is that there is ample

163

evidence that income distribution is important and that compensation tests can lead to serious errors. If a group of poor persons is worse off by $ 150,000 while a group of rich persons is better off by $ 250,000, the fact that the poor can be compensated for their loss must be considered completely irrelevant if the poor are in fact not compensated. In such circumstance the only meaningful measure of whether the change is good or bad, is by evaluating the losses and the gains at the appropriate social marginal utilities of income. If compensation payments do take place, losses and gains should be measured after compensation transfers, but still the issue of the social values remains. Suppose, for instance, that after compensation payments a certain project results in a gain of $ 200,000 for the rich while another project results in a gain of $ 100,000 for the poor. Then again we cannot say that the first project is better than the second without referring to a social welfare function. In our opinion, therefore, compensation tests are worse than useless.

7.2. THE CONCEPT OF A SOCIAL WELFARE FUNCTION

Every Government project will result in some redistribution of income because, on the one hand, it curtails either consumption or investment and, on the other hand, it provides benefits either to the Government itself or to individuals. For that matter, any economic change will alter the relative income positions of various groups in the population. As we have seen, even the ingenious compensation tests cannot evaluate a change without referring to a value judgment, i.e., a social welfare function.

The social welfare function was first described by BERGSON,[11] who postulated its existence to determine in a precise form the value judgements required for the derivation of the conditions of maximum economic welfare. BERGSON started his analysis by postulating that, 'Among the elements affecting the welfare of the community during any given period of time are the amounts of each of the factors of production, other than labor, employed in the different production units, the amounts of the various commodities consumed, the amounts of the different kinds of work done, and the production unit for which this work is performed by each individual in the community during that period of time.'[12] For a position of maximum welfare, the first derivative of welfare must equal zero subject to the limitations of the given production techniques and the given resources. It is thus possible to find in general terms the conditions for maximum welfare. Any set of value propositions may be introduced and this will, of course, affect the optimum conditions. However, as BERGSON states, '... in any particular case the selection of one of them must be determined by its compatibility with the values prevailing in the community, the welfare of which is being studied. For only if the welfare principles are based upon prevailing values can they be relevant to the activity of the community in question.'[13]

SAMUELSON[14] has further clarified the concept of the social welfare function with the help of utility possibility curves. In any country there are, of course, a whole range of utility possibility curves corresponding to all the various production possibilities, given the resources. Any single utility possibility curve corresponds to a single point on the country's production possibility curve. If we take all the production possibilities with a given resource basket into account, a whole series of utility possibility curves will be obtained which, for the greater part, will overlap. The outer envelope of this family of schedules may be called the utility possibility frontier. Each point on this frontier represents a PARETO optimum – it is impossible to put an individual on a higher satisfaction level without making someone else worse off – because each point on the frontier is a tangency point with a certain utility possibility curve. But the optimum point from a social welfare point of view can only be found if we know the social welfare function which defines the most desirable distribution of welfare in the economy. Furthermore, it is even possible that the social optimum will be inside the utility-possibility frontier, e.g., if society is willing to accept a trade-off between production and a more equitable income distribution. Consequently, welfare economics cannot give rules for changes without taking into account the desired distribution of welfare. We must look at every proposed change to determine who the losers and gainers are, and then evaluate the gain of the gainers and the loss of the losers in accordance with a specified distributional criterion in order to evaluate the change.

How is the distributional criterion to be found? SAMUELSON assumes that the value judgments defining the criterion are those given by 'some ethical belief – that of a benevolent despot or a complete egotist, or 'all men of good will,' a misanthrope, the state, race, or group mind, God, etc.'[15] Clearly, this is not very helpful for operational work.

7.3. OBJECTIONS TO THE CONCEPT

The BERGSON-SAMUELSON concept of a social welfare function has given rise to substantial criticism by those who consider it too general to be useful as an operational tool. The following quote from DOBB may illustrate this: 'The social welfare function (if one has understood it correctly) is an elegant example of the kind of formalism, so much in vogue today, which greatly facilitates analysis by supposing crucial problems to be solved by some ingenious (but undisclosed) device, without providing any actual means of their solution.'[16] We subscribe to this criticism to a large extent. If we are to make use of the concept, then we have to be much more specific than BERGSON and SAMUELSON are. The question, therefore, arises of how the social welfare function can be determined?

ARROW[17] sees the social welfare function as a collective choice rule to be derived from individual preferences. He postulates that five conditions are necessary to accept individual preferences for social decision-making. Three of these conditions concern 'citizen sovereignty' and imply that a social welfare function should not be dictatorial or imposed on the community, and that there should be consumer sovereignty, i.e., the social choice must not be independent

165

of the individual preferences. As such, although being value judgments, they are very appealing. The fourth condition relating to non-transitivity of social choice also appears plausible at first sight. It means that in the social decision-making process, if A is preferred over B, and B over C, then C should not be preferred over A. Finally, there is the condition of 'the independence of irrelevant alternatives,' which means that when individuals are ranking a set of possible decisions, they should consider this set only so that the social ranking which is derived from the individual rankings will not be affected by some alternative beyond those under consideration. ARROW shows by means of symbolic logic that in proceeding from individual preferences to social decisions, one or another of the conditions will always be violated.

The following example regarding an investment decision in the hypothetical republic of Xalandia, which recently achieved its independence, may be useful. Its Planning Department, recently established, has three projects in the pipeline, each costing about Xalandia dollar (X$) 50 million, and each having about the same economic rate of return of about 15 percent. The first project is an irrigation project that mainly favors the lower income groups, the second a road improvement program that is distributionally neutral, and the third a bridge that would mainly favor high income suburban communities. Since the Planning Department is new and a Development Plan reflecting the wants and needs of the population has not been drawn up, it is decided to poll the three political parties – each of equal strength – as to the priority they attach to the projects. The Action Party is rather conservative, the Freedom Party follows a middle of the road policy, the Progress Party is labor-oriented. There is uniformity of opinion within each party but opinions differ between the parties. The parties' priorities – indicated by high (H), medium (M), or low (L) for each project – are shown in the table below.

Unfortunately, as shown in the table, the poll has not been very helpful. The Action and the Progress parties prefer the irrigation project over the roads project; the Freedom and the Progress parties prefer the roads project over the bridge; and the Action and the Freedom parties prefer the bridge over the irrigation project. There is thus complete circularity and, since the parties are of equal strength, no majority decision can be reached. In other words, it is not possible to aggregate the individual votes without violating the principle of non-transitivity of social choice.

Is there a way out of this dilemma? Several writers[18] have argued that

TABLE 7.1.

Parties	Project		
	Irrigation	Roads	Bridge
Action (conservative)	M	L	H
Freedom (middle)	L	H	M
Progress (labor)	H	M	L

166

ARROW's problem has nothing to do with the concept of a social welfare function. We tend to agree. ARROW's dilemma belongs more to the realm of political decision-making. In this context it may be pointed out that ARROW's five conditions are value judgements and that they thus do not need to be universally accepted. Indeed, further analysis shows that they are rather restrictive. For instance, three of ARROW's conditions refer to citizen sovereignty. But does this really exist in the way ARROW suggests? Consumer sovereignty is, of course, a very appealing concept, especially to the Western World. But even in the Western world it is doubtful that social choices are never imposed. In our Xalandia example it might well be possible that two of the political parties band together and that the political leadership imposes its will on the individual members to solve the dilemma. As to the condition of non-transitivity, empirical observation confirms that inconsistencies do appear in the political decision-making process, so why should they not be allowed as ARROW postulates. Finally, it has been argued by some writers that the condition of independence of irrelevant alternatives, as defined by ARROW, means that the ranking of social preferences depends only on individual orderings and not, for instance, on the individuals' intensities of preference. This is also restrictive. In the Xalandia example, for instance, there would be no dilemma if the Progress Party's vote was weighted more heavily than those of the other parties because, for example, there was a general consensus that the poor should be represented more heavily than under the one-man, one-vote rule. This, of course, is again a value judgment. The condition of independence of irrelevant alternatives also implies, to give an example from ROTHENBERG,[19] that 'modern (non-Faustian) man should make his choice of a wife between two women on the basis of which of the two he prefers, and not be unduly influenced by the fact that what he would really prefer is Helen of Troy.' But such an irrelevant alternative may very well influence his choice and also, therefore, the condition may be too restrictive. The analysis of whether a condition is acceptable is subtle. What is clear is that the conditions as originally postulated by Arrow are too restrictive for general analysis of political decision-making.

7.4. The Need for a Positive Approach

ARROW's conditions are value judgments and, as such, much too specific to lead to a meaningful aggregation. How then should we proceed in constructing the community's social welfare function? As ROTHENBERG has pointed out, findings in allied sciences like anthropology, sociology and social psychology suggest that there are generally accepted values in a community from which most other, more specific, values flow. The search according to ROTHENBERG is thus for a generalization about the valuation rules of the population at large; that is, for the values which are strategic in that they form a matrix from which most other values in the community flow. ROTHENBERG adds that this value consensus should be derived from the social decision-making process and that 'a Social Welfare Function is acceptable only when it accurately describes a social decision-making process for which there exists in the observable real world a matrix-value consensus supporting it.'[20]

BERGSON disagrees with ROTHENBERG on this latter point and feels that the welfare economist should only refer to prevailing values and not to social decisions since the former may or may not be expressed in social decisions. He points out that, 'carried to its logical extreme, ROTHENBERG's analysis actually leaves welfare economics devoid of both ethics and counselling. What is there for the welfare economist to do but count ballots if the collective choices are taken as data?'[21] BERGSON appears to be very much afraid that individuals will not always choose consistently in the light of their own values when complex social questions are involved and sees the principal task of the welfare economist as one of counselling individuals. If the objective is to counsel any and all citizens at the same time, then the counsel should be based on the values held in common. If the objective is to counsel individual citizens, then one should take as data in counselling the person in question. The welfare economist may wish to consider his own values in the counselling but, as a social scientist, he should make his own values explicit. If there is disagreement on values, the extent of the disagreement is a matter for enquiry and the welfare economist may then even criticize the individually held values. Thus, according to BERGSON, welfare economics includes value criticism and it is, therefore, necessarily of an ethical nature. A frequent topic of concern for economic analysis is whether utilities are empirically comparable. But this is not the relevant question. What we should be looking for is the common dimensional unit, and '... just as the common dimensional unit of apples and nuts is found in utility, the common dimensional unit of utilities is found in the welfare of Social Man.'[22]

We very much tend to agree with BERGSON. Social questions are complex and the social decision-making process may often give wrong answers. ROTHENBERG's position that the social welfare function should be derived from an empirical analysis of social decisions, therefore, does not appear justified as a general rule. In every community, there are prevailing general values and in constructing the social welfare function, one should go beyond the individual values to discover it. In trying to do so, one should not, of course, follow the noted economist who, as BAUMOL[23] reported, asked the Chief Minister of a lesser developed country for a description of the country's social welfare function. Prevailing values can and should be found by experiments, interviews and analysis of social decisions, writings and actions of politicians, economists, community leaders and the public at large. In all of this, good common sense is just as important as theoretical insight.

We differ with BERGSON on the counselling function of the welfare economist. Whilst there is no doubt that welfare criteria are ethical in nature, it seems too much to suppose that the welfare economist is also a thought leader in ethics. The welfare economist may, of course, use other values – even his own values – to investigate to what this would lead to for an individual or a community, but he should not criticize. However ethical the welfare economist may be, who

168

is he to say that his thoughts are right?

A very important task of the welfare economist is to discern the prevailing values of a community and how they change over time, to define norms based on such values for operational work, and to point out inconsistencies that may occur in operational work due to confusion, ignorance or a misunderstanding of basic value precepts. Herewith we have come to the two basic questions in connection with this study. Does income distribution count in a Government's investment decision and, if so, can such considerations be expressed in a form which makes it suitable for decision-making at a lower level? As mentioned before, we believe the answer to the first question is clear. When we look at the types of projects that Governments are implementing, we see that many of them have as their sole objective the raising of the income levels of certain groups of beneficiaries. Sometimes, some trade-off between output increases and improvement in income distribution seems to be accepted. Even in a competitive economy such as the USA, HAVEMAN found that equity considerations play a role. Of some 147 water resource development projects in the ten southern states – the nation's lowest income region – some 50 percent had an economic rate of return of less than 5.5 percent.[24] In the developing countries we frequently find that in land settlement projects smallholder land is not as efficient as plantations. In irrigation projects water charges are often not levied, or the water is distributed over so many smallholdings that clearly a higher output could be achieved by concentrating the available water on a more limited number of smallholdings. Preference is often given to investment in roads in underdeveloped areas although the rates of return may be lower than if the investment took place in a developed area. The strategy of directing industry to less developed regions is also clearly based on income distribution considerations. And so on.

Income redistribution objectives are thus important; many would say of overriding importance. Recently, the belief that the pursuit of national income growth alone is not enough has received more emphasis.[25] As MCNAMARA, President of the World Bank, has stated: 'Despite a decade of unprecedented increase in the gross national product of the developing countries, the poorest segment of their populations have received little benefit. Nearly 800 million individuals – 40 percent out of a total of two billion – survive on incomes estimated (in U.S. purchasing power) at 30 cents per day, in conditions of malnutrition, illiteracy and squalor. They are suffering poverty in the absolute sense.'[26]

In general we might say then that the search is not one for economic growth alone but for growth in which the benefits of growth are equitably distributed in accordance with some prevailing distributional criterion. Assuming that this is correct, it is not justified to base project evaluation criteria on the objective of maximizing output without considering the distributional aspects of output increases.

We come now to the second question, which we may rephrase as follows. Is it possible to draw up an objective function that should be maximized which includes income distribution aspects? We believe it is, but wish to add imme-

169

diately that certain assumptions are necessary which are, to a certain extent, speculative. The function we have in mind is not an aggregation of individual utilities – we will show that this cannot be correct – but a social welfare function which assumes that there is indeed a value consensus in the community as regards what an equitable income distribution should be. Our present state of knowledge is such that it is inevitable that the income distribution weights we will propose are speculative. However, if we indeed wish to proceed further in this field, we should be willing to accept this. Sensitivity testing of the weights can show whether the proposed decision rules should be applied with caution. Our function assumes that efficiency counts. A substantial part of our review, therefore, will be concerned with whether there will be a trade-off between growth and equity.

Income distribution may have intertemporal as well as interpersonal aspects. In many countries we find that the growth rate of national income is considered inadequate or, in other words, that the distribution of income over time needs to be improved. In Chapter 8 we will review this matter. Chapter 9 will discuss how the interpersonal distribution aspects can be incorporated in benefit-cost analysis.

It may be asked why this study emphasizes the growth and equity aspects of social welfare since there are, of course, other dimensions of social welfare. Most plans set targets such as reducing the rate of inflation, obtaining self-sufficiency in certain products, improving the balance of payments, and raising employment. As regards inflation, benefit-cost analysis is clearly not the right instrument with which to combat inflation problems. Self-sufficiency objectives have been discussed in this study: they are determined at a higher level of the planning process and should be taken as given to the project evaluator so that the analysis becomes a cost effectiveness analysis. As regards the objectives of improving the balance of payments and increasing employment, we believe these are inherently the same as the objectives of growth and equity. In other words, balance of payments and employment objectives are derived from the principal objectives of increasing income and improving the distribution of income at least cost to the economy.

[1] MISHAN, 'Cost-Benefit Analysis,' 2nd revised new ed., Chapters 59 and 60. See also: MISHAN, E. J., 'Economics for Social Decisions,' Praeger Publishers, New York, Washington, 1973, Chapter 2.

[2] ROBBINS, L., 'An Essay on the Nature and Significance of Economic Science,' Second ed., 1935. Reprinted by MacMillan and Company Ltd., London, 1952.

[3] KALDOR, N., 'Welfare Propositions in Economics,' The Economic Journal, September 1939.

[4] HICKS, J. R., 'The Foundation of Welfare Economics,' The Economic Journal, December 1939.

[5] SCITOVSKY, T., 'A Note on Welfare Propositions in Economics,' The Review of Economics and Statistics, November 1941.

[6] LITTLE, 'A Critique,' pp. 84–116.

[7] SAMUELSON, P. A., 'Evaluation of Real National Income,' Oxford Economic Papers (New Series) Vol. II, No. 1, January 1950. Reprinted in 'The Collected Scientific Papers of Paul A. Samuelson,' The M.I.T. Press, 1966, pp. 1044–1072.

[8] GORMAN, W. M., 'The Intransitivity of Certain Criteria Used in Welfare Economics,' Oxford Economic Papers, New Series, Vol. 7, 1955.

[9] For a summary of the discussions see NATH, S. K., 'Are Formal Welfare Criteria Required?', The Economic Journal, September 1964.

[10] KENNEDY, C., 'The Welfare Criteria that Aren't,' The Economic Journal, December 1964.

[11] BERGSON, A., 'A Reformulation of Certain Aspects of Welfare Economics,' The Quarterly Journal of Economics, February 1938, reprinted in 'Essays in Normative Economics,' The Belknap Press of Harvard University Press, Cambridge, Massachusetts, 1966, pp. 3–26.

[12] Ibid., p. 4.

[13] Ibid., p. 15.

[14] SAMUELSON, 'Evaluation of Real National Income,' Collected Scientific Papers, p. 1056.

[15] SAMUELSON, P. A., 'Foundations of Economic Analysis,' Harvard University Press, 1947, reprint ed., Athenaeum, New York, 1965, pp. 221.

[16] DOBB, M., 'Welfare Economics and the Economics of Socialism,' Cambridge University Press, Cambridge, 1965, p. 112.

[17] ARROW, K. J., 'Social Choice and Individual Values,' 2nd ed., John Wiley and Sons, New York, 1963.

[18] For instance, LITTLE, I. M. D.,' Social Choice and Individual Values,' The Journal of Political Economy, October 1952, pp. 422–432; and BERGSON, A., 'Collective Decision-Making and Social Welfare,' The Quarterly Journal of Economics, May 1954, reprinted in 'Essays in Normative Economics,' p. 35.

[19] ROTHENBERG, J., 'The Measurement of Social Welfare,' Prentice-Hall, Inc., Englewood Cliffs, New Jersey, 1961, p. 22.

[20] Ibid., p. 335.

[21] BERGSON, 'Collective Decision-Making and Social Welfare,' in 'Essays in Normative Economics,' p. 45.

[22] Ibid., p. 48.

[23] BAUMOL, W. J., – 'Economic Theory and Operations Analysis,' 2nd ed., Prentice-Hall, Inc., Englewood Cliffs, New Jersey, 1965, p. 380.

[24] HAVEMAN, R. H., 'Water Resource Investment and the Public Interest,' Vanderbilt University Press, Nashville, Tennessee, 1965, pp. 147–148.

[25] In this respect it is interesting to note that MYRDAHL feels that a more equitable income distribution is a prerequisite for economic growth. This is thus an argument based on efficiency grounds. (MYRDAL, G., 'The Challenge of World Poverty,' Pantheon Books, New York, 1970, p. 54).

[26] McNAMARA, R. S., 'Address to the Board of Governors of the International Bank for Reconstruction and Development,' Nairobi, Kenya, September 24, 1973.

8. INTERTEMPORAL INCOME DISTRIBUTION ASPECTS

8.1. THE CONCEPT OF A SOCIAL DISCOUNT RATE

Under conditions of perfect competition, the market interest rate equates individuals' marginal time preferences with the marginal rate of return on investment. But, in the real world capital markets have many 'imperfections'. Corporate and personal income taxes, risk elements, government interventions, limited access to capital markets and monopoly elements are just a few of the many factors that drive a wedge between the time productivity of capital (the rates of return) and lenders' time preference rates. In Chapter 3 we argued that when investments are optimal for the country as a whole, the opportunity cost of capital to the Government should be measured by the rates of return foregone in the private sector. This argumentation is valid under the stipulated condition. However, it may be possible that the investments of the country as a whole are considered suboptimal, and several writers have argued that in such a case public sector investment decisions should not be based on rates of return foregone in the private sector, but on a discount rate – which we shall call the social discount rate – that takes into account that investments should be promoted.

KRUTILLA and ECKSTEIN proposed, as discussed in Chapter 3, that the social discount rate should be equal to the estimated time preference rates of the suppliers of capital to the Government, and estimated the value of the social discount rate to be between 5 and 6 percent in the United States. However, in a subsequent study, ECKSTEIN[1] revised his former position and argued that the estimate had no normative significance because it was based on the mistaken assumption that only the individual time preferences of the present generation count for intertemporal decisions. This is, of course, a familiar argument that had already been postulated a long time before by PIGOU.

In his monumental work on the economics of welfare, PIGOU stated[2] that there are two reasons for rejecting individuals' time preferences. The first is that we see future pleasures on a diminished scale, even though they may be of the same magnitude as our present satisfaction. As a result, people will often devote themselves to satisfying a present want now rather than a larger one several years hence. Second: 'Our desire for future satisfaction would often be less intense than for present satisfaction, because it is very likely that the future satisfaction will not be our own.' In other words, in making our present decisions we do not count the preferences of the unborn generation. PIGOU and ECKSTEIN feel, therefore, that the time preferences of the present generation should be rejected as a basis for collective intertemporal decision-making.

Regarding the first part of PIGOU's argumentation, we will discuss in Section 8.2 that there are perfectly good reasons for an individual or a country to have a time preference rate, and that it is unfair to treat this as a kind of 'myopia.'

172

Regarding the second part of PIGOU's argumentation, it should be noted that almost every country shows some growth in per capita incomes. Hence, in general, the future generation will be richer than the present, and one may question, therefore, whether the preferences of the future generation should be counted. In many countries we see that funds are transferred from the rich to the poor and similarly it might seem logical to reduce the rate of transfer of funds to the future rather than to increase it.

PIGOU's and ECKSTEIN's argument that the time preference of the present generation should be rejected is unfortunate because it may lead to rejection of citizens' sovereignty in favor of an authoritarian social welfare function[3]. However, in many cases we see that democratic governments are indeed trying to increase the savings rate of their countries. Development plans include target growth rates and investment programs designed to reach them. Hence, we should accept the possibility that prevailing social values, as expressed in a social welfare function which recognizes citizen sovereignty, may indeed reflect the view that the consumption-investment division of the community's income is not optimal.

We may illustrate this possibility with the help of Figure 8.1. The curve AB represents the possibility in the economy of transferring present consumption goods into next year's consumption goods. Suppose we find ourselves at a point like C. If we denote the slope of the transformation curve at C by $1 + q$, then the marginal rate of return which investments earn in that situation is q. Total consumption in the economy will be OD, and total investments DB. The marginal investment close to D will earn q, but intra-marginal investments will earn more, so that the total investments DB will produce CD in future consumption goods. Under conditions of perfect competition, the market interest rate – and there would be only one market interest rate – would be the same as the opportunity cost of capital q and there would be an equilibrium situation in the sense that lenders' time preference rates would equal the time productivity of capital. It is still possible, however, that the social welfare function expressing the collective preference as to the division of national income between consumption and investment indicates that investments are not optimal. Let the social welfare function be represented by a set of indifference curves W. Then, at point C, the slope of the indifference curve, as depicted by dd, is equal to one plus the social discount rate. Hence, more consumption goods should be transferred to the future than takes place in accordance with the market interest rate q.

Thus, even under conditions of perfect competition, the market interest rate may not represent the optimal interest rate. This is not surprising, since we have seen already that such questions as to whether there is an optimal interpersonal distribution of national income can only be answered by referring to a social welfare function. Similarly, the optimum of the intertemporal distribution of national income can also only be found by considering prevailing social values. In Figure 8.1, the optimum point would be at F, where the social indifference curve is tangent to the transformation curve.

FIGURE 8.1.

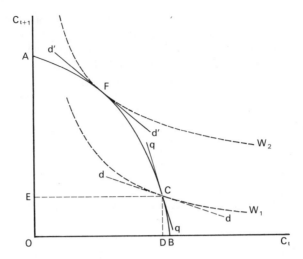

How then can we proceed from a position like C to the optimal point F? The point C is characterized by high consumption and a low rate of investment. Traditional economic theory prescribes that Government should move from C to F by curtailing consumption by means of, for instance, increasing taxes on consumption; by tax breaks stimulating investment such as extra depreciation allowances; or by an easy money policy using open market operations by the Central Bank. These fiscal and monetary policies would result in a lowering of the opportunity cost of capital in successive time periods and finally lead to a position where the consumption-investment ratio would be in agreement with collective preferences. There would, therefore, be no need to take the social discount rate into account for public investment decisions because the discount rate would be determined by the projected opportunity cost of capital rates[4].

However, proponents of the social discount rate approach to benefit-cost analysis – as elaborated in the UNIDO Guidelines and the OECD Manual – contend that governments often will not be able, because of political constraints, to apply appropriate fiscal and monetary policies, and that in such a case the only way to proceed from C to F is choosing more longer-life projects than would be undertaken under the opportunity cost of capital approach. Both the UNIDO Guidelines and the OECD Manual develop a special investment algorithm to ensure that this capital deepening will indeed take place.

The UNIDO and OECD approaches are both of current operational significance and deserve further scrutiny. We will, therefore, focus for the remainder of this chapter on the two approaches with the objective of revealing a variety of dichotomies and inconsistencies that would be involved in their operational application and with a view towards arriving at our own recommendations. Section 8.2 will review how UNIDO and OECD propose to estimate the social discount rate, and Sections 8.3 and 8.4 will discuss the operational implications of the proposed criteria. Finally, Section 8.5 will critically review the approaches from an immanent point of view.

174

8.2. The Value of the Social Discount Rate

Both the OECD Manual and UNIDO Guidelines maintain that there exist direct relationships between the social discount rate, on the one hand, and the elasticity of the marginal utility of consumption and the rate of growth of per capita consumption (UNIDO) and the pure time preference rate (OECD), on the other hand. The first of the recent writers who pointed out the usefulness of such relationships in connection with public investment decisions was again ECKSTEIN,[5] but the theory dates back to RAMSEY's classic paper of 1928 on optimal savings,[6] and has recently been discussed extensively in this connection.[7] Rather than repeating the mathematical exposition of the theory, we will try to clarify the concepts by analyzing in detail the individual consumer's consumption-investment decision.

The most elementary form of consumer equilibrium is characterized by the condition that the consumer equalizes the marginal utility per dollar spent on different commodities. The underlying premise is that the more a consumer consumes of a good, the less is his marginal utility. The time element is brought in if we, similarly, accept that a consumer discounts the future utility of a unit of consumption, i.e., that he attaches less utility to a future unit of consumption than to a present unit.

A consumer's consumption-saving decision can be expressed in terms of benefit-cost analysis. Consider Figure 8.2. Assuming that the consumer consumes his entire income, then the marginal utility of the last dollar spent on consumption may be represented by OA. Every dollar that is withdrawn from present consumption, i.e., saved, will be valued by him at an increasingly higher marginal utility because his present consumption is decreasing. Thus, if we denote the present marginal utility of a dollar saved by u_o, then every subsequent dollar saved will have a higher u_o as indicated by the curve ACE. Let us look now at what happens with the saved dollars. Since the consumer can invest a dollar at the interest rate i which he faces – a constant for him – he will receive t periods from now $(1 + i)^t$ dollars per dollar saved or expressed in continuous compounding terms e^{it} dollars.[8] However, the utility of a dollar which the consumer will receive in period t may be quite different from the utility of a present dollar because, for instance, he may have become much richer. If we denote the future utility of a dollar by u_t, then we can denote the consumer's future utility per dollar saved by $u_t \cdot e^{it}$ because of the interest he receives. Further, as discussed, the consumer will discount that future utility by his time preference rate which we denote by p, and the present value of the future utility is thus $u_t \cdot e^{(i-p)t}$.

Since the consumer's future marginal utility curve is downward sloping, the present worth of the future utility of each subsequent dollar saved will decrease, as indicated by curve BCF. An equilibrium position will be reached at the point C, where $u_o = u_t \cdot e^{(i-p)t}$, or in words, where the present utility of a dollar of consumption foregone equals the time preference discounted value of that dollar's interest-compounded future utility.

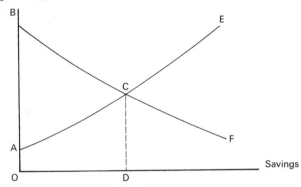

FIGURE 8.2. Present value of marginal utility

The consumer will thus save OD dollars when the interest rate is i. The curve BCF will move to the right when the interest rate increases and more will be saved and will move to the left inducing lower savings when the interest rate decreases. This analysis also allows for consumers who will not save at all because their time preference rate is so high that the curve BCF will be outside the savings quadrant so that they borrow funds. For each consumer, a savings curve can be constructed showing the savings of that consumer as a function of the interest rate. Summation for all savers will produce the savings curve for the country as a whole and intersection of that curve with the demand curve for capital will show the savings of the country.

So far, the classical theory. Suppose now that our consumer represents the community as a whole and that his consumption equals the per capita consumption of the community. Then his marginal utility u refers to the marginal utility of per capita consumption. Furthermore, we may assume, since our consumer speaks for the community, that he knows the value of the social discount rate d. Then the equilibrium position will be represented by the formula $u_o = u_t \cdot e^{(d-p)t}$ or, alternatively $u_t = u_o e^{-(d-p)t}$. From this it follows that the rate of decrease of marginal utility over time must equal $p - d$. Thus $(du/dt)/u = p - d$. For $(du/dt)/u$ we may write:

$$\frac{du/dt}{u} = \left(\frac{du/dt}{u} \cdot \frac{c}{dc/dt}\right) \cdot \frac{dc/dt}{c}$$

The bracketed expression in the formula represents the elasticity of the marginal utility of consumption with respect to per capita consumption, and the last term represents the growth rate of per capita consumption. The value of the marginal utility of consumption can, of course, only be found if we know the marginal utility function showing the consumer's marginal utility as a function of his 'richness.' One such function[9] would be $u = (b/c)^x$ where b is a constant representing base level consumption, c is the actual consumption level of the

176

consumer and, as is well known, α is the elasticity of the marginal utility of consumption with respect to consumption.[10] If we denote the growth rate of per capita consumption by g, it follows that: $(du/dt)/u = p - d = - \alpha g$, so that $d = p + \alpha g$. Or in words, the social discount rate must equal the sum of the pure time preference rate and the decrease over time of the marginal utility of per capita consumption – expressed as the product of its elasticity with respect to per capita consumption and the growth rate of per capita consumption. This formula is intuitively easy to understand. If the marginal utility of consumption decreases over time at the rate $p + \alpha g$, then future consumption should be discounted at this rate to find its present value.

Let us review now how the various writers have used this formula. ECKSTEIN[11] assumes that the elasticity of the marginal utility of consumption (α) lies between 0.5 and 2.0.[12] Hence with a growth rate of per capita consumption of, say, 2 percent – in his opinion a not unreasonable figure for developing countries – the value of αg varies from 1.0 to 4.0 percent. Regarding the pure time preference rate, ECKSTEIN suggests that it can be computed from mortality statistics. Any individual should prefer a consumption plan that stresses early years to a plan that stresses later years, since the probability of survival is greater in the earlier years.[13] For consumption one year after the present, the time preference rate is equal to the probability of not surviving the next year. ECKSTEIN found that the probabilities of not surviving the next year for a country like India vary from 1 to 5 percent over a range of ages, which includes most of the population. Hence, there appears to be a perfectly rational explanation for individuals' time preferences. ECKSTEIN then discusses whether planners should take individual pure time preferences into account. On the one hand, society goes on forever and ignoring individuals' pure time preferences may well be in the long-run interest of society. On the other hand, ignoring individuals' preferences implies a dictatorial social welfare function. Moreover, there is evidence that the people in developing countries prefer projects yielding immediate benefits to projects yielding benefits at a later stage – such as large scale construction works. In ECKSTEIN's opinion, the choice of the social discount rate remains essentially a value judgment. There are objective factors that enter into the choice, such as the values of α, g and p, but these must be combined with value judgments.

The OECD Manual suggests that the social discount rate should be set at 4 or 5 percent. In its first example, the Manual assumes that $\alpha = 2.0$, $g = 2$ percent and $p = 0$ percent, so that the social discount rate equals 4 percent.[14] In its second example, the Manual distinguishes between workers in the traditional and in the modern sector and assumes that the elasticity of the marginal utility of consumption varies from 3.0 for the low-paid workers in the traditional sector to 0.67 for the high-paid workers in the modern sector. As typical annual income growth rates for the two sectors are 0.5 and 1.8 percent, respectively, the rate of fall over time of the marginal utility of consumption in the two sectors will be 1.5 and 1.2 percent per annum, respectively. Postulating that there is a pure time preference rate of around 2.5 percent, the Manual suggests that the social discount rate cannot assume a higher value than about 5 percent.[15]

The UNIDO Guidelines sees the social discount rate as being determined solely by αg and does not pay any attention to the pure time preference rate, presumably because of the 'myopia' of individuals. It states explicitly that the determination of the social discount rate is a value judgment. However, since 'it is unlikely that the political process, such as it is presently, is capable of quantitative articulation of such value judgments as the elasticity of marginal utility embodies,'[16] the UNIDO Guidelines recommends that the social discount rate, like redistribution weights, be treated as an unknown in project formulation and evaluation. The hope is that by focusing policymakers' attention on the relevant social choices, the weights will eventually become known.

Is there anything that can be added to all this? It has been shown[17] that an intertemporal utility theory is not possible without considering at the same time a rate of pure time preference. This can best be demonstrated as follows. Assume that the economy is on an optimal growth path. Then, as is customary in growth theory, we may treat wages – expressed in terms of used-up consumption goods – as interest on the 'capitalized value of labor.' Hence, we may define the value of the capital stock as the sum of the discounted value of consumption from zero to infinity, and this is presented by:

$$K_o = \int C_t e^{-dt} \cdot dt = C_o \int e^{-(d-g)t} \cdot dt$$

If $d = g$, this expression will be infinite, which obviously cannot be correct. Because $d = \alpha g + p$, it follows that if $\alpha = 1$ there must be a pure time preference rate p in order to have a finite value for the capital stock.

Let us assume now that $p = o$, but that $\alpha \neq 1$. Integration of the expression is then possible because $d \neq g$ and the formula for the capital stock is then $K_o = C_o/(d - g)$. However, if $p = o$ and $\alpha < 1$, it is readily seen from $d = \alpha g + p$ that $d < g$ so that the value of K_o will be negative. Obviously, this cannot be correct and we may, therefore, conclude that in this case also p should be positive. This could also be illustrated by considering savings. The equation for K_o may be written as $d \cdot K_o = C_o + g \cdot K_o$, from which follows, because $Y_o = C_o + I_o$ and $d \cdot K_o = Y_o$, the well-known growth theory formula that the optimal proportion of income saved $s = I_o/Y_o = g \cdot K_o/d \cdot K_o = g/d$. Substituting the value of d, this formula may be written as $s = g/(\alpha g + p)$. Hence, if $p = o$, and $\alpha < 1$, we would arrive at the untenable result that more than present consumption should be saved. Thus, if $\alpha < 1$, there must be a positive pure time preference rate p to get a finite value for the capital stock and a savings ratio of less than 1.

Let us turn now to the case where $\alpha > 1$. Then, if $p = o$, d will be larger than g and K_o will be positive. However, it is useful here to consider the total utility function. Integration of the marginal utility of consumption function $u = (b/C)^\alpha$, gives two total utility functions:

$$U = b^\alpha \ln C + A \text{ for } \alpha = 1, \text{ and}$$

$$U = Z - \frac{b^\alpha}{\alpha - 1} C^{-(\alpha - 1)} \text{ for } \alpha \neq 1.$$

where A and Z are constants of integration. Consideration of the second equation shows that when $\alpha > 1$, total utility approaches Z – the bliss level – when C assumes large values. Since $C_t = C_o \cdot e^{gt}$, so that $C_t^{(1-\alpha)} = C_o^{\cdot(1-\alpha)} \cdot e^{(g-\alpha g)t}$, the discounted value of the utility at a certain time t is:

$$\left[Z - \frac{b^\alpha}{\alpha - 1} C_o^{(1-\alpha)} \cdot e^{(g-\alpha g)t} \right] e^{-pt}$$

$$= Z e^{-pt} - \frac{b^\alpha}{\alpha - 1} \cdot C_o^{(1-\alpha)} \cdot e^{-(d-g)t}$$

The integral of this from zero to infinity is the present value of the total expected utility. So long as $d > g$, the negative term will have a finite value. However, $Z e^{-pt}$ will only be finite if p is positive. Because it is total utility that must be maximized and one cannot maximize something which is infinite, it is clear that in the case $\alpha > 1$ the pure time preference rate must also have a positive value.

Thus, in all cases, whether $\alpha < 1$, $= 1$ or > 1, there must be a positive pure time preference rate. As a result, the social discount rate cannot have extremely low values. As regards the pure time preference rate, we would be surprised if it were, say, lower than 5 percent. If $\alpha = 1$, which, as discussed in the next Chapter, is probably the minimum value it can assume for low-income groups, which represent the bulk of the population, and the growth rate of per capita income is about 2–3 percent, which is normal for developing countries, then the social discount rate will be about seven to eight percent. If one is not willing to accept this and wishes to use a lower time preference rate and a lower α, then the social discount rate would still probably not be lower than about five percent.

Various objections can be raised to the intertemporal utility analysis used above. The use of marginal utility of consumption curves with constant elasticity is mathematically convenient, but there is no reason why the curves must take this form. In addition, it is unrealistic to assume that the intertemporal optimum position is determined by equating the present marginal utility foregone with the discounted value of the marginal utility at a certain future time. In reality, one does not normally give up present consumption for an increase in future consumption in a certain year, but for a flow of consumption in the future.[18] No satisfactory way of handling these problems has yet been devised. The theory which was presented here is, therefore, incomplete and presents only a partial description of reality. Furthermore, as will be discussed in the last section of this Chapter, we doubt seriously the validity of using a single discount rate for the community as a whole. In the next two sections, however, we will follow the literature in its use of a single social discount rate and will see where this leads us.

As was briefly mentioned, the first of the recent writers who proposed to base public investment decisions on a social discount rate lower than the market interest rate was ECKSTEIN. However, ECKSTEIN was well aware of the dangers of such an approach, i.e., that a naive use of a low cut-off rate would justify many projects of little economic value. He, therefore, makes the following suggestion: 'I propose the following compromise, which is designed to preserve the long-time perspective of the federal program, yet would assure that only projects are undertaken in which capital yields as great a value as it would in its alternative employments: let the Government use a relatively low interest rate for the design and evaluation of projects, but let projects be considered justified only if the benefit-cost ratio is well in excess of 1.0.'[19]

In the study just quoted, ECKSTEIN seems to feel that in the United States the social discount rate – d – is about $2^1/_2$ to 3 percent, and that the rate of return in the private sector – q – is about 6 percent. It may be remarked immediately that ECKSTEIN's estimate of the return in the private sector appears rather low compared with those in most other studies. Be that as it may, ECKSTEIN uses the above quoted values of d and q. He assumes that investment and operating costs of the different projects are to be borne by the Government budget and he then shows that a typical Government project with an economic life of 50 to 100 years must have a B/C ratio of about 1.3 if it is to produce a rate of return of 6 percent when its benefits are discounted at 3 percent. ECKSTEIN proposes that this ratio of 1.3 should be used as the cut-off B/C ratio for all Government projects.

What ECKSTEIN has done is to put a shadow price on Government investments so that all Government projects should be evaluated in accordance with the norm:

$$\sum_{t=1}^{n} \frac{B_t}{(1.03)^t} \geqslant 1.3 \sum_{t=1}^{n} \frac{C_t}{(1.03)^t}$$

It may immediately be pointed out that ECKSTEIN's criterion discriminates against projects with a short economic life for such projects must earn substantially more than six percent to pass the 1.3 cut-off test. This can most easily be shown if we use in the calculation of the shadow price of investment the N/K ratio which we believe is more in line with reality than the B/C ratio.[20] If we calculate the shadow price of investment (P_{inv}) for a project with a very long economic life as ECKSTEIN suggests, say 100 years or more for simplicity's sake, the value of $P_{inv} = 0.06/0.03 = 2$. Hence, in case of constancy of benefits, ECKSTEIN's criterion is $N_A a_{\overline{n}|3} \geqslant 2\,K$ which can be written for the marginal project as: $^1/_2 N_A a_{\overline{n}|3} = K$. The internal rate of return criterion is: $N_A a_{\overline{n}|r} = K$. Thus, for the marginal project: $^1/_2 a_{\overline{n}|3} = a_{\overline{n}|r}$. Hence, we can calculate r which has been done below for a few projects with different economic lives. As the Table shows, the economic internal rates of return vary inversely with project

TABLE 8.2. Minimum internal rates of return of projects according to Eckstein's criterion.
$(P_{inv} = 2)$

Project Life	
∞ years	6.0%
50 years	7.6%
25 years	10.5%
10 years	19.5%

life. In practice this means that under ECKSTEIN's criterion Governments will mainly undertake projects with long lives so that it can be expected that the capital structure of a country will be deepened.

While ECKSTEIN's criterion was principally designed to preserve the efficiency of the federal program and the capital-deepening effect appeared as a byproduct, other writers saw this effect as the principal justification for applying the criterion. It became, therefore, necessary to justify the criterion on theoretical grounds, rather than to base it on a suggestion. SEN, STEINER, MARGLIN and FELDSTEIN[21] have cast the benefit-cost analysis of public projects in terms of consumption created or foregone and have tried therewith to provide the theoretical foundation for the ECKSTEIN proposal. The benefit of a project should be measured in terms of the consumption it generates; its cost in terms of the consumption it foregos. MARGLIN, particularly, has written extensively about the social discount rate concept, and it may, therefore, be useful to review the concept as it appeared in his 1967 book on Public Investment Criteria[22] and in the 1972 UNIDO Guidelines[23] which he coauthored.

The concept as such is relatively simple. The basic principle to remember is that consumption is to be taken as the numéraire. Suppose that the rate of return in the private sector is q percent and that this rate of return is entirely consumed. It then follows immediately that, if the public project displaces private investment, the shadow price of public investment is q/d, where d represents the social discount rate at which consumption is to be valued. Assume that the opportunity cost of capital – the rate of return in the private sector – is 12.5 percent and that the social discount rate has the value of 5.0 percent. Then the shadow price of public investment is 2.5. Hence, the present worth of the benefits of the government project should be 150 percent higher than the present value of the investments – where both present values are calculated at the social discount rate of 5.0 percent. Or, expressed as a formula:

$$\sum_{t=1}^{n} \frac{N_t}{(1 + d)^t} \geqslant 2.5 \sum_{t=1}^{n} \frac{K_t}{(1 + d)^t}$$

However, the rate of return in the private sector is never entirely consumed, part of it is reinvested. MARGLIN has shown[24] that then the shadow price of investment – P_{inv} – can be represented by the formula $(q - sq)/(d - sq)$, where s is the reinvested part, i.e., the marginal savings coefficient of the private sector.

The proof is easy to follow. The numerator $q - sq$ represents that part of the returns that will immediately be consumed. The remainder sq will immediately be reinvested. However, since sq will produce an annual return, it should also be valued at the shadow price of investment. The annual return from a dollar of investment is thus $(q - sq) + P_{inv} sq$. Since the present value of that annual return must be equal to P_{inv}, we have

$$P_{inv} = \frac{(q - sq) + P_{inv}sq}{d}$$ which when solved for P_{inv} reduces to:

$$P_{inv} = \frac{q - sq}{d - sq}$$

Thus, if $q = 12.5$ percent, $d = 5$ percent and $s = 20$ percent, the shadow price of public investment is $(12.5 - 2.5)/(5 - 2.5) = 4.0$ and any public investment should be valued at a premium of 300 percent.

Let us illustrate the principle with an example using the shadow price of investment found above. Assume that the public investments are 100 and the annual returns – for simplicity's sake in perpetuity – are 12.5. Assume that of those particular returns, 20 percent will be reinvested. What is then the social rate of return of the project? Consider the following cost-benefit stream:

TABLE 8.3.

	Yr. 0	Annually Yrs 1 thru ∞
Costs		
Investment	100	
Premium on Investment (300%)	300	
Social Value of Investment	400	
Net Benefits		
Consumption Part of Benefits		10.0
Investment Part of Benefits		2.5
Premium on Investment Part (300%)		7.5
Social Value of Benefits		20.0

The social rate of return is $20/400 = 5$ percent and equal to the social discount rate. This result is, of course, not very surprising because the values of the benefit stream are exactly the same as those used for the calculation of the shadow price of investment.

Following the procedures outlined above for estimating the social rate of return of a project, we may write the general criterion for acceptance/rejection of a Government project as:

$$(8.1.) \quad \sum_{t=1}^{n} \frac{N_t (1 - s^*) + N_t s^* P_{inv}}{(1 + d)^t} \geqslant K P_{inv}$$

182

where $s*$ is the invested part of the net benefits and as before N is net benefits, P_{inv} is the shadow price of investments, d is the social discount rate, and K is the present value of the investments, found by discounting at the rate d.

Before proceeding further we must mention that MARGLIN in the UNIDO Guidelines also mentions briefly that the resources required for public investment may come out of consumption rather than alternative investment.[25] It is stated that in such a case, the righthand side of formula 8.1 should read $K(a^{inv}P_{inv} + a^{cons})$ rather than KP_{inv}, where a^{inv} and a^{cons} represent the proportions of private investment and private consumption displaced, respectively. However, the Guidelines do not consider this possibility further[26] and seem to assume that the funds for the Government investment come entirely from foregone private investments. The same assumption is implicity made in the OECD Manual. We will discuss this matter further in Section 8.5.

Finally, we may mention that the OECD Manual does not follow the approach outlined above but that it takes savings instead of consumption as the numéraire. Since the present value of the consumption generated by \$ 1 of investment is P_{inv}, the value of a dollar of present consumption expressed in terms of savings is $1/P_{inv}$. Furthermore, the benefits of a project are not discounted at the social discount rate d – which the Manual calls the consumption rate of interest – but at a so-called investment or accounting rate of interest a.[27] The use of this accounting rate of interest is necessary because under the OECD approach savings are used as the numeraire. Hence, the discount rate to be used – the accounting rate of interest – should be the rate at which the weight on savings relative to consumption falls over time. In terms of a formula, the relationship between a and d may be written as:

$$a_t = d_t + \frac{P_{inv(t)} - P_{inv(t+1)}}{P_{inv(t)}}$$

In words, this formula tells us that the accounting rate of interest is equal to the consumption rate of interest plus the rate of fall over time of the premium on savings. Thus, only if P_{inv} is constant over time will the accounting rate of interest be equal to the social discount rate.

The difference between the OECD approach and UNIDO formula 8.1 may be illustrated with a simple example.[28] Consider a two period cost-benefit stream. Then the OECD criterion is:

$$\frac{\dfrac{N_1(1-s*)}{P_{inv(1)}} + N_1 s*}{(1+a)} \geqslant K$$

For the above formula of the accounting rate of interest we may also write[29]:

$$(1+a_t) = (1+d_t) \cdot \frac{P_{inv(t)}}{P_{inv(t+1)}}$$

Substituting this into the OECD formula, we get

$$\frac{N_1 (1 - s^*) + N_1 s^* P_{inv(1)}}{(1 + d)} \geqslant K \cdot P_{inv(o)}$$

This is the same as the UNIDO formula 8.1 which assumes that the value of P_{inv} is constant over time. The OECD Manual is, of course, quite right that over time P_{inv} should assume lower values so that eventually $P_{inv} = 1$ when indeed an optimum savings situation has been reached. Also, the social discount rate for discounting the benefits of period t is then not $(1 + d)$ but $(1 + d_1) \ldots$ $(1 + d_{t-1}) (1 + d_t)$. However, the Manual gives no guidance as to how the successive discount rates should be determined. In fact, in all its case studies it assumes a constant shadow price of investment and a constant discount rate.

The OECD Manual also derives a shadow price of investment by considering reinvestments. However, the Manual emphasizes that within a reasonable time period – its examples are 10 years and 20 years – consumption and investment will be equally desirable. Its standard formula is, therefore, different from the standard UNIDO formula, which assumes that the relevant parameters d, q, and s remain unchanged over time.[30] It should be noted that the OECD Manual makes an error[31] in deriving P_{inv} and that in our annotation it should be presented by:[32]

$$P_{inv} = \frac{(1 + sq)^T}{(1 + d)^T} \left\{ \frac{(q - sq)(1 + d)}{(sq - d)} + 1 \right\} - \frac{(q - sq)(1 + d)}{(sq - d)}$$

The OECD formula will lead to much lower values for P_{inv} than the UNIDO formula. For instance, if we use values of $q = 12.5$ percent, $d = 5$ percent and $s = 20$ percent, and if we take T at 20 years as OECD suggests, then the OECD shadow price of investment will be 2.2, while UNIDO's value is 4.0. Two different assumptions underly these formulas. The UNIDO approach assumes that the Government faces severe constraints in expanding its budget so that the optimum investment situation is a long way off. OECD assumes a more flexible Government budget. It seems to us that the OECD assumption that it takes only 10 to 20 years before the optimum investment level is reached, is rather optimistic in that one could have made the same assumption 10 or 20 years ago as regards the present situation. The UNIDO assumption may, therefore, be more realistic.

8.4. Comparison of the UNIDO and OECD Criteria with the Traditional Criterion

We have so far discussed the principles of the social discount rate approach and how the various manuals propose to estimate the social discount rate and the shadow price of investment. It will now be useful to analyze what the consequences are of the application of the social discount rate cum shadow price of investment criterion in terms of the traditional economic rate of return criterion.

To analyze this matter we will make the simplifying assumption that the net benefits of the project in question are constant. Denoting as before the invested part of the benefits by $s*$, the social discount rate cum shadow price of investment criterion for the marginal project is

$$N_A(1 - s*)a_{n\;d} + N_A s* P_{inv} a_{n\;d} = KP_{inv}$$

The internal rate of return criterion is $N_A a_{n\;r} = K$. Hence, it follows that for the marginal projects:

$$a_{\overline{n}|r} = \frac{(1 - s*)a_{\overline{n}|d} + s* P_{inv}\, a_{\overline{n}|d}}{P_{inv}}$$

If we calculate the values of $a_{\overline{n}|r}$ for various values of $a_{\overline{n}|d}$, P_{inv} and $s*$, we can find the minimum internal rate of return which a project should have before it qualifies for acceptance under the social rate of return criterion. It should be noted that this minimum internal rate of return is calculated in the conventional way, i.e., the benefit and cost streams do not include the shadow price of investment.

We may illustrate the approach with two examples. What we are interested in finding is the economic internal rate of return of a Government project that would just be accepted under the social rate of return criterion proposed by UNIDO and OECD. Thus, if the social discount rate d is 5 percent, then the social internal rate of return of such a project should be 5 percent. Consider the following two cost-benefit streams. In both cases the social internal rates of return of the projects are 5 percent, but the economic internal rates of return are 9 percent and 19.6 percent, respectively.

The calculation illustrated in Table 8.5 has been done for a number of projects with varying parameters. Consider Tables 8.6 and 8.7. We have taken the previously used values for the opportunity cost of capital q of 12.5 percent and

TABLE 8.5.

	Project A Project Life ∞	Project B Project Life 10 years
Costs in Year 0		
Investments	100	100
Premium on Investments (300%)	300	300
	400	400
Annual Benefit Stream		
Consumption Part of Benefits (60%)	5.4	14.1
Reinvestment Part of Benefits (40%)	3.6	9.4
Premium on Reinv. Benefits (300%)	10.8	28.2
Social Benefits	19.8	51.7
Social Internal Rate of Return	5% (from 19.8/400)	5% (from $51.7 \times a_{\overline{n}|r} = 400$)
Economic Internal Rate of Return	9% (from 9/100)	19.6% (from $23.5 \times a_{\overline{n}|r} = 100$)

for the overall savings ratio of 20 percent. However, the social discount rate d is assumed to take values of 5 percent through 15.0 percent. Table 8.6 follows the UNIDO approach in calculating P_{inv}, Table 8.7 the OECD approach.[33] With the given values for q, s and d, the UNIDO values for P_{inv} are 0.8 through 4; the OECD values 0.93 through 2.22. Both tables include three series of calculations. The first assumes that all the project benefits will be consumed ($s^* = 0$ percent); the second that 20 percent of the benefits – the same as the national marginal savings rate – will be invested ($s^* = 20$ percent); and the third that 40 percent of the benefits – a very high rate – will be invested ($s^* = 40$ percent).

Let us analyze the tables for the cases $d = q$, $d > q$ and $d < q$. As is to be expected, each table shows that when $d = q$, then q – the opportunity cost of capital – represents the cut-off rate. This case represents no special features and we may turn, therefore, immediately to the other cases.

A series of interesting conclusions can be drawn when $d < q$. In all examples, the economic rates of return of the projects should be higher than d. But the series $s^* = 0$ percent has a higher cut-off rate of return than the series $s^* = 20$ percent and the series $s^* = 20$ percent a higher cut-off rate than the series $s^* = 40$ percent. In other words, there is a penalty on projects when the benefits

TABLE 8.6. Minimum internal rates of return of projects according to UNIDO Intertemporal Social Analysis[1].

$s^* = 0\%$					Project Life in Years			
T	q	s	d	P_{inv}	∞	50	25	10
∞	12.5%	20%	5%	4	20.0%	21.9%	28.2%	54.7%
∞	12.5%	20%	7.5%	2	15.0%	15.4%	18.0%	26.4%
∞	12.5%	20%	12.5%	1	12.5%	12.5%	12.5%	12.5%
∞	12.5%	20%	15.0%	0.8	12.0%	12.0%	11.6%	9.5%

$s^* = 20\%$					Project Life in Years			
T	q	s	d	P_{inv}	∞	50	25	10
∞	12.5%	20%	5%	4	12.5%	13.7%	17.6%	30.0%
∞	12.5%	20%	7.5%	2	12.5%	12.8%	14.4%	20.5%
∞	12.5%	20%	12.5%	1	12.5%	12.5%	12.5%	12.5%
∞	12.5%	20%	15.0%	0.8	12.5%	12.5%	12.2%	10.5%

$s^* = 40\%$					Project Life in Years			
T	q	s	d	P_{inv}	∞	50	25	10
∞	12.5%	20%	5%	4	9.0%	9.9%	12.2%	19.6%
∞	12.5%	20%	7.5%	2	10.7%	11.0%	12.1%	16.2%
∞	12.5%	20%	12.5%	1	12.5%	12.5%	12.5%	12.5%
∞	12.5%	20%	15.0%	0.8	13.0%	13.0%	12.8%	11.5%

[1] Formula:

$$a_{\overline{n}|r} = \frac{(1 - s^*)a_{\overline{n}|d} + s^* P_{inv} a_{\overline{n}|d}}{P_{inv}}$$

TABLE 8.7. Minimum internal rates of return of projects according to OECD Intertemporal Social Analysis.[1]

$s^* = 0\%$ T	q	s	d	P_{inv}	Project Life in Years ∞	50	25	10
20	12.5%	20%	5%	2.22	11.1%	12.1%	15.3%	26.0%
20	12.5%	20%	7.5%	1.71	12.8%	13.2%	14.9%	21.3%
20	12.5%	20%	12.5%	1.00	12.5%	12.5%	12.5%	12.5%
20	12.5%	20%	15.0%	0.93	13.9%	13.9%	13.8%	13.1%

$s^* = 20\%$ T	q	s	d	P_{inv}	Project Life in Years ∞	50	25	10
20	12.5%	20%	5%	2.22	8.9%	9.7%	11.9%	19.1%
20	12.5%	20%	7.5%	1.71	11.2%	11.5%	12.8%	17.4%
20	12.5%	20%	12.5%	1.00	12.5%	12.5%	12.5%	12.5%
20	12.5%	20%	15.0%	0.93	14.1%	14.1%	14.0%	13.5%

$s^* = 40\%$ T	q	s	d	P_{inv}	Project Life in Years ∞	50	25	10
20	12.5%	20%	5%	2.22	7.5%	8.0%	9.6%	14.2%
20	12.5%	20%	7.5%	1.71	10.0%	10.2%	11.1%	14.7%
20	12.5%	20%	12.5%	1.00	12.5%	12.5%	12.5%	12.5%
20	12.5%	20%	15.0%	0.93	14.4%	14.4%	14.3%	13.8%

[1] Formula:

$$a_{\bar{n}|r} = \frac{(1 - s^*)a_{\bar{n}|d} + s^* P_{inv} \cdot a_{\bar{n}|d}}{P_{inv}}$$

In this Table, P_{inv} has been calculated as per the OECD formula quoted in the main text, except for the case that $d = q$ where P_{inv} has been set at 1. OECD's value of P_{inv} in this case would be slightly higher than 1. This is due to the simplifying assumption which was made in deriving the OECD formula for P_{inv} that the consumption stream is instantaneously generated.

are consumed rather than invested. Second, the lowest cut-off rates are found for projects with long lives. Hence, there is a penalty on projects with a short life. All of these conclusions are to be expected if we accept the criteria. However, both tables, in particular the UNIDO table, show surprising results. For instance, the UNIDO approach implies that the Government should not undertake a project with a short life of 10 years and zero reinvestment unless the project's rate of return is at least 54 percent. In the OECD case the rate of return should be at least 26 percent. This means that unless one attaches weights to the income increase of project beneficiaries, which would increase the rates of return, such projects should not be undertaken. In practice, Governments should thus not undertake projects for middle-income groups – the groups on whose incomes no distributional weights can be placed. Thus Governments, for instance, should never undertake a tube-well program or construct feeder roads and the like for average income farmers.

Let us now turn to the case where $d > q$. None of the manuals mention this possibility, but it is quite possible – namely, if the investment program is considered too large – and we see, therefore, no reason not to discuss it. Both tables show that the cut-off rates are lower than d. Furthermore, short-life projects are favored and depending on the value of P_{inv}, the cut-off rate may even be lower than the opportunity cost of capital rate q (Table 8.6). Thus, tube-well and feederroad programs would not even need to earn the opportunity cost of capital rate q.

It thus appears that the social discount rate cum shadow price of investment approach results in dichotomies. In the case of $d < q$, we find that Governments should not undertake short-life projects for average income groups unless the economic rate of return is extremely high. In the cases where $d > q$, short-life projects do not even need to earn the opportunity cost of capital rate q. Regarding the first possibility, which is normally the case, we see of course that Governments in developing countries undertake short-life projects. Regarding the second possibility, we would expect that Governments would not undertake short-life projects for average income groups if they intend to curtail their investment programs. It is clear that something is wrong with the proposed criteria and that the UNIDO and OECD analyses should be reconsidered.[34]

8.5. CRITICISM OF THE UNIDO AND OECD CRITERIA

Our criticism of the UNIDO and OECD criteria for investment planning will be brief. We believe that the distribution of income between consumption and investment is not the relevant concept for analyzing the intertemporal income distribution problem, but that the correct concept should be the distribution of income between persons. In other words, we see the intertemporal income distribution problem as a special aspect of the interpersonal income distribution problem. We will illustrate this by reviewing in detail (a) the shadow price of investment; (b) the so-called shadow wage rate; and (c) the social discount rate.

To start our critical review of the shadow price of investment concept, it may be useful to reconsider briefly the general formula for the acceptance of a project:

$$(8.1.) \quad \sum_{t=1}^{t=n} \frac{N_t(1 - s^*) + N_t s^* P_{inv}}{(1 + d)^t} \geqslant K P_{inv}$$

The underlying assumption for Government projects with respect to the right-hand side of the formula is that the Government investment displaces an equivalent amount of private investment. Is this correct? The criterion seems rather odd because in many developing countries, Government funds are obtained from export duties and import duties which displace private consumption rather than private investment. It is worthwhile then to review the few cases where the literature discusses the possibility that public investments displace private consumption.

As mentioned in Section 8.3, MARGLIN mentions explicitly the possibility that private consumption can be displaced. The right-hand side of (8.1) is then $K(a^{inv}P_{inv} + a^{cons})$ rather than $K P_{inv}$. However, it also seems that he does not attach much importance to it. In the Harvard study[35] MARGLIN shows an example where the amount of private investment displaced by each dollar of public investment is 75 percent, so that the amount of private consumption displaced is 25 percent. In an example in his Public Investment Criteria,[36] the amount of private investment displaced has risen to 90 percent. In the UNIDO Guidelines the examples assume that public investment displaces only private investment and not consumption, and one is led to believe that MARGLIN feels that this must be true in approximation.[37] Why this should be so is nowhere explained.

In the first edition of his book MISHAN[38] seems to feel that public investment can displace private consumption to a considerable extent. He quotes MARGLIN's general displacement formula and then makes the distinction that the public funds can be raised by taxes or by borrowing. In the latter case, he states that the Government investment would displace private investment. However, if the funds were raised by direct taxation and the aggregate marginal propensity to save of the country were 20 percent, then 80 percent of the funds required for a public project would displace consumption and 20 percent private investment. Nevertheless, MISHAN then argues that since the funds taken from consumption could just as well have been invested instead in the private sector, these funds should be valued similarly to the funds taken from private investment. In other words, MISHAN feels that the right-hand side of (8.1) should remain P_{inv} even if 80 percent of the public investment represents consumption foregone.

As FELDSTEIN[39] has pointed out, MISHAN's reasoning is not correct. The actual opportunity cost of any resource is its value in the alternative use to which it *would* have been put and not to which it *could* have been put. The funds taken from consumption can indeed be invested by Government in the private sector but if there is a constraint on public funds, Government will use the resources for public investments. It is this second-best consideration that should be instrumental in valuing the appropriated funds as displaced consumption. In MISHAN's example then, if the funds raised by the Government displace private investment for 20 percent and private consumption for 80 percent, the correct shadow price of Government funds would be $(0.2 P_{inv} + 0.8)$.[40]

The sources from which the Government obtains its funds are thus important. As MUSGRAVE[41] has pointed out, if the funds are withdrawn from consumption, the likelihood that a public investment would qualify would be much greater than if the funds are largely withdrawn from private investment. FELDSTEIN[42] accepts this and analyzes in detail the relation between the sources of finance and the value of public projects. However, this very interesting analysis does not concern us here. The point we wish to make is that if the shadow price of Government funds does depend on the relative displacements of consumption and investment, then it is also crucially important to know whose consumption and whose investment is being displaced. In other words, interpersonal income distribution considerations must be taken into account.

Let us turn now to the so-called shadow wage rate formula. Both the OECD Manual and the UNIDO Guidelines seem to have been inspired for the derivation of this formula by the LEWIS labor surplus theory. We reviewed this theory in Chapter 3 and saw there that the opportunity cost of a laborer in the urban area is not equal to his foregone marginal product in agriculture because other agricultural workers are induced to migrate to the cities. This subject is not discussed in the Manual or the Guidelines; it is assumed in both that it is economically advantageous to transfer a laborer from the agricultural sector to the industrial sector as long as his marginal product in agriculture is lower than in industry.

Let us assume that the creation of one new job causes indeed only one man to shift out of agriculture. Then if investments are optimal in the economy, the traditional theory would argue that investments in industry are justified when

$$\frac{y - lm}{q} \geqslant 1$$

where the incremental output to capital ratio in the industrial sector is y, the number of laborers per dollar of investment is l, the marginal product of labor in agriculture is m, and the opportunity cost of capital is q. Let us now assume that the country's investment program is not optimal and that the Government funds displace an equivalent amount of private investments. Then the OECD Manual argues that the relevant formula should be:

$$\frac{(y - lw) + \dfrac{l(w - m)}{P_{inv}}}{a} \geqslant 1$$

In this formula w represents the wage rate, a the accounting rate of interest, $y - lw$ the capitalists' profits which the OECD Manual assumes will all be reinvested, and $lw - lm$ the increase in consumption of the laborers, which incurs a penalty (it should be recalled that OECD uses investment as the numéraire).[43] The numerator of the formula can be rearranged as follows:

$$y - l\left(w - \frac{w - m}{P_{inv}}\right)$$

This is easy to understand. Employing a laborer reduces capitalists' investments by w and increases a laborer's consumption by $w - m$. Since consumption is worth $1/P_{inv}$ of investments, the social cost of employing a laborer must be the

190

bracketed expression. The OECD Manual calls this the shadow wage rate.[44]

In their sequel volume[45] to the OECD Manual, LITTLE and MIRRLEES consider the matter further. There are now two ways to estimate P_{inv}. The first, as discussed in Section 8.3, and the second by analyzing what the social value of the consumption increase of the workers would be. Denoting the utility increase of a worker by $U_w - U_m$, it follows from the shadow wage rate formula that $U_w - U_m = (w - m)/P_{inv}$. The utility increase can, of course, only be measured if a marginal utility of consumption function is specified.[46] L and M suggest that the function $u = (b/c)^{\alpha}$ should be used, where u is marginal utility of consumption, b the base consumption level, c the per capita consumption of the group being analyzed, and α the elasticity of the marginal utility of consumption with respect to consumption. As regards b, L and M postulate that this is the level at which the Government makes subsidy payments to the poor.[47] Hence, by estimating b, w, m and α, the value of P_{inv} can also be calculated in this alternative manner.

Let us see how the actual calculation takes place. We will use values for b, w, m and α from an example of L and M, and will ignore such complications as the possibility that the consumption level of the migrants in the backward sector may be higher than their marginal product of labor or that an increase of demand for labor in the modern sector may cause an increase in the urban wage rates. These complications can easily be introduced into the formula but will only clutter the example. Assuming the following values:

b = Rs 600
w = Rs 1500
m = Rs 750
α = 2.

then $w - m = $ Rs 750, and $U_w - U_m = 240$ utils,[48] and from $P_{inv} = (w - m)/(U_w - U_m)$, it follows that the value of P_{inv} is 3.1.

L and M's analysis invites comment. First, it seems to us that the alternative method for estimating P_{inv} is not very helpful for operational work, since the estimate of b – the base consumption level – will always be very haphazard. Furthermore, in most developing countries no direct subsidy payments are made to the poor. Nor is there much sense in looking at the income level at which a man just escapes the direct income tax – as also suggested by L and M[49] –, because income tax levels are notoriously rigid, seldom adjusted. As regards the elasticity of the marginal utility of consumption function, L and M suggest that α may assume values varying from 0.67 to 3, but no guidance is given as to which value should be chosen. Much more fundamental, however, is the question why L and M choose the subsidy to the poor level as a measure of base consumption. The answer is, of course, that only then will the alternative method of estimating P_{inv} give values comparable to the P_{inv} estimates of Section 8.3. Furthermore, only by choosing the subsidy to the poor level as the base consumption level does the shadow wage rate formula continue to be valid. As the marginal utility of consumption function $u = (b/c)^{\alpha}$ shows, if c is much

FIGURE 8.3.

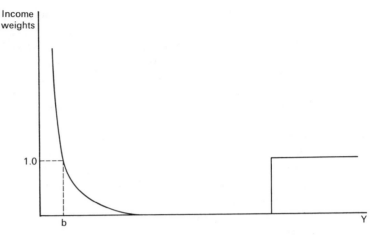

larger than b, as would be the case for capitalist consumption, then the interpersonal distribution weight for that class would be zero. But since savings are reckoned at face value, capitalists' income – which is supposed to be saved – receives again the weight of one. Thus, in the shadow rate formula, capitalists' income ($y - lw$) continues to receive the weight of one, even though from an interpersonal income distribution point of view the weight should be zero.

The discriminatory nature of L and M's method will by now, have become very clear. Figure 8.3 depicts the income weights which L and M use: the weights are greater than 1 for incomes below the base level income b, they decrease rapidly to 0 and rise to 1 for the rich groups who save almost all of their incomes. It appears then that the social discount rate cum shadow price of investment methodology does after all include interpersonal income distribution weights. However, these are so discriminatory that it needs no elaboration that the methodology will probably not be accepted by the body politic if the values of the weights are brought out into the open.

Finally, a few words about the social discount rate concept. In Section 8.2 we defined the social discount rate as the rate of fall of the marginal utility of consumption of the representative consumer over time. Hence, if the marginal utility of consumption function is $u = (b/c)^\alpha$, we get

$$\frac{du/dt}{u} = \frac{du/dt}{u} \cdot \frac{c}{dc/dt} \cdot \frac{dc/dt}{c} = -\alpha g$$

The same result is obtained if we work with a marginal utility of income schedule of the form given above instead of a marginal utility of consumption schedule.

We would like to show now that the social discount rate can also be derived from the general formula for the derivation of interpersonal income distribution

192

weights, and we will proceed as follows. The social weight (v_p) to be attached to additions to income of a person at a certain income level is, of course, determined by the formula $v_p = u_p/u_b$ where u_p is the marginal utility of additions to the income level y_p and u_b is the marginal utility of additions to the base income level y_b. Hence, with a marginal utility of income schedule of the form $u = (b/y)^\alpha$ we get $v_p = y_p^{-\alpha}/y_b^{-\alpha} = y_b/y_p$.

Essentially the same formula can be used to derive the social discount rate by applying it to utility levels at different points in time. The relevant formula is then:

$$z_{at} = \frac{u_{at}}{u_{ao}} = \frac{(y_{at})^{-\alpha}}{(y_{ao})^{-\alpha}} = \frac{(y_{ao} \cdot e^{g_a t})^{-\alpha}}{(y_{ao})^{-\alpha}} = e^{-\alpha g_a t}$$

where the subscript a denotes that we are dealing with our representative consumer and $z_t =$ the intertemporal weight, $u_t =$ the marginal utility of income at time t, $u_o =$ the marginal utility of income at time o, and $g_a =$ the growth rate of income. We thus obtain the familiar result that the marginal utility of future income falls at the rate $-\alpha g_a$. Hence, if there is also a pure time preference rate p_a, project benefits and costs should be discounted at the rate $d_a = p_a + \alpha g_a$.

Let us now suppose that we wish to calculate the intertemporal weight on the incomes of a group of persons whose incomes are not representative and whose incomes grow at a rate different to g_a, let us say the poor. Then the intertemporal weight for the poor over time will be presented by the formula $d_p = p_p + \alpha_p g_p$[50]. Benefits and costs of projects geared toward raising the incomes of the poor should not, therefore, be discounted at the rate d_a but at a different rate d_p. The upshot of this discussion is that we cannot speak of a single social discount rate when incomes of different income classes grow at different rates, since there are then as many social discount rates as there are income classes. This is not surprising of course. In the real world we cannot identify a representative income earner or consumer and the concept of a single social discount rate based on such an average person, therefore, breaks down.

It may be argued that there is still the possibility that the social discount rate would equal the rate of fall of the marginal utility of total income. Although it may well be possible that a planner has somehow dreamed up a function of the marginal utility of the economy's total income, we believe that such a function cannot be defended because it is not the growth of national income that is important but the growth of the different income classes. HAQ[51] has discussed this point in detail. The hot pursuit of growth in the Sixties has indeed resulted in fairly respectable GNP growth rates, especially by historical standards, but at the same time has increased income disparities. Pakistan, for instance, which was considered a model of development, showed during the Sixties an increase in unemployment, a decline in real wages in the industrial sector by one-third, a doubling of the income disparity between East and West, and an increased concentration of industrial wealth. As a result, according to HAQ, the system exploded in 1968, not only for political reasons, but also because of economic unrest.

If we are so critical of the social discount rate cum shadow price of investment methodology and its growth of national income approach, the question arises – what then? The difference between the UNIDO and OECD criteria and the approach we propose can be brought back to our view of the role of Government. Both the UNIDO and OECD approaches see Governments as having all-encompassing powers with respect to what type of investments should be undertaken. Because in the UNIDO approach no guidance is given as to the estimate of the interpersonal consumption weights, all the decisions have to be taken at the top level. In the OECD approach, decentralized decision-making is possible. However, both criteria are discriminatory. LITTLE and MIRLEES consider their system specially suitable for a well-managed socialist economy[52] but, in reality, of course it can only be applied if the Government assumes a dictatorial role, discriminating against average income earners.

In our approach, the level of investments as well as the distribution between persons of the benefits of investments are the relevant concepts and the role of Government is seen as that of an intermediary which should implement the population's value consensus objectives. If the investments of a country are considered too low, then the Government's role is to promote private investments by appropriate monetary and fiscal policies. Often we see in the developing countries that Governments do use these instruments and that they are able to influence the profit rate of the private sector and therewith the overall investment level. As discussed in Section 8.1, there is then no need to introduce the concept of a social discount rate and, in the absence of budget constraints, the opportunity cost of capital is then the relevant concept. A budget constraint would become binding if the Government is not allowed to transfer funds from the private sector and it wishes to undertake more projects than it has funds available. As discussed in Chapter 5, the relevant cut-off rate for the evaluation of Government projects is then no longer the opportunity cost of capital q but the budget constraint rate b.

If the Government is not allowed to use fiscal and monetary policies to expand the overall investment level, then it may well be that the consensus of opinion in the country is that investments should not be expanded. Also, in this case, there is then no need to apply the shadow price of investment algorithm.

Suppose, however, that the consensus of opinion is that investments are suboptimal. Suppose further that the body politic does not allow the Government the use of fiscal and monetary policies to promote investments. Then the algorithm could be used to deepen the capital structure of the country provided at the same time appropriate personal weights are attached to additions to the incomes of the poorest and the richest income groups in order to adhere to the principle that these groups should have social discount rates different from that of the middle income group. However, even then it would remain valid that this system of project evaluation discriminates against the middle income groups.

194

It seems to us, therefore, that usually the body politic will reject the system if it becomes aware of the system's discriminatory nature, and that it will prefer to achieve its objectives through the use of fiscal and monetary policies.

Our analysis thus leads us to conclude that the social discount rate cum shadow price of investment approach to public investment decisions should usually be rejected and that usually the normal traditional discount rates should be used to evaluate Government projects. However, the analysis of which investments – public as well as private – are acceptable and which are not, can only be undertaken if interpersonal income distribution aspects are taken into account. How this should be done will be discussed in the next Chapter.

[1] ECKSTEIN, 'Water Resource Development,' p. 99.

[2] PIGOU, 'The Economics of Welfare,' pp. 25–26.

[3] In a subsequent article, ECKSTEIN is much more careful in his wording and accepts the principle of citizen sovereignty (see Section 8.2).

[4] The discount rate at time n would be $(1 + q_1)(1 + q_2) \ldots (1 + q_n)$, where $q_1, q_2, \ldots$, etc., are the projected opportunity costs of capital in the successive time periods.

[5] ECKSTEIN, O., 'A Survey of the Theory of Public Expenditure Criteria' in 'Public Finances: Needs, Sources and Utilization,' A Conference of the Universities National Bureau Committee for Economic Research, published by Princeton University Press, Princeton, 1961, pp. 454–460.

[6] RAMSEY, F. P., 'A Mathematical Theory of Savings,' The Economic Journal, December 1928.

[7] e.g., HICKS, J., 'Capital and Growth,' Oxford University Press, New York and Oxford, 1965, Chapter XXI.

[8] It should be noted that we assume that our consumer receives a certain sum in a certain future year rather than a stream of future sums. We will return to this point at the end of this section.

[9] For a detailed discussion of marginal utility functions, see Chapter 9.

[10] Since $u = b^x c^{-\alpha}$, it follows that $du/dc = -\alpha b^x c^{-\alpha-1}$. Hence,

$$\alpha = -\frac{du}{dc} \cdot \frac{1}{b^x c^{-\alpha-1}} = -\frac{du}{dc} \cdot \frac{c}{b^x c^{-\alpha}} = -\frac{du}{dc} \cdot \frac{c}{u}.$$

[11] ECKSTEIN, O., 'A Survey of the Theory of Public Expenditure Criteria,' pp. 454–460.

[12] The likely values of the elasticity of the marginal utility of consumption function at different levels of consumption will be discussed in detail in Chapter 9. ECKSTEIN's assumption as to the order of magnitude of the elasticity values is in line with with empirical investigations.

[13] As ECKSTEIN notes (p. 456) this assumes that individuals are narrowly selfish, caring nothing about the wealth they leave behind when they die. It also assumes that individuals do not invest in education for their children to give them a better life than they themselves have. These factors would thus tend to lower an individual's pure time preference rate.

[14] LITTLE and MIRRLEES, 'Manual for Industrial Project Analysis in Developing Countries,' p. 167.

[15] Ibid., pp. 175–176.

[16] DASGUPTA, SEN and MARGLIN, 'Guidelines for Project Evaluation,' p. 167.

[17] For a detailed discussion, see HICKS, 'Capital and Growth,' Chapter XXI.

[18] See HICKS, 'Capital and Growth, p. 262.

[19] ECKSTEIN, 'Water Resources Development,' p. 101.

[20] See Section 5.5.

[21] SEN, 'Choice of Techniques'; STEINER, P. O. 'Choosing Among Alternative Public Investments in the Water Resource Field,' The American Economic Review, December 1959, p. 893; MARGLIN, S. A., 'The Opportunity Costs of Public Investment,' The Quarterly Journal of Economics, May 1963; FELDSTEIN, M. S., 'Net Social Benefits Calculation and the Public Investment Decision,' Oxford Economic Papers, March 1964, p. 114; and FELDSTEIN, M. S., 'The Social Time Preference Discount Rate in Cost-Benefit Analysis,' The Economic Journal, June 1964, p. 36.

[22] MARGLIN, S. A., 'Public Investment Criteria,' MIT Press, Cambridge, Massachusetts, 1967.

[23] DASGUPTA, SEN and MARGLIN, 'Guidelines for Project Evaluation.'

[24] DASGUPTA, SEN and MARGLIN, 'Guidelines,' p. 177.

[25] DASGUPTA, SEN and MARGLIN, 'Guidelines,' p. 181.

[26] See, for instance, its example on page 243.

[27] LITTLE and MIRRLEES, 'Manual,' pp. 178–179.

[28] See LAL, D., 'Methods of Project Analysis: A Review,' World Bank Staff Occasional Papers No. 16, distributed by The Johns Hopkins University Press, Baltimore and London, 1974, p. 29.

[29] LITTLE and MIRRLEES, 'Manual,' pp. 178–179.

[30] The UNIDO Guidelines also mentions the possibility that s and q may change within a relatively short time period (UNIDO Guidelines, pp. 196–198). However, the Guidelines seems to feel that this is not a realistic possibility and uses in all its studies the formula quoted in the text above.

[31] LITTLE and MIRRLEES, 'Manual,' footnote p. 167. The geometric sum should be:

$$(c - m)n \left\{ \frac{(1 + r)^T}{(1 + i)^T} - 1 \right\} \frac{1 + i}{r - i}.$$ OECD's $(c - m)n$ is the consumption part of the

benefit stream ($q - sq$ in our notation), r the reinvestment part (sq) and i the social discount rate (d).

[32] This can easily be proven. Consider the following division of the benefit stream per \$ 1 initially invested:

TABLE 8.4.

	yr 0	1	2	3	T
(1) Net Benefits	–	q	$q(1 + sq)$	$q(1 + sq)^2$	$q(1 + sq)^{T-1}$
(2) Reinvestments	–	sq	$sq(1 + sq)$	$sq(1 + sq)^2$	$sq(1 + sq)^{T-1}$
(3) Accumulated Capital	1	$(1 + sq)$	$(1 + sq)^2$	$(1 + sq)^3$	$(1 + sq)^T$
(4) Consumption (1)–(2)	–	$(q - sq)$	$(q - sq)(1 + sq)$	$(q - sq)(1 + sq)^2$	$(q - sq)(1 + sq)^{T-1}$

The value of the accumulated capital at the end of year T, discounted at the social discount rate d, will be

(i) $\dfrac{(1 + sq)^T}{(1 + d)^T}$ and since capital in year T is just as valuable as consumption, this term also

represents the discounted value of the final capital in terms of consumption. Consider now the consumption stream. To simplify matters, it is assumed that the investments generate their returns instantaneously, so that we can write for the present value of the consumption stream:

$$(q - sq) \left\{ 1 + \frac{(1 + sq)}{(1 + d)} + \ldots \frac{(1 + sq)^T}{(1 + d)^T} \right\}$$

As the second bracketed expression can be summed, the above expression can be reduced to:

(ii) $(q - sq) \left\{ \dfrac{(1 + sq)^T (1 + d)}{(1 + d)^T (sq - d)} - \dfrac{(1 + d)}{(sq - d)} \right\}$

P_{inv} is the sum of (i) and (ii), and it can easily be seen that this reduces to the formula presented in the main text.

[33] It should be mentioned that the OECD approach on which Table 8.7 is based is logically not consistent. P_{inv} in the OECD approach is calculated under the assumption that $T = 20$

years. As P_{inv} will decrease over time, it cannot be assumed that s^*P_{inv} will remain constant during the life of a project.

[34] The odd results of the UNIDO and OECD criteria for the case $d<q$ may be explained as follows. In case a project has to recover in addition to its capital costs a premium on these capital costs, then its cash flow must be larger than if no premium were to be recovered. Evidently, of two projects with different life times, the one with the shortest life needs to earn more per annum than the other one if the same premium were to be recovered. Hence, the project with the shortest life must have the highest rate of return. Putting a premium on the reinvestment part of the cash flow will reduce the required rate of return, the higher the reinvestment ratio the lower the required rate of return. A more meaningful calculation of the social rate of return of a project would be to apply the shadow price of investment to net savings, i.e. the savings that take place after the necessary allowance for depreciation has been made. However, neither UNIDO nor OECD make this suggestion. For the case $d > q$, consumption is at a premium. Hence, short-life projects, which produce consumption goods quickly, will have lower cut-off rates than long-life projects.

[35] MAASS et al., 'Design of Water Resource Systems,' p. 202.

[36] MARGLIN, 'Public Investment Criteria,' p. 61.

[37] DASGUPTA, SEN and MARGLIN, 'Guidelines,' p. 163.

[38] MISHAN, 'Cost-Benefit Analysis,' 1st ed., pp. 216–219.

[39] FELDSTEIN, M. S., 'The Inadequacy of Weighted Discount Rates,' excerpt from Feldstein, M. S., 'Financing in the Evaluation of Public Expenditure,' written for a forthcoming volume of essays in honor of Richard A. Musgrave, ed. Smith, W. L.; reprinted in 'Cost-Benefit Analysis,' ed., Layard, R., Penguin Education, Middlesex, England, reprinted with revisions, 1974.

[40] It may be noted in passing that the acceptance condition for a Government project becomes a very simple criterion if the consumption and investment propensities of the beneficiaries of the project are the same as those of the private sector as a whole. For then we would get

$$\sum_{t=1}^{n} \frac{N_t\{sP_{inv} + (1-s)\}}{(1+d)^t} \geq K\{sP_{inv} + (1-s)\}$$

which reduces to

$$\sum_{t=1}^{n} \frac{N_t}{(1+d)^t} \geq K$$

In other words, the Government project is acceptable as long as it has a positive net present value, present values found by discounting at the social discount rate. (In the case of a budget constraint, the projects should, of course, be ranked by their N/K ratios.) However, it must be added immediately that, in general, the consumption and investment propensities of the beneficiaries will not be the same as those of the private sector as a whole because it is the purpose of the investment algorithm to find projects with a high reinvestment ratio. So, even if we were to apply the law of large numbers to all Government projects, the assumption underlying the above formula would not be fulfilled.

[41] MUSGRAVE, R. A., 'Cost-Benefit Analysis and the Theory of Public Finance,' The Journal of Economic Literature, September 1969, pp. 798–807.

[42] FELDSTEIN, 'The Inadequacy of Weighted Discount Rates.'

[43] As the UNIDO Guidelines uses consumption as the numéraire, its formula is:

$$\frac{(y - lw)P_{inv} + l(w - m)}{d} \geq P_{inv}$$

[44] LITTLE and MIRRLEES, 'Manual,' footnote page 160.

[45] LITTLE and MIRRLEES, 'Project Appraisal and Planning for Developing Countries,' pp. 261–265.

[46] For a detailed discussion of marginal utility functions, see Chapter 9.

[47] In their sequel volume L and M postulate that a dollar of Government funds should be considered not only socially equal in value to a dollar of private investment, but also equal to a dollar used for either: (a) public consumption (defence, health, education, etc.,) which is not further analyzed because such expenditures are hard to evaluate; or (b) public investments; or (c) subsidies to the poor.

[48]
$$U_w - U_m = \int_m^w u \, dc = \frac{b^\alpha \cdot w^{-\alpha+1}}{-\alpha+1} - \frac{b^\alpha \cdot m^{-\alpha+1}}{-\alpha+1} = \frac{b^\alpha}{\alpha-1}\left(\frac{1}{m^{\alpha-1}} - \frac{1}{w^{\alpha-1}}\right) =$$
$$= \frac{b}{\alpha-1}\left\{\left(\frac{b}{m}\right)^{\alpha-1} - \left(\frac{b}{w}\right)^{\alpha-1}\right\}$$

If $\alpha = 2$, this reduces to $U_w - U_m = b^2(1/m - 1/w)$. Substituting the value of m and w, we get $U_w - U_m = 600^2 \,(1/750 - 1/1500) = 240$ utils.

[49] LITTLE and MIRRLEES, 'Project Appraisal and Planning for Developing Countries,' p. 244.

[50] It may be noted that we assume that the pure time preference rate of the poor p_p will differ from the pure time preference rate of the average income earner p_a. However, as discussed further below, these time preference rates are not relevant in our system because we believe that normally the projected opportunity costs of capital or budget constraint rates should be used for the evaluation of Government projects. There are persons who feel that the pure time preference rate of the poor should play a role in such evaluation. This is, in our opinion, not correct. The evaluation procedures we propose emphasize the necessity of increasing the incomes of the poor by attaching weights to increments in income of the poor and by discounting at the traditional discount rates. The use of an individual discount rate does not acknowledge that for project evaluation purposes the social rather than the individual rate should be used. It may furthermore be remarked that generally the time preference rate of the poor has a high value (e.g. they are often willing to repay the one bag of rice borrowed before the harvest with two bags of rice after the harvest), so that very few projects would be accepted if this rate were used.

[51] HAQ, M. ul, 'Employment in the 1970s: A New Perspective,' Speech at World Conference, Ottawa, May 1971.

[52] LITTLE and MIRRLEES, 'Project Appraisal and Planning for Developing Countries,' p. 350.

9. INTERPERSONAL INCOME DISTRIBUTION ASPECTS

9.1. PROJECT PLANNING AND THE DISTRIBUTION OF INCOME BETWEEN PERSONS

So far the discussion in this study has centered on the rules to be followed for project planning purposes if interpersonal income distribution considerations are not taken into account. Often, however, the purpose of a project is to raise the incomes of certain groups of people – rural poor, urban poor, target groups in particular regions, and the like. How should such projects be designed, evaluated and ranked?

The basic objective of the theory of project planning is to find rules for the maximization of national welfare. Where income distribution is neglected, the marginal utility of income of every individual either benefitting or losing from a project is assumed to be the same and constant. Hence, the net benefit of a project is then the sum of the gains and losses in real income accruing to the participants, which is represented by the area between the demand and cost curves. The objective function can be written as: $W = Y_p + Y_a$ where Y_p and Y_a are the gains in real income of consumers and producers, respectively. Since Y_p equals $(B - R)$ and Y_a equals $(R - C)$, where B is benefits, R revenues and C costs, this can also be written as $W = (B - R) + (R - C)$, which is, of course, the familiar criterion that $B - C$ should be maximized.

In cases where income distribution is deemed to have an influence on national welfare, the objective function becomes more complex. Traditionally, it has been held that income distribution was not important in project planning and evaluation because an appropriate distribution of income between persons could always be achieved through the transfer mechanism, i.e., by taxing high-income persons and transferring to low-income persons. In other words, the baking of the pie was to be considered separately from the slicing of the pie. The traditional benefit-cost analysis would ensure that the largest possible pie would be baked; the transfer mechanism would ensure that it would be distributed in appropriate slices. ECKSTEIN and others, however, believe that income distribution considerations should be included in the objective function. If the policymaker specifies some detailed rules, such as one that states that a certain minimum amount of income must accrue to a particular group, the formulation of the objective function is a relatively simple task. Often, however, no such rules are provided. ECKSTEIN suggests that the economist should then try to draw up specific objective functions and experiment with these. The following quote may illustrate this. 'For example, he (the economist) can assume a certain shape for the marginal utility of income function. He may assume some elasticity to his curve, or he may choose to use a form of the function that has been implicitly produced by the political process. The effective marginal rates of the personal income tax at different income levels can be interpreted as implying a marginal utility of income curve. If the Government is assumed to act on the principle of equi-marginal sacrifice, then marginal effective tax rates can be the basis for deriving a measure of the Government's notion of marginal utilities of income.'[1]

Accepting ECKSTEIN's suggestion, HAVEMAN[2] analyzed some 147 water resource development projects in the 10 southern states of the USA and found that the rate of return of 72 projects, about 50 percent of the total number, was less than 5.5 percent. When, however, welfare weights based on personal income taxes were attached to the benefits and costs of the different projects, it appeared that only 25 of the projects, about 18 percent, earned less than a 5.5 percent rate of return.[3] HAVEMAN concluded that the redistribution of income through some economically inefficient projects may well be a desirable technique.[4]

MARGLIN also maintains that the objective function should include income redistribution considerations. According to him, income cannot be redistributed by means of a transfer mechanism without violating institutional and political barriers. Direct subsidies are often vigorously opposed and lump-sum taxes are politically even more undesirable. Thus MARGLIN concludes that 'income must be redistributed through such means as development of water resource projects with accompanying inefficiencies, if desired income redistribution goals are to be achieved without violating institutional and political arrangements valued in the community.'[5] MARGLIN accepts as an established fact that the price of a project's output will be determined at a higher level of the planning process and discusses three alternative ways of formulating the objective function.

The first is that net benefits should be maximized with respect to project size, subject to the constraint that the income of system beneficiaries should be raised to at least a certain specified level. Using the notation followed here, this may be expressed as:

$$\text{Max. } B - C \text{ subject to } B - R \geqslant A_1$$

The second is that the income distribution weighted sum of the net benefits should be maximized. If the consumers of the project's product are a homogeneous group, we may write this as:

$$\text{Max. } v(B - R) + (R - C)$$

where the weight v is determined in relation to the Government's income $(R - C)$ which assumes a weight of unity. Finally, the third alternative: this states that the objective is to maximize the redistribution benefits subject to the constraint that the loss in efficiency should not exceed a certain level. The objective function is then:

$$\text{Max. } (B - R) \text{ subject to } B - C \geqslant A_2$$

Assuming that the constraints are binding, and solving the Lagrangean formulations of the first and third alternatives, the first order condition as regards λ is: $\lambda = (dC - dB)/(dB - dR)$. The same value is found for $(v - 1)$

when the first order condition for the maximization of the second objective function is determined. It means that project size should be expanded until the marginal loss in efficiency $(dC - dB)$ equals the marginal net redistribution gain $(dB - dR)$ weighted with the distribution premium $(v - 1)$. The condition may also be written as $1 + \lambda = v = (dC - dR)/(dB - dR)$, which is perhaps intuitively more clear. In words, it means that project size should be expanded until the marginal loss in income of the producer equals the marginal redistribution gain weighted with the distribution weight v. Under the first and third formulation, the constraints are expressed in amounts of income and the value of the constrained income – as represented by $1 + \lambda$ – is then the value which one additional (or foregone) unit of the constrained income would have in the rest of the economy. Or, in other words, the value of the constrained income is then determined by the costs that must be incurred to increase or decrease the constrained income by one unit. Under the second formulation one specifies in advance the costs – as represented by the weight v – that one is willing to incur to increase the constrained income and the optimization procedure will then show the amount of additional income by which the constraint can be relaxed. The three formulations are, therefore, theoretically equivalent, leading to the same result.

MARGLIN seems to prefer the use of either the first or third formulation. If some indication of the levels of either A_1 or A_2 can be elicited from the decision-maker, then the problem is solved. It seems to us, however, that even if the policymaker were willing to specify these levels, the procedure could easily lead to confusion because A_1 may not be consistent with A_2. Furthermore, in practice it is highly unlikely that any policymaker would be willing to indicate what additional income a certain target group should receive or what the maximum loss in efficiency benefits should be. It would, therefore, appear preferable to work with the second formulation and to make the welfare weights explicit. An artificiality which MARGLIN introduces is that he sees the repayments R as determined by a higher authority so that the project planner has only one instrument variable – the size of the project – at his disposal. If the objective is indeed to increase the incomes of a certain target group, then the lowering of repayments must surely be an efficient way of increasing the incomes of such a group even though this means that the Government would receive less revenues. In our opinion, R should, therefore, also be considered an instrument variable, albeit perhaps only over a certain range.[6] The analysis can easily be extended to take account of the repayment variable. The first order condition for the maximization of the weighted objective function when R is a function of the market clearing price is $v = (dC - dR)/(dB - dR)$. It would be pure chance, of course, if v would equal unity at the efficiency size of the project and normally repayments should be lowered to increase the income of the target group. If, however, with zero repayments, v is still greater than unity, then project size should be expanded. As dB would then represent the marginal redistribution gain rather than $dB - dR$, the expansion of project size should continue until the gain dB weighted with v equals the marginal increase in costs dC. Some-

202

times a constraint has been set on the lowering of repayments. For instance, the Government may insist, for administrative reasons, that operating costs should be recovered. The optimum condition is then $v = (dC - dO)/(dB - dO) = dK/dN$. If the target group's income at the efficiency optimum size is still considered to be below the norm when repayments have been reduced to the level of operating costs, then again project size should be expanded.

The above discussion is far from exhaustive, but it may have made it clear that there is a trend in the recent literature towards accepting that income distribution aspects should count in the design and selection of projects, a trend which is also reflected in the recent manuals on project evaluation. The UNIDO Guidelines state explicitly that income distribution counts, and the sequel to the OECD Manual also considers income distribution aspects. This trend also seems to be followed by the practitioners of benefit-cost analysis, those who have the hard task of designing projects and of determining which projects meet stated economic and social objectives. In a speech to the Board of Governors, the President of the World Bank states that the question of equity should be an integral part of project evaluation procedures both within the developing countries and the lending agencies, and that the World Bank is beginning to develop this approach.[7] Also, several of the OECD case studies consider income distribution an integral part of project analysis.[8]

On the other hand, there are still writers such as HARBERGER – albeit heavily criticized[9] – who do not consider income distribution weight adjustments and who firmly believe that only the traditional benefit-cost analysis leads to useful results. Is it possible that the truth lies somewhere between the two extreme positions?

The remainder of this Chapter will be devoted to this question. Since the level of the distribution weights determines the extent to which efficiency losses should be accepted to comply with the equity criteria, the next two sections will review how such weights can be determined. Having obtained some understanding of this matter, the Chapter concludes with a critical review of the proposed new criteria and an attempt to reconcile these with the traditional analysis.

9.2. The Marginal Utility of Income Schedule

Probably the simplest method of estimating the marginal utility of income, if it were a correct method, would be to follow ECKSTEIN's suggestion to calculate it from the personal income tax rates under the assumption that the Government fixes tax structure on the principle of equal sacrifice. If we denote by u_1, T_1 and Y_1, the marginal utility of income, the income tax rate and the income level of individual 1 respectively, ECKSTEIN's proposal is that it should hold for individuals 1, 2, 3, etc., that $u_1(dT_1/dY_1) = u_2(dT_2/dY_2) = \ldots$ etc.

Hence, by choosing a base level of income subject to income tax and setting the marginal utility of that income at unity, the marginal utility of all other incomes subject to income tax can be determined relative to the base level. For instance, if the marginal income tax is 0.50 at a level of income of $ 15,000 which we choose as the base level, and 0.25 at a level of income of $ 5,000, it would follow from $u_1 = (dT_2/dY_2) \cdot (dY_1/dT_1) = 0.50\,(1/0.25) = 2$, that the marginal utility of income at the $ 5,000 level would be twice as much as that at the $ 15,000 level.

There are, however, several objections to this method. First, a practical one. Income taxes start only at a certain level of income so that, in many cases, especially for the ultra poor, no income weights can be determined. The method therefore has not much operational value. Second, if the principle of equal sacrifice is accepted, then the indirect taxes which an individual pays should also be taken into account. The procedure then becomes very complicated and is probably, again, no longer operational. Third, this method assumes that the incidence of the income tax will be fully borne by the taxpayer; in reality, of course, the tax will be passed on to others. Fourth, it may be questioned whether indeed the principle underlying the methodology – equal absolute sacrifice – is a correct one. While there are writers who have defended this on the grounds that it is, in their opinion, the most equitable principle, other writers have postulated different principles: for instance, that of equi-proportional sacrifice, which should leave relative positions in terms of total utility unchanged; or that of equal marginal sacrifice in which each individual after paying the tax should end up with the same marginal utility of income level.[10] Finally, of course, none of these principles takes into account that different levels of income may well have been obtained with different levels of effort. The principles can, therefore, be applied only to effortless incomes. All in all, it must be concluded that ECKSTEIN's suggestion does not present an appropriate basis on which to determine income distribution weights.

The question arises, what then? There are, of course, many possible marginal utility of income functions. Are there any a priori reasons why a certain one should be chosen? Some writers believe so and it may, therefore, be useful to review briefly some of the possible functions. A very convenient table has been produced by FREEMAN,[11] showing alongside the type of function, the weights that should be placed on marginal additions to incomes of persons at various income levels. A slightly revised version of the FREEMAN table is presented below: the weights have been normalized to give a weight of 1 to US $ 1 of income accruing to families with US $ 2,000 current income.

The base against which the income weights were calculated was purposely put in the revised table at US $ 2,000 of annual income, so that the weights would have some relevance for developing countries where average annual family income of a typical middle income level country was about US $ 2,000 in 1974. All the functions – except function 5 – are downward sloping, so that the weights decline with income levels. Function 5 is the one assumed by the traditional benefit-cost analysis: all incomes have the same weight. Other functions in the table would value a dollar to a family earning only US $ 200 per annum at from 100 to $2^1/_2$ times more than a dollar accruing to a family

TABLE 9.1.

Marginal Social Utility Function	Value Placed on US$ 1 Extra Income to a Family with an Annual Income (in 1974 US dollars) of:			
	US $ 200	US $ 2,000	US $ 20,000	US $ 200,000
1. Y^{-2}	100.00	1.00	0.01	0.0001
2. $Y^{-1.5}$	31.62	1.00	0.03	0.001
3. Y^{-1}	10.00	1.00	0.10	0.01
4. $Y^{-0.5}$	3.16	1.00	0.32	0.10
5. Y^0	1.00	1.00	1.00	1.00
6. $e^{-(Y/2,000)}$	2.46	1.00	0.001	Nil
7. $(\frac{Y}{1,000} + 1)^{-1}$	2.50	1.00	0.14	0.01
8. $(\frac{Y}{1,000} + 1)^{-2}$	6.25	1.00	0.02	0.0002

with an income of US $ 2,000 per annum.

Which of the several functions shown have some a priori grounds for preference? In an interesting study,[12] CHENERY et al. propose that the so-called Equal Weights Index should be used to measure whether the welfare of a country has increased. Under that index, a one percent increase in income at a low income level is considered as valuable socially as a one percent increase in income at a high income level. Hence, an increase of one percent at the US $200 income level should be weighted with the factor 10 to make it equally valuable as an increase of one percent at the US $2,000 level. As may be seen in Table 9.1. CHENERY et al. thus favor function 3. TINBERGEN also seems inclined to accept this function, which – it should be noted – had already been postulated as a plausible one in the 18th Century by BERNOULLI and in the 19th Century by WEBER and FECHNER. TINBERGEN proposes it as follows: 'When it comes to specifying in explicit mathematical shape my concept of welfare, I am inclined to use Weber-Fechner's law, and propose that the welfare feeling derived from income available per consumer rises with the logarithm of that income, that is, by equal steps for equal percentage increases of income.'[13] Since neither CHENERY nor TINBERGEN discuss the immanent reasons for preferring this function, let us see what BERNOULLI and WEBER and FECHNER had to say on the subject.

BERNOULLI postulated the existence of a downward sloping individual marginal utility of income function in connection with the so-called St. Petersburg paradox. As it would lead us too far from our main line of discussion to present this paradox here, we have relegated it to the Annex to this Chapter and it may suffice to mention that BERNOULLI believed that the function he proposed (function 3 in Table 9.1) would be highly probable but that he had no specific reasons for defending the postulate. In fact, he found a different function proposed by Gabriel CRAMER, a contemporary – who also solved the paradox, independently of him – quite acceptable. For an explanation as to why the marginal utility of income should assume a particular shape, we must, therefore, look elsewhere.

In fact, further advances in the field had to wait until the next century. In 1846, WEBER[14] published the results of his experiments on touch and concluded that the just noticeable difference of an increase in a stimulus bears a constant ratio to the original level of the stimulus. If we denote the just noticeable difference by $\triangle Y$ and the stimuls by Y, then his finding may be expressed as: $\triangle Y/Y =$ constant. FECHNER, a philosopher, physicist, psychophysicist and mathematician, believed that WEBER's law, as he called it, had universal validity applicable to probability analysis, stellar magnitudes, tonal pitch, and such[15] and developed it as follows.[16] He postulated that just noticeable differences in stimuli would cause constant increments in sensations. If we denote sensation by U, FECHNER's fundamental law may be written as $\triangle U = b \cdot \triangle Y/Y$, where b is a constant. Or, in other words, geometric increases in a stimulus produce only arithmetic increases in sensation. The equation can also be written as $u = \mathrm{d}U/\mathrm{d}Y = b/Y$. The integral of this is: $U = b \ln Y + C$, where C is the constant of integration. By setting this constant at $- b \ln \overline{Y}$, where $\overline{Y}$ is the value of Y at which $U = 0$, the formula for U becomes $U = b \ln Y$. Transforming this formula from a natural logarithmic expression into a common logarithmic one, it becomes $U = 2.3026\, b \log Y$. This equation has important operational value. Although it contains the unknown parameter b, we can dispose of it by using two such equations. If the sensation levels of two stimuli are denoted by U_1 and U_2 and the stimuli by Y_1 and Y_2, then it follows from the formula that $U_1/U_2 = \log Y_1/\log Y_2$. Hence, if we know the levels of two stimuli Y_1 and Y_2, then we can always calculate the corresponding levels of sensation.

The WEBER-FECHNER formula – as it is now called – is, of course, the same as the one postulated by BERNOULLI a century before. While BERNOULLI – a mathematician – developed the formula only as a hypothesis to solve the St. Petersburg paradox, FECHNER derived the formula from WEBER's actual observations. FECHNER's work has been invaluable for psychology and gave rise to the entire new field of quantitative experimental psychology.[17]

The WEBER-FECHNER law has mathematical properties which are very convenient for utility theory. Proportional increases in income produce arithmetic increases in utility. Also, income multiplied by the marginal utility of income is a constant. Further, a one percent increase in income results in a one percent decrease in marginal utility, or, in other words, the elasticity of the marginal utility of income with respect to income always equals unity.[18] If the WEBER-FECHNER law were universally applicable, then income distribution weights could easily be determined: they would be inversely proportionate with income. Recent experiments in psychophysics by STEVENS[19] have cast some doubts, however, on the validity of the WEBER-FECHNER law.

STEVENS's fundamental contribution to psychophysics is that he queried why proportionate increases in a stimulus should increase sensation by constant increments. Although constant percentage increases in a stimulus may be necessary to find the just noticeable difference, this does not necessarily imply that the sensation increases are constant. STEVENS invented a method of experimentation – the so-called magnitude estimation – whereby the observer is free to assign any number to his subjective impression of the sensation a particular stimulus produces. In pathbreaking experiments, he showed that our sensation as a function of variations in stimulus appear to follow a power function rather than the logarithmic function postulated by BERNOULLI. In terms of a formula, the relationship may be written as $U = bY^\beta$, where the exponent β – the elasticity of sensation with respect to stimulus[20] – determines the curvature of the function. When the exponent is greater than 1, the U function curves upwards and reaches an infinite value at a certain limit of Y. On the other hand, when the exponent is smaller than 1, additions to Y beyond a certain value of Y will not increase U. When the exponent equals 1, the U function becomes a straight line. STEVENS's law tells us that constant percentage changes in a stimulus do not produce constant increases in sensation as FECHNER believed, but constant percentage changes.

STEVENS is eloquent in his explanation of why this relationship seems plausible. Suppose that the law does not apply. Then, when we walk towards a house, the proportions of the house would become distorted. Or, similarly, when the sun goes behind a cloud and the light intensity falls, pictures become unrecognizable. Perhaps the power law – which allows us to perceive relations among objects as they are – is the only reason why we are able to survive in our heterogeneous environment.

The power law seems to apply to such sensory continuums as taste, smell, warmth, cold, vibration, shock, and also – according to STEVENS – to the utility of income. A simple experiment STEVENS repeated many times with classroom students was the following. A student is supposed to receive $ 10 and to answer how much he would need to receive to make him twice as happy. The answers ranged from about $ 35 to about $ 50. STEVENS concludes that this corresponds very well with the result obtained from the power function which CRAMER postulated for the solution of the St. Petersburg paradox because CRAMER's function,[21] which has an exponent of 1/2, gives the answer as $ 40.[22] It is interesting to note that, according to the WEBER-FECHNER law, the answer should be $ 100.[23]

If the utility of income function is indeed a power function, as proposed by CRAMER and STEVENS, then the function has the interesting property[24] that the elasticity of the marginal utility of income is a constant equal to $\beta - 1$. Hence, if the exponent of the total utility function is 0.5, the elasticity of the marginal utility of income would be minus 0.5. However, whether this is the correct value is, in our opinion, open to dispute. STEVENS's classroom experiment is a very crude one. Moreover, it does not take into account a person's income position.

Turning from psychophysics to economics, the values postulated by CRAMER and STEVENS for the elasticity of the marginal utility of income appear indeed to be on the low side. In pathbreaking work, FISHER[25] and FRISCH[26] showed, independently of each other, that there is a method by which the marginal utility of income can be measured directly. The procedure, which was subsequently further refined by FELLNER,[27] is basically as follows.

It is generally accepted that the consumers equilibrium position is characterized by the condition that $MU_x/P_x = MU_y/P_y = MU_z/P_z = \ldots = u$, where MU_x and P_x are the marginal utility of good x and the price of good x, respectively, and u the marginal utility of income. Suppose now that two consumers are observed consuming the same food package, but each is in a different price and income situation than the other. Assuming that these two consumers have identical tastes, it must hold that the marginal utility of food MU_f is the same for both consumers. The equilibrium conditions for the two consumers are: $MU_f/P_1 = u_1$ and $MU_f/P_2 = u_2$ where P_1 and P_2 indicate the different prices the two consumers pay, and u_1 and u_2 indicate the different marginal utilities of income they have. Since MU_f is the same in both cases, it follows that: $u_2 = (p_1/p_2) \cdot u_1$. This simple equation can also be written as: $u_2 - u_1 = u_1\{(p_1/p_2) - 1\}$. Substituting this in the formula of the elasticity of the marginal utility of real income, $e_u = (du/dY) \cdot (Y/u)$, gives $e_u = \{(p_1 - p_2)/p_2\} \cdot (Y/dY)$. In words, e_u is the percentage change in food prices necessary to compensate a one percent change in real income in order to keep the quantity of food consumed constant. Taking data on the cost of living for a couple and two children in 14 large cities in the USA and combining these with price and income data, FELLNER used basically this equation to estimate e_u and found a value of 1.8 for incomes ranging from about $ 4000 to $ 12,000 (fall 1959).

The elasticity of the marginal utility of income can also, however, be measured in another way since e_u also equals e_2/e_1, where $e_2 = \%$ change in quantity of food consumed due to a one percent change in real income while prices are kept constant, and $e_1 = \%$ change in quantity of food consumed due to a one percent change in food prices while real income is kept constant. This identity can perhaps best be shown by the following reasoning. A one percent change in real income (prices constant) will increase the quantity of food consumed by e_2 percent. However, to measure e_u, the quantity of food consumed must be kept at the same level. From the definition of e_1, it follows that if the quantity of food consumed has to decrease by e_2 percent, food prices should change by e_2/e_1 percent (real income constant). Hence, to keep the quantity of food consumed constant, a one-percent change in real income should be compensated by an e_2/e_1 percent change in food prices. Since this is the definition of e_u, we have $e_u = e_2/e_1$.

The difficulty with this equation is that demand elasticities are normally calculated under the assumption that money income does not change, whereas e_1 is the demand elasticity with respect to price under the assumption that real income does not change. Hence, to estimate e_1, the effect of a price change on real income should be eliminated from the normal demand elasticity. FELLNER did this as follows. The elasticities he used were those determined by TOBIN[28] for the United States as a whole, namely, 0.56 for e_2 and 0.53 for the normal demand elasticity. The real income effect had to be eliminated from the latter. Since the propensity to consume food in the United States is 25 percent, a one percent increase in food prices reduces real income by 0.25 percent. This reduction will itself lead to a reduction of $0.25.e_2 = 0.14$ percent in food consumption. Hence, $e_1 = 0.53 - 0.14 = 0.39$. It follows that $e_u = e_2/e_1 = 0.56/0.39 =$ about 1.5.

FELLNER thus derived two values for the elasticity of the marginal utility of income, namely, 1.8 and 1.5. However, as FELLNER pointed out, taste differences were not completely eliminated from the data on the cost of living and this tended to cause a slight over-estimation of the first estimate. Another factor leading to over-estimation is the following. The FISHER-FRISCH-FELLNER procedure of estimating the marginal utility of income works only if it can be assumed that food consumption is independent of the consumption of any other consumer item. Suppose that there is complementarity between food and non-food. Then the marginal utility of food for two families consuming the same food package but different non-food packages would not be equal. The family with the largest non-food package (and the higher real income) would have in reality a higher marginal utility of food than the other family because of the complementarity relationship. In reality, therefore, the fall in the marginal utility of income when real income rises would be slower than under the FISHER-FRISCH-FELLNER assumption. Also, the estimate of 1.5 may thus be somewhat too high. Nevertheless, taking into account that the first estimate is higher, FELLNER feels that 1.5 should remain the most reasonable estimate of the elasticity of the marginal utility of income.

FELLNER's estimate is not consistent with those of FRISCH, who estimated the elasticity of the marginal utility of income at 3.5 for a French group of workers and at 1 for a wealthier group of American workers. FRISCH concluded that the elasticities would decline (in absolute terms) with increases in real income. FELLNER, on the other hand, feels that his analysis confirms that the elasticity of the marginal utility of income is constant over a wide range of incomes. The data which FRISCH used were much less sound than those of FELLNER. Nevertheless, FELLNER's data also leave much to be desired, and, as FELLNER himself mentions, the results of his investigations 'continue to be speculative to a considerable extent.'

While the original findings of FRISCH were almost generally rejected because of the shaky data base, in a later article FRISCH[29] has affirmed his belief that the elasticity of the marginal utility of income would decrease (in absolute terms) with increases in real income. FRISCH conjectures that the elasticity of the marginal utility of income would vary from 10 for the extremely poor and apathetic part of the poluation to 0.1 for the rich part of the population with ambitions towards conspicuous consumption, while a value of 2 would apply to the middle income bracket. THEIL and BROOKS[30] have tried to verify this conjecture by analyzing empirically determined demand equations for the Netherlands in the period 1922–1963. They found a point elasticity of 1.56 for the median of the income distribution, which compares with a value of 2 conjectured by FRISCH, but also found that the elasticity increases (in absolute terms) when real income rises, which is the opposite of FRISCH's conjecture. However, the estimates were subject to so much error that on equally plausible assumptions a constant elasticity of 1.79 could be estimated. The degree of variation of real income was not large in their sample: the largest value of real income per capita exceeded the lowest value by about two-thirds. All in all, the estimates by THEIL and BROOKS must also be considered quite speculative.

Finally, we may mention that a new theory as regards consumer behavior has recently been put forward by VAN PRAAG,[31] who postulated that the individual utility function of income will tend to a lognormal distribution. In subsequent empirical investigations in Belgium,[32] VAN PRAAG found that this hypothesis could not be rejected and, at the same time, inter alia that the empirical findings of others as regards the value of the elasticity of the marginal utility of income were consistent with his own estimates of values of somewhere between 1.6 and 2.9. However, under VAN PRAAG's theory, the elasticity would increase (in absolute terms) if income rises.[33] To VAN PRAAG such an increase is more appealing than FRISCH's conjecture that it would decrease, although he does not state on what grounds he bases his preference.[34]

We have now reviewed what the rather scarce literature has to say about the value of the individual marginal utility of income schedule. At the lower end of the scale are the experiments of STEVENS, resulting in an estimated value of the elasticity of 0.5. However, these experiments were crude, and the findings of FRISCH, FELLNER, THEIL and BROOKS, and VAN PRAAG contradict this low estimate.

In our opinion, the matter of what elasticity the marginal utility of income schedule may assume is still an open question; we can speculate but further empirical studies are necessary before a definitive answer can be given. It seems to us, however, that it can generally be accepted that the elasticity has at least a value of unity for the low income groups and we will, therefore, work in the following parts of this study with a value of unity. We thus accept the proposition of BERNOULLI, WEBER-FECHNER, and CHENERY and TINBERGEN that the individual marginal utility of income is inversely proportional to income level, but with the proviso that the so found marginal utilities of income should be considered minimum values for the poorest income classes.

9.3. THE DERIVATION OF SOCIAL INCOME DISTRIBUTION WEIGHTS

We will begin this section by attempting to derive social income distribution weights from the individual marginal utility of income schedule – the procedure generally adopted in the literature. We will see where this leads us, show that the method cannot be correct, and propose how it should be amended to arrive at plausible social weights.

Social weights are the social utilities to be attached to additions to different levels of income. A meaningful aggregation of utilities is, of course, only possible if each utility is determined in the same way, i.e., expressed in terms of some numéraire level of utility. If we denote that numéraire level by u_b, the social weight of a marginal increase to any given level of income can be represented by $v_p = u_p/u_b$, where u_p is the social utility of additions to income level Y_p, and u_b the social utility of additions to the base income Y_b. Using the function $u = (b/Y)^\alpha$ for the individual schedule, the formula for the weight to be imputed to a marginal addition to a certain income is $v_p = u_p/u_b = bY_p^{-\alpha}/bY_b^{-\alpha} = (Y_b/Y_p)^\alpha$. Since this is a monotonically decreasing function when Y_p increases, the choice of Y_b – the base level income – is completely arbitrary. Varying Y_b shifts the function, but does not change the slopes of the function; hence, the absolute value of v_p will change when Y_b changes but the ratios of the v_p's will remain the same. In the literature's view, any income and its marginal utility level can be used as a base provided the social values of all income changes are calculated with respect to the same base.

Let us review an example of how the weights are to be calculated. If we assume that the elasticity of the individual marginal utility of income function equals unity, which, as discussed in the previous section is a reasonable assumption for operational work, then the formula for the derivation of the weights to be attached to marginal changes in income may be represented by $v = b/Y$, where $b = Y_b$. Suppose that b equals $\$ 1,200$ per annum and that the incomes of a certain target group are $\$ 300$ per annum. Then the weight in the case of a marginal change of this income level is $\$ 1,200/\$ 300 = 4.0$. For cases of non-marginal changes, however, the weights are to be derived from the total utility function, as may be shown as follows. Suppose that the incomes of our target group increase from $\$ 300$ to $\$ 500$ per annum. Then the weights in case of marginal changes of these two income levels are 4 and 2.4, respectively. However, it would be wrong to calculate the utility increase on the basis of the apparent average weight of 3.2. The marginal utility curve is not linear but concave and the increase in total utility is, therefore, somewhat less than the 640 'utils' ($\$ 200 \times 3.2$) which this method indicates. The total utility function when $u = b/Y$ is represented by $U = 2.3b \log Y$. Hence, the increase in total utility is represented by $\triangle U = 2.3b \log Y_2 - 2.3b \log Y_1$, and, in our example, $\triangle U$ is, therefore, 607 utils.[35] As the increase in income $\triangle Y = \$ 200$, the weight on the additional income is $607/200 = 3.0$, rather than 3.2.

After these preliminary remarks we can turn to the issue as to how project costs and benefits should be weighted. As an example, let us assume that the beneficiaries of a certain project consist of a homogeneous group of low income people – the poor – and that their incomes can be increased by providing them with an input, for instance, irrigation water, which will enable them to expand their production. There are then two parties – the target group and the Government (the supplier of the input) – and the objective function that should be maximized is the welfare function $\triangle W = v_p Y_p + v_a Y_a$, where Y_p is the increase in income of the target group, Y_a the increase or decrease in income of the Government, and v_p and v_a the respective welfare weights.

How can we determine the weights? The literature is divided in its approach. SETON[36] uses values for the elasticity of the individual marginal utility of income schedule varying from 1 to 2, and assumes that the Government will obtain its funds through some package deal of direct and indirect taxation which will diminish every worker's consumption by the same proportion. In his system, the foregone utility of the workers is the numéraire, and the weight v_a – the value at the margin of Government funds – is equal to the value of the numéraire, while the weight v_p – the value of an addition to the income of the poor – is derived from the individual marginal utility of income schedule by calculating the marginal utility of the poor relative to the numéraire. FELDSTEIN[37] takes as the numéraire the uniformly distributed dollar, that is, a single dollar divided equally among all the families in the nation, and assumes that all incremental projects are financed by a proportional increase in the personal income tax. The weights v_a and v_p are then again derived from the individual marginal utility of income schedule. In our opinion, both models are not logically consistent. As FELDSTEIN himself states, the attachment of weights to income increases of the poor will lead in his model, and we may add also in the SETON model, to the acceptance of uneconomic projects, i.e., projects with economic rates of return lower than the opportunity cost of capital. This appears contradictory to us. Both writers seem to assume that the Government budget is flexible and we see then no reason why the Government would not be able to transfer its funds to the poor. As will be discussed in detail below, if such transfers are possible, then there is no need to accept uneconomic projects. There is further the important point that both writers work with the individual marginal utility of income schedule. As will be discussed below, this cannot be correct.

The SQUIRE and VAN DER TAK[38] methodology is, in our opinion, also subject to criticism. They take as the numéraire the marginal utility of consumption at the average level of consumption and postulate that the value of public income – the weight v_a – is determined by applying to Government investments the P_{inv} formula, a formula which we discussed in the preceding chapter for private sector investments. Furthermore, they derive the weight v_p from the individual marginal utility of income schedule, the elasticity of which they assume varies from 0 to 2. As it is not entirely clear which assumptions SQUIRE and VAN DER TAK apply as regards constraints, it may be useful to analyze their system under the assumption that the Government has a flexible budget as well as that the Government has an absolute constraint on its funds. In the first case, there is, as extensively discussed in the preceding Chapter, no need to work with a shadow price of investment and the value of public income should then be determined by the foregone marginal utilities of income. As SQUIRE and VAN DER TAK take average consumption as the numéraire, it would appear as if they assume implicitly that the Government funds are obtained by taxing average consumers. This is obviously not correct. In this case, the SETON and FELDSTEIN assumptions are more realistic but, as discussed above, there is then no need to accept uneconomic projects, which SQUIRE and VAN DER TAK appear willing to do. Let us assume then that they assume that public investment is absolutely constrained. Then, as discussed in Chapter 5, the value of public funds is determined by the rate of return of the marginal Government project and we believe, as discussed in Chapter 8, that usually also there is no need to introduce a

212

shadow price of public investment.

As a final remark concerning the logical consistency of the three methodologies, we may point out that under these systems the social rates of return of projects geared towards increasing the incomes of the poor may be extremely high, even when the very reasonable value of 1 is assumed for the elasticity of the marginal utility of income schedule. Under the SETON and FELDSTEIN methodologies, these high rates of return are obtained because the incomes of the poor are low compared to numéraire income so that high weights will be attached to income increases of the poor. Under the SQUIRE and VAN DER TAK methodology, the high rates of return will appear if the investment program in the relevant country is optimal. In that case, the value of public funds is equal to that of average consumption and the value of additions to the incomes of the poor, which is high relative to the value of average consumption, will then also be high relative to the value of public funds. As a matter of interest, it may be noted that under the SQUIRE and VAN DER TAK methodology the land settlement projects in Malaysia, which will be discussed in Chapter 10, have social rates of return of more than 50 percent under the stipulated assumptions, i.e., Government expenditures as valuable as private consumption and an elasticity of the marginal utility of income schedule of 1. This result is obtained because the average family income in Malaysia in 1974 was about M\$ 5,000, whereas the income of the prospective settlers was only about M\$ 900, so that the weight of an additional settler dollar assumes the very high value of 5.6. Other examples with even more extreme results could have been taken from recent project analyses. We believe, however, that this example will suffice to suggest that the methodologies lead to results with very little meaning.

The inconsistencies of the above methodologies stem, in our opinion, to a great extent, from one fundamental point that these approaches have overlooked: namely, that weights based on the individual marginal utility of income schedule are not necessarily those accepted by the community as a whole. For if they were, then every person in the community should have the same income level. This can best be shown with the help of the so-called LERNER-box,[39] presented in Figure 9.1. The total amount of income of two persons equals AB. The first person has an income of AO measured in the direction of AB and the second person B has an income BO, measured in the direction of BA. Both persons have identical marginal utility of income schedules uu' which, for simplicity's sake, have been drawn as straight lines. What would be the position of optimum income distribution? At point O, A's total utility is only Au_AQO, while B's is Bu_BPO. A's marginal utility OQ is much higher than B's, which is only OP. It, therefore, makes sense to transfer a dollar from B where it has a low marginal utility to A, where it has a high marginal utility. The optimum position will be reached at R, where A and B have the same marginal utility of income RS.

The use of income distribution weights based on the individual marginal utility of income schedule thus leads inevitably to the conclusion that all persons should have equal incomes. Since equality of income does not exist in any

FIGURE 9.1.

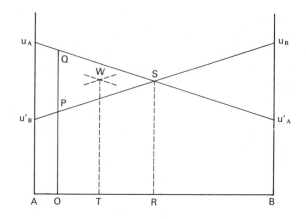

society, not even in the centrally planned ones, it is clear that society does not accept transfers leading to complete equality. On the other hand, some transfers may be acceptable. For instance, turning again to Figure 9.1, it may well be possible that, while equality is rejected, it is socially acceptable to end up with an income for A of AT and for B of BT. What this means is that the distribution weights based on the individual marginal utility of income schedule have been replaced by social weights. A's individual marginal utility of income has been lowered, B's increased, so that, at the equilibrium position, the marginal utility of A's income as well as that of B's is considered socially equal (TW in Figure 9.1).

Our analysis has led us to conclude that, in order to arrive at a position of optimum income distribution, social weights instead of individual income distribution weights should be used. The task at hand is, therefore, to discuss how these weights can be determined. To us it is immanently acceptable that societies, although concerned about the incomes of the poor and the rich, do not strive towards equality of incomes so that we can assume that over a wide range of middle incomes they are indifferent as to how incomes are actually distributed. To others, perhaps, this point of view is not so readily acceptable. However, because education and own efforts cause divergences in income and unacceptable losses in efficiency would occur if everyone had the same income, they would nevertheless agree that equality cannot be reached in practice. Thus, even if we tend towards a philosophy of complete egalitarianism we still arrive at the conclusion that income differences must be accepted for a wide range of middle incomes. It is, therefore, only with respect to the poorest and the richest groups that income distribution considerations play a role, so that the matter is essentially one of choosing social weights for these groups.

One method of determining these social weights would be to interview a select sample of the population as to what they believe the social weights for the poorest and richest groups should be. However, this technique is more suitable for developed than developing countries as it is a rather sophisticated and costly method which needs to be repeated periodically because of the inflation

214

factor. Furthermore, such interviews have not been undertaken. Therefore, it seems to us that a more practical method is in order. To illustrate how we would propose to derive the weights, it is perhaps useful to discuss an example. PAUKERT[40] has calculated the income shares of each quintile of the population for 56 countries at different levels of development and AHLUWALIA[41] provides similar data for selected countries. Expanding on their findings as regards the top level incomes – albeit speculative to a certain extent – the following table (figures in 1974 US dollars) can be established for a typical middle level developing country. In such a country, mean family income would be about US $ 2,000, modal family income about US $ 1,200, unskilled labor income about US $ 600, and subsistence level family income about US $ 250 per annum. If we use WEBER-FECHNER's function with modal income as the base, the individual weights would vary as shown in the Table, from about 0.11 for the top 5 percent of the population to 4.8 for subsistence level incomes. The income of a subsistence level farmer would thus have an individual weight over 40 times that of a person in the richest group. However, the social weights are the ones that count and, as discussed, we believe that for a wide range of incomes these weights approximate unity. At the lower end of the income scale, it seems to us that most societies do not attach a weight to the income of a fully employed unskilled laborer. Taking this income as a base, and applying WEBER-FECHNER's law, the minimum[42] social weights can then be found for the lower level incomes. At the high income end of the scale, we may assume that the incomes of highly trained professionals such as physicians, cabinet members, and managers receive a unit weight. Taking that income level as the base, and applying WEBER-FECHNER's law, the weights on the incomes of the richest groups can again be determined. Government salaries provide the best means of determining the range

TABLE 9.2.

Income Class	Share in Total Income	Average Family Income per Class	Individual Income Distribution Weights (US$1200 = 1)	Social Weights (b_r = US$4,800) ($b_p$ = US$600)
(Top 5%)	(27%)	(US$10,800)	(0.11)	(0.44)
(Next 5%)	(12%)	(4,800)	(0.25)	(1.00)
(Next 10%)	(14%)	(2,800)	(0.43)	(1.00)
Top 20%	53%	5,300	0.23	0.91
Next 20%	22%	2,200	0.54	1.00
Middle 20%	13%	1,300	0.92	1.00
Next 20%	7%	700	1.71	1.00
Poorest 20%	5%	500	2.40	1.20
Average Income		US$2,000	0.60	1.00
Modal Income		1,200	1.00	1.00
Income Unskilled Laborer		600	2.00	1.00
Subsistence Level Income		250	4.80	2.40
Income Highly Trained Professional		4,800	0.25	1.00

FIGURE 9.2.

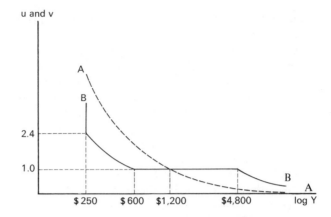

of the unit weighted incomes, since it may be assumed that these are the socially acceptable salaries. The various social weights for our typical country are shown in the table and are half of the individual weights for the poorest groups.

The procedure may also be clarified with the help of Figure 9.2, which presents the two different welfare functions in graphical form. The individual and social marginal utilities of income are on the vertical axis and income is on the horizontal axis, the latter with a logarithmic scale. The curve AA represents the individual weighting function, taking modal income as the base, the curve BB the social welfare function that we are proposing. BB is, in our opinion, quite a plausible social welfare function. If income distribution considerations are indeed to be incorporated into project planning, then one should work with a function which approaches reality to the maximum extent possible. BB shows that, over quite a range of incomes, income distribution considerations do not count[43] and realistic weights for the lowest and highest incomes are assumed. No weights are shown, on purpose, for lower than subsistence level incomes. If one, nevertheless, wishes to do so, a weight of infinity might be attached to such incomes because, in the face of starvation and misery, economic considerations recede and any weight derivation is a rather meaningless exercise. There would also seem to be little merit in attaching a weight to the richest incomes, and a weight of zero might be appropriate for the incomes of the ultra rich.

The social weights indicated by the curve BB should not be considered precise and absolute. For instance, it may well be that the unit weighted income range should be somewhat extended to the lower end as well as to the higher end of its range. On the other hand, this would not influence the weights very much. If, for instance, the base were $ 500 at the lower end, then subsistence income would have a weight of 2.0 rather than 2.4. Another open question is whether one can indeed apply WEBER-FECHNER's law. If, for instance, the elasticity of the marginal utility of income were greater than unity for low incomes, then the weights should be somewhat larger for the low incomes than indicated in the graph. With our present state of knowledge, these matters remain open to dispute. However, as discussed in the previous section, in our opinion, it seems likely that

216

the minimum range of the social weights for the poorest groups is as indicated in the table and the graph.

There are two more remarks we would like to make about the postulated social welfare function. First, although in our opinion the function sets forth the prevailing values of most countries in the world, there are exceptions. For instance, it has happened that Government officials have exploited the poorer groups to enrich themselves. We do maintain, however, that such cases do not occur often and that the normal situation is one of serious concern about the lot of the poor. Second, we would like to mention that the middle segment of our function does not take account of sudden income changes. This implies that if an engineer loses his job and has to live on a fraction of his salary, the loss of his income is valued socially the same as it is economically. Or, to take another example, if somebody at a subsistence level of \$ 250 per annum receives annually, because of a Government project, an additional \$ 3,350, a weight is attached only on the income additions up to the unskilled wage level of \$ 600, and the subsequent addition of \$ 3,000 is valued at unit weight. Is this correct? It seems to us that there is much to be said for an income weighting related to a worker's profession so that, for example, any underpayment to an engineer or overpayment to a subsistence level worker would be valued in accordance with their role in society. Rather than having one social welfare function of the type depicted in Figure 9.2, there might then be as many functions of this type as there are professions. Unfortunately, however, our present state of knowledge is such that no meaningful estimates can be made of the income range per profession that should receive a unit weight. For our purposes, this is also not necessary. In this study we are interested mainly in projects geared towards raising the incomes of the poor and we cannot imagine that overpayments will be made to such an extent that they should be discounted. We see our function as applicable to a society where the poor receive substandard incomes, the middle classes earn in accordance with their profession a range of salaries that are socially acceptable, and the rich earn rather high incomes. From all points of view, we feel that the postulated function is a reasonable one and the most feasible for practical work.

The difference between, on the one hand, the traditional as well as the approach of the most recent literature and, on the other hand, our approach may now be explained as follows. In the traditional approach, the income distribution in an economy is assumed to be optimized by means of income transfers between persons so that willingness to pay can be used as the guiding principle for the allocation of resources. In the recent version of benefit-cost analysis, it is assumed that income distribution is not optimized by means of income transfers and it is, therefore, postulated that projects should be used for this optimization process. In these approaches, the individual marginal utility of income schedule which underlies, for instance, the taxation principles in the distribution branch of government is also used as the guiding principle for investment planning. That this leads to unacceptable conclusions has been discussed above. The fundamental principle that is overlooked in suggesting the use of individual weights is that the valuations which individuals use in their personal decisions do not necessarily reflect the valuations which individuals use in making decisions that concern the community at large. Such a discrepancy is most notable in the case of the marginal utility of income schedule: the use of the individual weighting function leads to the inevitable conclusion that incomes in the economy should be equal. As we have discussed, no community is willing to accept this proposition, either on practical or on principal grounds. In contrast to the traditional and more recent approaches, we believe that for large groups of the population, the existing income distribution can be considered optimal and that, therefore, the allocation of resources should take income distribution aspects into account only when the poorest and the richest groups are involved. We accept that the individual marginal utility of income schedule is the guiding principle for the distribution branch of government, but reject it for the allocation branch. We attach, therefore, no weight to uncommitted government income, i.e., the weight v_a assumes in our approach the value of unity, and we only attach a weight $-v_p$ – on the change in income of project beneficiaries if they consist of ultra-poor or ultra-rich persons. The weight v_p assumes in our system a value larger than unity in case of the ultra-poor and smaller than unity in case of the ultra-rich. As discussed, it is not possible to determine the precise values of these weights with our present state of knowledge and the best we can do is to accept the values as indicated by the BB function. Efficiency considerations play an important role in our system, and we will therefore review in the next two sections what implications the social weights will have for project design and project selection.

9.4. Redistribution Through Project Design

In Section 9.1 we observed that if we follow the literature's approach of including distribution weights in the objective function, the condition for a maximum is presented by $v = dC/dB$ when no repayments are levied, or $v = dK/dN$ when repayments should cover operating costs. What are the implications of this regarding project size? If we make the simplifying assumption that project benefits are constant over time, we may write for the first case $v = dC/dB = dB_{Aa_{\bar{m}}r}/dB_{Aa_{\bar{m}}q}$ where C is the present value of costs, B the present value of benefits, $dB_{Aa_{\bar{m}}r}$ the annual benefit stream of the marginal invested dollar discounted at the marginal invested dollar's rate of return, and $dB_{Aa_{\bar{m}}q}$ the same benefit stream but discounted at the opportunity cost of capital rate q. From this it follows that $a_{\bar{m}r} = v \cdot a_{\bar{m}q}$. Using the optimum condition $v = dK/dN$ would lead to the same result, since then dN_A would drop out of the formula.

Let us assume that the project we wish to analyze is geared towards raising the incomes of a group of poor persons and that the weight at the margin which should be attached to an increase in income of the project beneficiaries is 1.5. Let us assume also that the opportunity cost of capital is 10 percent and that the project's life is about 20 to 25 years. Then, from the above formula $a_{\bar{m}r} = v \cdot a_{\bar{m}q}$

218

and from discount and compound tables, we find that r should be about 5 percent. If the weight were about 2, then r should be about 2 percent. If the project life were shorter, then the required rate of return would still be lower and with a very short life it could even become negative. What all this would mean is that, if we really wish to incorporate income distribution weights into project analysis, projects should be oversized to the point that in many cases the rate of return on the marginal investment dollar should be negligible or even negative.

According to the literature, oversized projects should thus be quite normal. Can this be true? We would like to clarify the matter with the help of Figure 9.3, which may be considered a graph of the income transfer which a certain Government project would make possible from the Government to project beneficiaries. The various values which $R-C$, i.e., repayments by project beneficiaries minus Government costs, can assume as repayments are lowered or project size is expanded are set out on the vertical axis on a positive and negative scale. These values are thus what the Government can expect to get back from the project if it levied a normal market clearing price, or what it should be willing to lose if it reduced the price of the project's output. The net benefits of the project beneficiaries equal $B-R$, i.e., gross benefits minus repayments, and are set out on the horizontal axis. These net benefits would increase if either repayments are lowered or project size is expanded.

The curve OMEAP shows the relationship between Government income $(R-C)$ and beneficiary income $(B-R)$ under the assumption that, while project size is being expanded, the Government charges the normal market clearing price. The values of $R-C$ and $B-R$ are, of course, determined by the normal cost and demand functions such as, for instance, in Figure 4.1. At the point M in Figure 9.3 the Government would make maximum profits but, as we discussed in Chapter 4, it is not the position of maximum total net benefits. This optimum position is found by maximizing benefits minus costs or, in our present model, by maximizing $(B-R) + (R-C)$ and the first order condition may thus be written as $d(B-R) = -d(R-C)$. In Figure 9.3 this condition is fulfilled at the point E: the tangent line to the OMEAP curve has a negative slope of $45°$. At that position Government income is ES_1, beneficiaries' income is OS_1 and the combined income is at a maximum. Beneficiaries' income can be increased by increasing plant size but the Government income will then be reduced. For instance, at position A project size has been expanded until average cost is equal to price. The Government income is then zero but beneficiaries' income OA has been increased by S_1A. Further expansion of project size means that average costs rise above the demand curve, and the Government is then losing money. The curve OMEAP has, therefore, a negative part AP.

Suppose now that the Government does not charge any price at all for the project's output so that R is zero. Then, by increasing project size we would develop the normal cost-benefit curve. By turning Figure 9.3 one-quarter to the left, one can see that the curve OE'D is such a curve. The efficiency optimum on this curve is represented by E', a position which fulfills the condition that

FIGURE 9.3.

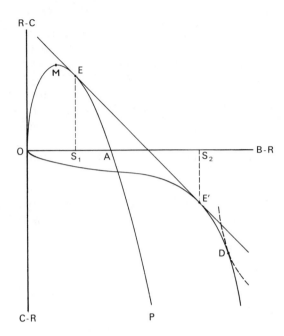

$-dC/dB = 1$. The relationship between the points E and E′ may now be shown as follows. Suppose we are at position E, i.e., the situation where beneficiaries pay the normal market clearing price and the size of the project is optimal. Then the income of the beneficiaries can be increased by lowering price and therewith repayments to the Government. As this is a pure transfer from the Government to the project beneficiaries, this is represented in graphical form by a movement to the right along the EE′ line. At point E′ repayments are zero, all the costs – $S_2E′$ – are borne by the Government, all the benefits – OS_2 – accrue to project beneficiaries, and we find ourselves on the normal cost-benefit curve. It is thus obvious that the EE′ line is a tangent line to the two curves.

The analysis has thus made it clear that it is much more efficient to lower repayments than to expand project size while insisting on repayments: E′ provides the project beneficiaries with more benefits than any other position on EAP would make possible. So far so good. Suppose now that the income of project beneficiaries should be still further increased. Then, if we follow those writers who are willing to accept inefficiency for redistribution purposes, the optimum should be at a point such as D, where the social welfare function is tangent to the benefit curve. This is, however, a very inefficient way of transferring income. As shown in Figure 9.3, beyond the efficiency point E′, costs continue to rise, while the income of project beneficiaries increases only marginally. It is, therefore, not surprising that we found that the rate of return on the marginal invested dollar becomes negligible if the optimum condition is adhered to by expanding the size of the project in question.

It seems to us that it has been overlooked that the income of the project's target group can also be increased by other means than expanding project size beyond the efficiency optimum. It is simply not true that institutional or political constraints would bar the raising of incomes of the target group except by the expansion of one specific project. The one method of income transfer that may, perhaps, not be feasible is the extension of the line EE′ to the right of E′, i.e., the normal transfer of money. However, an equally efficient way of transferring money to the target group would be to start another project, also geared towards raising the group's income. Such a project would start from E′ as the origin, or somewhere to the left of E′ on the tangent line EE′ if operating costs were to be covered, and its transfer curve would be similar to the curve OMEE′. Also, the price of that project's output can then be lowered if at the efficiency optimum the group's income would still remain below the norm. There are, of course, many possible projects of this nature in education, family planning, roads, power, housing, and other fields. Furthermore, there may be the possibility of increasing incomes by means of transfers in kind, price-subsidy or price-support programs. It is, therefore, not necessary to expand project size beyond the efficiency optimum size except in the case that other methods of income transfer are excluded. We believe that such situations seldom occur in real life.

We can now recapitulate the argument. Projects are a highly efficient way of transferring income to the poor. When at the optimum size of a project – the size where the rate of return on the marginal investment dollar equals the appropriate discount rate – incomes of the target group are still below the norm, either the price of the output should be lowered or other means of income transfer should be used to increase these incomes. Which method to choose will depend on efficiency considerations. For instance, if price reductions of the project's output cause rationing to be necessary, then this method may be more costly than starting another project or using a subsidy. In reality, we believe that the opportunities to raise incomes with the help of other types of projects are abundant. Usually there is thus, in our opinion, no need to build oversized projects.

9.5. REDISTRIBUTION THROUGH PROJECT SELECTION

We have seen in the previous section that interpersonal income distribution weights should not be considered when designing the size of a project. The question now is whether they should also be ignored in the selection of a project; in other words, should economic rates of return rather than social rates of return be used for project selection? We assume that there is no budget constraint and would like to clarify the matter with the help of Figures 9.4A and 9.4B.

The curves EROR represent the economic rates of return of Government projects, the beneficiaries of which are the poor in Figure 9.4A, and the rich in Figure 9.4B. For ease of exposition, it has been assumed that the curves are smooth and that successively lower rates of return are obtained if investments are increased. The social rates of return are found by attaching income distri-

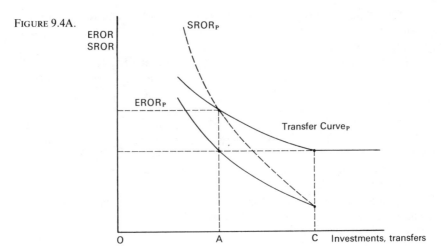

FIGURE 9.4A.

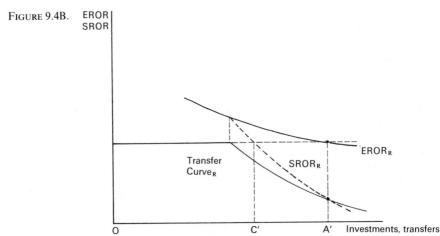

FIGURE 9.4B.

bution weights to the benefits and are represented by the SROR curves. The 'Transfer' curves show the values of transferred dollars in terms of yield. For transfers to middle income groups the transfer curve is horizontal because the values of transferred dollars in terms of yield are then equal to the opportunity cost of capital. Transfers to the poor, however, are worth more. For instance, suppose that the opportunity cost of capital is 10 percent and that at income position A, in Figure 9.4A, the marginal utility of income of the poor is 1.5 utils. Then, as shown by the Transfer curve in Figure 9.4A, the value in terms of yield of an additional dollar at income position A is equal to a social rate of return of 15 percent.[44] At point C, the weight on income accruing to the poor is unity, and the social rate of return of a transfer is then 10 percent. The transfer curve in Figure 9.4B is similar, but since the weights on income accruing to the rich are lower than unity starting somewhat to the left of C', the curve lies below the 10 percent line to the right of this point.

222

Turning again to Figure 9.4A, we see that the minimum target income of the poor is at point C where their marginal utility of income is unity. How can they be brought to this position? Investing in projects geared towards raising the incomes of the poor appears to be highly efficient up to point A, since the economic rates of return are above the opportunity cost of capital. Beyond this point, however, the economic rates of return are lower than the opportunity cost of capital and the transfer curve rises above the social rate of return curve. In other words, transfer of income to the poor by other means than the project method is then a much more efficient way of redistributing income. Hence, in order to maximize total utility, the policy to be followed should be one of investing up to A, and then transferring AC. Although the mechanism of direct money transfers may then perhaps not be used because of political constraints, the indirect method of supporting the prices of farm outputs or subsidizing such farm inputs as credit, fertilizers and extension services, is commonly used and there is much to be said for this approach. Turning to Figure 9.4B, we see that from a social point of view OC' should be invested. It is theoretically possible to invest up to A' and then mulcting from the rich the returns generated by C'A', but it is then essential that appropriate taxation measures be devised to obtain these returns. If this is not feasible, then it seems to us that such projects should be abandoned rather than going ahead to benefit the rich.

The basic principle which has emerged is that – irrespective of whether the projects are geared towards the poor, the rich or the middle classes – only those projects whose economic rates of return are higher than the opportunity cost of capital should be accepted. This is logical because we have assumed in all cases that there are more efficient ways of transferring income than by expanding project size unduly or selecting projects with low rates of return.

Is there then no need at all for a social rate of return analysis? We believe there is because usually incomes can not be sufficiently increased by means of transfers so that then indeed the social rate of return analysis of projects becomes important. Caution is, however, necessary. A naive use of social weights can lead to the acceptance of many unsound projects and can even put into jeopardy the credit worthiness of the country in question. As in reality, in our opinion, poverty projects with reasonable economic rates of return usually can be found, we would like to propose as a pragmatic rule – in order to induce project planners to follow sound principles – that projects should only be subjected to a social rate of return analysis if they have satisfactory economic rates of return. The acceptable projects should then be ranked according to their social rates of return and those with unsatisfactory social rates of return should be rejected. Since under this procedure each project will have an economic rate of return higher than the cutoff efficiency rate of return, a minimum efficiency rate of return is ensured for each project. At the same time, since only projects with high social rates of return will be chosen, the social priority of the projects will also be ensured. This procedure has important implications with respect to a country's development strategy because many projects that would not be considered under the traditional analysis may now well appear to have higher social values than their alternatives. For instance, while according to the normal analysis, in many cases, land settlement projects[45] should not be undertaken because they may be less efficient than plantations, under our methodology these projects should be preferred if their social rates of return are higher than those of plantations. In other words, under our methodology there may well be some trade-off between efficiency and equity but not to the extent that projects earn less than the opportunity cost of capital q[46]. The latter would only be acceptable if no projects can be found with satisfactory economic rates of return. However, as we have stated, we believe that such cases do not occur often. Our procedure also underlines what we have argued before: projects cannot be considered in isolation; they form part of an overall investment program. The macro-economic goals set by the Central Planning Unit regarding employment, income growth of the economy as a whole and per income class, foreign exchange earnings, and the like can be attained only if the overall investment program is successful. It is the task of the micro-planners to assess whether the proposed individual investments are likely to succeed, economically as well as socially. By calculating the expected economic and social rates of return of individual projects one can ensure that these objectives will be attained. In the next Chapter we will illustrate the methodology with the help of a number of actual case studies.

9.6. Review of the Different Transfer Mechanisms

Reference has been made in the preceding sections to the several possible ways in which the Government can increase the incomes of the poor. In devising such measures, efficiency counts and the question, therefore, is: How can the incomes of the target group be raised with least cost to the rest of the community? In the following we will discuss this matter but without pretension that the discussion will be exhaustive. There are so many ways of increasing income, each with its own peculiarities, that only a global review can be undertaken in the space of this study. Several classifications are possible; a useful one for our purpose is to distinguish among Government policies that intervene directly at the income level, the price level and the investment level, and we will discuss each of these. First, however, it may be useful to give some indication of the order of magnitudes that are involved in raising the incomes of the poor. Assume that a country's per capita income is about US $ 400 and its income distribution is as shown in Table 9.2. Then, in such a typical country, the per capita income of at least 10 percent of the population (US $ 40) would be about US $ 80 below per capita base level income (US $ 120). Hence, if one were to use the normal transfer method to wipe out poverty, the annual income transfer would amount to at least 2 percent of national income. On the other hand, if one were to follow the project method, investments in projects for the poor would amount to at least 20 percent of national income, assuming that the economic rate of return is 10 percent. Obviously this is not possible and it must, therefore, be accepted that a combination of the various possible transfer mechanisms should be used, the actual mixture depending on efficiency and social considerations.

In principle, the allocation of Government funds over the various expenditure categories should be such that the social value of the last dollar spent in every category has the same value. Budget constraints complicate the principle, but do not present a theoretical problem. We discussed in Chapter 5 that in the case of a single period budget constraint the cut-off N/K ratio assumes a higher value than unity and that in the case of multiple period budget constraints the cut-off rate of return assumes a higher value than the opportunity cost of capital. As regards transfers the same principle applies. Suppose, for instance, that the cut-off N/K ratio must be set at 1.2 instead of at the normal ratio of 1.0. Then, the social value of the last transferred dollar should be 1.2 rather than 1.0. The same would be true in the case of multiple period budget constraints if the cut-off rate of return had to be set at 12 percent. Budget constraints limit thus the amount of public investments as well as the amount of transfers that can be undertaken.

A curtailment of the transfers under a certain transfer method will also occur if the transfers involve additional costs. A simple example may illustrate this. Assume that there is no budget constraint, and that the opportunity cost of capital is 10 percent, so that the social rate of return of the last dollar spent in any direction should be 10 percent. Suppose now that, for a certain method of transfer, costs of $ 0.20 are incurred. Then $ 1.20 must be foregone to give to the poor the last additional dollar of unit weight, and the social rate of return of the last transferred dollar would thus be 8.33 percent, which makes it inefficient compared to the other possible methods of transfer. Hence, to the extent that additional costs are incurred, expenditures will be curtailed. Additional costs in the form of dead weight losses may arise in the case of a subsidy program and we will discuss this matter further in detail below. A special issue is posed by the administrative costs of Government programs. Should they be taken into account when considering the efficiency of the various possible transfer methods? In our opinion, this is, in general, not necessary because the administrative Government apparatus does exist and the marginal cost of administering either normal transfers, subsidy programs or public projects may be assumed – as is generally done in the literature – to be negligible. We maintain, therefore, that when transfers are possible projects geared towards increasing the incomes of the poor should have satisfactory economic rates of return because otherwise normal transfers or subsidies with negligible deadweight losses will be more efficient.

The direct method of income transfer can take many forms: it may be a straight money transfer; it may also be a transfer in kind, such as in the case of school feeding, housing and health care programs or where consumption goods – food, electricity, water supply – are provided to the poor. In all such cases, the analysis is the same as if it were a direct money transfer.

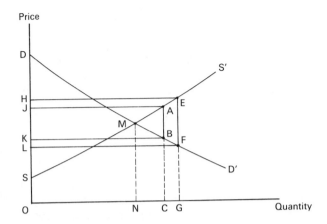

FIGURE 9.5.

We may turn our attention now to measures that intervene at the price level. Our objective is to analyze whether such measures are feasible, and it is useful for this purpose to classify them as to whether the goods and services are: (a) produced by the poor; or, (b) consumed or used as an input by the poor for the production of other goods and services. As regards the first case, an example would be a general price subsidy on an agricultural product produced by the poor. If we denote the extra income of the poor due to the price subsidy by Y_p, then the benefit of the poor is presented by $v_p Y_p$. On the cost side, the community must pay Y_p plus the costs of the subsidy program – which we denote by X. Hence, the objective function is: $v_p Y_p - (Y_p + X)$. This is maximized when $v_p d Y_p - d Y_p - dX = 0$, which may be written as $v_p = (d Y_p + dX)/d Y_p$. It may be noted that this is basically the same formulation we used when we considered the cost of a project expansion beyond the optimum size (Section 9.3).

The above analysis lends itself to graphical presentation. Consider Figure 9.5. The curve SS′ represents the supply curve of the goods produced by the poor, the curve DD′ the demand curve of the rest of the community. We are interested in the costs of a subsidy program and assume that the Government pays a subsidy of AB per unit. Producers receive then AC per unit while consumers pay BC per unit and the output level is, therefore, OC. The total amount paid by the Government is JABK, by consumers KBCO, so that producers receive a total of JACO, of which OSAC is used to pay the factors of production. On the other hand, at the output level OC, the value of the goods produced as valued by the consumers is ODBC. Hence, the net surplus of producing OC is ODBC minus OSAC, which equals DMS minus MAB. It should be noted that this is equal to the producers' surplus SJA plus the consumers' surplus DBK minus the Government payment JABK. Without the subsidy, the output level is ON and the surplus SDM; with the subsidy the output level is OC and the surplus SDM minus MAB. The effect of the subsidy is thus that a loss is incurred of MAB. This can also be seen by considering the costs and

226

benefits of the extra output NC. While its cost of production is NMAC, its value is only NMBC, the difference MAB representing the loss resulting from expanding the output beyond the optimal point.

Since the optimum for an income transfer is a marginal condition, let us assume now that the subsidy of AB per unit is increased to a level of EF per unit. Producers' surplus and hence producers' income increases then by HEAJ, which is equal to the dY_p of our formula. On the other hand, the Government pays an extra amount equal to HEFL minus JABK. Assuming that the weight on the Government's as well as consumers' income equals unity, the Government's loss may be compensated with the gain in the surplus of the consumer, which is KBFL. Hence, the effect of the subsidy on the income of the rest of the community (Government and consumers) is a loss in income equal to HEAJ plus AEFB, which is the $dY_p + dX$ of our formula. Neglecting changes of the second order of smallness, it can be seen in the figure that $dY_p = $ HEAJ $= OC \cdot \triangle P_s = Q \cdot \triangle P_s$, and $dX = $ AEFB $= $ AB $\cdot \triangle Q = T \cdot \triangle Q$, where Q is output, P_s the supply price and T the subsidy per unit. Hence, our formula reduces to $v_p = (Q \cdot \triangle P_s + T \cdot \triangle Q)/(Q \cdot \triangle P_s)$, which may be written as $(v_p - 1) = (T \cdot \triangle Q)/(Q \cdot \triangle P_s)$. Since the elasticity of supply $e_s = (dQ/dP_s) \cdot (P_s/Q)$, we may write $(v_p - 1) = (T/P_s) \cdot e_s$.[47]

As the equation shows, the relative subsidy (T/P_s) is a function of the elasticity of supply of the product produced by the poor and the weight on the poor's income. Hence, if this procedure of subsidizing the poor's production were to be followed consistently, each different type of product produced by the poor should receive a different subsidy. In rural areas where the poor produce only one or two products, this may well be feasible. However, such subsidies may need to assume very high values. For instance, let us assume that the weight on the targeted income increase is 1.5 and that the elasticity of supply of the product produced by the poor is less then unity as it is for most food grains, say, 0.2. Then it follows that the Government should provide a subsidy equal to 250 percent of the price ($T/P_s = 2.5$). Even if the elasticity of supply were unity – a most unlikely possibility for goods produced by the poor – the subsidy should be 50 percent of the price.

The same analysis applies regarding the subsidization of the prices of goods or services used by the poor as inputs or for consumption purposes. In Figure 9.5, let the curve DD' represent the demand curve of the poor and the curve SS' the supply curve of the good in question. Increasing the subsidy from the level AB to EF per unit results then in an increase in consumer surplus of KBFL, which is equal to $Q \cdot \triangle P_d$ where P_d is the demand price, and a loss of income in the rest of the community of KBFL plus AEFB, which is equal to $Q \cdot \triangle P_d$ plus $T \cdot \triangle Q$. Hence $(v_p - 1) = (T \cdot \triangle Q)/(Q \cdot \triangle P_d) = (T/P_d) \cdot e_d$ where e_d is now the elasticity of demand of the poor for inputs or consumption goods. Also, since this elasticity is normally much less than unity, high subsidies would be necessary.

Why is it that we do not find such high subsidies in practice? The reason is that if the T/P ratios increase the deadweight losses also increase, making the

227

price subsidy method more and more inefficient. Price subsidies are, however, an efficient method of income transfer if the deadweight loss is small and they are then well worth considering in conjunction with other methods of income transfer. In fact, the entire subsidy goes to the producers where the supply curve has zero elasticity and to the consumers where the demand curve has zero elasticity, and no deadweight losses occur then at all. In practice, this means that if the curves are relatively inelastic – which they often are for goods produced or consumed by the poor – the price subsidies for very reasonable T/P ratios incur only very small deadweight losses, say of the order of one or two percent of the transferred amounts. For all practical purposes this makes such subsidies comparable to direct transfer payments.

A problem with many price subsidies is that other groups than the target groups benefit. The challenge is, therefore, to ensure that the subsidies will raise solely the incomes of the target group. In the case of subsidies on goods consumed by the poor, an extensive system of discriminatory rationing would be necessary to ensure that only the poor benefit, something which most Governments are unwilling to do. Regarding goods produced by the poor, a system of production quotas and differential payments based on, for instance, size of landholdings, seems theoretically possible but, again, such a system would seldom be acceptable. With regard to inputs used by the poor, however, a scheme of price subsidies and input rationing may well be feasible. In this connection, we have noted already that a relatively efficient way of increasing incomes is to subsidize the price of a project output used as an input by the poor, e.g., irrigation water. The same applies to other inputs not specifically produced in the context of a project for the poor. In the rural sector, the inputs that come immediately to mind are such things as extension services, agricultural credit and fertilizers; in the urban sector probably the only input of significance in this respect is training programs to improve the skills of the poor. In all these cases some form of rationing would be necessary, but its cost in many cases may be small and such schemes are then well justified.

Before turning to the discussion of investment policies, a few words about the use of tariffs to raise the incomes of target groups. In this connection, it needs no elaboration that export duties are not very useful. Import duties, however, are a highly efficient method of raising the price level of selected commodities. There will, of course, be a loss in consumer surplus but this is offset, except for the deadweight losses, by the increase in Government revenues and the increase in producers' incomes. Let us review an example. In Figure 9.6, SS' is the domestic supply curve, DD' is the domestic demand curve and II' is the import curve. An increase in the tariff on imported goods from GJ to EJ will result in a decrease of consumer surplus equal to ABCD. This is, however, compensated by the increase in producer income of ABEF, so that the additional loss is equal to FECD. However, as the Government receives GECH in the form of tariffs, the net result is an increase in the deadweight loss equal to the areas FEG and HCD. Assuming that the additional producer income receives a weight and applying our familiar formula, we get $v_p \cdot dY_p = dY_p (ABEF) + dX (FEG + CHD)$.

228

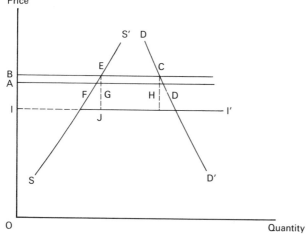

FIGURE 9.6. Price

Since the horizontal difference between the SS′ curve and the DD′ curve is the import demand curve, dX is equal to $\frac{1}{2} \cdot \Delta M_m \cdot \Delta P$ where M_m is volume of imports. Import elasticities are in general not higher than 5, and a 10 percent increase in the import price amounts thus, at the most, to a deadweight loss of 2.5 percent of the import bill[48] and a yet smaller percentage of national income. If we assume, as may well be the case, that imports are small in comparison with domestic production, the loss amounts also to only a small percentage of the income transfer. Furthermore, most Governments use tariffs to increase their revenues and to limit foreign exchange expenditures and we may, therefore, consider the deadweight loss an inevitable cost of these objectives. Tariffs are thus well worth considering to increase the incomes of the poor, provided, of course, that commodities can be identified which are mainly produced and not consumed by the poor[49].

Finally, let us examine Government policies that intervene at the investment level. It is useful here to distinguish among the ownership of capital assets. Government policies to help the poor may be directed towards: (a) capital assets held by the poor (mainly land); (b) other private capital – mainly industrial; or (c) Government capital. Since the bulk of the poor are often nonviable farmers and landless rural laborers, the ownership of land is an important factor. In many countries the ratio of land to population is such that land reform or land settlement can solve the problem by providing land to smallholders and landless workers. In others, however, there is just not enough land available to provide the landless and submarginal farmers with viable units, and other strategies must be devised. The determination of viable farm size is vital because too many mistakes have been made in the past by assuming that smallholdings can be made viable merely by increasing farm inputs. On the other hand, in land settlement projects, oversized holdings are often provided, creating a rural

229

elite. In principle, we maintain that the holding should provide an income sufficient to provide a reasonable return on invested capital as well as to farm labor.

Let us turn now to Government policies concerning private industrial investment. The problem of poverty is to a large extent the problem of unemployment and underemployment, and many Governments have, therefore, followed a policy of employment generation by promoting modern private manufacturing. Such policies are important but cannot alone solve the problem because the elasticity of modern industrial output with respect to employment – the Verdoorn elasticity – is high, often between 1.5 and 2.5. To give an example: Assume that the output of the industrial sector grows at the rate of 10 percent per annum, surely a high rate. Then industrial employment would grow by 5 percent per annum if the Verdoorn elasticity is 2. Assume further that employment in manufacturing accounts for 10 percent of total employment, a figure typical for a developing country at the first stage of industrialization, and that the total labor force grows at the conservative rate of 2.5 percent per annum. Then industrial employment would absorb only 20 percent of the increase in the labor force. In other words, some 80 percent of the increase in the labor force must be absorbed by sectors other than modern manufacturing. Services, for which the Verdoorn elasticity would certainly be lower than for manufacturing, can perhaps reduce this target by half, but this would still leave a substantial amount of unemployment. It is, therefore, not surprising that many Governments have tried to promote labor-intensive techniques of production. Unfortunately, in the modern manufacturing sector there are few opportunities to increase labor intensity because, in any one production process, the pace of the machine determines the employment of labor, and the elasticity of subsitution between capital and labor is low. More promising is the promotion of labor-intensive small-scale manufacturing, and cottage and handicraft industries, and to the extent that such industries have an adequate economic rate of return, such a strategy is well justified, even if some subsidy is necessary to ensure financial viability.

As regards Government investments, we have noted already that such investments may be a highly efficient method of raising the poor's income insofar as inputs or services are produced which will be used by the poor. Many possibilities exist in such fields as irrigation, land drainage and consolidation, agricultural processing, marketing, transportation, education, water supply and electrification, and after our discussion in the preceding sections there is no need to discuss this category further. It is also possible, however, that Governments embark on a program of investments to provide the poor with subsidized consumption goods and services, such as housing. According to the traditional analysis, such programs are often not justified because the willingness of the poor to pay may be so low – due to their limited incomes – that the program may not have an acceptable rate of return. This is not correct. To give an example: Assume that housing can be built – either by private enterprise or the Government – at a cost of $ 1,000 per house, the house being of the type used by those with incomes equal to that of an unskilled laborer. Assume further that the rent normally charged for such a house is $ 100 per annum, this rent amounting to one-sixth of the income of an unskilled laborer (a reasonable charge), which would provide a satisfactory economic rate of return of about 9 percent. Assume now that Government wishes to make such houses available to the poor at a rental fee of $ 40 per annum, the maximum they can pay.[50] Then the program would not be acceptable according to the traditional benefit-cost analysis, since the rate of return is only 1.2 percent. What this analysis overlooks is that the program includes an investment component as well as an income transfer component, and that the latter is well justified because the incomes of the poor are below base-level income. The subsidy of $ 60 on the rental fee is an acceptable income transfer, and the annual benefit stream of the housing program should, therefore, be considered to consist of $ 40 paid directly by the poor and $ 60 paid by the distribution branch of the Government. The economic rate of return of the program remains 9 percent, whether the houses will be used by unskilled laborers or the poor.

To end our review, a few words about public works projects such as roads, bridges, and dams. Quite a controversy exists in Government circles and the economic literature as to whether such projects should be undertaken with labor-intensive or capital-intensive techniques. The proponents of the labor-intensive method point out that it would create employment and raise the incomes of the poor, while opponents claim that such methods are extremely costly. The controversy is in reality a non-controversy. A public works project is, of course, open to the same type of scrutiny as any other project. Its optimum size should be determined by comparing at the margin investment costs and returns, and its acceptability should be based on its economic and social rates of return. Its investment costs are the costs of the most efficient production technique determined on the basis of the appropriate opportunity costs and whether a public works program should be labor-intensive or capital-intensive depends, therefore, on the actual circumstances. Labor-intensive techniques are often justified, especially if unemployment exists and the opportunity cost of foreign exchange is high. Since we have discussed such situations in Chapter 6, Section 4, we need not spend further time on them. As a last remark, it may be noted that a problem can arise if the works are to be undertaken by private contractors. Because they prepare their work programs and bids on the basis of the financially least costly technique, which may well be the economically inferior capital-intensive production method, it is advisable in cases where labor-intensive methods are justified to specify in the invitation to tender that labor-intensive techniques should be followed and to grant the contracts on a cost plus basis.

ANNEX TO CHAPTER 9

THE ST. PETERSBURG PARADOX

The paradox – a problem which arises in connection with a simple gamble – is important because it can only be solved by postulating – as DANIEL BERNOULLI and GABRIEL CRAMER saw independently of each other – the existence of a downward sloping marginal utility of income function. It may therefore be useful to discuss it in some detail.

The paradox is as follows. A person is tossing a coin and continues to do so until 'heads' appears. He is paid one ducat if 'heads' appears on the first toss of the coin, two ducats if it appears for the first time on the second toss and so on, so that 2^{n-1} ducats will be paid if 'heads' appears for the first time on the nth toss. The probabilities of seeing 'heads' appear for the first time on the first, second, or third toss are $1/2$, $1/2^2$ and $1/2^3$ respectively, so that, in general, the probability of 'heads' on the nth toss is $1/2^n$. Since the sum of the probabilities multiplied by the corresponding money gain is the maximum amount of money a person should be willing to pay for the privilege of playing the game, the value of the game is

$$\sum_{n=1}^{\infty} \frac{2^{n-1}}{2^n} = \frac{1}{2} + \frac{1}{2} + \frac{1}{2} + - - - - - = \infty$$

Clearly, no sane person would be willing to pay an infinite amount for the privilege of playing such a game.

BERNOULLI understood that the expected utility gains count rather than the expected money gains. In his 1738 paper[1] he states: 'It is highly probable that that any increase in wealth, no matter how insignificant, will always result in an increase in utility which is inversely proportionate to the quantity of goods already possessed.' If we denote total utility by U and wealth by R, BERNOULLI's proposition is: $dU/dR = b/R$, where b is a constant. This condition is fulfilled when total utility is a natural logarithmic function of wealth, of the form $U = b \ln R/R^*$ where b and R^* are constants.

The figure below presents such a curve. The constant b is the projection on the U axis of that segment of the tanget to the U curve that lies between the tangent's point of intersection with the U axis and its tangency point and equals HJ in Figure 9.7. The constant R^* is the value of R when U assumes the value of zero and equals OA in Figure 9.7.

It is easy to show that any logarithmic curve of the form presented in Figure 9.7 fulfills BERNOULLI's proposition regarding the marginal utility of a gain. Suppose that a person's initial wealth is OB, and that he expects to gain a sum of BC. Then the total utility before and after the gain is BD and CE, respectively, and the increase in utility is FE. Since triangle DFE is congruent to triangle

FIGURE 9.7.

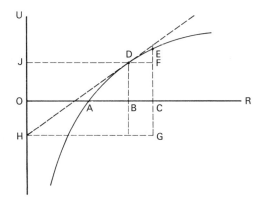

HGE, it must hold that $FE/BC = \Delta U/\Delta R = GE/OC$. Suppose that the gain BC is infinitesimally small, so that GE is almost equal to HJ and OC almost equal to OB. Then we obtain $dU/dR = b/R$ which is what BERNOULLI proposed.

The paradox can now easily be solved by calculating not the expected value of the money gain, but the expected value of the utility gain. The utility value of any gain is, of course, the difference between total utility after and before the gain. Hence, if the fortune of the person playing the game is initially A, then the utility value of a gain of 2^{n-1} ducats is:

$$b \ln \frac{A + 2^{n-1}}{R^*} - b \ln \frac{A}{R^*} = b \ln \frac{A + 2^{n-1}}{A}$$

Since the probability of a money gain of 2^{n-1} ducats in the St. Petersburg game is $1/2^n$, the mathematical value of the utility gain is $(b/2^n) \ln (A + 2^{n-1})/A$. Hence, the mathematical expectation of the utility gain of the game is:

$$\Delta U = \sum_{n=1}^{\infty} \frac{b}{2^n} \ln \frac{A + 2^{n-1}}{A}$$

If A – the value of the fortune with which a person is starting the game – is known, this expression can be solved. This can be done by writing it out so that we obtain:

$$\Delta U = \frac{b}{2} \ln \frac{A + 1}{A} + \frac{b}{4} \ln \frac{A + 2}{A} + \dots \frac{b}{2^n} \ln \frac{A + 2^{n-1}}{A} + \dots$$

$$= b \ln [(A + 1)^{1/2} \cdot (A + 2)^{1/4} \dots (A + 2^{n-1})^{1/2^n} \dots] - b \ln A$$

Since the utility of an additional sum of sure money D is presented by $\Delta U = b \ln (A + D) - b \ln A$, the bracketed expression in the written out formula is equal to $A + D$. If $A = 0$, it is easy to see that $D = \sqrt[2]{1} \cdot \sqrt[4]{2} \cdot \sqrt[8]{4} \cdot \sqrt[16]{8} \dots$, which amounts to exactly two ducats. Hence, if a person had no money to start the game, he would be happy to receive two ducats rather than to play the game. The

233

utility represented by these two ducats would be the same as the mathematical expectation of the utility he could gain by playing the game.

BERNOULLI mentions in his paper also that GABRIEL CRAMER – at about the same time and independently of BERNOULLI – solved the problem. CRAMER, however, assumed that the utility of a sum of money would be directly proportionate to the square root of the sum, i.e., $U = b\sqrt{R}$. Hence, the mathematical expectation of the utility gain of the game is $\Delta U = b\sqrt{(A + D)} - b\sqrt{A}$. If we assume that $A = 0$, then

$$\Delta U = \sum_{n=1}^{\infty} \frac{b\sqrt{2^{n-1}}}{2^n} = b\left[\frac{1}{2}\sqrt{1} + \frac{1}{4}\sqrt{2} + \frac{1}{8}\sqrt{4} + \frac{1}{16}\sqrt{8} + \ldots\right] =$$

$$= \frac{b}{2 - \sqrt{2}}$$

Hence, the value of the game is presented by $\sqrt{D} = \dfrac{1}{2 - \sqrt{2}}$. Solving for D,

we find that the value of the game amounts to about three ducats.

The difference between BERNOULLI's and CRAMER's solution is, of course, due to the difference in assumption as to the shape of the marginal utility of money curve. BERNOULLI assumes $dU/dR = bR^{-1}$, whereas CRAMER assumes $dU/dR = bR^{-0.5}$. Therefore, as can be seen in Table 9.1 in the main text, a small money gain represents less utility for BERNOULLI than for CRAMER, and the game is thus worth less to BERNOULLI than to CRAMER. BERNOULLI finds CRAMER's solution very plausible. In his words: 'Indeed, I have found his theory so similar to mine that it seems miraculous that we independently reached so close agreement on this sort of subject.' Neither BERNOULLI nor CRAMER gave any other reasons for their choice of function than that it was plausible that the marginal utility of money curve is downward sloping. To them the matter arose in connection with risk and, having solved the problem, they saw no need to investigate further the slope of the function. Their work has been, however, of fundamental importance for risk analysis and they may be considered the forerunners of modern subjective probability theory which uses essentially the same method.

[1] ECKSTEIN, 'Survey of the Theory of Public Expenditure Criteria,' p. 448.   —

[2] HAVEMAN, 'Water Resource Investment and the Public Interest,' pp. 111–112.

[3] Ibid., pp. 147–148.

[4] Ibid., p. 151.

[5] MARGLIN, 'Objectives of Water Resource Development,' in Maass et al., 'Design of Water Resource Systems,' p. 67.

[6] See also FREEMAN, who takes the same position: FREEMAN, A. M., 'Income Distribution and Public Investment,' The American Economic Review, June 1967, pp. 495–508.

[7] McNAMARA, 'Address to the Board of Governors,' Nairobi, 1973.

[8] For instance, SETON, F., 'Shadow Wages in the Chilean Economy,' Series on Cost-Benefit Analysis, Case Study No. 4 ,Development Center of the Organization for Economic Cooperation and Development, Paris, 1972.

[9] See, for instance, David BARKIN's review of Harberger's Collected Papers on Project Evaluation in the Journal of Economic Literature, June 1974.

[10] For a discussion of the different principles, see MUSGRAVE, R. A., 'The Theory of Public Finance – A Study in Public Economy,' McGraw-Hill Book Company, New York, Toronto, London, 1959, Chapter V.

[11] FREEMAN, A. M., 'Project Design and Evaluation with Multiple Objectives,' in 'Public Expenditures and Policy Analysis,' eds. Haveman, R. H. and Margolis, G., Markham Publishing Company, Chicago, 1970, pp. 347–363.

[12] CHENERY, H. et al., 'Redistribution with Growth – Policies to improve Income Distribution in Developing Countries in the Context of Economic Growth,' A joint study by the World Bank's Development Research Center and the Institute of Development Studies of the University of Sussex, Oxford University Press, London, 1974.

[13] TINBERGEN, J., 'Some Features of the Optimum Regime,' in 'Optimum Social Welfare and Productivity,' The Charles Moskowitz Lectures, New York University Press, New York, 1972.

[14] WEBER, E. H., 'Tastsinn und Gemeingefuhl,' Leipzig, 1846.

[15] Interesting cases where the law seems to apply are mentioned by AITCHISON, J. and BROWN, J. A. C., 'The Log Normal Distribution,' Cambridge University Press, London and New York, 1957, Chapter 10.

[16] FECHNER, G. T., 'Elemente der Psychophysik,' Leipzig, 1860.

[17] BORING, E. G., 'A History of Experimental Psychology,' 2nd ed., Appleton-Century Crafts Inc., New York, 1950, pp. 275–296.

[18] If $u = bY^{-1}$, then $du/dY = -bY^{-2} = -(b \cdot Y^{-1}) \cdot Y^{-1} = -u/Y$, Hence, $e_u = du/dY \cdot Y/u = -1$.

[19] STEVENS, S. S., 'Psychophysics, Introduction to Perceptual, Neural and Social Prospects,' edited by Geraldine Stevens, John Wiley and Sons, New York, London, Sydney, Toronto, 1975.

[20] If $U = bY^{\beta}$, then $dU/dY \cdot Y/U = \beta bY^{\beta-1} \cdot Y/bY^{\beta} = \beta$

[21] See the Annex to this Chapter. CRAMER postulated that $U = \sqrt{Y}$.

[22] If $U_1 = b \, 10^{1/2}$ and $2U_1 = b \, Y_2^{1/2}$, it follows that $2.10^{1/2} = Y_2^{1/2}$. Hence, $\log 2 + \frac{1}{2} \log 10 = \frac{1}{2} \log Y_2$. Taking logs we get $0.3 + 0.5 = \frac{1}{2} \log Y_2$, so that $\log Y_2 = 1.6$ and $Y_2 = \$ 40$.

[23] If $U_1 = 2.3\, b \log 10$ and $2U_1 = 2.3\, b \log Y_2$, it follows that $4.6 = 2.3 \log Y_2$, so that $\log Y_2 = 2$ and $Y_2 = \$ 100$.

[24] If $U = b \, Y^{\beta}$, then $u = \beta bY^{\beta-1}$ and $du/dY = (\beta - 1)\beta bY^{\beta-2}$. Writing e_u for the elasticity of the marginal utility of income, i.e., $e_u = du/dY \cdot Y/u$, we get $\{(\beta - 1)\beta bY^{\beta-2}Y\}/\beta bY^{\beta-1} = \beta - 1$.

[25] FISHER, I., 'A Statistical Method for Measuring Marginal Utility and the Justice of the Progressive Income Tax' in 'Economic Essays in Honor of John Bates Clark,' The Macmillan Co., New York, 1927, pp. 157–193.

[26] FRISCH, R., 'New Methods of Measuring Marginal Utility' in 'Beitrage zur Okonomischen Theorie' (No. 3), J. C. B. Mohr (Paul Siebeck), Tubingen, 1932.

[27] FELLNER, W., 'Operational Utility: The Theoretical Background and a Measurement' in 'Ten Economic Studies in the Tradition of Irving Fischer,' John Wiley and Sons, New York, London, Sydney, 1967.

[28] TOBIN, Y., 'The Statistical Demand Function for Food in the USA,' Journal of the Royal Statistical Society, Series A, Vol. CXIII, Part II, 1950.

[29] FRISCH, R., 'A Complete Scheme for Computing all Direct and Cross Demand Elasticities in a Model with Many Sectors,' Econometrica, April 1959.

[30] THEIL, H. and BROOKS, R. B., 'How Does the Marginal Utility of Income Change When Real Income Changes?', European Economic Review, Vol. II, No. 2, Winter 1970–71.

[31] VAN PRAAG, B. M. S., 'Individual Welfare Functions and Consumer Behavior,' North-Holland Publishing Company, Amsterdam, 1968.

[32] VAN PRAAG, B. M. S., 'The Welfare Function of Income in Belgium: An Empirical Investigation,' European Economic Review, Vol. II, No. 3, Spring 1971, pp. 337–369.

[33] The elasticity of the marginal utility of income is in this case represented by $e_u = -[\ln Y - \mu)/\sigma^2]- 1$, where the values of the parameters μ and σ are individually determined. Hence, if Y increases, e_u increases (in absolute terms).

[34] Ibid., p. 368.

[35] As $b = \$ 1,200$, $Y_2 = \$ 500$, and $Y_1 = \$ 300$, it follows that $\triangle U = 2.3 \times 1200 \times \log 500/300 = 607$ utils.

[36] SETON, F., 'Shadow Wages in the Chilean Economy,' p. 167.

[37] FELDSTEIN, M. S., 'Distribution Preferences in Public Expenditure Analysis' in 'Redistribution Through Public Choice,' eds. Hochman, J. M. and Peterson, G. D., Columbia University Press, New York and London, 1974.

[38] SQUIRE and VAN DER TAK, 'Economic Analysis of Projects.'

[39] LERNER, A. P., 'The Economics of Control,' The MacMillan Company, New York, 1944.

[40] PAUKERT, F., 'Income Distribution at Different Levels of Development, A Survey of Evidence,' International Labor Review, Aug.-Sept. 1973.

[41] AHLUWALIA, M. S., 'Income Inequality: Some Dimensions of the Problem,' in Chenery et al., 'Redistribution with Growth,' Chapter I, pp. 3–37.

[42] See Section 9.2.

[43] Those who believe that societies should strive towards income equality will not, probably, accept this premise and will argue that the curve BB should show a slight slope over the middle income range. However, as fine tuning of middle income levels is often difficult and is seldom explicitly stated as a government objective, we believe that, even if we accept this egalitarian point of view, the horizontal segment is adequate for operational purposes.

[44] We may also express it in this way: that the annual yield of $ 1 generated by a long-life investment of $ 10 represents an economic rate of return of 10 percent if this dollar accrues to the economy at large but a social rate of return of 15 percent if this dollar is transferred to the poor.

[45] See Chapter 10 for a detailed analysis of such a project.

[46] The case of budget constraints will be discussed briefly in the next section.

[47] We would like to mention here that we became aware of this formula through a lecture (unpublished) given by Harberger in Washington, D.C., in the fall of 1974. Needless to say, the responsibility for any errors in its derivation, or in the discussion of its implications, rests with us.

[48] As $dP = 0.1P$ and $dM_m = 0.5M_m$, the loss is $1/2 \times 0.5 \ M_m \times 0.1P = 0.025 \ M_mP$.

[49] Tariffs are also popular in the developed world. Until about 1971 agricultural products were heavily protected in the EEC. Zeylstra reports that during a certain period the EEC protected sugar to the extent of 240 % and butter to the extent of 290 % above world market prices (Zeylstra, 'Aid or Development,' p. 155).

[50] In principle, we maintain that the rental should be set at such a level that when weighted with the marginal utility of income it would be equal to the rental paid by someone with a base-level income.

236

[1] Translated from Latin into English by Dr. Louise Sommer, The American University, Washington, D.C., as 'Exposition of a New Theory on the Measurement of Risk,' Econometrica, January 1954.

10. SOCIAL BENEFIT-COST ANALYSIS IN PRACTICE

10.1. INTRODUCTION

The social rate of return approach to investment decisions is fairly straightforward: the parties who benefit and lose because of the project should be identified, and appropriate income distribution weights should be attached to the gains and losses. To illustrate the methodology we will review a hypothetical example, namely, a land settlement project in the hypothetical country Xalandia. The analysis is unfolded in the form of a parable.

Hypothetical Example of the Analyses of the Financial, Economic and Social Return of the Xalandia Oil Palm Project

The proposed project was identified by the Planning Department and would be the first of its kind in Xalandia. It would consist of the settling of 5,000 families on about 65,000 acres of land, 60,000 acres of which would be planted with oil palm. The settlers would be recruited from among the rural poor and would each be provided with 12 acres of planted oil palm, for which they would pay an appropriate rent. The Government would undertake all the investments except housing (clearing of land, planting of oil palm, and construction of a palm oil mill and feeder roads) and would operate the mill and provide the extension services; settlers would take care of their housing. All of the products produced under the proposed project, some 105,000 tons of palm oil and 20,000 tons of kernels per annum, would be exported.

The Prime Minister had asked the Treasury's opinion as to the feasibility of the project and Treasury officials had calculated that the financial return on the Government's funds would be only 6 percent (see Table 10.1). They, therefore, stated that the project should not be undertaken because at least 8 percent could be earned in the international capital markets. However, the Planning Department was not convinced by this reasoning and stated that the project should be evaluated from a national point of view. Consultants were, therefore, hired to do a detailed feasibility study.

The consultants started by measuring the rates of return on capital in the country and, with their usual precision, estimated the opportunity cost of capital at 12 percent. The foreign exchange situation of the country was also examined. The merchandise and services accounts were found to be in equilibrium and there was only an insignificant outflow of domestic capital. As the price level of tradeables in the country appeared to be about 40 percent above world market prices, the consultants recommended using a shadow price for foreign exchange of 1.4. Further, the consultants found that the average annual income of the prospective settlers in their old occupations amounted to about

X$ 680 and they recommended using this as the opportunity cost of labor. The economic rate of return of the proposed project was calculated and found to be about 13 percent. Since the opportunity cost of capital in the country was estimated at 12 percent, the consultants considered the proposed project marginal.

The Planning Department remained unconvinced and pointed out that the settlers all belonged to the bottom 5 percent of the income groups in Xalandia and that, if something was not done, disturbances could surely be expected. Furthermore, the country's investment program was much too low and, although there were other investment opportunities for the Government, the Planning Department was not aware of any other project that could raise incomes so much as the proposed project. Settlers' incomes were expected to increase to four times the original income level of the settlers (about X$ 2,720). The Planning Department proposed hiring a new consultant who could, it had heard, quantify these considerations. The Prime Minister agreed.

The new consultant reviewed the economic rate of return calculation, the parameters of which he accepted, and undertook to make a social benefit-cost calculation. He pointed out that the wage rate of an unskilled worker in the rural area was about X$ 4,500 and interviewed the Cabinet as to whether this was considered excessive. It appeared that all the Ministers considered X$ 4,500 the minimum income level. The consultant explained that several functions could be used to measure the utility of an additional Xalandia dollar at various income levels and after·much discussion the Cabinet felt that the Bernoulli-Weber-Fechner function presented the best estimate of their value judgment as to how much more a Xalandia dollar accruing to the settlers should be worth than a Xalandia dollar accruing to a person at the X$ 4,500 income level.

The consultant made the necessary calculations and arrived at the result that a premium of 200 percent should be placed on the income increase of the settlers.[1] Incorporating this premium in the benefit-cost calculation, the consultant found that from a social point of view the project was highly valuable. Whereas the economic rate of return was only 13 percent, the social rate of return appeared to be about 19 percent. Sensitivity tests confirmed the plausibility of these values. On the basis of the Planning Department's advice, the Prime Minister accepted the consultant's recommendations and approached one of the international institutions for a loan.

The staff of that institution visited the country shortly thereafter to appraise the project. They found the technical, financial, managerial and economic aspects of the project well presented and acceptable, but expressed no opinion as to the validity of the social benefit-cost analysis. The Government of Xalandia understands that the appraisal report is being prepared and hopes to hear soon whether the request for a loan will be granted.

So far the discussion of our hypothetical example, and the reader may wish to guess what position the international lending institution is likely to take. The calculations are summarized in Table 10.1 and should not present a problem. All values are corrected for inflation. For ease of exposition, it is assumed

TABLE 10.1. Hypothetical example: Analyses of the financial, economic, and social return of the Xalandia oil palm project.

		Financial Return		Economic Return	Social Return
		Govt.	Settlers		
Years 1–6 (Total):			X$ Million		
Domestic value of investments	128.0	128.0	–	128.0	
Premium on foreign exchange component of 102.4	40.0%			41.0	
Economic value of investments	169.0			169.0	169.0
Years 7–30 (Annual):					
Sales (125,000 tons at X$ 257 f.o.b. – FE 100%)	32.1			45.0	
Export duties	0.5	0.5			
Transport, mill operating, and additional extension costs (FE 80%)	5.0			6.6	
Revenues accruing to settlers	26.6				
Settler operating costs (materials – FE 65%)	2.0			2.5	
Land rent	10.5	10.5			
Income taxes	0.5	0.5			
Net cash income settlers	13.6		13.6		
Settler labor cost (opportunity cost of labor X$ 680)	3.4		3.4	3.4	
Financial benefits	21.7	11.5	10.2		
Economic benefits				32.5	32.5
Premium on income increase of settlers	2.0 × 10.2				20.4
Social benefits	52.9				52.9
Internal rates of return:		6%		13%	19%

that the investments are evenly distributed over the six-year investment period, while the benefits remain constant during years 7 to 30. Since we are interested in highlighting the social issues, only the internal rates of return of the project have been calculated and we have not bothered to calculate present values and probability distributions. The example is, of course, simplified and in real life the calculations would be more bothersome, but we hope to have shown that, with a minimum of investigation, fairly accurate financial, economic and social rates of return analyses can be made.

As a last remark, it may be underlined that the example is entirely hypothetical. The values of the variables have been chosen such that the social rate of return is significantly higher than the economic rate of return. As we will see in the next Section, in which a real land settlement project will be discussed, this is not necessarily always the case.

240

The example of the previous Section is not as hypothetical as it might at first sight seem to be. Malaysia, Indonesia, the Philippines, Papua New Guinea and many African countries have land settlement programs quite similar to the example discussed. Of these, the Malaysia program is probably the largest and the best planned and organized, and it will be well worthwhile to review it in some detail.

Malaysia, a country with a population of about 12 million, is generally regarded a successful case in development.[2] During the 1960s, its GNP growth rate was between 6 and 7 percent, and its per capita income in 1974 was more than US$ 700. Nevertheless, it has a severe social problem. According to a 1970 survey, in Peninsular Malaysia[3] the incomes of the Malays (55 percent of the population) is only half that of the Chinese (34 percent of the population), while the Indians (accounting almost entirely for the remaining 11 percent) occupy a middle position. Furthermore, Malays and Indians own only 2.4 and 1.1 percent, respectively, of the share capital of limited companies, while the Chinese own 27.2 percent. In the non-corporate sectors, Malays own 2.3 percent of the fixed assets in manufacturing, construction and mining, and 47.1 percent of the acreage under cultivation. On the other hand, the Chinese ownership is 92.2 percent in manufacturing, construction and mining, and 32.8 percent in agriculture. The survey also indicated that, out of a total of 1.6 million households in Peninsular Malaysia, some 590,000 had incomes below the poverty line and that 79 percent of these were Malay households.

The increasing concern with this structural problem led the Government of Malaysia to formulate the New Economic Policy, which is well described in the Mid-Term Review of the Second Malaysia Plan, 1971–1975.[4] The two-pronged strategy of development is the 'eradication of poverty' and 'the restructuring of Malaysian society to correct imbalance, so as to reduce and eventually eliminate the identification of race with economic function.' The strategy is to be accomplished through 'the modernization of rural life, the rapid and balanced development of urban activities, and the creation of a Malay commercial, industrial community in all categories and at all levels of operation.' The modernization of rural life is a very important element of the New Economic Policy. Of the 590,000 poor households, some 520,000 were in the rural areas. The largest number was found among rubber smallholders (176,000), followed by padi cultivators (104,000), mixed agriculture farmers (102,000), and a residual group (138,000), in which non-estate laborers, fishermen and coconut smallholders formed the more important occupational groups.

Malaysia is in the fortunate position of being endowed with ample land resources. Some 34 million acres of land are suitable for agricultural development but, so far, only about half have been developed, leaving about 17 million acres to be opened up (6 million acres in Peninsular Malaysia and 11 million acres in Sabah and Sarawak). Land development is, therefore, an eminently feasible method of reducing the pressure of population on existing farming areas and providing the poverty farmers new opportunities to raise their standard of living. From 1956, the year when land development as a program really started (the Federal Land Development Authority – FELDA – the most successful and most important of the land development agencies, was established in that year), through 1974, public agencies developed a total of some 1.6 million acres of land and settled some 150,000 families. At present, some 200,000 acres are annually being developed, some 80,000 acres of this by FELDA. The pace of development has accelerated in the past. Public sector allocations for land development increased from 4.5 percent of total public expenditures in the First Malaysia Plan (1966–1970) to 8.3 percent in the Second Malaysia Plan (1971–1975).

Are these land settlement projects good or bad? To analyze this, we will review a typical land settlement project as undertaken by FELDA during 1974. FELDA develops oil palm as well as rubber holdings but we will limit our analysis to the oil palm schemes, the more profitable of the two types. The investment costs per settler over the six-year investment period, the period during which no palm oil is produced, are of the order of US$ 14,000 (1974 US dollars), surely not a negligible amount. About 56 percent of this amount is for infrastructure, land clearing, nurseries and planting of seedlings; about 24 percent for the oil mill; about 13 percent for management costs (supervision) of FELDA, and about 7 percent for settler housing.

The full bearing of the trees begins in the seventh year of the scheme; yields increase until the tree is about 13 years old, decrease somewhat thereafter but are still very substantial until the tree is about 30 years old, which is considered the end of the fruit-bearing period. Rather than calculating benefits and costs for each individual year, we will not be far off the mark if we show the calculations for an average year. Table 10.2 summarizes the basic data.

A problem with such calculations, of course, is the price projection. The f.o.b. prices of palm oil and kernels shown in the table are in 1974 dollars and are based on an extrapolation of historical trends, adjusted for expected changes in demand and supply. In 1974, they were generally accepted as reasonable in price-forecasting circles. As the table shows, the settlers – they all have a holding of 14 acres – can expect to receive an average gross cash income during the years that the trees are bearing fruit (years 7 to 30) of about M$ 4,540 (about US$ 2,000). Under the FELDA schemes, the settlers move in during the fourth year after planting and, during the next two years when no income is being produced, receive a subsistence allowance of about M$ 1,080 (US$ 470) per annum, which they are obliged to repay. In addition, they have to repay part of the agricultural development costs of the holding and the cost of the house they receive. All in all, the repayable amount at the end of the six-year investment period amounts to about M$ 19,400 (US$ 8,435) and the annual debt amortization (loan to be repaid over 15 years at $6^{1}/_{2}$ percent) to about M$ 2,000 (US$ 900). The spendable cash income of the settlers during the greater part of the productive lifetime of the trees is thus about M$ 2,500 (US$ 1,100).

The economic rate of return calculation for this type of project is rather

TABLE 10.2. Basic data on the Malaysian oil palm projects (1974 Malaysian Dollars).

I. *Yields and Prices at Full Bearing*

Date of full bearing (years after clearing)	7 years	
Yield (average quantity of fresh fruit bunches – ffb – per acre)	7.7 tons	
	(21 % oil; 4.2 % kernels)	

Per ton	*Palm oil*	*Kernels*
F.o.b. price	M$ 407	M$ 250
Export tax	32	–
Marketing/distr. charges	18	14
Ex-mill value	357	236

Per acre		
Production	1.6 tons	0.3 tons
Ex-mill value	M$ 571	M$ 70
Ex-mill value per acre of production	M$ 640	
Processing costs	M$ 100	
Price to settlers per acre of production	M$ 540	

II. *Average Annual Revenues at Full Bearing per* 14-*acre Holding*

1. F.o.b. value of production per holding	M$ 10,140
2. Export tax	715
3. Marketing/distr. charges	465
4. Ex-mill value	M$ 8,960
5. Processing costs	1,400
6. Revenues settlers (14 ac. × M$ 540)	M$ 7,560
7. Transport costs (holding to mill)	540
8. Replanting fund charge	540
9. Fertilizers, pesticides	1,740
10. State land tax	150
11. Settler Devt. Fund charge	50
12. Gross cash income, settler	M$ 4,540
13. Debt amortization (principal and interest)	2,000
14. Net cash income settler	M$ 2,540 (yrs. 7–21)
15. Net cash income settler	4,500 (yrs. 22–30)

tedious because the values of benefits and costs are different for every year. We will not repeat the calculation here and it may, therefore, suffice to state that the numerous calculations which have been made for these schemes all arrive at economic rates of return between about 14 and 18 percent, say, an average of about 15 percent.[5]

A few comments, however, are in order. Normally, no foreign exchange shadow rate is used in the calculations. In Malaysia, import duties are, on average, 13 percent; export duties about 5 percent. If we assume that import and export elasticities are equal, the shadow rate would be 104 percent of the

243

official rate.[6] If it is assumed that an additional dollar of foreign exchange would be used entirely for increasing imports, the shadow rate would be about 113 percent of the official rate. This is certainly not negligible. On the other hand, the foreign exchange component of the investments is low (about 25 percent) while the foreign exchange component of the net benefit stream is high (the products are exported). The use of a foreign exchange shadow rate thus tends to increase the economic rate of return. There is, further, the point that the price projections are subject to a wide margin of error and that these errors may be larger than the foreign exchange adjustment. All in all, on practical grounds, we believe that it does not make much difference whether the official exchange rate or a shadow rate is used for this type of project in Malaysia.

In the rate of return calculation, the f.o.b. value of the exports should, of course, be taken gross of the export duty, since this accrues to the Government and is therefore a benefit; similarly, the various taxes paid by the settlers should not be considered costs – they are transfer payments from the settlers to the Government. Also, the settlers' labor cost must be evaluated. FELDA surveyed the settlers carefully before they joined the schemes and found that settlers' average income was about M$ 870 per annum. This may thus be taken to represent the opportunity cost of the settlers' labor.

A short-cut method may be used to show that the economic rate of return will indeed be about 15 percent. As shown in Table 10.2, the f.o.b. value of the annual production of a holding is about M$ 10,140. The costs consist of the real costs of items 3, 5, 7 and 9 in Table 10.2 and the opportunity cost of the settlers' labor (M$ 870). Taking the figures of Table 10.2 we obtain a total cost of M$ 5,015. However, about M$ 1,000 of depreciation, interest charges and taxes are included in the figures for processing, transporting and distributing, and the real total cost is therefore about M$ 4,000. The value of the net benefit stream during years 7 to 30 is thus about M$ 6,000 (US$ 2,600). The investments of M$ 32,000 (US$ 14,000) per holding take place about evenly during years 1 to 6. Adjusting for taxes and compounding the yearly investments at an interest rate of 15 percent, we obtain, as the real value of the investments at the end of year 6, about M$ 39,000. Comparison of the benefit stream of M$ 6,000 per annum during years 7 to 30 with the terminal investment in year 6 of M$ 39,000 shows that the economic internal rate of return is indeed about 15 percent.

We are now in a position to analyze the social rate of return of this type of project, and the first question which arises is: which income level should be taken as the base income level? We have two pieces of evidence to determine this base level. First, in 1974, the wage paid by the Government for unskilled workers in the rural areas was about M$ 2,500 per annum. Second, the bulk of the unskilled workers on private estates received a cash income of about M$ 1,800 in 1974, to which must be added payments in kind such as housing and food. One would not be far off the mark if one evaluated the total income of an estate worker at about M$ 2,500. Taking all these points into account, it seems to us that a base level of M$ 2,500 represents a fairly accurate estimate of what in Malaysia was considered a reasonable income in 1974 for an unskilled

244

worker in the rural areas.

For the social rate of return calculation, we should write out, year by year, the social value of the benefits, because these are a function of base level income, which may change over time. To simplify the exposition, we assume that there are no general productivity increases which would increase benefits and base level income. This may well be justified because, in the last decade, productivity increases have not been significant and this may well be so in the future. In any case, our assumption will not lead to large errors. Under our assumption then, an income distribution weight is to be attached to the increase in settlers' annual income from about M$ 900 without the project to the base income level of M$ 2,500 with the project. Using our usual formula, we may set the weight on the additional annual income of M$ 1,600 at 1.6[7] or, in other words, we may attach to settlers' additional income of M$ 1,600 a social premium of about 60 percent (about M$ 1,000). The net economic benefit of the project of M$ 6,000 per annum becomes thus a social net benefit stream of about M$ 7,000. While the economic rate of return of this type of project is about 15 percent, the social rate of return appears to be slightly less than 17 percent.

Why is it that the social analysis for this type of project results in a social rate of return only marginally different from the economic rate of return? The principal reason is that, whereas the relatively high investments (US$ 14,000 per settler) take place in the early years, the benefits of the schemes appear late in time: it takes six years after clearing before the settlers' income will increase. It would be of much interest to compare the land settlement type of project with projects also geared towards raising the incomes of the rural poor but with more immediate benefits. Malaysia has concentrated its efforts so far almost entirely on land settlement, and it is, therefore, difficult to find other types of projects. There are, however, two rural projects – the Muda and Kemubu Irrigation Projects – where the objective was to increase the incomes of padi farmers. In the next section we will analyze the Muda project – the larger of the two.

10.3. MALAYSIA – IRRIGATION

One of the most spectacular projects in Malaysia is the Muda Irrigation project. It is located in the States of Kedah and Perlis in the northwest of Peninsular Malaysia and covers some 245,000 acres of land, on which some 51,000 farmers cultivate padi. The objective of the project is to make double-cropping of padi possible. The major works include the Muda and Pedu Dams of concrete and rockfill, respectively, with a tunnel connecting them; a head-works and main canal system; improvement of existing and construction of new distributory canals; and drainage construction and ancillary works. Construction began in 1966 and was completed in 1970. In current Malaysian dollars, the total cost was M$ 245 million (US$ 106 million). In 1974 Malaysian dollars,

TABLE 10.3. Basic data: Malaysia-Muda irrigation project.

	Without Project	With Project	Change
Farm Data, 1980			
Number of farmers	51,000	51,000	–
Area	245,000 ac	245,000 ac	–
Annual cropped area	237,000 ac	490,000 ac	253,000 ac
Cropping intensity	96%	196%	–
Yield per acre	1.5 tons	1.5 tons	–
Padi output (tons)	347,000	710,000	363,000
Annual Benefits and Costs by 1980		M$ Million[1]	
Gross value of production	122.8	251.3	128.5
Operating costs farmers	30.0	51.7	21.7
Value added	92.8	199.6	106.8
Labor cost farmers (hired labor and farmers' own labor)	19.8	55.3	35.5
Net economic benefits, farmers	73.0	144.3	71.3
Operating and maintenance costs, project works	–	8.9	8.9
Net economic benefit of project	73.0	135.4	62.4
Investment Costs			313.0
Economic Rate of Return 18%			
Net Social Benefit of Project			83.6
Social Rate of Return 24%			313.0

[1] In 1974 Malaysian dollars.

the total cost is M$ 313 million (US$ 136 million) or about US$ 2,650 per farmer.

Although there are some leakages at the Muda Dam which are presently being sealed, and water control needs improvement, the project must be considered a great success. In 1965, the year before construction started, padi production was about 277,000 tons, and in 1971, the first full year when off-season irrigation water was available, about 452,000 tons. It is expected that by 1980 the full potential of off-season irrigation will be realized and that padi production then will be about 710,000 tons, accounting for about 60 percent of total padi production in Malaysia. A second-phase project, scheduled to start within the next few years, is expected to increase yields and lower production costs through improvements in water flows and agricultural supporting services.

The economic rate of return analysis of the project is straightforward and the benefits and costs of the project for 1980, the year of full production, are recapitulated in Table 10.3. The area is analyzed without and with the project, and the incremental net benefit stream compared with the investments. The economic rate of return appears to be 18 percent.

The social rate of return analysis is more difficult since we need to differentiate between the various income classes. The income distribution pattern in the area is presently being studied but it will be several years before the results will

246

be available and the best we can do at present is to make some educated guesses. It is known that about 40 percent of the farmers are tenants and 60 percent owner-farmers. Furthermore, based on a sample survey of 4-acre holdings, it has been estimated that the incomes of the farmers operating this size of farm with and without the project would be as follows by 1980:

TABLE 10.4. Net cash incomes 4-acre farmers by 1980 (1974 Malaysian dollars).

		Without Project	With Project	Change
Tenant-farmers	M$	1,800	3,500	1,700
Owner-farmers		2,000	4,000	2,000

While the owner-farmers have in general larger holdings than four acres, the tenants in general have smaller farms. Since the base income level is M$ 2,500 (as discussed in the previous section), we assume that no income distribution weight is to be placed on the income increase of the 30,000 owner-farmers. As regards the tenants, we may calculate a conservative income distribution weight by assuming that the income of all tenants without and with the project are M$ 1,800 and M$ 3,500, respectively. Applying the usual formula[8] we find that the increase from M$ 1,800 to M$ 2,500 should receive a weight of 1.17. The total social premium is then 20,000 × M$ 700 × 0.17 = M$ 2.4 million, which is a marginal addition to the economic benefits of about M$ 62.4 million. This is, however, not surprising since the farmers have a relatively high annual income without the project of M$ 1,800. As discussed in the previous section, the settlers under the land settlement projects have incomes without the projects of about M$ 900 only.

There is, however, another very important social benefit. Detailed investigations have shown that, because of the double-cropping, the labor requirement of the farmers has increased significantly. Again, only very rough estimates can be made, but the following labor situation for 1980 without and with the project may well be considered a realistic estimate.

TABLE 10.5. Farm labor requirements and costs (in 1974 Malaysian dollars) by 1980.

	Without Project	With Project	Change
Total farm labor, including farmers' own labor (in manyears)	36.350	73.700	37.350
Total labor cost (M$ million)	19.8	55.3	35.5
Hired labor cost per manyear	M$ 570	M$ 750	M$ 950
Total cost of hired labor (M$ million)	12.0	28.0	16.0
Total hired labor in manyears	21.000	37.350	16.350

It appears thus that some 16,350 additional manyears of hired labor may be necessary by 1980 and it has been estimated that the cost of this additional labor would be the equivalent of M$ 950 per manyear, as compared to a normal cost equivalent to M$ 570 per manyear. As a result, the average cost per man-year would rise from M$ 570 to M$ 750. If we assume conservatively that the 37,350 laborers equivalent in 1980 will experience this rise in income of M$ 180, the social weight to be attached to this increase is 3.8[9] and the social premium is thus 37,350 $\times$ 180 $\times$ 2.8 = M$ 18.8 million.

A rough estimate of the total social value of the annual net benefits of the project is thus M$ 84 million, compared with an annual net economic benefit of M$ 62 million, and the social rate of return of the project is therefore approximately 24 percent, compared to the economic rate of return of 18 percent.

More will be said about the land settlement projects vis-a-vis irrigation projects in Section 6 where we wish to draw some further conclusions, but first it will be useful to study two other cases.

10.4. West Africa – Mechanical Clearing versus Hand Clearing of Jungle Forests

During one of our visits to a West African country in the late 1960s, we became aware of a very controversial problem that arose in connection with a planned oil palm project, namely, whether the area for the project that consisted of jungle forest should be cleared mechanically or by hand. The mechanical method of clearing consists of the mechanical felling of forests with specialized equipment, windrowing of the felled woods with bulldozers, and light burning of the area between the windrows. Furthermore, no stumps are left in the field and the area between the windrows can be traveled by car. On the other hand, the manual method consists of the cutting of undergrowth, smaller trees and larger trees by successive worker teams. The trees are felled in only one direction and later on burned, leaving only the largest stumps standing. A path of 2.40 m width is opened after every row of oil palm trees, but this is only a foot-path which cannot be traveled by car.

The dispute was fierce. The proponents of mechanical clearing claimed that complete burning in the case of hand clearing would affect the humus content of the soil, possibly leading to a reduction of yields, and that motorized inspection of the trees would not be possible. The proponents of hand clearing claimed that burning had a favorable effect on yields and auto transport between blocks of trees was possible, and that, as regards the trees in the blocks, a good manager should do his inspection on foot and not by car, and so on. In the end, after considerable discussion, both parties agreed that there was no evidence that the two methods of clearing would produce different yields. Furthermore, the inspection issue appeared not to be relevant at all, both parties eventually agreeing that neither of the clearing methods really had any advantage over the other.

The dispute thereafter centered on the financial rates of return of both methods. Projects with mechanical clearing appeared to have a rate of return of about 11 percent, while projects with hand clearing had a rate of return of about 9 percent. Further analysis showed that the higher financial rate of return of mechanical clearing was based on the fact that a larger area could be cleared per annum than under hand clearing so that the benefits of the project would materialize sooner. The higher cost per hectare of mechanical clearing appeared thus to be more than compensated by the earlier sales. It was pointed out, of course, that the economic rate of return rather than the financial rate of return was relevant for the decision, and it was finally agreed to undertake such a calculation.

Much time was spent on estimating the relevant shadow prices. This does not concern us here, except that it should be noted that the costs of mechanical clearing were entirely foreign exchange costs and the output of the project would be exported. All the foreign exchange elements were, therefore, evaluated at the opportunity cost of foreign exchange, which differed markedly from the official exchange rate because the national currency was overvalued. As regards labor, it was found after detailed investigation that the wages which would be paid under the hand clearing method were about twice as high as the laborers' normal earnings. The opportunity cost of labor was therefore set at 0.5 of the wage rate. In order to compare the two methods of land clearing, a differential analysis was made using different values for the most significant variables (sensitivity tests). The base values of this analysis are presented in Table 10.6. As the calculations show, it was found that the base estimate of the economic rate of return on the incremental cost of mechanical clearing was only about 3 percent, and it was, therefore, concluded by several of the participants in the debate that mechanical clearing was not justified. Nevertheless, this conclusion was challenged by others because the calculations appeared to be very sensitive to the chosen values.

There is not much sense in reviewing all the different calculations. The point we wish to make is that the debate could easily have been settled if one had calculated the social rates of return of the two methods. It has already been pointed out that the workers under the land clearing method would be paid about twice what they would earn in their next best alternative. As the normal unskilled labor income was about 50 percent higher than the earnings of the workers, the social weight that should be attached to an increase in their income would be about 2.0.[10] This means thus that land clearing would have an additional benefit stream equal to the opportunity cost of land clearing (the stream 14, 32, 33 and so on, in Table 10.6) and, as shown at the bottom of Table 10.6, the incremental cost of mechanical clearing would then have a negative rate of return, making hand clearing definitely the more preferable method of clearing the forests.

TABLE 10.6. West Africa— Oil palm development project.
Differential Cost – Benefit Analysis Mechanical Clearing versus Manual Clearing.

	1 69/70	2 1971	3 1972	4 1973	5 1974	6 1975	7 1976	8 1977	9 1978	10 1979	11 1980	12 1981	13 1982	14 1983
Mechanical clearing of 9,000 ha – annually	1,200	1,800	2,000	2,000	2,000									
Hand clearing of 9,000 ha – annually	600	1,400	1,400	1,400	1,400	1,400	1,400							
Differential Cost/Benefit Analysis (X$ million)														
Investments, mechanical clearing	109	164	182	182	182									
Investments, manual clearing	14	32	32	32	32	32	32							
Higher economic investment costs, mechanical	(95)	(132)	(150)	(150)	(150)	32	32							
Higher economic revenue, mechanical clearing	–	–	–	16	34	66	99	150	150	126	100	54	18	
Differential stream	(95)	(132)	(150)	(150)	(134)	66	98	99	150	150	126	100	54	18
Economic Return on Incremental Costs, Mechanical Clearing – 3%														
Differential stream adjusted with income distribution weights	(109)	(164)	(182)	(182)	(166)	34	66	99	150	150	126	100	54	18
Social Return on Incremental Costs, Mechanical Clearing – negative														

250

Beginning in the latter part of the 1960s, the International Development Association (the sister organization of the World Bank) made three credits on soft terms available to the Government of Pakistan for the procurement of tractors by farmers. These credits resulted in the introduction into Pakistan of some 18,000 tractors between 1966 and 1973. Although the appraisal reports indicated that the projects had high financial and economic rates of return, the Government of Pakistan and the Association became seriously concerned about possible adverse social effects of farm mechanization and, therefore, initiated a study[11] following approval of the third credit in 1970.

The study consisted of two parts, the first being a field survey. From the 3,868 farms which received tractors from the first credit in 1967-1968, 202 farms were randomly selected and field survey data collected on farm situation, resource use, production processes and output in both the 'before' and 'after' tractor situations.[12] The second part consisted of an analysis of the financial and economic returns on investment in tractors.

One of the principal findings of the study was that farm mechanization leads to a substantial increase in farm size. The 202 survey farms encompassed an area of 9,083 cultivated acres before acquiring tractors, compared to 22,025 acres at the end of the period, thereby increasing the mean size of farms from some 45 acres to some 109 acres. The bulk of the increase in farm size came about because the mechanizing farmers took over the land formerly leased out to their tenants, thereby displacing some 879 tenant farmers.

To make a meaningful calculation of the economic rate of return of farm mechanization, the authors of the study took as their base the final area of land (22,025 acres), and calculated inputs and outputs of this area before and after mechanization began. Appropriate shadow prices were introduced (for instance, the opportunity cost of foreign exchange was set at Rs. 9,50 to the US dollar, while the official rate was Rs. 4.50 to the US dollar) and the surprising result is that the authors found an economic rate of return for the program of about 24 percent even though some 1,707 full-time employment opportunities were lost as a result of the mechanization – well over eight jobs per tractor.

The authors are at a loss as to what conclusions can be drawn from the analysis. On the one hand, they state that farm mechanization has been a very mixed blessing to the Pakistan economy because of this employment displacement. On the other hand, there is this rather satisfactory economic rate of return. The authors conclude that 'no definitive judgment is possible as to whether tractor mechanization in Pakistan (or similar) agriculture is good or bad.'

To make this judgment, a social rate of return analysis should, of course, be undertaken. But let us start with a review of the methodology the authors followed for the calculation of the economic rate of return. Table 10.7 presents in summary form all the relevant data. We do not wish to quarrel with the evaluation of benefits and costs other than labor, and assume that these have

251

TABLE 10.7. Calculation of the economic rate of return of farm mechanization in Pakistan. Valuation using Shadow Prices.

	Before	After	Change
		Rs. Million	
I. *Annual Benefit and Cost Flows*			
Benefits (value of output)	13.8	19.1	5.3
Costs other than Labor	1.6	3.9	2.3
Financial Costs of Labor	3.7	2.3	−1.4
Total Unadjusted Costs	5.3	6.2	0.9
Net Benefits before Labor Cost			
Adjustment	8.5	12.9	4.4
Adjustment to price Labor at			
Opportunity Cost	+3.7	+2.3	−1.4
Net Economic Benefit	12.2	15.2	3.0
II. *Capital Costs*			
Investment year 0 in tractors,			
tube wells, etc.	Rs. 10.5 million		
Bullock sales: Year 1	Rs. 0.4 million		
2	Rs. 0.4 million		
3	Rs. 0.04 million		

III. *Cost-Benefit Stream*

Year 0	− 10.5	Year 4	3.0
1	3.4	5	3.0
2	3.4	6	3.0
3	3.0	7	3.0

Economic Rate of Return: 24 percent.

been correctly calculated. As regards labor, the implicit assumption of the authors was that the annual wage rate of Rs 844, which a casual worker makes, represents the opportunity cost of labor for hired labor as well as for farmers and tenants. As shown in Table 10.8, before the program, the labor requirements were 4,379 manyears and the total labor cost Rs 3.7 million, whereas, after the program, the labor requirements are 2,672 manyears and the total labor cost Rs 2.3 million. The authors state that the labor displaced from the area has no significant employment opportunities elsewhere and they propose to treat the displaced labor as representing neither costs nor benefits to the economy. They continue, therefore, to evaluate labor costs after the program at Rs 3.7 million. We prefer a different presentation and show, therefore, in Table 10.7 the financial cost of labor as well as the adjustment which must be made to arrive at the opportunity cost of labor which, if there are really no employment opportunities, must be set at zero.[13] Both methods arrive at the same net economic benefit stream of Rs 3.0 million per annum. As Table 10.7 shows, the economic rate of return of the program is then about 24 percent.

It is very unfortunate that the authors of the study were not able to collect separate data on the incomes of the mechanizing farmers and the tenant farmers

TABLE 10.8. Labor use on 22,025 acres of farm land before and after farm mechanization program.

	Acres	Labor Use – manyears			Total Labor Cost Rs million
		Owners/ Tenants	Hired Labor	Total Labor	
Before					
202 mechanizing farmers	9,083	714	1,029	1,743	
879 tenant farmers	10,095	2,197	439	2,636	
New land acquired	2,847	–		–	
	22,025	2,911	1,468	4,379	3.7
After					
202 tractor farms	22,025	853	1,819	2,672	2.3
Change	–	– 2,058	+ 351	– 1,707	– 1.4

before and after the program. For the social evaluation it would have been of great help if we knew what the loss in income was of the displaced farmers, how long they remained unemployed, whether they migrated to the city and found another job, and so on. In the absence of these data, we can only accept the statement of the authors that there was no significant employment opportunity for the displaced 1,707 manyears of labor. Evaluating this at the rate of Rs 844 per annum, we find that there was annually a loss in income of about Rs 1.4 million which, socially, should be valued at the appropriate income distribution weight. We have no data for Pakistan to calculate these weights but can show the effect of the weights as follows. Let us assume that a socially acceptable project should have a rate of return of 10 percent, surely a low return for Pakistan. Then the social net benefit should be about Rs 2 million per annum,[14] which will be the case if the displaced labor of Rs 1.4 million has socially a cost of Rs 2.4 million. Or, in other words, the loss of income should be valued at a weight of 1.7 only to make the entire mechanization program unacceptable. Since the weights in case of a decrease in income of the indicated order of magnitude will be substantially higher than that (see Chapter 9), it may definitely be concluded that, if the data of the study are correct and displaced labor indeed has no alternative employment opportunities, the program should not have been undertaken.

Another matter that should have been investigated is whether the tenant farmers had viable units. Unfortunately, the study does not provide any data on this point and the only observation we can make is that we would not be surprised if indeed the holdings of the tenants were submarginal. If additional employment opportunities were in fact as scarce as the authors believe, land reform would probably provide the best measure to remedy the situation.

10.6. Implications of the Analysis

The examples studied in the previous sections are all isolated case studies. However, as this study has tried to emphasize, projects should not be considered in isolation; they should be ranked against each other to determine what the composition of a country's investment program should be. To make such a comparative analysis, a larger project data base is needed than the few analyzed examples provide. Many more examples could have been taken from the files of consultants and international lending agencies; they would, however, have even greater shortcomings than the previous examples in that they would have even less information. In fact, it is extremely rare to find a feasibility study that addresses itself to the question of who benefits and who loses, and that provides any detail on income levels. Because of this scarce data base, only a sketch of the implications of the social benefit cost approach with respect to a country's development strategy can be given. As two of the cases studied above refer to Malaysia, we will take this country as an example and comment briefly on its agricultural development strategy.

For the last 20 years, the Malaysian Government has tried to reduce the pressure of the population on existing land by developing new land for agricultural settlement. Increasing concern for rural poverty and income distribution, and a recognition that the land settlement programs have not made as much of a dent in poverty as was hoped, have led recently to a re-evaluation of the costs of land settlement schemes and a questioning as to whether it would not be better to develop smallholder agriculture in situ or to take other measures of combating rural poverty. What can social benefit-cost analysis tell us in this regard?

The analysis of the FELDA schemes in Section 2 showed clearly that the social rate of return of the land settlement projects (17 percent) is not significantly higher than their economic rate of return (about 15 percent). An example of a project in situ is the Muda Scheme discussed in Section 3; its economic rate of return is about 18 percent. Surprisingly enough, it appeared that this project dealt to a large extent with relatively well-to-do farmers, so that for these beneficiaries the additional social benefit is not large. However, the double cropping made possible by the project is leading to a significant additional demand for hired labor and very possibly to an increase in the incomes of the hired laborers. Applying some conservative weights, the overall social rate of return of the project was estimated to be about 24 percent. Nevertheless, this project also has its drawbacks. Incomes of hired labor are only half those of the smaller farmers and are far below what should be considered a reasonable minimum income.

Are there any other possible schemes that can alleviate poverty in the rural areas? In Section 10.2 it was mentioned that a substantial part of the poverty groups consisted of smallholder farmers. The problem with these farmers is not only that their productivity is low but also that, unless they receive additional land, it cannot be expected that they will be able to rise above the poverty line. But additional land is hard to find in the populated areas where these farmers live. Furthermore, alienation of existing land is probably not the solution since Malaysia does not have the extreme variation in landholdings that exists, for instance, in several Latin American countries. We believe, therefore, that a combination of measures is necessary.

The non-viable farmers should be transferred to the settlement schemes and should surrender their existing holdings – the value of which should, of course, be deducted from their loan repayment obligation – so that the freed land can be used to increase the farm size of those staying behind. At the same time, measures should be taken to increase the productivity of those staying behind.

Hence, to provide non-viable farmers with a livelihood and also to absorb the growth in the labor force, the development of new land should continue. However, Government should try to develop low-cost schemes, based on the principle of more farmer self-help and less Government assistance. Also, it should not be necessary to provide at the start the sometimes luxurious infrastructure which the Government presently provides. If, for instance, the investment cost per settler could be reduced from about US$ 14,000 to about US$ 10,000, the social rate of return of this type of project would be about 24 percent.

As regards measures to raise the productivity of smallholders in situ, numerous possibilities exist. For instance, the existing replanting program with improved planting material for rubber smallholders can be substantially expanded; whereas it was formerly believed that the potential for irrigation was limited, it now appears that there is considerable scope for constructing small-scale irrigation works for existing padi smallholders; the technique of interplanting with cocoa for coconut growers is only now becoming known and can be greatly expanded; and so on. In general, there is ample room for further developing the agricultural production potential of the existing smallholders, not only with specific technical measures but also by providing agricultural credit, and access to fertilizers and other farm inputs.

The social rate of return of in situ farm development is high. Although we have no specific data on all the different possibilities, an example regarding padi farming may be useful. Some pilot schemes have shown that small-scale irrigation works can be constructed at less than M$ 4,500 (US$ 2,000) per farmer. A padi farmer with two acres of land may be expected to produce some six tons of padi when his land is irrigated, which gives him gross revenues of about M$ 2,100 and a net income of about M$ 1,600, as compared to a maximum production of three tons of padi under dryland conditions, which gives him gross revenues of M$ 1,050 and a net income of about M$ 800. Such a scheme would have an economic rate of return of about 15 to 16 percent, but a social rate of return of at least 35 percent.[15]

We, therefore, definitely believe that, in order to combat rural poverty, much more should be done for existing smallholders. The social benefits of smallholder schemes are so much higher than those of the land settlement projects that a change in strategy appears well justified. This does not mean that land settlement projects should not be undertaken at all. Rather, we believe that the Government should try to identify and prepare more in situ projects, and that at least part of the additional resources otherwise used for land settlement should be used for the in situ projects.[16] The right strategy would in principle be attained when investments for existing smallholders would have been so much expanded and would have become so costly that their social rates of return would have become equal to the social rates of return of the land settlement projects.

We have tried to show in this Chapter that the social benefit-cost approach to investment decisions is a powerful tool. Even though, in all the cases discussed, the data base was scarce and educated guesses had to be made, it was possible to analyze the social impact of such programs as farm mechanization; mechanical and hand clearing of forests; rural development-type projects, varying from the rather costly land settlement project to a simple irrigation project; and, most importantly, how a sensible social development strategy should be drawn up. We hope that this study has shown that the social analysis should be as much a part of the instruments of those responsible for determining investment programs as the economic analysis.

SENSITIVITY TESTING OF THE SOCIAL RATES OF
RETURN OF THE DISCUSSED EXAMPLES

As mentioned in Chapter 9, the income distribut˙on weights which we have used for the social rate of return analysis of the discussed examples are somewhat speculative because of our lack of empirical data. It is, therefore, of interest to know to what extent our conclusions should be modified if we use CRAMER's rather than BERNOULLI's function for the derivation of the weights. To normalize CRAMER's function so that the weight on base level income equals unity, we write for his marginal utility of income function $u = \sqrt{b}/Y$, so that total utility $U = 2\sqrt{bY}$. The weights on the income changes of the poor can then be calculated from $v_p \times \Delta Y = 2\sqrt{b}(\sqrt{Y_2} - \sqrt{Y_1})$.

Table 10.9 tabulates for each discussed project its economic rate of return, the social weight on the benefits or losses of the poverty groups if the weight is based on BERNOULLI's function, and its corresponding social rate of return, as well as the social weight and corresponding social rate of return if the CRAMER function is applied. The social weights and the social rates of return are, of course, lower in the latter case. Nevertheless, our conclusions remain the same. For instance, as regards Malaysia, even the use of CRAMER's function gives a social rate of return of in situ development (25%) which is much higher than that of land settlement (16%). Our recommendation of a strategy change thus remains well justified. As extensively discussed before, we nevertheless believe that the BERNOULLI function is, on social grounds, more acceptable and we would recommend this function for the social rate of return analysis.

TABLE 10.9. Economic rates of return as well as social weights and social rates of return of the discussed examples according to Bernoulli and Cramer.

	Economic Rates of Return	Social Weights on Benefits (Losses) of Poverty Groups According to:		Social Rates of Return According to:	
		Bernoulli	Cramer	Bernoulli	Cramer
Xalandia Land Settlement	13%	3.00	1.72	19%	15.5%
Malaysia Land Settlement	15%	1.60	1.25	17%	16%
Malaysia Irrigation	18%	3.80	1.95	24%	20%
W. Africa Land Clearing	3%	2.07	1.44	neg.	1.5%
Pakistan Farm Tractors	24%	>1.70	>1.70	<10%	<10%
Malaysia Padifarming	16%	2.15	1.46	35%	25%

[1] This was calculated from $v_p \times \triangle Y = \triangle U$, where $\triangle U = 2.3\ b \log Y_2/Y_1$. Since $\triangle Y =$ \$ 2,720 - \$ 680 = \$ 2,040, while $b = \$ 4,500$ and $\triangle U = 2.3 \times 4,500 \log 2,720/680 = 6,230$ utils, it was found that $v_p = 6,230/2,040 = 3.0$.

[2] See, for instance, KASPER, W., 'Malaysia: A Study in Successful Economic Development,' American Enterprise Institute for Public Policy Research, Foreign Affairs Studies, Washington, D.C., 1974.

[3] Malaysia consists of Peninsular Malaysia and the States of Sabah and Sarawak.

[4] GOVERNMENT OF MALAYSIA, 'Mid-Term Review of the Second Malaysia Plan, 1971–75,' Kuala Lumpur, 1973.

[5] For instance, during the period 1966–1973, the World Bank made four loans to FELDA for this type of project; the economic rates of return were estimated at 16 percent, 13.8 percent, 17.5 percent, and 14.8 percent, respectively.

[6] As discussed in Chapter 3, the simplified formula for the shadow foreign exchange rate is
$$\frac{(M + T) + (X - D)}{M + X}$$
Government statistics show the following values of M, X, T and D:

M\$ Million		1971	1972	1973	1971–1973
Value imports	(M)	4,422	4,543	5,899	14,864
Value exports	(X)	5,017	4,884	7,342	17,243
Value taxes on imports	(T)	582	589	720	1,891 (13%)
Value taxes on exports	(D)	231	232	371	834 (5%)

The shadow rate is thus $\dfrac{16,755 + 16,409}{14,864 + 17,243} = 104$

[7] The formula is $v_p \times \triangle Y = \triangle U.$, where $\triangle U = 2.3\ b \log Y_2/Y_1$. Since $b = M\$ 2,500$, $Y_2 = M\$ 2,500$, $Y_1 = M\$ 900$, and $\triangle Y = M\$ 1,600$, we obtain: $v_p \times 1,600 = 2.3 \times 2,500 \log 2,500/900$, from which follows that $v_p = 1.6$.

[8] $v_p \times \triangle Y = \triangle U$, where $\triangle U = 2.3\ b \log Y_2/Y_1$. Substituting $b = M\$ 2,500$, $Y_2 = M\$ 2,500$, $Y_1 = M\$ 1,800$, and $\triangle Y = M\$ 700$, we get $v_p \times 700 = 2.3 \times 2,500 \log 2,500/ 1,800$, so that $v_p = 1.17$.

[9] $v_p \times \triangle Y = 2.3\ b \log Y_2/Y_1$ where $b = M\$ 2,500$, $Y_2 = M\$ 750$, $Y_1 = M\$ 570$ and $\triangle Y = M\$ 180$. Hence, $v_p \times 180 = 2.3 \times 2,500 \log 750/570$, from which follows that $v_p = 3.8$.

[10] Our formula is $v_p \times \triangle Y = 2.3\ b \log Y_2/Y_1$, where $Y_1 = 100$, $Y_2 = 200$, and $b = 300$. Hence: $v_p \times 100 = 2.3 \times 300 \log 200/100$, from which follows $v_p = 2.07$.

[11] McINERNEY, J. P. (Consultant) and DONALDSON, G. F., 'The Consequences of Farm Tractors in Pakistan,' World Bank Staff Working Paper No. 210, February 1975.

[12] We will not quibble with the words 'before' and 'after.' As discussed in Chapter I, we prefer the terms 'without' and 'with' the project.

[13] We may also express this as follows. If labor can be fully employed throughout the economy, then the cost saving of Rs 1.4 million worth of labor represents a real saving in resources because this labor can be employed elsewhere. If this labor has, however, no employment elsewhere, then there is from an economic point of view no saving at all.

[14] The cost and benefit stream would then be: – 10.5 (Year 0), 2.4 (Year 1), 2.4 (Year 2), and 2.0 (Years 3–7), representing a rate of return of 10 percent.

[15] Since $v_p \times \triangle Y = 2.3\ b \log Y_2/Y_1$, we get $v_p \times 800 = 2.3 \times 2,500 \log 1600/800$, so that $v_p = 2.15$. Hence, the differential social net benefit stream is $800 \times 2.15 = M\$ 1,720$. Since the investment costs are less than M\$ 4,500, the social rate of return will be at least 35 percent.

[16] It should be mentioned here that the Third Malaysia Plan (TMP) was published at the time this study was being finalized. The TMP sets the target for land settlement during the period 1976–1980 at 1 million acres, i.e., the same target as under the Second Malaysia Plan (SMP), and fixes the target for in situ development at 1.7 million acres or double that under the SMP. The new strategy of the Malaysian Government is thus well in line with the strategy outlined above (Third Malaysia Plan, 1976–1980, Kuala Lumpur, 1976, p. 170).

CONCLUDING REMARKS

The gap between the rich countries and the poor countries has been widening for at least the last hundred years. ZIMMERMAN calculated that the 25 percent of the world population that lived in the lowest income areas of the world earned 12.5 percent of the world income in 1860, against 3.2 percent in 1960.[1] Annual per capita income of the industrialized countries was about US$ 4,550 in 1974 whereas per capita income of the poorest developing countries (mostly in Africa and Asia where more than one billion persons live) was only US$ 116.[2] This gap between rich and poor has caused the developing countries to demand a larger share of the world's production. HAQ,[3] who must be considered one of the most eloquent spokesmen for the group, sees this as part of an historical process and feels that a new economic order is in the making. A larger share of the liquidity created by the International Monetary Fund should be made available to the developing countries, taxes on nonrenewable resources (oil, minerals, and the like) and on multinational corporation activities should be collected for the benefit of the developing countries, and more international assistance should be given to the poorest countries in the form of grants. Furthermore, according to HAQ, the slate must be wiped clean: a major settlement should be reached between creditors and debtors to ease past debt burdens, particularly for the poorest countries, and the contracts and concessions that multinational corporations obtained in the past through strength should be renegotiated.

It is, however, becoming increasingly clear from the present discussions on the new economic order that the expectations of the developing countries will not be fulfilled. The most important of the developed countries are quite willing to enter into new arrangements where this is mutually beneficial, but far from agreeable to increase their transfers to the developing world. Although disappointing, this is not a reason for despair on the part of the developing countries because, as KAHN has pointed out, they are now entering a stage of higher income and lower population growth rates. While it took the United States about 200 years to go from about US$ 250 to about US$ 7,000 in per capita GNP, there is every reason to believe that today the process will take place much more rapidly in many of the developing countries since the gap that now exists between the developed and the developing countries acts as a powerful force to pull the latter forward. The industrialized world needs the raw materials, other products and labor of the developing countries, and it can, therefore, be expected that the latter will gradually obtain better bargaining positions to secure the capital, technology and institutions necessary to help develop these resources. Furthermore, population growth rates are expected to go down in the developing world because rearing children is becoming costlier while increasing incomes are making parents less dependent for their old age livelihood on their children, thereby reducing the need for children.[4]

Although we thus expect that substantial economic growth will take place in the developing world, it has been stated that such growth will not benefit the lower income groups. KUZNETS[5] advanced the hypothesis that a U-shaped relationship exists between income distribution and income, or, in other words, that if we plot the shares of total income for the lowest 30 or 40 percent of income earners over time, we should find that for subsistence societies at a low level of income the shares are high; that when overall income increases, the shares decrease; and that, in the last stages of development, the shares start to rise. AHLUWALIA[6] found indeed such a secular relationship but found also that, although the relative shares of the poorer groups may decline during the early structural stages of development, there is no cross-country evidence that the incomes of the poorer groups decline in absolute terms in this phase. Furthermore, there did not appear to be any evidence that faster growing countries show higher inequality at the same level of development than slower growing countries. As AHLUWALIA states, '... policy makers are perhaps best advised to think of the rate of growth as determining essentially the speed of transition through the different phases of development and inequality; higher growth rates accelerate the transition without necessarily generating greater inequality than can be structurally expected in each phase.' AHLUWALIA's findings confirm that high levels of growth can have a positive effect on the share of total income for the poorest income groups.

What instruments should be used to achieve an improvement in income distribution without trading off growth for equity? We discussed the several possible transfer mechanisms in Chapter 9 and found that the investment method of transferring income proved to be a highly efficient method of raising the incomes of the poor. The same conclusion was reached by AHLUWALIA and CHENERY[7] but their analysis gives the impression that a mere increase of capital stock in the areas where the poor live would be sufficient to increase their incomes. Such investments may be for the improvement of water supply, electrification, health, nutrition, education, roads, marketing and grain storage facilities, irrigation, drainage, and the like. In our opinion, however, extreme caution is in order if the above policy prescription is to be followed for rural areas. For instance, some 80 percent of the land usually belongs to the top 20 percent of the farmers, and it must, therefore, be expected that the benefits of general infrastructure investments will accrue mainly to the richest groups.

Another criticism we might direct at the CHENERY et al. study is that they are willing to accept low productivity investments where the objective is to raise the incomes of the poor. For instance, their income growth model assumes that, initially, the investments undertaken by the Government for the poor have an output-capital ratio of 0.22, with output being produced after 5 years, while the investments undertaken by the richest groups of the population have an output-capital ratio of 0.33 to 0.35, with output being produced after one year.[8] It is stated in so many words that this trade-off between growth and equity is perfectly acceptable as long as the relative weight on the incomes of the project beneficiaries justifies it.[9] This means in practice that CHENERY et al. are willing to accept any project with a satisfactory social rate of return so that the economic rate of return appears to have lost its significance. In the same study, DULOY writes: 'For large investments which are at the core of a poverty program – those which are designed to increase the access to income earning assets of the poor – we suggest that the appropriate procedure should include, first, the setting of aggregate levels of investment funds to be allocated for this purpose and, second, the evaluation of projects utilizing a weighting system for benefits according to the income level of the recipients.'[10] Hence, DULOY also negates the function of the economic rate of return in project evaluation. Although SQUIRE and VAN DER TAK mention that the economic rate of return of a project should be calculated, a careful reading of their study leads us to conclude that, in their opinion, the social rate of return is the only one that counts.[11] We believe that the approach of all these writers to the poverty problem is unfortunate. Because sound investment possibilities almost always exist in reality, public investments should usually have satisfactory economic as well as social rates of return. If the economic criterion is overlooked, the result is not only that the international lending agencies will be open to the criticism of LINDER[12] that they exacerbate the balance of payments problems of the developing countries, but also to the criticism that their lending will lead to a serious waste of resources.

There is, in our opinion, no short-cut method to social development. A poverty-focussed strategy is necessarily a micro-economic strategy and must rely on project analysis to help determine which projects and which programs will indeed raise the incomes of the poor and which must be rejected. This study has tried to show that in the drawing up of a poverty eradication strategy, efficiency as well as equity counts, and that the calculation of economic and social rates of return makes it possible to choose investment programs geared towards raising the incomes of the poor without neglecting efficiency.

Looking at the actual development experience of the last decade, there have indeed been several countries which have followed development strategies based on efficiency as well as equity criteria. These countries have done well in economic terms while their income distribution has also become much more equitable. Others have paid attention mainly to distributive considerations, putting emphasis on extensive subsidy programs to help the poor, while neglecting the investment method of raising incomes. Although income distribution has perhaps improved, the economic performance of these countries has been poor. Other developing countries focussed principally on the economic justification of their investment programs. Their economic performance has been good but progress towards a more equitable income distribution has lagged behind.

In our opinion, the choice between the different strategies is clear. The essence of the development process is the achievement of growth, not only of national income but also of the incomes of the lowest income groups. It is only in this way that social stability can be ensured. By basing investment decisions on both an economic and a social rate of return analysis, this objective can be attained.

[1] ZIMMERMAN, L. J., 'Poor Lands, Rich Lands: The Widening Gap,' Random House, Inc., New York, 1965, p. 38.

[2] For details see 'World Bank Atlas-Population, Per Capita Product and Growth Rates,' World Bank, Washington, D. C., 1975, Annex II.

[3] See HAQ, M. ul, 'Toward a New Framework for International Resource Transfers,' Finance and Development, September 1975.

[4] For a detailed analysis of all these factors, see KAHN, H., BROWN, W. and MARTEL, L., 'The Next 200 Years – A Scenario for America and the World.' William Morrow and Company, Inc., New York, 1976.

[5] KUZNETS, S., 'Economic Growth and Income Inequality,' The American Economic Review, March 1955, pp. 1–28.

[6] AHLUWALIA, M. S., 'Income Distribution and Development: Some Stylized Facts,' The American Economic Review, May 1976, Papers and Proceedings of the Eighty-Eighth Annual Meeting. See also AHLUWALIA, M. S., 'Income Inequality: Some Dimensions of the Problem,' in Chenery et al., 'Redistribution with Growth,' Chapter 1.

[7] AHLUWALIA, M. S. and CHENERY, H., 'A Model of Distribution and Growth,' in Chenery et al., 'Redistribution with Growth,' Chapter XI.

[8] Ibid., p. 237.

[9] Ibid., p. 234.

[10] DULOY, J. H., 'Sectoral, Regional and Project Analysis' in Chenery et al., 'Redistribution with Growth,' Chapter X, p. 207.

[11] SQUIRE and VAN DER TAK, 'Economic Analysis of Projects.' This study is further subject to the criticism that it is operationally not very useful. The project evaluators are supposed to estimate the elasticity of the marginal utility of income schedule in a particular country and project evaluation becomes therewith a rather subjective matter.

[12] See Chapter VI, Section 3.

SUMMARY

This study concerns project planning or, as it may also be called, project evaluation or benefit-cost analysis. It is a study of criteria for the design, selection and implementation of projects, with the basic objective of maximizing national welfare. Chapter 1 discusses that national welfare is not synonymous with national income and that the maximization of national income should not be accepted as a strategy for development since it excludes a number of important welfare dimensions. Specifically, consumer surpluses, disutilities of effort, scarcity values of goods and services, externalities, and the distribution of income between persons and over time are aspects of welfare which are not incorporated in the concept of national income. There is, therefore, a fundamental difference between a normal profitability analysis which uses basically the price data entering the national income accounts, and benefit-cost analysis. While profitability analysis uses market prices for inputs and outputs, benefit-cost analysis uses imputed values – the real values of benefits and costs – to determine whether an investment is worth undertaking. Traditional benefit-cost analysis – the economic evaluation of projects which considers all the above mentioned aspects of welfare except income distribution – is discussed in Part I of the study. Income distribution considerations are taken into account in Part II, and the analysis there is referred to as the social evaluation of projects.

Chapter 1 also discusses some of the broader principles of project planning; for example, the fundamental efficiency principle: any expansion of a project's production is justified as long as incremental units of production have higher benefits than costs. But what are benefits and costs? Benefits may be defined as willingness to pay and thus are identical to the gross consumer surplus. In an economy without distortions, costs can be measured at market prices, but such economies do not exist and the use of shadow prices, therefore, becomes mandatory to measure the real scarcity values of goods and services. It has been suggested that programming models could generate these shadow prices but such models are as yet insufficiently developed to be of practical use. The opportunity cost doctrine is, therefore, accepted as the starting point for the measurement of costs of production. The cost of a factor of production is defined as the maximum return which would be earned by that factor in its next best alternative use.

It is important for a project evaluator to know which variables are under his control. Suboptimal situations often exist and the project evaluator may find, for instance, that it would be more economical to import a certain product than to produce it domestically. However, it may be that the Government intends the country to be self-sufficient in a certain product. Although this may not be optimal in a strict economic sense, it may well be sensible from a national point of view, and the project evaluator should then base his analysis on actual policies rather than on imaginary optimal policies.

264

The last subject which is discussed in Chapter 1 concerns the relationship between national planning and project planning. Benefit-cost analysis is an important tool for determining the priority of projects and national planning cannot do without project planning since the project data are essential for the derivation of national parameters. At the same time, project planning cannot proceed without a knowledge of the national parameters. In a well run administration, this circularity will strengthen the drawing up of national plans as well as plans for regions and income groups. The central planning unit would make tentative projections of national parameters and submit these to departments responsible for project planning; the latter would formulate their tentative investment program and submit these to the center, which would in turn correct the national plan and submit new parameters to the departments, and so on. As a result of this interaction, the likelihood of success for the nation's total investment program will be greatly increased.

The valuation of benefits is reviewed in Chapter 2. After a discussion of the criticisms directed at the consumer surplus concept, it is concluded that changes in consumer welfare due to a price change cannot be measured if the consumer's marginal utility of income is not known. Anticipating the discussion in Part II, it is postulated that a social marginal utility of income function can be derived from the prevailing value concepts in the community. Welfare changes can then be found by evaluating the change in consumer surplus at the appropriate marginal utilities of income. If income distribution considerations are not important, then the social marginal utilities of income can be assumed to be constant and an additional dollar at a low income level will have socially the same value as an additional dollar at a high income level. This is the justification for using, in such cases, the traditional benefit-cost analysis, even if goods have substantial income effects. Hence, when income distribution does not count, willingness to pay is the relevant concept and a consumer's welfare change can then be measured by the change in consumer surplus under the Marshallian demand curve. It is further discussed that the value of an intermediate product should be derived from the consumer's willingness to pay for the final product that the intermediate product helps to produce.

The concept of willingness to pay, which is a concept of domestic prices, appears at first sight to have been challenged by LITTLE and MIRRLEES in their Manual on Industrial Project Analysis, where they suggest that all goods should be valued at border prices. Further review reveals, however, that the difference in approach is merely one of choosing different numéraires. Both methods have the same information requirements and will lead theoretically to the same result. Nevertheless, in practice, the LITTLE-MIRRLEES method can easily lead to inappropriate pricing. Moreover, due to the use of aggregated conversion factors, it will not be as precise as the normal method which undertakes to evaluate for each individual project its impact on the balance of payments.

HARBERGER's methodology is adopted in the first two sections of Chapter 3 for the determination of the opportunity costs of inputs and foreign exchange. The opportunity cost of an input is shown to be the weighted average of the demand and supply prices, the weights being the fractions of demand displaced and supply induced. The opportunity cost of foreign exchange appears to be the weighted average of the domestic values of the country's import and export prices, the weights being the fractions in which an additional dollar of foreign exchange will be used to increase imports and reduce exports.

Labor as a production factor is unique in that the laborer's services are tied to the laborer, so that earnings as well as disutility of effort determine the welfare position of the laborer. With the help of the indifference curve analysis it is shown in section 3.3 that the opportunity cost of labor generally cannot be said to equal the foregone marginal product of labor, since this does not acknowledge that labor may incur an extra disutility of effort. Three institutional frameworks are analyzed. The first is that of over-populated developing countries, and the doctrine that in such countries the marginal productivity of labor in the agricultural sector is zero (the LEWIS labor surplus model) is challenged on the basis of production principles and on the ground that it cannot be assumed that farmers have no disutility from work. SEN's hypothesis that the marginal utility of income schedule and the marginal disutility of labor schedule are flat in the relevant region is also rejected as unrealistic and in contradiction with empirical observation. HANSEN's supply and demand model provides a clarifying analysis as to how wages are determined in the agricultural sector, and the opportunity cost of labor in the agricultural sector can be assumed to be a weighted average of observed actual rural wage rates and a reservation wage which may be set at the subsistence level. The second case concerns the cities. When calculating the opportunity cost of hiring a laborer in the city, it must be taken into account that the institutionally-determined high urban wage rates will result in an inflow of rural workers, not all of whom can find employment. An equilibrium situation is reached when the increase in urban unemployment reduces the expected earnings of the rural workers to such a level that migration is no longer attractive. Several migration functions proposed in the economic literature are discussed and, although sufficient empirical data are not available to determine the precise migration function, it is clear that the opportunity cost of labor in the urban areas must be set at a substantially higher level than the supply price of the rural migrants. The hiring of one migrant induces other rural workers to migrate to the urban area. The total opportunity cost must, therefore, include not only the direct opportunity cost of the worker hired but also the loss in welfare of those who become unemployed. The last institutional framework studied is that of the so-called 'primitive affluence' societies, where the subsistence farmer is able to produce as much as he can consume of the normal staple foods with a minimum of work – 19 to 25 hours per week in Papua New Guinea according to MOULIK – and is not willing to work, even at relatively high wages, in the modern sector. Following NAKAJIMA, FISK and others, this last phenomenon is explained by introducing the concept of a demand ceiling. As soon as this level of consumption has been reached, the labor-supply curve will start to slope backward. The opportunity cost of labor in such a society is high; furthermore, to make a modern man out of the subsistence farmer, the demand ceiling must be raised by bringing the farmer into contact with the modern world and inducing greater demand for goods and services.

As regards the opportunity cost of the factor capital (section 3.4), the economic literature is divided in its approach. On the one hand, there are those writers who feel that the relevant concept is the subjective time preference rate of lenders; on the other hand, there are those who feel that it should be the rates of return on private investment (gross of corporate taxes). It is pointed out that the individual time preferences do not necessarily reflect the social time preference rate of society as a whole and that the latter is the relevant concept. In Part I of the study it is assumed that the country in question has an optimal investment program and if resources are then transferred from the private sector to the public sector, the value of the goods produced in the public sector with these resources must at least be equal to the value of the goods that would be produced with these resources in the private sector. Hence, the social time preference rate is then the weighted average of the private rates of return foregone, the weights being the amounts of investments which would have been necessary to produce the private sector products. The production function approach of estimating the rates of return on investment in an economy is discussed, and it is concluded that this approach must be rejected on practical as well as on theoretical grounds. The only correct method is the direct analysis of the rates of return on private investment. A complication arises in that industrial surveys publish nominal data whereas capital, labor, other inputs and outputs should be measured in real terms, or, in other words, at their appropriate shadow prices. Theoretically, the approach is clear, but lack of empirical data will often result in rather rough estimates of the opportunity cost of capital, and sensitivity tests should, therefore, generally be applied.

Chapter 4 is concerned with the analytics of project planning. The first two sections review the optimal scale and the optimal timing of a project; the third section reviews more complicated cases such as competing projects, joint production, peak-load demand problems, decreasing average cost projects and projects which earn or save foreign exchange. Great emphasis is placed in the fourth section on the analysis of non-optimal situations. This section is an elaboration of what was briefly discussed in Chapter 1, namely, that in all cases where the Government is not willing to eliminate distortions, the project evaluator should base his analysis on actual policies rather than on hypothetical optimal policies.

Chapter 5 reviews the various project ranking criteria which have been proposed by the economic literature, specifically the internal rate of return, the present value and the benefit-cost ratio methods. It is shown that in the absence of budget constraints, the present value method is the only correct way to evaluate a project. In the event of a single period budget constraint, projects should be ranked on the basis of their ratios of present value of net benefits to present value of investment, priority being given to the project with the highest ratio and so proceeding down the line until the budget is exhausted. The same result can be obtained by ranking projects on the basis of what the study calls their modified internal rates of return. While the unmodified internal rate of return is calculated by valuing the cash flow generated by a project at the internal rate of return, the modified internal rate of return is calculated by valuing the cash flow at the opportunity cost of capital rate. When the budget constraint prevails over multiple periods, the opportunity cost of capital can no longer be used for discounting the benefits and costs of projects and the discount rate should then be the rate at which the number of projects accepted just exhausts the investment funds available. In other words, it is the rate which equilibrates total investments with available funds. In many cases the values of a project's inputs and outputs cannot be projected with precision but are subject to a margin of uncertainty. Probability distributions of each of the significant variables about which uncertainty exists should then be drawn up, and the probability distribution of the net present value of the project calculated. The value of the project is then its expected value, i.e., the aggregate of each net present value multiplied by its probability. There is a substantial theoretical literature about decision rules to be followed in the case of complete uncertainty. The author believes, however, that in reality decisions are always based on subjective judgments and it is then difficult to imagine, as decision theory does, that no opinion can be formed about the probable value of a certain variable.

How linkage effects, externalities, and foreign labor and capital are to be handled in benefit-cost analysis is discussed in the first three sections of Chapter 6; none of these present a theoretical problem although, in practice, of course, estimation problems arise. The last section of Chapter 6 reviews how the opportunity costs of the factors of production differ from their normal values when the economy is not in a situation of internal and external balance. It is shown that the micro-economic project decision rules proposed in the study are consistent with the macro-economic policies that Governments should follow to attain overall balance.

Part II of the study starts with a review in Chapter 7 of the so-called compensation tests and it becomes clear immediately that they are worse than useless if income distribution counts. If a group of poor persons is worse off by $ 100,000 while a group of rich persons is better off by $ 250,000, the fact that the poor could have been compensated for their loss is completely irrelevant if they are not, and one cannot say, therefore, that there is a net gain in welfare of $ 150,000. If compensation does not take place – and it is difficult to find a project where it takes place – the loss of the poor as well as the gain of the rich should be valued at the appropriate social marginal utilities of income to determine whether there is a net gain in welfare. Furthermore, even if compensation would take place, the same procedure should be followed since, otherwise, projects cannot be compared on the basis of their social values. In other words, the determination of whether a project will result in a welfare gain should always be based on a country's social welfare function. ARROW's objection to the concept, namely that the function cannot be derived from individual preferences, is discussed but it appears that his conditions for constructing the function are much too restrictive. There are in every community prevailing general values and they can be found by experiments, interviews and analyses of the actions of thought leaders and the public at large. Income distribution is an important aspect of social welfare, and there can be no doubt that it is taken into consideration by Governments when making investment decisions. It is, therefore, accepted that social income distribution weights do exist, and the task at hand is to determine these and to incorporate them in the project planning framework.

In the opinion of several writers, income distribution has an intertemporal as well as an interpersonal aspect. Chapter 8 reviews the so-called social discount literature which argues that when investments and therewith income and consumption growth are not considered optimal, a special investment algorithm should be used for the evaluation of investment projects to ensure that a quick deepening of the capital structure of the economy takes place. Under normal circumstances it may be assumed that the Government will apply appropriate monetary and fiscal policies to promote investments if expansion of investment is considered necessary, in which case the projected opportunity costs of capital determine the discount rate for evaluating public investment projects. The social discount rate literature, however, maintains that political and institutional constraints make such a policy not feasible, especially in the developing countries, so that then investment is socially worth more than consumption, and proceeds to analyze the situation as follows.

First of all, it is contended that the objective of development is the maximization of aggregate consumption – present as well as future consumption – and the problem is, therefore, to determine how aggregate consumption should grow over time. Dividing aggregate consumption by population and taking present per capita consumption as the numéraire, the literature shows that the rate of fall over time of the marginal utility of per capita consumption is equal to the product of the growth rate of per capita consumption g and the elasticity of the marginal utility of consumption with respect to consumption α. For instance, if the growth rate of per capita consumption is 3 percent per annum while for every one percent increase in per capita consumption the marginal utility of per capita consumption decreases by one percent, the rate of fall of the marginal utility of per capita consumption will be 3 percent per annum. If there is a pure time preference rate p – and there are good reasons to believe that there is – future consumption must increase at the rate $p + \alpha g$ if it is to be on the optimal growth path. This means, of course, that future consumption should be discounted at the rate $p + \alpha g$ to find its present value. This rate, which is denoted by d, is known as the social discount rate or sometimes also as the consumption rate of interest. Although it is assumed in the literature that the values of p vary from 1 to 5 percent, of α from $\frac{1}{2}$ to $2\frac{1}{2}$ percent, and of g from 2 to 3 percent, so that the value of the social discount rate d may be set at anywhere between 2 and $12\frac{1}{2}$ percent, the literature seems to feel that generally d is of the order of 5 percent or less.

The second point made in the social discount literature is that, because there exists the constraint on expanding investments to the optimal level, private investments will generate consumption streams much larger than the rate of return d. Suppose that the rate of return of the private sector is q percent and that this rate of return is entirely consumed. Then it follows immediately that the present value of this consumption stream is q/d. Assuming that the opportunity cost of private capital q is 12.5 percent and that d is 5 percent, the literature concludes that in this case investments have a shadow price P_{inv} of 2.5 times their nominal value. However, this example is not entirely correct because the rate of return in the private sector is never entirely consumed. Part of it, sq, will be reinvested, where s is the savings coefficient. Since this reinvested part should be valued at the shadow price of investment, the return on private investment is socially worth $(q - sq) + sq\, P_{inv}$. The present value of this stream discounted at the rate d is equal to P_{inv}, and it thus follows that $P_{inv} = (q - sq)/(d - sq)$. Assuming that the marginal savings coefficient of the private sector s equals 20 percent and using the values for q and d assumed above, the shadow price of investment in this example would be 4.0 and any investment should thus, according to the literature, be valued at a premium of 300 percent.

It is now clear how the proponents of the social discount rate method evaluate public investment projects. Since benefits and costs should be measured in terms of consumption, the benefit-cost stream of a particular project should be divided into its consumption and investment parts and, while the consumption part should be valued at its face value, the investment part should be valued at the shadow price of investment. Assuming, as the literature does, that the public investment displaces for the full hundred percent private investments, the social discount rate cum shadow price of investment algorithm of evaluating public investment projects may be written as:

$$\sum_{t=1}^{n} \frac{N_t(1 - s^*) + N_t s^* P_{inv}}{(1 + d)^t} \geqslant KP_{inv}$$

where N is net benefits of the project under scrutiny, s^* is the invested part of the net benefits, K is the investment costs of the project and, as before, P_{inv} is the shadow price of investment, and d is the social discount rate.

The above discussion of the social discount rate sets out the approach taken in the UNIDO Guidelines. The OECD Manual takes savings as the numéraire instead of consumption, but it is shown that the two approaches are theoretically identical. There are, however, serious difficulties with both procedures for evaluating public investments. Section 8.4 compares the algorithm with the traditional criterion and concludes that with very reasonable values of s^*, q, d and P_{inv}, short life projects (10 years) should have very high internal rates of return (26 percent to more than 50 percent) before they are acceptable under the algorithm. Section 8.5 analyzes the algorithm in more detail. It is pointed out that public investment generally displaces not only private investment but also consumption and that the source of finance of a particular public project determines, therefore, to a large extent whether the project is acceptable. This means also that the algorithm cannot be diverged from interpersonal income distri-

270

bution considerations since it is of course of the utmost importance to know whose consumption and whose investment will be foregone. In their sequel volume to the OECD Manual, LITTLE and MIRRLEES have indeed introduced interpersonal weights but, as Section 8.5 discusses, it appears that these are highly discriminatory. The weights are greater than unity for incomes below the level at which the Government makes subsidy payments, decrease rapidly to zero above this level and rise to unity for the rich groups who save almost all of their incomes. Section 8.5 also points out that the concept of one single social discount rate is unrealistic. The intertemporal income distribution problem is a special aspect of the interpersonal income distribution problem since the intertemporal weights as well as the interpersonal weights are derived from the same marginal utility of consumption function. There are, therefore, as many social discount rates as there are income classes with different income growth rates. It is also pointed out that it is unrealistic to draw up a social marginal utility schedule as a function of the economy's aggregate consumption or income; the fallacy of the pursuit of growth for its own sake, without taking into account whose incomes should grow, has been amply demonstrated in the last decade.

If the UNIDO and OECD approaches of evaluating public investments have drawbacks, the question arises, what then? It is discussed that usually Governments do promote private investments by appropriate fiscal and monetary policies and that if they are allowed to transfer funds from the private sector, the weighted projected rates of return of the private sector represent the discount rate for public projects. If such transfers are not possible, there will be a budget constraint and, as discussed in Chapter 5 a budget constraint discount rate is then the relevant cut-off rate. There may be some use for the capital deepening algorithm if the body politic prohibits the use of fiscal and monetary policies and is willing to accept the discriminatory nature of the system. However, the writer believes that such cases are rare indeed.

Chapter 9 addresses itself to the question of whether income distribution between persons should be considered relevant for project planning. On the one hand, there are those who without further ado postulate that income distribution weights should be used; on the other hand, there are those who feel that only the traditional benefit-cost analysis leads to correct results. A detailed discussion of why this controversy exists is deferred to Sections 9.4 and 9.5 and the first problem which is analyzed is whether meaningful income distribution weights can be determined. Section 9.2 reviews the rather scarce literature which has postulated that individual marginal utility of income functions do exist. There is the BERNOULLI function, subsequently defended by WEBER and FECHNER and recently adopted by CHENERY et al. and TINBERGEN, which states that constant percentage increases in income produce constant arithmetic increases in welfare; there is also the function of CRAMER, recently defended by STEVENS, which states that constant percentage increases in income produce constant percentage increases in welfare. The marginal utility of income under the BERNOULLI function falls much faster than under the CRAMER function;

the elasticity of the marginal utility of income with respect to income is minus unity according to BERNOULLI and minus one-half according to CRAMER. While the functions were postulated by these writers to solve the so-called St. Petersburg Paradox – discussed in the Annex to Chapter 9 – they were presumably not based on empirical observations. The pathbreaking work of FISHER, FRISCH, FELLNER, THEIL and BROOKS, and VAN PRAAG on the measurement of the marginal utility of income from observable consumer behavior is discussed, but unfortunately it appears that the various findings are still quite speculative. It appears, however, very probable that the elasticity of the marginal utility of income with respect to income is larger than unity (in absolute terms) for the lower income groups.

Section 9.3 discusses whether the income distribution weights derived from the individual marginal utility of income schedule can be taken to represent the social weights which the Government should use for project planning purposes. It is shown that the individual marginal utility of income schedule cannot be relevant because the use of this schedule implies that every person in the community should have the same income. In reality, of course, for a wide range of incomes society is indifferent as to how incomes are actually distributed. Education and own efforts will cause differences in incomes and even in the most centrally planned economies such differences are accepted. Society, however, does attach weights to the incomes of the ultra-poor and the ultra-rich. Since unskilled labor income appears normally to be valued at unity, this may be taken as the base income for the calculation of the income distribution weights on the poor's income. Applying the BERNOULLI-WEBER-FECHNER law, these weights are inversely proportionate to income level. At the higher income levels, the incomes of professionals such as engineers, physicians and Cabinet members appear to be generally accepted socially as reasonable, and taking that level as a base, the weights on higher incomes can then again be calculated with the help of the BERNOULLI-WEBER-FECHNER function. For instance, in a typical middle-level developing country with a modal family income of about US$ 1,200 per annum, subsistence income is about US$ 250 per annum, unskilled labor income is about US$ 600 per annum, and professionals employed in the Government receive about US$ 4,800 per annum. Following the procedures discussed above, the range of incomes of US$ 600 to US$ 4,800 would receive a weight of unity; the incomes of the poor, i.e., incomes below US$ 600, would receive weights varying from 2.4 to 1; and the incomes of the rich, i.e., incomes above US$ 4,800, would receive weights varying from 1.0 to zero. In the opinion of the writer, the proposed procedure of estimating socially acceptable weights is reasonable. However, the found weights should not be considered precise and absolute, and sensitivity tests should be undertaken.

While the objective function for a project under the traditional benefit-cost criterion is written as $\triangle W = Y_p + Y_a$ where Y_p is the gain in real income of the different consumers of the product produced by the project and Y_a the gain in real income of the producer, the objective function in the case of welfare maximization is of the form $\triangle W = v_p Y_p + v_a Y_a$, where v_p is the income distribution weight on the additions to income of the consumers, and v_a the income distribution weight on the income of the producer. In the case of a public project, the weight v_a has the value of unity, while the weight v_p is derived as discussed in the previous paragraph. What are the implications of the use of the welfare maximization function for project size? Since $Y_p = B - R$, and $Y_a = R - C$, where B is benefits, R is revenues and C is costs, the first order condition for the maximization of the objective function is $v_p = (dC - dR)/(dB - dR)$ or, in words, project size should be expanded until the marginal loss in income of the producer equals the marginal redistribution gain of the consumers weighted with the distribution weight v_p. If no repayments are levied, this condition becomes $v_p = dC/dB$. In case of constancy of project benefits, this may be written as $v_p = dB_A \cdot a_{\overline{n}\,r}/dB_A \cdot a_{\overline{q}\,r}$, where $dB_A \cdot a_{\overline{n}\,r}$ is the annual benefit stream of the invested marginal dollar discounted at the marginal dollar's rate of return, and $dB_A \cdot a_{\overline{m}\,q}$ the same benefit stream but discounted at the opportunity cost of capital rate q. It follows that $a_{\overline{m}\,r} = v_p \cdot a_{\overline{m}\,q}$ and it is thus possible to calculate the internal rate of return r of the invested marginal dollar under varying assumptions as to the values of v_p, n and q. Suppose, for instance, that the incomes of a certain group of subsistence level farmers can be raised by providing them with irrigation water. Then, when the income distribution weight v_p on additions to this group's income equals 2.0, the lifetime of the irrigation works is about 25 years and the opportunity cost of capital is 10 percent, the irrigation works should be built oversized to the point that the rate of return on the marginal invested dollar is about 2 percent only.

The use of an income distribution weighted objective function thus leads inevitably to the conclusion that projects should be oversized to the point that in many cases the rate of return on the marginal invested dollar is negligible or even negative. It is, therefore, not surprising that many writers believe that income distribution considerations should not play a role in determining the optimum size of a project. The author tends to agree. There are almost always other projects possible to increase the incomes of the target groups so that usually there is no need to build oversized projects.

Should income distribution weights also be ignored in the selection of projects? Or, in other words, are only the economic rates of return relevant for project selection and not the social rates of return? When the possibility to transfer incomes is limited – which is usually the case – the only way of increasing incomes is by means of projects. The consequence of this is that all possible projects should be socially weighed against each other. As in practice almost always projects with satisfactory economic rates of return can be found, it is suggested as a basic principle that only projects with economic rates of return higher than the opportunity cost of capital should be accepted. All the economically acceptable projects should then be scrutinized as to their social priority, and those with unsatisfactory social rates of return should be rejected. Since under this procedure each project will have a satisfactory economic rate of return, a minimum efficiency is ensured for the overall program; by choosing projects with satisfactory social rates of return, the program will also be socially justified. To determine the overall investment program, it is thus necessary to calculate the economic as well as the social rates of return of the individual projects. This procedure has important consequences with respect to a country's development strategy. For instance, while according to the traditional analysis, the more efficient plantation development should be preferred to smallholder development, under the proposed methodology the latter should be preferred if it has the higher social rate of return. The methodology thus leads to some trade-off between growth and equity but not to the extent that projects earn less than the opportunity cost of capital, or the budget constraint rate if the assumption of absence of budget constraints is relaxed.

The final section of Chapter 9 reviews the different income transfer mechanisms that are available to a Government to increase the incomes of the poor. A useful classification is to distinguish among Government policies that intervene at the income level, the price level and the investment level. The policies that intervene directly at the income level are fairly straightforward: they may consist of direct money transfers or transfers in kind. As regards the policies that intervene at the price level, it is shown that price subsidies may be an efficient way of transferring income if the subsidy level is not too high. There is also the possibility of using tariffs to fix the price of a domestically produced good at a certain level. Although in such a case, a small deadweight loss exists, this can be considered to be the inherent cost of raising Government revenues by means of a tariff and this method of increasing the incomes of the poor is, therefore, well worth considering, provided that commodities can be identified which are mainly produced and not consumed by the poor. At the investment level, Government policies may be directed at: (a) capital held by the poor; (b) other private capital; and (c) Government capital. Since the bulk of the poor are often non-viable farmers, land reform or the opening up of new land may solve the problem of rural poverty to a large extent (where sufficient land is available). In many countries, however, the land to population ratio is so low that other strategies must be devised. Promotion of private manufacturing and services creates employment and thereby increases incomes but, in general, does not solve the entire problem. It is, therefore, not surprising that many Governments are promoting labor-intensive techniques of production. As regards Government investments, many Governments embark on programs of investments to provide the poor with inputs or other services. Many investment possibilities exist in such fields as irrigation, land drainage, agricultural processing, marketing, transportation, education, water supply and electrification, and this project method of increasing incomes has been amply demonstrated to be a highly efficient method of income transfer.

Chapter 10 applies the developed social methodology to several practical cases and the study ends with some concluding remarks. Any attack on poverty – and this is essential if social stability is to be ensured – should consist of a conglomerate of the various possible income transfer mechanisms, the actual mix to be determined on the basis of efficiency considerations. What this study is all about is that by calculating economic as well as social rates of return, it is possible to devise investment programs geared towards raising the incomes of the poor without neglecting efficiency, thus ensuring both growth and social stability.

Compound and Discount Tables
Present value of $ 1
$$1/(1 + i)^n$$

Years	2%	4%	5%	6%	8%	10%	12%	14%	15%	16%	18%	20%	25%	30%	35%	40%	45%	50%
2	0.961	0.925	0.907	0.890	0.857	0.826	0.797	0.769	0.756	0.743	0.718	0.694	0.640	0.592	0.549	0.510	0.476	0.444
4	0.924	0.855	0.823	0.792	0.735	0.683	0.636	0.592	0.572	0.552	0.516	0.482	0.410	0.350	0.301	0.260	0.226	0.198
5	0.906	0.822	0.784	0.747	0.681	0.621	0.567	0.519	0.497	0.476	0.437	0.402	0.328	0.269	0.223	0.186	0.156	0.132
6	0.888	0.790	0.746	0.705	0.630	0.564	0.507	0.456	0.432	0.410	0.370	0.335	0.262	0.207	0.165	0.133	0.108	0.088
8	0.853	0.731	0.677	0.627	0.540	0.467	0.404	0.351	0.327	0.305	0.266	0.233	0.168	0.123	0.091	0.068	0.051	0.039
10	0.820	0.676	0.614	0.558	0.463	0.386	0.322	0.270	0.247	0.227	0.191	0.162	0.107	0.073	0.050	0.035	0.024	0.017
12	0.788	0.625	0.557	0.497	0.397	0.319	0.257	0.208	0.187	0.168	0.137	0.112	0.069	0.043	0.027	0.018	0.012	0.008
14	0.758	0.577	0.505	0.442	0.340	0.263	0.205	0.160	0.141	0.125	0.099	0.078	0.044	0.025	0.015	0.009	0.006	0.003
15	0.743	0.555	0.481	0.417	0.315	0.239	0.183	0.140	0.123	0.108	0.084	0.065	0.035	0.020	0.011	0.006	0.004	0.002
16	0.728	0.534	0.458	0.394	0.292	0.218	0.163	0.123	0.107	0.093	0.071	0.054	0.028	0.015	0.008	0.005	0.003	0.002
18	0.700	0.494	0.416	0.350	0.250	0.180	0.130	0.095	0.081	0.069	0.051	0.038	0.018	0.009	0.005	0.002	0.001	0.001
20	0.673	0.456	0.377	0.312	0.215	0.149	0.104	0.073	0.061	0.051	0.037	0.026	0.012	0.005	0.002	0.001	0.001	
22	0.647	0.422	0.342	0.278	0.184	0.123	0.083	0.056	0.046	0.038	0.026	0.018	0.007	0.003	0.001	0.001		
24	0.622	0.390	0.310	0.247	0.158	0.102	0.066	0.043	0.035	0.028	0.019	0.013	0.005	0.002	0.001			
25	0.610	0.375	0.295	0.233	0.146	0.092	0.059	0.038	0.030	0.024	0.016	0.010	0.004	0.001	0.001			
26	0.598	0.361	0.281	0.220	0.135	0.084	0.053	0.033	0.026	0.021	0.014	0.009	0.003	0.001				
28	0.574	0.333	0.255	0.196	0.116	0.069	0.042	0.026	0.020	0.016	0.010	0.006	0.002	0.001				
30	0.552	0.308	0.231	0.174	0.099	0.057	0.033	0.020	0.015	0.012	0.007	0.004	0.001					
35	0.500	0.253	0.181	0.130	0.068	0.036	0.019	0.010	0.008	0.006	0.003	0.002						
40	0.453	0.208	0.142	0.097	0.046	0.022	0.011	0.005	0.004	0.003	0.001	0.001						
45	0.410	0.171	0.111	0.073	0.031	0.014	0.006	0.003	0.002	0.001	0.001							
50	0.372	0.141	0.087	0.054	0.021	0.009	0.003	0.001	0.001	0.001								

Compound and Discount Tables
Present value of $ 1 Cash flow per year during n years
$$a_{\overline{n}|i}$$

Years	2%	4%	5%	6%	8%	10%	12%	14%	15%	16%	18%	20%	25%	30%	35%	40%	45%	50%
2	1.942	1.886	1.859	1.833	1.783	1.736	1.690	1.647	1.626	1.605	1.566	1.528	1.440	1.361	1.289	1.224	1.165	1.111
4	3.808	3.630	3.546	3.465	3.312	3.170	3.037	2.914	2.855	2.798	2.690	2.589	2.362	2.166	1.997	1.849	1.720	1.605
5	4.713	4.452	4.329	4.212	3.993	3.791	3.605	3.433	3.352	3.274	3.127	2.991	2.689	2.436	2.220	2.035	1.876	1.737
6	5.601	5.242	5.076	4.917	4.623	4.355	4.111	3.889	3.784	3.685	3.498	3.326	2.951	2.643	2.385	2.168	1.983	1.824
8	7.325	6.733	6.463	6.210	5.747	5.335	4.968	4.639	4.487	4.344	4.078	3.837	3.329	2.925	2.598	2.331	2.108	1.922
10	8.983	8.111	7.722	7.360	6.710	6.145	5.650	5.216	5.019	4.833	4.494	4.192	3.571	3.092	2.715	2.414	2.168	1.965
12	10.575	9.385	8.863	8.384	7.536	6.814	6.194	5.660	5.421	5.197	4.793	4.439	3.725	3.190	2.779	2.456	2.196	1.985
14	12.106	10.563	9.899	9.295	8.244	7.367	6.628	6.002	5.724	5.468	5.008	4.611	3.824	3.249	2.814	2.478	2.210	1.993
15	12.849	11.118	10.380	9.712	8.559	7.606	6.811	6.142	5.847	5.575	5.092	4.675	3.859	3.268	2.825	2.484	2.214	1.995
16	13.578	11.652	10.838	10.106	8.851	7.824	6.974	6.265	5.954	5.669	5.162	4.730	3.887	3.283	2.834	2.489	2.216	1.997
18	14.992	12.659	11.690	10.828	9.372	8.201	7.250	6.467	6.128	5.818	5.273	4.812	3.928	3.304	2.844	2.494	2.219	1.999
20	16.351	13.590	12.462	11.470	9.818	8.514	7.469	6.623	6.259	5.929	5.353	4.870	3.954	3.316	2.850	2.497	2.221	1.999
22	17.658	14.451	13.163	12.042	10.201	8.772	7.645	6.743	6.359	6.011	5.410	4.909	3.970	3.323	2.853	2.498	2.222	2.000
24	18.914	15.247	13.799	12.550	10.529	8.985	7.784	6.835	6.434	6.073	5.451	4.937	3.981	3.327	2.855	2.499	2.222	2.000
25	19.523	15.622	14.094	12.783	10.675	9.077	7.843	6.873	6.464	6.097	5.467	4.948	3.985	3.329	2.856	2.499	2.222	2.000
26	20.121	15.983	14.375	13.003	10.810	9.161	7.896	6.906	6.491	6.118	5.480	4.956	3.988	3.330	2.856	2.500	2.222	2.000
28	21.281	16.663	14.898	13.406	11.051	9.307	7.984	6.961	6.534	6.152	5.502	4.970	3.992	3.331	2.857	2.500	2.222	2.000
30	22.396	17.292	15.372	13.765	11.258	9.427	8.055	7.003	6.566	6.177	5.517	4.979	3.995	3.332	2.857	2.500	2.222	2.000
35	24.999	18.665	16.374	14.498	11.655	9.644	8.176	7.070	6.617	6.215	5.539	4.992	3.998	3.333	2.857	2.500	2.222	2.000
40	27.355	19.793	17.159	15.046	11.925	9.779	8.244	7.105	6.642	6.233	5.548	4.997	3.999	3.333	2.857	2.500	2.222	2.000
45	29.490	20.720	17.774	15.456	12.108	9.863	8.283	7.123	6.654	6.242	5.552	4.999	4.000	3.333	2.857	2.500	2.222	2.000
50	31.424	21.482	18.256	15.762	12.233	9.915	8.304	7.133	6.661	6.246	5.554	4.999	4.000	3.333	2.857	2.500	2.222	2.000

Compound and Discount Tables
Compound amount of $1 single investment
$$(1 + i)^n$$

Years	2%	4%	5%	6%	8%	10%	12%	14%	15%	16%	18%	20%	25%	30%
2	1.040	1.082	1.103	1.124	1.166	1.210	1.254	1.300	1.32	1.35	1.39	1.44	1.56	1.69
4	1.082	1.170	1.216	1.262	1.360	1.464	1.574	1.699	1.75	1.81	1.94	2.07	2.44	2.86
5	1.104	1.217	1.276	1.338	1.469	1.610	1.762	1.925	2.01	2.10	2.29	2.49	3.05	3.71
6	1.126	1.265	1.340	1.419	1.587	1.772	1.974	2.195	2.31	2.44	2.70	2.99	3.81	4.83
8	1.172	1.369	1.477	1.594	1.851	2.144	2.476	2.853	3.06	3.28	3.76	4.30	5.96	8.16
10	1.219	1.480	1.629	1.791	2.159	2.594	3.106	3.707	4.05	4.41	5.23	6.19	9.31	13.79
12	1.268	1.601	1.796	2.012	2.518	3.138	3.896	4.818	5.35	5.94	7.29	8.92	14.55	23.30
14	1.319	1.732	1.980	2.261	2.937	3.797	4.887	6.261	7.08	7.99	10.15	12.84	22.74	39.37
15	1.346	1.801	2.079	2.397	3.172	4.177	5.474	7.138	8.14	9.27	11.97	15.41	28.42	51.19
16	1.373	1.873	2.183	2.540	3.426	4.595	6.130	8.137	9.36	10.75	14.13	18.49	35.53	66.54
18	1.428	2.026	2.407	2.854	3.996	5.560	7.690	10.575	12.38	14.46	19.67	26.62	55.51	112.46
20	1.486	2.191	2.653	3.207	4.661	6.728	9.646	13.743	16.37	19.46	27.39	38.34	86.74	190.05
22	1.546	2.370	2.925	3.604	5.437	8.140	12.100	17.861	21.64	26.19	38.14	55.21	135.53	321.18
24	1.608	2.563	3.225	4.049	6.341	9.850	15.179	23.212	28.63	35.24	53.11	79.50	211.76	542.80
25	1.641	2.666	3.386	4.292	6.848	10.835	17.000	26.462	32.92	40.87	62.67	95.40	264.70	705.64
26	1.673	2.772	3.556	4.549	7.396	11.918	19.040	30.167	37.86	47.41	73.95	114.48	330.87	917.33
28	1.741	2.999	3.920	5.112	8.627	14.421	23.884	39.204	50.07	63.80	102.97	164.84	516.99	1,550.29
30	1.811	3.243	4.322	5.743	10.063	17.449	29.960	50.950	66.21	85.85	143.37	237.38	807.79	2,620.00
35	2.000	3.946	5.516	7.686	14.785	28.102	52.800	98.100	133.18	180.31	328.00	590.67	2,465.19	9,727.86
40	2.208	4.801	7.040	10.286	21.724	45.259	93.051	188.883	267.86	378.72	750.38	1,469.77	7,523.16	36,118.86
45	2.438	5.841	8.985	13.765	31.920	72.890	163.988	363.679	538.77	795.44	1,716.68	3,657.26	22,958.87	134,106.82
50	2.692	7.107	11.467	18.420	46.902	117.391	289.002	700.233	1,083.66	1,670.70	3,927.36	9,100.44	70,064.92	497,929.22

Compound and Discount Tables
Compound amount of $ 1 invested per year during n years

$$s_{\overline{n}|i}$$

Years	2%	4%	5%	6%	8%	10%	12%	14%	15%	16%	18%	20%	25%	30%
2	2.020	2.040	2.050	2.060	2.080	2.100	2.120	2.140	2.15	2.16	2.18	2.20	2.25	2.30
4	4.122	4.246	4.310	4.375	4.506	4.641	4.779	4.921	4.99	5.07	5.22	5.37	5.77	6.19
5	5.204	5.416	5.526	5.637	5.867	6.105	6.353	6.610	6.74	6.88	7.15	7.44	8.21	9.04
6	6.308	6.633	6.802	6.975	7.336	7.716	8.115	8.536	8.75	8.98	9.44	9.93	11.26	12.76
8	8.583	9.214	9.549	9.897	10.637	11.436	12.300	13.233	13.73	14.24	15.33	16.50	19.84	23.86
10	10.950	12.006	12.578	13.181	14.487	15.937	17.549	19.337	20.30	21.32	23.52	25.96	33.25	42.62
12	13.412	15.026	15.917	16.870	18.977	21.384	24.133	27.271	29.00	30.85	34.93	39.58	54.21	74.33
14	15.974	18.292	19.599	21.015	24.215	27.975	32.393	37.581	40.50	43.67	50.82	59.20	86.95	127.91
15	17.293	20.024	21.579	23.276	27.152	31.772	37.280	43.842	47.58	51.66	60.97	72.04	109.69	167.29
16	18.639	21.825	23.675	25.673	30.324	35.950	42.753	50.980	55.72	60.93	72.94	87.44	138.11	218.47
18	21.412	25.645	28.132	30.906	37.450	45.599	55.750	68.394	75.84	81.14	103.74	128.12	218.04	371.52
20	24.297	29.778	33.066	36.786	45.762	57.275	72.052	91.025	102.44	115.38	146.63	186.69	342.94	630.17
22	27.299	34.248	38.505	43.392	55.457	71.403	92.503	120.436	137.63	157.41	206.34	271.03	538.10	1,067.28
24	30.422	39.083	44.502	50.816	66.765	88.497	118.155	158.659	184.17	213.98	289.49	392.48	843.03	1,806.00
25	32.030	41.646	47.727	54.865	73.106	98.347	133.334	181.871	212.79	249.21	342.60	471.98	1,054.79	2,348.80
26	33.671	44.312	51.113	59.156	79.954	109.182	150.334	208.333	245.71	290.09	405.27	567.38	1,319.49	3,054.44
28	37.051	49.968	58.403	68.528	95.339	134.210	190.699	272.889	327.10	392.50	566.48	819.22	2,063.95	5,164.31
30	40.568	56.085	66.439	79.058	113.283	164.494	241.333	356.787	434.75	530.31	790.95	1,181.88	3,227.17	8,729.99
35	49.994	73.652	90.320	111.435	172.317	271.024	431.663	693.573	881.17	1,120.71	1,816.65	2,948.34	9,856.76	32,422.87
40	60.402	95.026	120.800	154.762	259.057	442.593	767.091	1,342.025	1,779.09	2,360.76	4,163.21	7,343.86	30,088.66	120,392.88
45	71.893	121.029	159.700	212.744	386.506	718.905	1,358.230	2,590.565	3,585.13	4,965.27	9,531.58	18,281.31	91,831.50	447,019.39
50	84.579	152.667	209.348	290.336	573.770	1,163.909	2,400.018	4,994.521	7,217.72	10,435.65	21,813.09	45,497.19	280,255.69	1,659,760.74

Compound and Discount Tables
Investment required per year during n years to grow to compound amount of $ 1 (sinking fund factor)

$$1/s_{\overline{n}|i}$$

Years	2%	4%	5%	6%	8%	10%	12%	14%	15%	16%	18%	20%	25%	30%
2	0.4951	0.4902	0.4878	0.4854	0.4808	0.4762	0.4717	0.4673	0.4651	0.4630	0.4587	0.4545	0.4444	0.4348
4	0.2426	0.2355	0.2320	0.2286	0.2219	0.2155	0.2092	0.2032	0.2003	0.1974	0.1917	0.1863	0.1734	0.1616
5	0.1922	0.1846	0.1810	0.1774	0.1705	0.1638	0.1574	0.1513	0.1483	0.1454	0.1398	0.1344	0.1218	0.1106
6	0.1585	0.1508	0.1470	0.1434	0.1363	0.1296	0.1232	0.1172	0.1142	0.1114	0.1059	0.1007	0.0888	0.0784
8	0.1165	0.1085	0.1047	0.1010	0.0940	0.0874	0.0813	0.0756	0.0729	0.0702	0.0652	0.0606	0.0504	0.0419
10	0.0913	0.0833	0.0795	0.0759	0.0690	0.0627	0.0570	0.0517	0.0493	0.0469	0.0425	0.0385	0.0301	0.0235
12	0.0746	0.0665	0.0628	0.0593	0.0527	0.0468	0.0414	0.0367	0.0345	0.0324	0.0286	0.0253	0.0184	0.0135
14	0.0626	0.0547	0.0510	0.0476	0.0413	0.0357	0.0309	0.0266	0.0247	0.0229	0.0197	0.0169	0.0115	0.0078
15	0.0578	0.0499	0.0463	0.0430	0.0368	0.0315	0.0268	0.0228	0.0210	0.0194	0.0164	0.0139	0.0091	0.0060
16	0.0537	0.0458	0.0423	0.0390	0.0330	0.0278	0.0234	0.0196	0.0180	0.0164	0.0137	0.0114	0.0072	0.0046
18	0.0467	0.0390	0.0355	0.0324	0.0267	0.0219	0.0179	0.0146	0.0132	0.0119	0.0096	0.0078	0.0046	0.0027
20	0.0412	0.0336	0.0302	0.0272	0.0219	0.0175	0.0139	0.0110	0.0098	0.0087	0.0068	0.0054	0.0029	0.0016
22	0.0366	0.0292	0.0260	0.0230	0.0180	0.0140	0.0108	0.0083	0.0073	0.0064	0.0048	0.0037	0.0019	0.0009
24	0.0329	0.0256	0.0225	0.0197	0.0150	0.0113	0.0085	0.0063	0.0054	0.0047	0.0035	0.0025	0.0012	0.0006
25	0.0312	0.0240	0.0210	0.0182	0.0137	0.0102	0.0075	0.0055	0.0047	0.0040	0.0029	0.0021	0.0009	0.0004
26	0.0297	0.0226	0.0196	0.0169	0.0125	0.0092	0.0067	0.0048	0.0041	0.0034	0.0025	0.0018	0.0008	0.0003
28	0.0270	0.0200	0.0171	0.0146	0.0105	0.0075	0.0052	0.0037	0.0031	0.0025	0.0018	0.0012	0.0005	0.0002
30	0.0247	0.0178	0.0151	0.0126	0.0088	0.0061	0.0041	0.0028	0.0023	0.0019	0.0013	0.0008	0.0003	0.0001
35	0.0200	0.0136	0.0111	0.0090	0.0058	0.0037	0.0023	0.0014	0.0011	0.0009	0.0006	0.0003	0.0001	0.0000
40	0.0166	0.0105	0.0083	0.0065	0.0039	0.0023	0.0013	0.0007	0.0006	0.0004	0.0002	0.0001	0.0000	0.0000
45	0.0139	0.0083	0.0063	0.0047	0.0026	0.0014	0.0007	0.0004	0.0003	0.0002	0.0001	0.0001	0.0000	0.0000
50	0.0118	0.0066	0.0048	0.0034	0.0017	0.0009	0.0004	0.0002	0.0001	0.0001	0.0000	0.0000	0.0000	0.0000

Compound and Discount Tables
Cash flow required per year during n years
to recover an investment of \$ 1 (capital recovery factor)
$$1/a_{\overline{n}|i}$$

Years	2%	4%	5%	6%	8%	10%	12%	14%	15%	16%	18%	20%	25%	30%	35%	40%	45%	50%
2	0.5151	0.5302	0.5378	0.5454	0.5608	0.5762	0.5917	0.6073	0.6151	0.6230	0.6387	0.6545	0.6944	0.7348	0.7755	0.8167	0.8582	0.9000
4	0.2626	0.2755	0.2820	0.2886	0.3019	0.3155	0.3292	0.3432	0.3503	0.3574	0.3717	0.3863	0.4234	0.4616	0.5008	0.5408	0.5816	0.6231
5	0.2122	0.2246	0.2310	0.2374	0.2505	0.2638	0.2774	0.2913	0.2983	0.3054	0.3198	0.3344	0.3718	0.4106	0.4505	0.4914	0.5332	0.5758
6	0.1786	0.1908	0.1970	0.2034	0.2163	0.2296	0.2432	0.2572	0.2642	0.2714	0.2859	0.3007	0.3388	0.3784	0.4193	0.4613	0.5043	0.5481
8	0.1365	0.1485	0.1547	0.1610	0.1740	0.1874	0.2013	0.2156	0.2229	0.2302	0.2452	0.2606	0.3004	0.3419	0.3849	0.4291	0.4743	0.5203
10	0.1113	0.1233	0.1295	0.1359	0.1490	0.1627	0.1770	0.1917	0.1993	0.2069	0.2225	0.2385	0.2801	0.3235	0.3683	0.4143	0.4612	0.5088
12	0.0946	0.1066	0.1128	0.1193	0.1327	0.1468	0.1614	0.1767	0.1845	0.1924	0.2086	0.2253	0.2684	0.3135	0.3598	0.4072	0.4553	0.5039
14	0.0826	0.0947	0.1010	0.1076	0.1213	0.1358	0.1509	0.1666	0.1747	0.1829	0.1997	0.2169	0.2615	0.3078	0.3553	0.4036	0.4525	0.5017
15	0.0778	0.0899	0.0963	0.1030	0.1168	0.1315	0.1468	0.1628	0.1710	0.1794	0.1964	0.2139	0.2591	0.3060	0.3539	0.4026	0.4517	0.5011
16	0.0737	0.0858	0.0923	0.0990	0.1130	0.1278	0.1434	0.1596	0.1679	0.1764	0.1937	0.2114	0.2572	0.3046	0.3529	0.4018	0.4512	0.5008
18	0.0667	0.0790	0.0855	0.0924	0.1067	0.1219	0.1379	0.1546	0.1632	0.1719	0.1896	0.2078	0.2546	0.3027	0.3516	0.4009	0.4506	0.5003
20	0.0612	0.0736	0.0802	0.0872	0.1019	0.1175	0.1339	0.1510	0.1598	0.1687	0.1868	0.2054	0.2529	0.3016	0.3509	0.4005	0.4503	0.5002
22	0.0566	0.0692	0.0760	0.0830	0.0980	0.1140	0.1308	0.1483	0.1573	0.1664	0.1848	0.2037	0.2519	0.3009	0.3505	0.4002	0.4501	0.5001
24	0.0529	0.0656	0.0725	0.0797	0.0950	0.1113	0.1285	0.1463	0.1554	0.1647	0.1835	0.2025	0.2512	0.3006	0.3503	0.4001	0.4501	0.5000
25	0.0512	0.0640	0.0710	0.0782	0.0937	0.1102	0.1275	0.1455	0.1547	0.1640	0.1829	0.2021	0.2509	0.3004	0.3502	0.4001	0.4500	0.5000
26	0.0497	0.0626	0.0696	0.0769	0.0925	0.1092	0.1267	0.1448	0.1541	0.1634	0.1825	0.2018	0.2508	0.3003	0.3501	0.4001	0.4500	0.5000
28	0.0470	0.0600	0.0671	0.0746	0.0905	0.1075	0.1252	0.1437	0.1531	0.1625	0.1818	0.2012	0.2505	0.3002	0.3501	0.4000	0.4500	0.5000
30	0.0447	0.0578	0.0651	0.0726	0.0888	0.1061	0.1241	0.1428	0.1523	0.1619	0.1813	0.2008	0.2503	0.3001	0.3500	0.4000	0.4500	0.5000
35	0.0400	0.0536	0.0611	0.0690	0.0858	0.1037	0.1223	0.1414	0.1511	0.1609	0.1806	0.2003	0.2501	0.3000	0.3500	0.4000	0.4500	0.5000
40	0.0366	0.0505	0.0583	0.0665	0.0839	0.1023	0.1213	0.1407	0.1506	0.1604	0.1802	0.2001	0.2500	0.3000	0.3500	0.4000	0.4500	0.5000
45	0.0339	0.0483	0.0563	0.0647	0.0826	0.1014	0.1207	0.1404	0.1503	0.1602	0.1801	0.2001	0.2500	0.3000	0.3500	0.4000	0.4500	0.5000
50	0.0318	0.0466	0.0548	0.0634	0.0817	0.1009	0.1204	0.1402	0.1501	0.1601	0.1800	0.2000	0.2500	0.3000	0.3500	0.4000	0.4500	0.5000

SOCIAL WEIGHTS

The following Table, which covers most of the income increases resulting from a project geared towards poverty eradication if the increases are expressed in US dollars, has been included in this study to help the reader in the calculation of the Bernoulli social weights. As reviewed in Chapter 9, the Bernoulli function is

$$v_p \times \triangle Y = \triangle U \text{ where } \triangle U = 2.3\,b \log Y_2/Y_1$$

or in natural logarithmic form $v_p \times \triangle Y = b\,(1nY_2 - 1nY_1)$. As an example, assume that i) target minimum income $b = D5,000$, ii) incomes will increase from $Y_1 = D2,000$ to $Y_2 = D3,000$ and iii) the exchange rate is $D5 = US\$1$. Then we obtain in US dollars: $b = US\$1,000$, $Y_1 = US\$400$ and $Y_2 = US\$$ 600. Hence:

$$v_p \times 200 = 1,000\,(1n\,600 - 1n\,400) \text{ or } v_p \times 200 = 1,000\,(6.397 - 5.991)$$

so that $v_p = 2.03$. The weight on the income increase may thus be set at about 2. Due to rounding off, the found weights will differ slightly from those of the examples in Chapter 10. but these differences are inconsequential.

$Y(US\$\,s)$	$1nY$	$Y(US\$\,s)$	$1nY$	$Y(US\$\,s)$	$1nY$
250	5.521	850	6.745	1900	7.550
300	5.704	900	6.802	2000	7.601
350	5.858	950	6.856	2100	7.650
400	5.991	1000	6.908	2200	7.696
450	6.109	1100	7.003	2300	7.741
500	6.215	1200	7.090	2400	7.783
550	6.310	1300	7.170	2500	7.824
600	6.397	1400	7.244	2600	7.863
650	6.477	1500	7.313	2700	7.901
700	6.551	1600	7.378	2800	7.937
750	6.620	1700	7.438	2900	7.972
800	6.685	1800	7.496	3000	8.006

REFERENCES

ADLER, H. A., 'Sector and Project Planning in Transportation,' World Bank Staff Occasional Papers, No. 4, distributed by The Johns Hopkins Press, Baltimore 1967.

AHLUWALIA, M. S., 'Income Inequality: Some Dimensions of the Problem' in Chenery et al., 'Redistribution with Growth,' Chapter I, Oxford University Press, London, 1974.

AHLUWALIA, M. S., 'Income Distribution and Development: Some Stylized Facts,' The American Economic Review, May 1976, Papers and Proceedings of the Eighty-Eighth Annual Meeting.

AHLUWALIA, M. S. and CHENERY, H., 'A Model of Distribution and Growth,' in Chenery et al., 'Redistribution with Growth,' Chapter XI, Oxford University Press, London, 1974.

AITCHISON, J. and BROWN, J. A. C., 'The Log Normal Distribution,' Cambridge University Press, London and New York, 1957.

ALEXANDER, S. S., 'Effects of a Devaluation on a Trade Balance,' IMF Staff Papers, April 1952. Reprinted in 'Readings in International Economics,' published for the American Economic Association by Richard D. Irwin, Inc., Homewood, Illinois, 1968.

ALEXANDER, S. S., 'Effects of a Devaluation – A Simplified Synthesis of Elasticities and Absorption Approaches,' The American Economic Review, March 1959.

ARROW, K. J., 'Social Choice and Individual Values,' 2nd ed., John Wiley and Sons, New York, 1963.

BACHA, E. and TAYLOR, L., 'Foreign Exchange Shadow Prices: A Critical Review of Current Theories,' The Quarterly Journal of Economics, May 1971. Reprinted in 'Benefit-Cost Analysis 1971,' an Aldine Annual, Aldine-Atherton, Inc., Chicago, New York, 1972.

BALASSA, B., 'Estimating the Shadow Price of Foreign Exchange in Project Appraisal,' The Economic Journal, July 1974.

BALASSA, B. and Associates, 'The Structure of Protection in Developing Countries,' published for the International Bank for Reconstruction and Development and the Inter-American Development Bank by The Johns Hopkins University Press, Baltimore and London, 1971.

BARKIN, D., 'Review of Harberger's Collected Papers on Project Evaluation,' The Journal of Economic Literature, June 1974.

BATOR, F. M., 'The Anatomy of Market Failure,' The Quarterly Journal of Economics, August 1958.

BAUMOL, W. J., 'Economic Theory and Operations Analysis,' 2nd ed., Prentice-Hall, Inc., Englewood Cliffs, New Jersey, 1965.

BAUMOL, W. J., 'On the Social Rate of Discount,' The American Economic Review, September 1968.

BAUMOL, W. J. and OATES, W. E., 'The Theory of Environmental Policy,' Prentice-Hall, Inc., Englewood Cliffs, New Jersey, 1975.

BERGSON, A., 'A Reformulation of Certain Aspects of Welfare Economics,' The Quarterly Journal of Economics, February 1938, reprinted in 'Essays in Normative Economics,' The Belknap Press of Harvard University Press, Cambridge, Massachusetts, 1966.

BERGSON, A., 'Collective Decision-Making and Social Welfare,' The Quarterly Journal of Economics, May 1954, reprinted in 'Essays in Normative Economics,' The Belknap Press of Harvard University Press, Cambridge ,Massachusetts, 1966.

BERGSON, A., 'Essays in Normative Economics,' The Belknap Press of Harvard University Press, Cambridge, Massachusetts, 1966.

BERGSON, A., 'On Monopoly Welfare Losses,' The American Economic Review, December 1973.

BERNOULLI, D., 'Specimen Theoriae Novae de Mensura Sortis in Commentarii Academiae Scientarim Imperialis Petropolitanae, Tomus V (Papers of the Imperial Academy of Sciences in Petersburg, Vol. V), 1738, pp. 175–192. Translated from Latin into English by Dr. Louise Sommer, The American University, Washington, D.C., as 'Exposition of a New Theory on the Measurement of Risk,' Econometrica, January 1954.

BHADURI, A., 'On the Significance of Recent Controversies on Capital Theory: A Marxian View,' The Economic Journal, Vol. 79, 1969, reprinted in 'Capital and Growth – Selected Readings,' eds. Harcourt, G. C., and Laing, N. F., Penguin Books, 1971.

BORING, E. G., 'A History of Experimental Psychology,' 2nd ed. Appleton-Century-Crafts, Inc., New York, 1950.

BUCHANAN, J. H., 'External Diseconomies, Corrective Taxes and Market Structure,' The American Economic Review, March 1969.

BURNS, M. E., 'A Note on the Concept and Measure of Consumer's Surplus,' The American Economic Review, June 1973.

CHAKRAVARTY, S., 'The Use of Shadow Prices in Programme Evaluation' in 'Capital Formation and Economic Development,' ed. Rosenstein-Rodan, P. N., George Allen and Unwin, Ltd., London, 1964.

CHENERY, H., AHLUWALIA, M. S., BELL, C. L. G., DULOY, J. H. and JOLLY, R., 'Redistribution with Growth – Policies to Improve Income Distribution in Developing Countries in the Context of Economic Growth,' a joint study by the World Bank's Development Research Center and the Institute of Development Studies at the University of Sussex, Oxford University Press, London, 1974.

COASE, R. H., 'The Problem of Social Cost,' Journal of Law and Economics, October 1960.

DASGUPTA, A. K. and PEARCE, D. W., 'Cost-Benefit Analysis: Theory and Practice,' MacMillan Student Editions, London and Basingstoke, 1972.

DASGUPTA, P., 'A Comparative Analysis of the UNIDO Guidelines and the OECD Manual,' Bulletin of the Oxford University Institute of Economics and Statistics, February 1972.

DASGUPTA, P., SEN, A., and MARGLIN, S., 'Guidelines for Project Evaluation,' United Nations Industrial Development Organisation, Vienna, Project Formulation and Evaluation Series, No. 2, United Nations, New York, 1972.

DOBB, M., 'Welfare Economies and the Economics of Socialism,' Cambridge University Press, Cambridge, 1965.

DORFMAN, R., 'Basic Economic and Technologic Concepts: A General Statement' in Maass, A., et al., 'Design of Water Resource Systems – New Techniques for Relating Economic Objectives, Engineering Analysis and Governmental Planning,' Harvard University Press, Cambridge, Massachusetts, 1962.

DOUGLAS, P. H., 'Theory of Wages,' The MacMillan Company, New York, 1934.

DOUGLAS, P. H. and COBB, C. W., 'A Theory of Production,' The American Economic Review, Vol. 18, 1928, supplement.

DULOY, J. H., 'Sectoral, Regional and Project Analysis,' in Chenery et al., 'Redistribution with Growth,' Oxford University Press, London, 1974, Chapter X.

DUPUIT, J., 'De la Mesure de l'Utilité des Travaux Publics, Annales des Ponts et Chaussées,' 2nd series, Vol. 8, 1844. Translated by Barbach, R. H. as 'On the Measurement of the Utility of Public Works,' and reprinted in International Economic Papers, No. 2, The MacMillan Company, New York, 1952. Also reprinted in 'Readings in Welfare Economics,' published for the American Economic Association by Richard D. Irwin, Inc., Homewood, Illinois, 1969.

ECKSTEIN, O., 'Water Resource Development – The Economics of Project Evaluation,' Harvard University Press, Cambridge, Massachusetts, 1958.

ECKSTEIN, O., 'A Survey of the Theory of Public Expenditure Criteria,' in 'Public Finances: Needs, Sources and Utilization,' A Conference of the Universities National Bureau Committee for Economic research, published by Princeton University Press, Princeton, 1961.

ELLIS, H. S. and FELLNER, W., 'External Economies and Diseconomies,' The American Economic Review, 1943, reprinted in 'Readings in Price Theory,' published for the American Economic Association by George Allen and Unwin, Ltd., London, 1953.

FECHNER, G. T., 'Elemente der Psychophysik,' Leipzig, 1860, Vol. I. Translated into English as 'Elements of Psychophysics,' Holt, Rinehart and Winston, New York, 1966.

FELDSTEIN, M. S., 'Net Social Benefits Calculation and the Public Investment Decision,' Oxford Economic Papers, March 1964.

284

FELDSTEIN, M. S., 'The Social Time Preference Discount Rate in Cost-Benefit Analysis,' The Economic Journal, June 1964.

FELDSTEIN, M. S., 'Distribution Preferences in Public Expenditure Analysis' in 'Redistribution through Public Choice,' eds. Hochman, J. M., and Peterson, G. D., Columbia University Press, New York and London, 1974.

FELDSTEIN, M. S., 'The Inadequacy of Weighted Discount Rates,' excerpt from Feldstein, M. S., 'Financing in the Evaluation of Public Expenditure,' written for a forthcoming volume of essays in honour of Richard A. Musgrave, ed. Smith, W. L.; reprinted in 'Cost-Benefit Analysis,' ed., Layard, R., Penguin Education, Middlesex, England, reprinted with revisions, 1974.

FELLNER, W., 'Operational Utility: The Theoretical Background and a Measurement,' in 'Ten Economic Studies in the Tradition of Irving Fisher,' John Wiley and Sons, New York, London, Sydney, 1967.

FISHER, I., 'A Statistical Method for Measuring Marginal Utility and the Justice of the Progressive Income Tax' in 'Economic Essays in Honor of John Bates Clark,' The MacMillan Company, New York, 1927.

FISK, E. K., 'Response of Non-Monetary Production Units to Contact with the Exchange Economy,' Paper presented at the Conference on Agriculture in Development Theory at Villa Serbilloni, Bellagio, Italy, May 23–29, 1973.

FREEMAN, A. M., 'Income Distribution and Public Investment,' The American Economic Review, June 1967.

FREEMAN, A. M., 'Project Design and Evaluation with Multiple Objectives' in 'Public Expenditures and Policy Analysis,' eds. Haveman, R. H., and Margolis, G., Markham Publishing Company, Chicago, 1970.

FRIEDMAN, M., 'The Marshallian Demand Curve' in 'Essays in Positive Economics,' University of Chicago Press, Chicago, 1953.

FRISCH, R., 'New Methods of Measuring Marginal Utility' in 'Beitrage zur Okonomischen Theorie (No. 3).' Mohr, J. C. B. (Paul Siebeck), Tubingen, 1932.

FRISCH, R., 'A Complete Scheme for Computing all Direct and Cross Demand Elasticities in a Model with Many Sectors,' Econometrica, April 1959.

GORMAN, W. M., 'The Intransitivity of Certain Criteria Used in Welfare Economics,' Oxford Economic Papers, New Series, Vol. 7, 1955.

GOVERNMENT OF MALAYSIA, 'Mid-term Review of the Second Malaysia Plan, 1971–75,' Kuala Lumpur, 1973.

GOVERNMENT OF MALAYSIA, 'Third Malaysia Plan, 1976–1980.' Kuala Lumpur, 1976.

GRANT, E. L. and IRESON, W. G., 'Principles of Engineering Economy,' 4th ed., The Ronald Press Company, New York, 1960; 5th ed., The Ronald Press Company, New York, 1970.

GREEN, D. I., 'Pain Cost and Opportunity Cost,' The Quarterly Journal of Economics, Vol. VIII, (1893–1894).

HANSEN, B., 'Employment and Rural Wages in Egypt, Reply,' The American Economic Review, June 1971.

HAQ, M. ul, 'Employment in the 1970s: A New Perspective,' Speech at World Conference, Ottawa, May 1971.

HAQ, M. ul, 'Toward a New Framework for International Resource Transfers,' Finance and Development, September 1975.

HARBERGER, A. C., 'Some Evidence on the International Price Mechanism,' The Journal of Political Economy, Vol. 56, 1957. Reprinted in 'International Finance – Selected Readings,' ed. Cooper, R. N., Penguin Books, 1969.

HARBERGER, A. C., 'Investment in Men Versus Investment in Machinery: The Case of India,' in 'Education and Economic Development,' eds., Anderson, C. A. and Bowman, M. J., Aldine Publishing Company, Chicago, 1965. Reprinted in Harberger, A. C., 'Project Evaluation – Collected Papers,' Markham Publishing Company, Chicago, 1974.

HARBERGER, A. C., 'Professor Arrow on the Social Discount Rate' in 'Cost-Benefit Analysis of Manpower Policies,' eds. Somers, G. C. and Woods, W. D., Industrial Relations Centre, Queen's University, Kingston, Ontario, 1969. Excerpted in Harberger, A. C., 'Project

Evaluation – Collected Papers,' Markham Publishing Company, Chicago, 1974.

HARBERGER, A. C., 'On Measuring the Social Opportunity Cost of Public Funds,' in 'The Discount Rate in Public Investment Evaluation,' Conference Proceedings of the Committee on the Economics of Water Resource Development, Western Agricultural Research Council, Report No. 17, Denver, Colorado, 17–18 December 1969. Reprinted in Harberger, A. C., 'Project Evaluation – Collected Papers,' Markham Publishing Company, Chicago, 1974.

HARBERGER, A. C., 'On Measuring the Social Opportunity Cost of Labor,' Paper presented at a meeting of experts on Fiscal Policies for Employment Promotion, sponsored by the International Labor Office at Geneva, Switzerland, 1971. Reprinted in Harberger, A. C., 'Project Evaluation – Collected Papers,' Markham Publishing Company, Chicago, 1974.

HARBERGER, A. C., 'Three Basic Postulates for Applied Welfare Economics – An Interpretive Essay,' The Journal of Economic Literature, September 1971.

HARBERGER, A. C., 'Project Evaluation – Collected Papers,' Markham Publishing Company, Chicago, 1974.

HARCOURT, G. C., 'Some Cambridge Controversies in the Theory of Capital,' Cambridge University Press, London, New York, 1972.

HARCOURT, G. C. and LAING, N. F., eds., 'Capital and Growth – Selected Readings,' Penguin Books, 1971.

HARRIS, J. R. and TODARO, M. P., 'Migration, Unemployment and Development: A Two Sector Analysis,' The American Economic Review, March 1970.

HAVEMAN, R. H., 'Water Resource Investment and the Public Interest,' Vanderbilt University Press, Nashville, Tennessee, 1965.

HAWKINS, E. K., 'The Principles of Development Aid,' Penguin Books, 1970.

HELLEINER, G. K., 'Peasant Agriculture, Government and Economic Growth in Nigeria,' Richard D. Irwin, Inc., Homewood, Illinois, 1966.

HICKS, J. R., 'The Foundation of Welfare Economics,' The Economic Journal, December 1939.

HICKS, J. R., 'Value and Capital,' 2nd ed., Oxford University Press, London, 1946.

HICKS, J. R., 'A Revision of Demand Theory,' 2nd ed., Oxford University Press, London, 1959.

HICKS, J. R., 'Capital and Growth,' Oxford University Press, New York and London, 1965.

HINRICHS, H. H., 'Determinants of Government Revenue Shares Among Less Developed Countries,' The Economic Journal, September 1965.

HIRSHLEIFER, J., DE HAVEN, J. C., and MILLIMAN, J. W., 'Water Supply – Economics, Technology and Policy,' University of Chicago Press, Chicago, 1960.

HOTELLING, H', 'The General Welfare in Relation to Problems of Taxation and of Railway and Utility Rates,' Econometrica 6 (1938). Reprinted in 'Readings in Welfare Economics,' published for the American Economic Association by Richard D. Irwin, Inc., Homewood, Illinois, 1969.

JANSEN, F. P., 'Schaarse Middelen en Structurele Samenhangen,' Thesis, University of Tilburg, 1969.

JORGENSON, D. W., 'The role of Agriculture in Economic Development: Classical versus Neoclassical Models of Growth' in 'Subsistence Agriculture and Economic Development,' ed. Wharton Jr., C. R., Aldine Publishing Company, Chicago, 1969.

KAHN, H., BROWN, W., and MARTEL, L., 'The Next 200 Years – A Scenario for America and the World,' William Morrow and Company, Inc., New York, 1976.

KAHN, R. F., 'Some Notes on Ideal Output,' The Economic Journal, March 1935.

KALDOR, N., 'Welfare Propositions in Economics,' The Economic Journal, September 1939.

KAO, C. H., ANSCHEL, K. R. and EICHNER, C. K., 'Disguised Unemployment in Agriculture: A Survey' in 'Agriculture in Economic Development,' eds. Eicher, C. K. and Witt, L. W., McGraw-Hill, New York, 1964.

KASPER, W., 'Malaysia – A Study in Successful Economic Development,' American Enterprise Institute for Public Policy Research, Foreign Affairs Studies, Washington, D.C., 1974.

KENNEDY, C., 'The Welfare Criteria That Aren't,' The Economic Journal, December 1964.

KNIGHT, F. H., 'Risk, Uncertainty and Profit,' Sixth Impression, Houghton Mifflin Company, Boston and New York, 1946.

KRUTILLA, J. V. and ECKSTEIN, O., 'Multiple Purpose River Development,' published for the Resources for the Future by The Johns Hopkins Press, Baltimore, 1958.

KUZNETS, S., 'Economic Growth and Income Inequality,' The American Economic Review, March 1955.

LAL, D., 'Wells and Welfare – An Exploratory Cost-Benefit Study of the Economics of Small-Scale Irrigation in Maharashtra,' Series on Cost-Benefit Analysis, Case Study No. 1, Development Center of the Organisation for Economic Cooperation and Development, Paris, 1972.

LAL, D., 'Methods of Project Analysis: A Review,' World Bank Staff Occasional Papers No. 16, distributed by The Johns Hopkins University Press, Baltimore and London, 1974.

LAYARD, R., 'An Introduction to Cost-Benefit Analysis, Selected Readings,' ed. Layard, R., Penguin Education, reprinted with revisions, 1974.

LERNER, A. P., 'The Economics of Control,' The MacMillan Company, New York, 1944.

LEWIS, A. W., 'Economic Development with Unlimited Supplies of Labor,' The Manchester School of Economic and Social Studies, May 1954.

LEWIS, A. W., 'Unlimited Labor – Further Notes,' The Manchester School of Economic and Social Studies, January 1958.

LINDER, S. B., 'Trade and Trade Policy for Development,' Frederick A. Praeger, Publishers, New York, Washington, London, 1967.

LITTLE, I. M. D., 'Social Choice and Individual Values,' The Journal of Political Economy, October 1952.

LITTLE, I. M. D., 'A Critique of Welfare Economics,' 2nd ed., Clarendon Press, 1957; reprint ed., Oxford Paperbacks, 1963.

LITTLE, I. M. D. and MIRRLEES, J. A., 'Manual of Industrial Project Analysis in Developing Countries, Vol. II, Social Cost Benefit Analysis,' Development Center of the Organisation for Economic Cooperation and Development, Paris, 1968.

LITTLE, I. M. D. and MIRRLEES, J. A., 'A Reply to Some Criticisms of the OECD Manual,' Bulletin of the Oxford University Institute of Economics and Statistics, February 1972.

LITTLE, I. M. D. and MIRRLEES, J. A., 'Project Appraisal and Planning for Developing Countries,' Basic Books Inc., New York, 1974.

LITTLE, I. M. D., SCITOVSKY, T. and SCOTT, M., 'Industry and Trade in Some Developing Countries – A Comparative Study,' published for the Development Center of the Organization for Economic Cooperation and Development, Paris, by Oxford University Press, London, New York, Toronto, 1970.

LORIE, J. H. and SAVAGE, L. J., 'Three Problems in Capital Rationing,' The Journal of Business, University of Chicago, October 1955.

MAASS, A., HUFSCHMIDT, M. M., DORFMAN, R., THOMAS Jr., H. A., MARGLIN, S. A., and MASKEW FAIR, G., 'Design of Water Resource Systems – New Techniques for Relating Economic Objectives, Engineering Analysis and Governmental Planning,' Harvard University Press, Cambridge, Massachusetts, 1962.

McINERNEY, J. P. and DONALDSON, G. F., 'The Consequences of Farm Tractors in Pakistan,' World Bank Staff Working Paper, No. 210, February 1975.

McKEAN, R. N., 'Efficiency in Government through Systems Analysis, with Emphasis on Water Resources Development,' a Rand Corporation Study, John Wiley and Sons, Inc., New York, 1958.

McKENZIE, L. W., 'Ideal Output and the Interdependence of Firms,' The Economic Journal, December 1951.

McNAMARA, R. S., 'Address to the Board of Governors of the International Bank for Reconstruction and Development,' Nairobi, Kenya, September 24, 1973.

MARGLIN, S. A., 'Objectives of Water Resource Development: A General Statement' in Maass, A., et al., 'Design of Water Resource Systems – New Techniques for Relating Economic Objectives, Engineering Analysis and Governmental Planning,' Harvard

287

University Press, Cambridge, Massachusetts, 1962.

MARGLIN, S. A., 'The Opportunity Costs of Public Investment,' The Quarterly Journal of Economics, May 1963.

MARGLIN, S. A., 'Approaches to Dynamic Investment Planning,' North Holland Publishing Company, Amsterdam, 1963.

MARGLIN, S. A., 'Public Investment Criteria,' MIT Press, Cambridge, Massachusetts, 1967.

MARSHALL, A., 'Principles of Economics,' 8th ed., 1920; reprint ed., MacMillan and Company, Ltd., London, 1962.

MAZUMDAR, D., 'The Rural-Urban Wage Gap, Migration and the Shadow Wage,' World Bank Staff Working Paper No. 197, Washington, D.C., February 1975.

MILLWARD, R., 'Public Expenditure Economics – An Introductory Application of Welfare Economics,' McGraw Hill, London, 1971.

MISHAN, E. J., 'Economics for Social Decisions,' Praeger Publishers, New York, Washington, 1973.

MISHAN, E. J., 'Cost-Benefit Analysis,' 1st ed., Praeger Publishers, New York, Washington, 1971; revised new edition, George Allen and Unwin, Ltd., London, 1975.

MOULIK, E. K., 'Money, Motivation and Cash Cropping,' New Guinea Research Unit of the Australian National University, Bulletin No. 53, Port Moresby and Canberra, 1973.

MUSGRAVE, R. A., 'The Theory of Public Finance: A Study in Public Economy,' McGraw-Hill Book Company, New York, Toronto, London, 1959.

MUSGRAVE, R. A., 'Cost-Benefit Analysis and the Theory of Public Finance,' The Journal of Economic Literature, September 1969.

MYINT, H., 'The Economics of the Developing Countries,' 4th (revised) ed., Hutchison University Library, London, 1973.

MYRDAL, G., 'The Challenge of World Poverty,' Pantheon Books, New York, 1970.

NAKAJIMA, C., 'Subsistence and Commercial Family Farms' in 'Subsistence Agriculture and Economic Development,' ed. Wharton Jr., C. R., Aldine Publishing Company, Chicago, 1969.

NATH, S. K., 'Are Formal Welfare Criteria Required?' The Economic Journal, September 1964.

OORT, C. J., 'Decreasing Costs as a Problem of Welfare Economics,' Drukkerij Holland N.V., Amsterdam, 1958.

PAUKERT, F., 'Income Distribution at Different Levels of Development – A Survey of Evidence,' International Labour Review, Vol. 108, Nos. 2–3, International Labour Office, Geneva, 1973.

PIGOU, A. C., 'The Economics of Welfare,' 4th ed., MacMillan and Company Ltd., London, 1952.

POULIQUEN, L., 'Risk Analysis in Project Appraisal,' World Bank Staff Occasional Papers, No. 11, distributed by The John Hopkins Press, Baltimore and London, 1970.

PREST, A. R. and TURVEY, R., 'Cost-Benefit Analysis: A Survey,' The Economic Journal, December 1965.

RAMSEY, D. D., 'On the Social Rate of Discount – Comment,' The American Economic Review, December 1969.

RAMSEY, F. P., 'A Mathematical Theory of Savings,' The Economic Journal, December 1928.

REAUME, D. M., 'Cost-Benefit Techniques and Consumer Surplus – A Clarificatory Analysis,' Public Finance, Volume XXVIII, No. 2, 1973.

REINHARDT, U., 'Efficiency Tolls and the Problem of Equity,' Working Draft, 1973.

REUTLINGER, S., 'Techniques for Project Appraisal under Uncertainty,' World Bank Staff Occasional Papers, No. 10, distributed by The Johns Hopkins Press, Baltimore and London, 1970.

ROBBINS, L., 'An Essay on the Nature and Significance of Economic Science,' 2nd ed., 1935, reprinted by MacMillan and Company, Ltd., London, 1952.

ROBINSON, J., 'The Foreign Exchanges' in 'Essays in the Theory of Employment,' 2nd ed., Basil Blackwell, Oxford, 1974, Part III, Chapter 1. Reprinted in 'Readings in the Theory of International Trade,' published for the American Economic Association by George Allen and Unwin Ltd., London, 1950.

ROTHENBERG, J., 'The Measurement of Social Welfare,' Prentice-Hall, Inc., Englewood Cliffs, New Jersey, 1961.

SAMUELSON, P. A., 'Foundations of Economic Analysis,' Harvard University Press, 1947; reprint ed., Athenaeum, New York, 1965.

SAMUELSON, P. A., 'Evaluation of Real National Income,' Oxford Economic Papers (New Series) Vol. II, No. 1, January 1950. Reprinted in 'The Collected Scientific Papers of Paul A. Samuelson,' The MIT Press, Cambridge, Massachusetts, 1966.

SAMUELSON, P. A., 'Parable and Realism in Capital Theory: The Surrogate Production Function,' The Review of Economic Studies, Vol. 39, 1962. Reprinted in 'Capital and Growth,' eds. Harcourt, G. C. and Laing, N. F., Penguin Books Ltd., 1971.

SCHYDLOWSKY, D. M., 'On the Choice of a Shadow Price for Foreign Exchange,' Harvard University Development Advisory Service, Economic Development Report No. 108, Cambridge, Massachusetts, 1968.

SCITOVSKY, T., 'A Note on Welfare Propositions in Economics,' The Review of Economics and Statistics, Vol. 9, No. 1, November 1941.

SCITOVSKY, T., 'Two Concepts of External Economies,' The Journal of Political Economy, No. 17, 1954. Reprinted in 'Readings in Welfare Economics' published for the American Economic Association by Richard D. Irwin, Inc., Homewood, Illinois, 1969.

SEN, A. K., 'Choice of Techniques,' 1st ed., 1960; 3rd ed., Basic Blackwell, Oxford, 1968.

SEN, A. K., 'Peasants and Dualism with or without Surplus Labor,' The Journal of Political Economy, October 1966.

SEN, A. K., 'Control Areas and Accounting Prices: An Approach to Economic Evaluation,' The Economic Journal, March 1972 (supplement). Reprinted in 'Benefit-Cost and Policy Analysis, 1972,' an Aldine Manual on Forecasting, Decision-Making and Evaluation, Aldine Publishing Company, Chicago, 1973.

SETON, F., 'Shadow Wages in the Chilean Economy,' Series on Cost-Benefit Analysis, Case Study No. 4, Development Center of the Organization for Economic Cooperation and Development, Paris 1972.

SILBERBERG, E., 'Duality and the Many Consumer's Surpluses,' The American Economic Review, December 1972.

SOLOMON, E., 'The Arithmetic of Capital Budgeting Decisions,' The Journal of Business, University of Chicago, April 1956.

SOLOW, R. M., 'Capital Theory and the Rate of Return,' Professor Dr. F. de Vries Lectures, North Holland Publishing Company, Amsterdam, 1964.

SQUIRE, L. and VAN DER TAK, H. G., 'Economic Analysis of Projects,' A World Bank Research Publication distributed by The Johns Hopkins University Press, Baltimore and London, 1975.

STEINER, P. O., 'Choosing Among Alternative Public Investments in the Water Resource Field,' The American Economic Review, December 1959.

STEVENS, S. S., 'Psychophysics, Introduction to Perceptual, Neural and Social Prospects,' ed. Stevens, G., John Wiley and Sons, New York, London, Sydney, Toronto, 1975.

STEWART, F. and STREETEN, D., 'Little-Mirrlees Methods and Project Appraisal,' Bulletin of the Oxford University Institute of Economics and Statistics, February 1972.

STIGLITZ, J. E., 'Alternative Theories of Wage Determination and Employment in LDCs: The Labor Turnover Model,' The Quarterly Journal of Economics, May 1974.

SWAN, T. W., 'Longer-Run Problems of the Balance of Payments,' Paper presented to Section G of the Congress of the Australian and New Zealand Association for the Advancement of Science, Melbourne, 1955. Published in 'The Australian Economy – A Volume of Readings,' eds. Arndt, H. W. and Corder, M. W., Cheshire Press, Melbourne, 1963. Reprinted in 'Readings in International Economics,' published for the American Economic Association by Richard D. Irwin, Inc., Homewood, Illionis, 1968.

THEIL, H. and BROOKS, R. B., 'How Does the Marginal Utility of Income Change When Real Income Changes?', European Economic Review, Vol., II, No. 2, Winter 1970–71.

TINBERGEN, J., 'The Design of Development,' published for the International Bank for Reconstruction and Development by The Johns Hopkins Press, Baltimore, 1958.

TINBERGEN, J., 'Some Features of the Optimum Regime' in 'Optimum Social Welfare and Productivity,' The Charles Moskowitz Lectures, New York University Press, New York, 1972.

TOBIN, J., 'The Statistical Demand Function for Food in the USA,' Journal of the Royal Statistical Society, Series A, Vol. CXIII, Part II, 1950.

TODARO, M. P., 'A Model of Labor Migration and Urban Unemployment in Less Developed Countries,' The American Economic Review, March 1969.

USHER, D., 'On the Social Rate of Discount – Comment,' The American Economic Review, December 1969.

VAN DER TAK, H. G., 'The Economic Choice between Hydroelectric and Thermal Power Developments,' World Bank Staff Occasional Papers No. 1, distributed by The Johns Hopkins Press, Baltimore and London, 1966.

VAN PRAAG, B. M. S., 'Individual Welfare Functions and Consumer Behavior,' North-Holland Publishing Company, Amsterdam, 1968.

VAN PRAAG, B. M. S., 'The Welfare Function of Income in Belgium: An Empirical Investigation,' European Economic Review, Vol. II, No. 3, Spring 1971.

VINER, J., 'Cost Curves and Supply Curves,' Zeitschrift für National Okonomie, Vol. III, 1931. Reprinted in 'Readings in Price Theory,' published for the American Economic Association by George Allen and Unwin Ltd., London, 1953.

VINER, J., 'Some Reflections on the Concept of Disguised Unemployment' in 'Contribuicoes a Analise do Desenvolvimento Economico,' Livraria Agir Editoria, Rio de Janeiro, 1957. Reprinted in 'Leading Issues in Development Economics', ed. Meier, G. M., Oxford University Press, New York, 1964.

WEBER, E. H., 'Tastsinn und Gemeingefuhl,' Leipzig, 1846.

WEISBROD, B. A., 'The Valuation of Human Capital,' The Journal of Political Economy, October 1961.

WEITZMAN, M., 'Free Access vs. Private Ownership as Alternative Systems for Managing Common Property,' Working Draft, April 1972.

WILLIAMSON, O. E., 'Peak-Load Pricing and Optimal Capacity under Indivisibility Constraints,' The American Economic Review, September 1966.

WINCH, D. M., 'Consumer Surplus and the Compensating Principle,' The American Economic Review, June 1965.

WOHL, M. and MARTIN, B. V., 'Evaluation of Mutually Exclusive Design Projects,' Special Report 92, Highways Research Board, Washington, D.C., 1967.

WOLFSON, D. G., 'Fiscal Policy and Development Strategy,' Thesis, University of Amsterdam, 1974.

WORLD BANK, 'World Bank Atlas – Population, Per Capita Product and Growth Rates,' World Bank, Washington, D. C., 1975.

ZEYLSTRA, W. G., 'Aid or Development: The Relevance of Development Aid to the Problems of Developing Countries,' A. W. Sijthoff, Leyden, 1975.

ZIMMERMAN, L. J., 'Poor Lands, Rich Lands: The Widening Gap,' Random House, Inc., New York, 1965.

INDEX

accounting rate of interest, 183, 190
Adler, H. A., 17
Ahluwalia, M. S., 215, 236, 261, 263
Aitchison, J., 235
Alexander, S. S., 142, 143, 155
alternate cost savings method, 98–99
Anschel, K. R., 72
Arrow, K. J., 165, 167, 171
Asian Development Bank, 137

Bacha, E., 70
balance of payments, 138–145, 170
Balassa, B., 33, 70, 140, 141, 142, 154
Barkin, D., 235
Bator, F. M., 123, 153
Baumol, W. J., 57, 58, 59, 72, 73, 124, 153, 168, 171
benefit-cost ratios, 75, 99–100, 104–105, 110–111
Bergson, A., 33, 164, 165, 168, 171
Bernoulli, D., 205–210, 232–234, 237, 257
Bhaduri, A., 65, 73
border prices, 27–31
Boring, E. G., 235
bridge, 79
Brooks, R. B., 209, 210, 236
Brown, J. A. C., 235
Brown, W., 263
Buchanan, J. H., 122, 153
budget constraints, 96, 100–105, 109–111, 194, 199, 225
Burns, M. E., 24, 33

capital, 57–69
– foreign capital, 129–138
– marginal product of capital, 58, 60, 62–65
capital market, 59–61
capital recovery factor, 92, 95
capitalist sector, 43–45, 190–192
Chakravarty, S., 17, 73
Chenery, H., 205, 210, 235, 261, 263
Coase, R. H., 123, 153
Cobb, C. W., 63, 64, 73
Cobb-Douglas production function, 63, 64, 73
compensated demand curves, 20, 24
compensating surplus, 20, 32
compensating variation, 32, 40, 71, 128
compensation tests, 159–163
compound formulas, 91–95

congestion, 125–128
conversion factors, 28, 30, 31
constraints, 101, 132, 137 (*see also* budget constraints)
consumer surplus, 4, 5, 6, 7, 18–26, 27, 74–79, 81–89, 228
consumption, 45, 67, 142, 144, 172–176, 181, 183, 184, 188, 189
cost effectiveness analysis, 129 (*see also* alternate cost savings method)
cost reduction, 81, 86, 118–119
Cramer, G., 205, 207, 232, 234, 235, 257

Dasgupta, A. K., 17, 116
Dasgupta, P., 16, 28, 29, 33, 63, 73, 196, 197, 198
decreasing average costs, 10, 26, 84–85
De Haven, J. C., 5, 16, 57, 58, 59, 72, 104, 116
demand curve, 18, 27, 76, 77, 83, 84, 120
devaluation, 138–149
discount formulas, 91–95
distortions, 10, 27, 66, 172
Dobb, M., 165, 171
domestic prices, 27–31
Donaldson, G. F., 258
Dorfman, R., 117
Douglas, P. H., 63, 64, 73
Duloy, J. H., 262, 263
Dupuit, J., 5, 16, 18, 19, 26, 32
dynamic investment planning, 110–111

Eckstein, O., 5, 16, 57, 72, 81, 90, 116, 172, 173, 175, 177, 180, 181, 196, 200, 201, 203, 204, 235
economic evaluation of projects, 6
economic rate of return, (*see* rate of return)
Eicher, C. K., 72
elasticity approach to balance of payments problems, 138–150
elasticity of
– demand, 75, 76
– demand for foreign exchange, 37–38, 139–142
– export demand, 136, 139–142
– export supply, 38–39, 135, 139–142
– import demand, 38–39, 135, 139–142
– import supply, 139–142
– marginal utility of consumption, 177, 191
– marginal utility of income, 206, 207, 208,

Tobin, J., 236
Todaro, M. P., 49, 50, 51, 72
tradeables, 28, 88, 143–149
trade multiplier, 144
transfers (*see* income transfers)
Turvey, R., 5, 16

uncertainty, 96, 111–115
UNIDO, 5, 28, 29, 38, 63, 64, 70, 174, 175, 178, 181, 183, 184, 185, 186, 187, 188, 195, 197, 198, 203
urban wage, 49–52
Usher, D., 59, 73
utility-possibility curves, 160–163, 165

van der Tak, H. G., 17, 33, 116, 212, 213, 236, 262, 263
van Praag, B. M. S., 210, 236

Viner, J., 7, 17, 46, 71

Weber, E. H., 205, 206, 207, 210, 215, 216, 235
Weisbrod, B. A., 128, 153
Weitzman, M., 153
Williamson, O., 79, 90
willingness to pay, 6, 24, 26, 27, 28, 35, 36, 81, 124, 125, 129, 217
Winch, D. M., 24, 33
with and without approach, 9
Wohl, M., 26, 33
Wolfson, D. G., 136, 153
World Bank, 134, 135, 137, 169, 203

Zeylstra, W. G., 134, 153, 236
Zimmerman, L. J., 260, 263